MODERN ARTHURIAN LITERATURE

GARLAND REFERENCE LIBRARY
OF THE HUMANITIES
(VOL. 1420)

MODERN ARTHURIAN LITERATURE
An Anthology of English and American Arthuriana from the Renaissance to the Present

edited by
Alan Lupack

GARLAND PUBLISHING, INC. • NEW YORK & LONDON
1992

For Barbara

"Gwenivere Tells" and "The Death of Lancelot as Told by Gwenivere" from *Midsummer Night and Other Tales in Verse* by John Masefield are reprinted by permission of The Society of Authors as literary representative of The Estate of John Masefield.

"Mount Badon" and "The Coming of Galahad" from *Taliessin Through Logres* by Charles Williams, copyright The Estate of Charles Williams, 1938, 1944 are reprinted by permission of Watkins/Loomis Agency.

"Launcelot in Hell" from *In the Stoneworks* by John Ciardi is reprinted by permission of Ms. Judith H. Ciardi.

"Merlin Enthralled" from *Things of This World*, copyright 1953 and renewed 1981 by Richard Wilbur, is reprinted by permission of Harcourt Brace Jovanovich, Inc.

The selection from *Arthur Rex* by Thomas Berger, copyright (c) 1978 by Thomas Berger, is reprinted by permission of Little, Brown and Company.

"The Naming of the Lost" by Valerie Nieman Colander is reprinted by permission of the author.

"Guenever Speaks" by Wendy Mnookin is reprinted by permission of the author.

Library of Congress Cataloging-in-Publication Data

Modern Arthurian literature : an anthology of English and American
  Arthuriana from the Renaissance to the present /
  edited by Alan Lupack.
    p. cm. — (Garland reference library of the humanities ; vol.
1420)
    Includes bibliographical references.
    ISBN 0-8153-0055-7 (hardback). — ISBN 0-8153-0843-4 (pbk.)
    1. Arthurian romances—Adaptations. 2. English literature.
    3. American literature. I. Lupack, Alan. II. Series.
    PR1111.A85M63 1992   91-46442
    820.8'0352—dc20   CIP

Printed on acid-free, 250-year-life paper
Manufactured in the United States of America

Contents

Acknowledgments

My sincere thanks to:

Thomas Berger for editing the selection from his novel *Arthur Rex* so that it forms a discrete unit.

The graduate students at the University of Rochester who have helped me in the preparation of this book: Nandini Bhattacharya, Karen Saupe, and Pauline Alama.

Gary Kuris from Garland Publishing for his encouragement of my work and the work of many others on the Arthurian legends.

And, as always, to my wife, Barbara, for her critical acumen, careful eye, and constant support.

I.
The Renaissance to the Nineteenth Century

Introduction

The Middle Ages produced many brilliant and innovative Arthurian works. In the twelfth century the chronicle of Geoffrey of Monmouth and the courtly romances of Chrétien de Troyes established two modes of presenting the Arthurian material that have influenced the treatment of the legends ever since. The great Vulgate Cycle of the thirteenth century, some of the English alliterative works of the fourteenth, and of course Malory's *Morte Darthur* in the fifteenth are masterpieces whose power and artistry give them enduring appeal.

It is easy to see the following centuries in the shadow of such works and to declare the period from the Renaissance to the Victorian revival of interest in the Matter of Britain as an Arthurian Dark Age. These centuries were not, however, devoid of Arthurian literature; and perhaps only because the Victorian reinterpretation of the Arthurian world has imprinted itself so powerfully on our culture do we tend to overlook what came before.

Renaissance England, concerned as it was with questions of kingship and succession, turned primarily to chronicles for its Arthurian subject matter and sometimes used this material for political purposes. Henry VII, the first of the Tudor monarchs, traced his lineage and his claim to the throne back to Arthur and reinterpreted the legend so that not Arthur himself but his descendant, in the person of Henry VII, was said to have returned at a time of need (the War of the Roses) to restore stability to Britain. This Tudor myth was fostered by Henry VII, who named his first son Arthur, and also by his successors.

Thus it is not surprising that an Englishman like John Leland (?1503–1552) would feel a need to respond to the attacks on the historicity of Arthur written by the Italian Polydore Vergil. As King's Antiquary during the reign of Henry VIII, Leland had traveled throughout Britain gathering information on its past. This pursuit gave him the evidence he needed to refute Vergil's charges.

Leland's most detailed and documented refutation appeared in his *Assertio Inclytissimi Arturii Regis Britanniae* (Assertion of the Most Renowned King Arthur of Britain) published in 1544 and translated into English in 1582 (during the reign of Elizabeth I) by Richard Robinson. Leland's *Assertion* is the equivalent of a modern scholarly article based on both his personal observation and a reading and interpretation of earlier authors. From his personal travels Leland offered as proof of historicity a detailed description of Arthur's seal, a transcription of the legend on the cross found at Arthur's grave site, and reports of local lore associating Cadbury with Camelot.

But Leland also provides more objective evidence. He cites numerous historians, complete with the Renaissance equivalent of footnotes. He presents an impressive number of sources, from Gildas and Nennius to writers of his own day. Astute enough both as historian and as rhetorician to recognize that some of the marvels referred to in the medieval chronicles are beyond belief, he draws a distinction between the fantastic and the factual and concludes that while the excesses of some earlier writers are regrettable, the weight of the historical and archaeological evidence points to the historicity of Arthur.

This is an opinion that one might accept even today. And, as James Carley has said, "In the final analysis, we have not moved far beyond Leland in the solution to the Arthurian question. . . . Some modern conclusions may be closer to Vergil's, but the methodology resembles Leland's" ("Polydore Vergil . . . ," 91). In fact, many of the issues he raises are still being debated by scholars: why doesn't Gildas mention Arthur as the victor at Badon? how reliable on other matters are historians who will accept accounts of marvels that could not possibly be true? is Cadbury Camelot? how accurate are the accounts of the finding of Arthur's grave and the cross marking it at Glastonbury?

While one should not overstate the significance of the Tudor myth of descent from Arthur, it was a prop to the family's claim to the throne and to Henry VIII's assertion of independence from Rome, as well as a factor in shaping the spirit of the Elizabethan age and empire. It also provided the impetus for quite a few authors to incorporate Arthurian material into poems or plays. Allusions to Arthurian stories and sites make their way into such poems as Michael Drayton's *Poly-Olbion* (1612) and Thomas Churchyard's *The Worthines of Wales* (1587). Published just five years after Robinson's translation of Leland's *Assertion*, Churchyard's poem reads in one place like a versified version of the argument of the treatise. Churchyard questions Polydore Vergil's ability to write about Arthur ("this Pollidore, sawe never much of Wales," he says) and warns against relying on "the bookes that straungers [i.e., foreigners] make" when "our owne men," writers like Gildas and Bede, wrote so well "That honey seem'd to drop from Poets quill." Churchyard concludes that "Arthures raigne, the world cannot denye."

More propaganda than poetry, Churchyard's work nevertheless reveals the passion with which Arthur could be defended by some Englishmen. Another poem, Edmund Spenser's *Faerie Queene*, also contains elements of propaganda but has an epic scope and a mastery of verse that Churchyard's poem never approaches. Begun in the 1570s, the poem was only a little more than half finished when Spenser died in 1599. Of the twelve books traditionally found in an epic he completed only six and part of a seventh, each of which dealt with a particular virtue (holiness, temperance, chastity, etc.).

Spenser's poem is an allegory with each of the main characters representing a virtue or vice or some abstract quality. Even though he appears only sporadically throughout the poem, Arthur is the key figure in Spenser's scheme since he represents Magnificence, or the quality of being great-souled, which contains within it all the other virtues. After having had a vision of the Fairy Queen (Gloriana, who represents "Glory"), Arthur sets out in search of her and so rides as a knight errant through the allegorical world Spenser has created. Ultimately, had the poem been completed, Arthur was to have been united with Gloriana. The union of the two would have alluded to the Tudor myth of descent from Arthur and suggested that Elizabeth had brought back to England the glory of her famous ancestor.

But we do not follow Arthur throughout the poem. Book I, for example, begins with an account of how the Red Cross Knight, accompanied by Una (a symbol of revealed Truth) rides in search of a dragon, which the Fairy Queen has ordered him to slay. Arthur plays no role until Canto VII, when he comes upon Una and learns that her companion has been imprisoned by the giant Orgoglio. Arthur agrees to free the Red Cross Knight, which he does after killing the giant. Then Arthur leaves the scene and is absent from the rest of Book I, which proceeds with the slaying of the dragon by the Red Cross Knight.

Arthur makes similar cameo appearances in the later books and Merlin is introduced; but otherwise there is little that is recognizable as Arthurian in Spenser's epic. Nevertheless, *The Faerie Queene* is important in the Arthurian tradition. At a time when the traditional medieval romances were old-fashioned and so no longer a viable form, Spenser revitalized the Arthurian material by structuring it around the largely Aristotelian concepts of virtue and adapting it to the political concerns of his day. Not only did his approach appeal to the classical interests of his age, but it also did for the moral allegory what plays like *Respublica* did for the dramatic morality plays; that is, it transformed the religious concerns of the medieval world into the political concerns of Renaissance England.

Renaissance drama also made use of Arthurian material. In 1588 Thomas Hughes wrote a Senecan revenge play called *The Misfortunes of Arthur*, which begins with the ghost of Gorlois of Cornwall calling for vengeance on the line of Uther Pendragon. The ghost predicts the events of the play, which, based on Geoffrey of Monmouth, include the treachery of Mordred, the betrayal of Arthur by Guinevere, and the death of Arthur and Mordred. Thomas Middleton's play *Hengist, King of Kent*, sometimes referred to as *The Mayor of Queenborough* (first published in 1661, but written much earlier), also takes its subject matter from the chronicles. Middleton's play deals with the events prior to the reign of Arthur: the alliance of Vortiger (the Vortigern of earlier sources) with the Saxons; the poisoning of his son Vortimer by Vortiger's Saxon wife; the contract killing of Constantius so Vortiger can rule in his place; and the victory of Aurelius and Uther, which prevents this first of the Saxon invasions from being the end of Britain and the beginning of England. It also contains a comic subplot about Simon the tanner, who is the Mayor of Queenborough and the man who cut a hide into small strips so it would surround a large area for Hengist, who had asked as a reward for his mercenary services as much land as could be encompassed by a calf's hide.

But perhaps the best of the Renaissance Arthurian plays using chronicle material is William Rowley's *The Birth of Merlin*, a play in which the comic plot (which overwhelms the historical to such a degree that it seems inappropriate to call it a "subplot") involves a search by Merlin's mother for the father of her child. In this play she is not a nun, as is traditional, but a simple woman called Joan Goe-too't. Having gone to it with a stranger and bearing his child, Joan enlists the help of her brother, identified only as a "Clown," to find the father. Though the Devil is described in the stage directions as having "horrid" head and feet, she is unable to describe him, except to say that he was a gentleman who wore rich clothing and had a gilt sword and "most excellent hangers" ("hangers" being the loops or straps from which a sword was hung, but also having vulgar connotations as used by Joan and the Clown). Her lack of discernment about the father of her child leaves Joan unable to distinguish one "gentleman" from another, so that she thinks even Uther ("Uter" in the play) Pendragon may have been responsible.

Uter, on the other hand, who calls her "Witch, scullion, hag" because of her sin and her accusation, is unable to perceive, at least initially, that another woman is far more wicked and dangerous. He is attracted to Artesia, sister of the Saxon general Ostorius. Since Artesia is wed to Uter's brother Aurelius, she manipulates his affections to cause a breach between the brothers. Recognizing her evil, Uter says she is a "witch by nature, devil by art." Just as Joan was deceived by the Devil, so the devilish Artesia deceives Uter, temporarily, and Aurelius, fatally. (Later it is revealed that Aurelius has been poisoned by Artesia and Ostorius.)

In both plots Merlin helps to set things right. Through the familiar device of the red and white dragons that struggle beneath the site where Vortiger would build a castle, Merlin predicts the downfall of Vortiger and the victory of Uter as well as the birth to Uter of two children, one of whom will be Queen of Ireland, the other (Arthur) a great conqueror who will win thirteen crowns. In the comic plot, when the Devil returns to take advantage of Joan a second time, Merlin—in an action that echoes his own fate in other stories—seals him in a rock where he will never touch a woman again.

The play ends with another complex prediction: the Saxons will ultimately triumph, but first Arthur will win great fame, only to die "in the middest of all his glories." Uter, aware that Fate "must be observ'd," seems content with the prediction of his son's glory. While this final exchange may seem an inappropriate ending for a play so basically comic, it may not be inconsistent, given the historical perspective of the age in which the play was written. After all, the glory of Arthur was to be renewed through the line of the Tudors; thus the apparent tragedy of Arthur's death is balanced by the future glory of Arthur's line. In this context even Arthur's death can be seen as part of a larger comic pattern.

A similar historical perspective is evident again in Ben Jonson's masque *The Speeches at Prince Henries Barriers*. The "Barriers" were a celebration (at the Christmas festivities of 1609) in honor of the investiture of Henry, eldest son of James I, as Prince of Wales in 1610. The Stuarts, like the Tudors, traced their lineage back to Arthur. As James Merriman has written, "Like the Tudors before him, James I was quick to see the usefulness of Arthur in bolstering his throne. Through both the Tudor and the Stuart lines, he was able to trace himself to Arthur's blood, and by his relinquishment of separate titles to the two realms of Scotland and England and his taking instead the title of King of Great Britain, James made possible the assertion by his supporters that his accession fulfilled Merlin's prophecy that under the name of Brutus England and Scotland would be united once more as they had been under Arthur" (49). Thus it is fitting that the Lady of the Lake and Merlin instruct James's son as he becomes Prince of Wales.

In the masque the Lady of the Lake presents a shield to Meliadus (who represents Henry) and then calls on Merlin to explain the shield's images to him. The allusion to the shield of Achilles is obvious; and other classical echoes occur throughout (cf. Peacock, 175). But despite the references to the glorious Arthurian background and the recounting of the deeds of English rulers, Meliadus is advised that he is not meant to act according to the "bold stories" of Arthur's time but that "his arts must be to governe, and give lawes / To peace no less than armes." This emphasis on using "chivalrous attainments to guarantee peace rather than wage war unnecessarily" is one of the "three principal themes" of the *Barriers*, along with the notion of "revival of chivalry" and the "superiority of union to division" (Peacock, 172).

Didactic and celebratory, Jonson's masque is very different both from the medieval treatments of the legends and from the type of Arthurianism found in the Victorian period. Another play written in the latter part of the seventeenth century combines elements of the masque and of opera to produce a similarly unusual Arthurian work. John Dryden's "dramatic opera" *King Arthur* (with music by Henry Purcell) depicts a military struggle between Arthur and Oswald, who is "a Saxon and a heathen." This conflict is paralleled by a struggle between them for the beautiful Emmeline, daughter of the Duke of Cornwall. The conflict culminates in a single combat in which, of course, Arthur is victorious. The principal architect of Arthur's triumph is Merlin, who, more than any other character, is responsible for the harmonious conclusion to the events of the play. Unlike his Saxon counterpart Osmond, who uses his magic to deceive, Merlin enlightens Arthur and others, a function that is depicted symbolically by his literally curing Emmeline of the blindness that afflicts her at the beginning of the play. In the end Merlin restores order in such a way that even the enemy is accommodated. He predicts not only Arthur's fame as the first of the three Christian Worthies but even the eventual union of Britons and Saxons, who will be bound together "in perpetual peace" by "one common tongue, one common faith."

Dryden's Arthur is a far cry from Malory's, but he does embody the courage and faithfulness in love so important to the medieval knight. Thus a direct line extends from the medieval romances, through Spenser's Arthur and the Arthurian instruction provided for Jonson's Meliadus, to Dryden's noble king. But in the eighteenth century there is an interruption of this tradition. By the eighteenth century little of the heroism and romance and magic of the early Arthurian stories survives. King Arthur and his knights rarely receive serious treatment, even of the kind seen in Dryden's drama. The only memorable uses of Arthurian material are found in satiric pieces.

In the early seventeenth century there were two editions of the prophecies of Merlin (1603 and 1605) with commentary believed to be by Alanus de Insulis. The interest in Merlin's prophecies was undoubtedly fostered by James's use of them in support of his claim to the throne. But by the eighteenth century "Merlin" had become a name for any "prophet" wishing to sell copies of an almanac. Jonathan Swift parodies such almanac prophecies, purported to have been written by Merlin and proving true in the year of their actual writing, in "A Famous Prediction of Merlin, the British Wizard." Swift creates a typically obscure prophecy and twists and squeezes its language so that he can wring from it any meaning he wants merely by saying "this way of expression is after the usual dark manner of old astrological predictions."

Henry Fielding's burlesque play *Tom Thumb* (1730; rewritten in 1731 as *The Tragedy of Tragedies*) treats the legend in a similarly satiric manner. As part of his parody Fielding takes as his hero a character who appeared in the chapbooks of his day and makes reference to other chapbook heroes, like the giant-killing Tom

Hickathrift. The minuscule protagonist, who was "by Merlin's art begot," is called by Arthur "hero, giant-killing lad, / Preserver of my kingdom." But the greatest example of Tom Thumb's valor in the play is his killing of a bailiff who wants to arrest Tom's friend Noodle.

The satirizing of the debased form of valorous action found in the chapbooks and the heroic drama of Fielding's day is complemented by the satirizing of the love interest also found in both. Because of his service to the country Tom has been promised the hand of Princess Huncamunca. His decision to leave martial pursuits for "Hymeneal" ones is compared, in a mock-heroic epic simile, to a chimney sweeper washing his face and hands and changing his shirt before he lies with his wife. The love plot is complicated by the fact that Arthur's queen, in this version not Guinevere but Dollalolla, is also in love with Tom.

Both loves are frustrated when Tom is swallowed by a cow, but his ghost returns, only to be killed by a character named Grizzle, who has a grievance against Tom. Huncamunca then kills Grizzle and is herself killed by Doodle, who is then killed by the queen. In quick sucession Noodle kills the queen and is killed by a character named Cleora, who is killed in turn by one Mustacha. Arthur kills this last murderer and, to complete the parody of bloody dramatic endings, kills himself.

Fielding is obviously poking fun primarily at the heroic drama and the popular chapbooks of his time. His selection of the story of Tom Thumb, traditionally linked to Merlin and Arthur, is probably due more to its mock-heroic possibilities than to any particular dislike for the legend of Arthur, which was at a low point anyway in his day since eighteenth-century rationalism rejected many of the fantastic events of medieval romance. The age looked instead to the classics for models because Classical authors were believed to have captured universal truths. Thus the epic, as produced by Homer and Vergil, was considered the noblest form of poetry.

Yet there was another side to the eighteenth century, a pre-Romantic leaning toward the art of the Middle Ages and the emotion and inspiration that such art was thought to represent. There resulted an antiquarian movement that sought to preserve and to make available native romances and ballads. This movement was as important to the rediscovery of vernacular texts as Renaissance scholarship was to the rediscovery of the classics. One of the most influential works in this revival was Thomas Percy's

Reliques of Ancient English Poetry: Consisting of Old Heroic Ballads, Songs, and Other Pieces of Our Earlier Poets, (Chiefly of the Lyric Kind.) Together with Some Few of Later Date. Published in 1765, Percy's collection contained a wide range of material from the Middle Ages and the Renaissance. Included in its three volumes were six ballads that treated various aspects of the Arthurian legends, such as Lancelot's fight with Tarquin; King Ryence's demand that Arthur send his beard as a sign of submission; and Sir Gawain's marriage to a loathly lady who becomes fair, an analogue of the story told by the Wife of Bath in *The Canterbury Tales*. Though, strictly speaking, the ballads mostly date from an earlier period, they are a significant part of what the eighteenth and nineteenth centuries came to know as Arthurian; and the focus on specific incidents rather than on the epic scope of the legend undoubtedly provided a model for modern Arthurian poets.

But perhaps more influential than this approach is Percy's defense of medieval "romance" (a term he uses almost interchangeably with "ballad") in his introduction to the third volume of the collection. Percy says that though they are "full of the exploded fictions of Chivalry," the romances "frequently display great descriptive and inventive powers" and that "Many of them exhibit no mean attempts at Epic Poetry" (p. viii). This linking of the romances—which Percy feels often contain the "rich ore of an Ariosto or a Tasso" buried "among the rubbish and dross of barbarous times" (p. ix)—with the epic is a way of using eighteenth-century critical standards to argue for the quality of the medieval material. His claim is that "Nature and common sense had supplied to these old simple bards the want of critical art, and taught them some of the most essential rules of Epic Poetry" (p. xii).

Percy goes so far as to summarize the Arthurian romance *"Libius Disconius"* (better known as *Libeaus Desconus*) to show the courage and nobility of Gawain's son. He concludes that the romance is "as regular in its conduct, as any of the finest poems of classical antiquity" (p. xvi). This statement could easily be applied to the ballad that Percy calls "The Marriage of Sir Gawaine." In fact, a later writer, Howard Pyle, used the story, which he adapted from Percy's collection, as just such a model of conduct (see the selection printed below from *The Story of King Arthur and His Knights*).

But it took some time for the Arthurian material to pass from an object of antiquarian and scholarly interest to an inspiration for vital new art. Even among the Romantic writers there was relatively little use of Arthurian themes. John Thelwall, a radical thinker and a friend of Coleridge, published a play called *The Fairy of the Lake* (1801). Thomas Love Peacock looked to Celtic sources for his novel *The Misfortunes of Elphin* (1829). Sir Walter Scott devoted a portion of "The Bridal of Triermain" (1813) to an Arthurian story, but the poem is a minor piece and ultimately not as important as Scott's edition of *Sir Tristrem* (published in 1804). The only complete Arthurian poem by a major British Romantic poet is William Wordsworth's "The Egyptian Maid," which appeared in his collection *Yarrow Revisited and Other Poems* in 1835. Perhaps this scarcity is a response to what every poet attempting to deal with any aspect of the legend must feel: the weight of the tradition. In writings about England's most famous king the Romantic inclination toward originality and individuality would have to yield at least a little to the powerful and well-known traditions that surrounded him.

Wordsworth asserts his originality by creating an incident not found in Malory or any other source and by taking liberties with the traditional characters. He indicates that for everything but the "Names and persons" in the poem, "the Author is answerable." His narrative tells of an Egyptian maiden who is coming to Arthur's court to marry one of his knights because of the assistance that Arthur had given the maiden's father. When Merlin's "freakish will" leads him to destroy her ship, he must be instructed by Nina, the Lady of the Lake, and then must correct the wrong done by his arbitrary use of power. The poem thus becomes a comment on the responsibility of those who wield power.

The liberties he took with tradition, the focus on a single (and original) incident, and the molding of the material to a particular theme make Wordsworth's modest poem a significant beginning for nineteenth-century Arthurian poetry. At the same time it is, like most of the best Arthurian poetry, very much a product of its age. Romantic elements abound: the exotic, the power of nature, the death of a beautiful woman, and others. Yet, though clearly of its age, it does not seem to achieve the perfect melding of medieval and modern that makes Tennyson's *Idylls* and some of the other Victorian poems treating the Matter of Britain masterpieces of Arthurian literature.

The Assertion of King Arthure

translated by
RICHARD ROBINSON
from the Latin of
JOHN LELAND

Chapter 3.
The Twelve Battelles Fought by Arthure.

Nennius the Brittaine[1] a writer of good and auncient credit,[2] amongst many others maketh most lightsome[3] mention of his battels: whose wordes although by the negligence of printers and injurie of time, they be somewhat displaced, yet notwithstandinge because they make much for our present matter, and bring with them a certaine reverent antiquitie, I will here set them downe, and in their order. Arthure fought in deed against those Saxones, with the governours of the Britaines, but he himselfe was generall. The first battell was at the entraunce of the floude[4] called Gleyn, alias Gledy. The second, third, fourth, and fift, was upon an other floud called Dugles, which is in the countrie of Lynieux. The sixt was upon the floud which is called Bassas. The seaventh was in the wood Caledon, that is, Catcoit Celidon. The eight in the Castle of Gwynyon. The nynth was fought in the cittie of Caerlegion upon Uske. The tenth on the sea shore, which is called Traitheurith, otherwise Rhydrwyd. The eleaventh in the hill which is called Agned Cathregonion. The twelfth in the mount Badonis, wherein many

---

1. Welsh cleric said to be the author of the *Historia Brittonum*, a ninth-century chronicle that lists the twelve battles in which, according to tradition, Arthur was victorious. The locations of some of the sites of these battles are uncertain. Even the location of Mount Badon, identified below as Bath, is a subject of debate.

2. Long-established credibility.

3. Clear.

4. River.

were slaine by one assault of Arthure. Thus farre witnesseth Nennius.

. . . .

And so these are the wordes of Henry sirnamed of Huntington[5] in the second booke of his history. Arthure the warrier, in those dayes the captaine generall of soldiours, and of the rulers in Brittaine, fought most valiantly against the Saxons. Twelve times was he generall of the battell, and twelve times got he the victory. And there also. But the battels and places wherein they were fought a certaine historiographer declareth.

Henry of Huntington seemeth here to have hitte upon the breefe history of Nennius, the name of whose exemplar[6] (as it seemeth) was not set downe. Herehence came that silence. Neyther was that booke common in mens handes at that time, and in this our age is surely most rare: only three exemplars[7] do I remember that I have seene, John Rhesus[8] a lover of antiquitie, and the same a diligent setter forth thereof, hath a little booke entituled *Gilde*, which booke (so farre as I gather by his speach) had not to author Gildas,[9] but Nennius.

The Elenchus[10] or Registred Table of the librarie at Batle Abbey, accounteth the historie of Gildas among there treasures, I have diligently enquyred for the booke: but as yet have I not found it. The reporte is, that the exemplar was translated or carried to Brecknocke[11] there to be kept.

---

5. Henry of Huntingdon (?1084–1155) wrote a chronicle of England that covered events from the invasion of Julius Caesar to the twelfth century.

6. Source.

7. Examples or copies.

8. Probably John ap Rice or ap Rhys (Price) (d. ?1573), who wrote *Historiae Britannicae Defensio* (c. 1553, published 1573), which counters the criticisms of Polydore Vergil.

9. Gildas, a cleric born c. 500, was the first to write about the Battle of Mount Badon (though he does not name Arthur as the victorious general).

10. An index or analytical table of contents.

11. A town in Brecknockshire in southeast Wales on the Usk River.

Now must we report the battels.

The writer of the life of the reverent Dubritius,[12] Archebishop of the cittie Caerlegion upon Usk,[13] not unelegantly, doth commemorate such like matters. When at length Aurelius[14] the King was made away by poyson, (and that Uther, his brother ruled a few yeares) Arthure his sonne by the helpe of Dubritius succeded in governement, who with bold courage set upon the Saxones in many battels, and yet could he not utterly roote them out of his kingdome. For the Saxones had subdued unto them selves the whole compasse of the island which stretcheth from the water of Humber unto the Sea Cattenessinum or Scottish Sea. For that cause the Peares[15] of the realme being called together, he determined by their counsell what he might best do, against the irruption of the pagane Saxones. At length by common counsell he sendeth into Armorica,[16] (that is to say, the leser Brittaine,) unto King Hoel[17] his ambassadors, which advertised him at full, touching[18] the calamitie of the Brittaines, who comming with fiftene thousand of armed men into Brittaine was honorably entertayned of Arthure, and D. Dubritius: going unto the cittie of Lincolne beseeged of the Saxones, having fought the battell, there were six thousand of Saxones which eyther being drowned or wounded with weapons, dyed. But the others flying away unto the wood of Caledon, being besseged by the Brittaines, were constrayned to yeeld themselves: and pledges being taken for tribute yearely to be paied, he gave them leave with their shippes onely to returne into their countrie. Afterwardes within a short time the Saxones were ashamed of the league[19] made: and having recovered their strength, they made their league as voyde, and beseeged the cittie Badon rounde aboute, which now is called Bathe: this when Arthure hearde of,

---

12. A sixth-century Welsh bishop (later Saint Dubritius or Dyfrig in the Welsh). Geoffrey of Monmouth established the tradition that he crowned Arthur.

13. Caerleon, a town in Gwent on the Usk River, often referred to as the site of Arthur's court.

14. Ruler of Britain who is poisoned by a Saxon acting in league with Vortigern. Aurelius is succeeded by his brother, Uther Pendragon.

15. Nobles.

16. A region in northwest France corresponding roughly to Brittany.

17. King of Brittany and an ally of Arthur.

18. Who reported to him fully concerning . . . .

19. Agreement.

havinge gathered his hoaste together, and beholding the tentes of his enemies, he spake thus unto them.

"Because the most ungodly Saxones, disdaine to keepe promise with me, I keeping faith with my God, will endevoure to be advenged of them for the bloud and slaughter of my citizens: Let us therefore manfully set upon those traytours whom by the mediation of Christ out of all doubt we shall overcome with a wished triumphe." And hee rushing upon the ranckes of the Saxones, beinge helped by the prayers of Dubritius in overthrowing many thousandes, obtayned the victorie: and the few which fled this garboyle,[20] he caused them to yeelde to his mercy.

. . . .

Chapter 4.
King Arthures Expedition Towardes the French.

The sixte booke of the *History of Brittaine* speaketh copiously touching things done by Arthure in Fraunce: unto which countrie he went not, before hee had forseene (as it seemed then in deede) with advised counsell, the immunitie or disburdenance[21] of Brittaines troubles. He had to nephewe one Mordred by name, sonne of Lotho,[22] King of the Pictes and of Anna sister of Aurelius Ambrosius King of Brittaine. Unto this man, because hee was most nearest in bloodde,[23] and familiar in acquaintance, did hee committe all his kingdome, together with Guenhera his most loving wife. For Mordred, in respect of fortitude or magnanimitie, was most commendable, and besides this for his quicke and prompt witte, in accomplishing his affayres: which vertues, had hee not obscured with most ardent lust of ruling, and offence of adultery, (but in meane time at first kept close for feare) hee had in deede beene worthie to have beene accompted amongst the most famous personages. Nowe had Arthure entered into Fraunce, and the governors being subdued, hee had left a notable testimony of his prowesse there. Behold, now commeth a savage tyraunt, cruell and fierce, who had ravished Helen the neece of Hoel of Armorica, or the Lesse Brittaine (stolen away and brought out of Brittaine) at the

---

20. Tumult.

21. The freedom from or removal of.

22. King of Lothian, a region in Scotland. In Malory his name is Lot and he is married to Morgawse, Arthur's half-sister.

23. Most closely related.

coaste of Fraunce, and where upon she died. Arthure could not take well this so heynous a reproach done unto Helen, and straight way gotte the tyraunte by the throate, that hee utterly destroyed this greate and horrible monster. And not longe after did Hoel cause to bee erected a sacred tombe for Helen in the islande where she died, and a name fitly given unto the place where Helens tombe was made, which serveth even till this daye. The Cronicles of the writer of Digion in Burgonie, doe with greate commendation extolle Arthure warring in Fraunce, by these like wordes.

> Arthure for nine yeeres space, subdued Fraunce unto him, having betaken his kingdome and Queene unto Mordred his nephew. But he desiring ambitiously to raigne (yet fearing only Cerdicius)[24] gave him, to the end hee should favour his doinges, seaven other provinces. Viz. Sudo Saxony or Southsex, Sudorheiam or Southery, Berrochiam or Barckeshyre: Vilugiam or Wiltshier: Duriam or Dorcetshier: Devoniam or Devonshier: and Corineam Cornwale.[25] And Cerdicius consenting unto these (sending for the Englishmen) restored his provinces, and was crowned after the manner of the countrie at Wintchester. But Mordred was crowned over the Brittaines at London. And so Cerdicius, when he had raigned three yeeres, died, while Arthure yet remayned amongest the French: unto whome Kinrichus succeeded. In the seaventh yeere of whose raigne Arthure, returned into Englande.

Thus farre out of the Cronicles. These which I have nowe recited, have not onely their antiquitie, but also credite,[26] and with a certaine circumstance are consonant to the history.
. . . .

Chapter 9.
King Arthures Returne out of Fraunce.

Arthure had advertisement both by letters and also by messengers of spetiall credit, that Mordred his too much familier friend was with Guenhera, whiles himselfe was absent: and besides this, that he had entered a league (against the oath of his aleageance) with Cerdicius the King and with the Saxons: yeelding up unto them (to the

---

24. Cerdic was the leader of the second wave of Saxon invasions of Britain and the founder of the West Saxon dynasty.

25. Sussex, Surrey, Berkshire, Wiltshire, Dorset, Devon, and Cornwall.

26. Credibility.

infinite daunger of the common weale) almost all the countrie which extendeth towardes the south part of Brittaine. An other mischeefe also happened hereunto: then[27] which more pernicious was none. This same most lewde[28] revolt, and most ungracious betrayer of his lord, and land, (al bondes of amitie, aliance and alegeance being broken) takes upon him the purple roabe not fitte for those his sholders, and trusting to a new upstart tyranny of his, mountes up to the royall seate. Arthure could no longer abide so notable an injury howsoever done unto him by this perjured person: although he also a few yeares before had determined his just revenge upon him, (being yet letted[29] by his warres in Fraunce) but that he would utterly subvert by might and maine, so horrible, so ingent,[30] and so cruell a monster. His navy therefore being prepared, from the cittie Bononia[31] bordering upon the coastes of Belgia unto the shoare of Richeborow[32] (as witnesseth Mattheus Florilegus[33] together with others) he laboureth the seaes with prosperouse windes. The most lewdest servant of all understood before,[34] the comming of his gracious lord, and with a full appoynted hoast not without counsell and helpe of Pictes, Scottes, and West Saxones, most boldly meetes him, returning home. The coast of Kent ratled with all manner noyse of weapons: and now the captaines stood orderly before their ensignes: the troupe of chevalliers also conquerours of the world with chearefull[35] assaults tossed their weapons, parte of them drew out their fierie flashing blades, and part shaked their shivering speares with strong handes. They had all one voyce. The battells were warrelike fightes. Arthure most jocund with this prompt alacritie and stoute courages of his

---

27. Than.

28. Wicked.

29. Prevented.

30. Great.

31. Boulogne-sur-Mer, at the mouth of the Liane River on the English Channel.

32. A port two miles north of Sandwich.

33. The *Flores Historiarum* (Flowers of History), long believed to have been written by one Matthew of Westminster, is a Latin chronicle dealing with English history up to 1326. The name Matthew of Westminster was apparently a blending of "Matthew of Paris," from whose *Chronica Major* a part of the *Flores* was copied, and Westminster, the abbey in which part of the work was written.

34. Knew about beforehand.

35. Lively.

souldiours, as the miracle both of all manhood, and also of ripe wisdome by experience, made such a like oration unto them by lifting up his eyes from the earth unto heaven, and with cherefulnesse of countenance together with a certaine majestie mixed, saying on this manner.

Yee Chevaliers the most noble lightes[36] of martiall prowesse, and you the other multitude of most approved valiancie, do see whither our fortune and associate of so great victories hath brought us, as what we have with most strong hand gotten abroade, wee may not onely keepe upright, but also get us more greater booties with some straunge[37] and large increase: the which thing that it may at this instant be brought to passe and more easely, such occasion is now offered us, as all good happes[38] could not in deede, if they would, more plentifully, nor more prosperously offer themselves to favour us frendly.[39] Let us therefore go to this geare[40] with most manly courages, whither as Fortune, valiancie, and finally victory calleth us. Now is the most impudent Mordred at hand, yet one most nearest to me in bloude, whome I have brought up and loved in hope of greate fame, and so far forth made much of, and that in very many booties bestowed upon him in deede, and those no lesse beneficiall as when I should passe into France to advenge me of mine enemies, he so seeming to be then undoubtedly of profound counsell, unto him I did both commit my wife and state, (and that which is much more) my native country to keepe, and to governe our affaires as our deputie, finally to defend the same most valiantly from the dayly assault of Saxones, Scottes, and Pictes. But he in meane time forgetfull of my most bountiful liberallity towards him, and of our familiaritie, (which for most part in humaine affaires, hath undoubtedly cheefest importance) and not remembring the solemne oath of warelike[41] order, wherby he is to me most deeply bounden, like a false perjured and mightie contemner of God and man, yea an adulter also, (as Fame reporteth) now entertayneth[42] me, a king and conqueror of nations, and his liege soveraigne lord returning into mine owne countrie (if God so would permit him)

---

36. Luminaries.

37. Very great.

38. Chances.

39. Be favorably disposed toward us.

40. Affair.

41. Martial. (The martial order referred to is the Knights of the Round Table.)

42. Meets.

even with open hostilitie, having ready for his complices[43] the Pictes his kinsmen, the Scottes their neighbours, and last of all the Saxones to helpe him.

And neither doth this so notable mischeefe only touch me, but in deede it toucheth you all. Wherfore you most invincible champions, my only care, and you most valiant fellow souldiers, with present prowesse, handle your comune cause, and let vertue now shine forth in you, which I have hetherunto perceived to be ready, valiant and wonderful alwayes. Sir Gallouinus[44] you the most praise worthy garland of warlike prowesse, whose glory for manie causes, and cheefly this, is most commendable unto the world (in that you have set at nought, Mordred our commune enemie, and in respect of equitie and oath of your alegeance to us made, have despised him your brother in law.) Stand you here on your right hand, as the most apt furnished horne with strength of souldiours. For the first shares of hand stroakes and of renome[45] shal light in this troupe of yours. Sir Augusellus[46] as the bulwarke of most approved valiancie shall cast himselfe to encounter with our enemies at the left wing. I my selfe (and God to friend) will in the middest of you fight it out continually and will be present as your onely safegard, but to the enemies will I be a terrour, a scourge, and a deserved destruction. But what neede many wordes,[47] which neyther in deede adde nor take away valiant courage. Your valiancy is enlarged by custome, exercise, and sustayning of labour, watchinges[48] and penury, yea finallie by shedding of the enemies bloud, and spoyling the same enemies: For the which considerations both I to you, and you to me againe (God favouring so just a cause) do promise assured victory. Go to, make immortall tryall of your manhoodes, and slay down right those traytours at a pinch.[49]

When he had thus saide, they altogether at their governours commaundement showted aloude, and with a cherefull onsette, bestowing in order their ensignes, far and wide shewed forth the valiant tokens of warlike attempt. So at the length partly their enemies being slaine, and partly put to flight, Arthure obtayned the

---

43. Accomplices.

44. Gawain.

45. Renown.

46. King of Scotland and brother to Lot and Urien, Augusellus is at first Arthur's enemy but becomes his ally.

47. What necessity is there for many words?

48. "Watching" here means "guarding against attack."

49. At a [i.e., this] critical juncture.

victory with an horrible overthrow of his enemies. But there were slaine in that battell fought at the haven of Dorcester, both Gallouinus and Augusellus the two thunderbolts of the battell, as Graius[50] maketh mention in his booke called *Scalecronica*, and as other authours of fame not to be despysed, do witnesse. Mordred blaming Fortunes untowardnesse,[51] with a navy recovered, and the remnant of his hoast therein, got him with shame enough to the haven of Tammeroth on the sea coaste of Cornwaile. The noble coarse[52] of Gallouinus was entombed in a certaine chappell within the Castle of Dorcester. But Arthure, (the death of two so excellent famouse men being fully knowne to him) sore bewailed the same: and with often prayer as, also with very deepe greefe of heart, suppressing sorrow from their handes, (nobly minded and of Godly disposition as he was) fatherly tooke care over them. And then in deed having a fresh prepared with incredible expedition a full hoast and army, he determined with long jorneyes to pursue his lewde[53] enemie, and as it were upon the snappe[54] to overthrowe the fugetive. Mordred yet was more craftie, then of power able to withstand: hereupon found he out a meane for unacustomed inventions. He had manifest knowledge given him by espyals,[55] that Arthure most absolutly furnished for the battell, was comming at hand. Wherefore he commanded every souldier wearied upon the land, and againe with toile upon the sea, as also penury of corne,[56] to departe for a season, and having refreshed their industrie, labour, and dilligence, as also furnishing them with munition, so well as he could through the mountayny soiles of Cornwale, by the way that leadeth to the banckes of Severne, not farre thence distant conducteth he his hoast with easie jornies: and in a place which of the common sorte of writers is called Camblan[57] (where as are waste grounds and partly a natural moist plaine, and a little hill rising up to the use of a watch or a prospect) did he pitch his tents. Here am I

---

50. Thomas Gray of Heton, author of a fourteenth-century Anglo-Norman chronicle that relates events from the early history of Britain until 1362.

51. Unpropitiousness.

52. Corpse.

53. Wicked.

54. Suddenly.

55. Spies.

56. Scarcity of grain.

57. Camlann, the site of Arthur's final battle with Mordred.

compelled to interpose or set downe by the way my judgment concerning the place where it was fought by both parts: and for the cause that I should not thinke to bring hether anything amongst the rest, as if it were out of Jupiters braine,[58] but that with the good leave of the learned sort I might explane my conjecture, without all bitternes or disdaine as it were touching it by the way. In which behalfe I freely confes my selfe hardly to hold opinion with Hector Boetius the Scot,[59] which (as his maner is) applieth all most famous facts of antiquity in Brittaine to the commendation of his owne country, beyond all meane and measure. And here he boldly affirmeth that Arthure (with his last ensignes) fought it out not far from the great flowing river of Severne, which he barbarously calleth Humbar not knowing the circumstance of the phrase. But the history of Brittaine beleeveth otherwise, and affirmeth that he scourged his enemies in his last battle in Cornwale: so yet notwithstanding as he mentioneth how Mordred was the second time vanquished and put to flight by Arthure at Winchester.

Graius undoubtedly an excellent champion in behalfe of the truth and a stoute assertor of Arthures glory, holdes the same opinion. Neither singeth the sound censured society of learned witnesses any other song.[60] But truely our conjecture is not of the places, but of the name of the place. Surelie I am almost brought to that poynte, to beleeve that the River Alaune[61] is easily chaunged by the faulte of unlearned lybraryes[62] into Camblan. This river ryseth in Cornewale a fewe myles above the towne Athelstowe otherwise Padstowe, a fisher towne not farre scituate[63] from the salte water of Severne: by meanes wherof, (but yet mixed with salte waters) it runneth downe lower into the countrie. Aboute the heade springes of that originall in champion[64] grounde, and a certaine waste plaine, there is a famous place, somewhat more fruitfull of grasse then of corne. The reporte (amongest the inhabitants so many ages

---

58. The allusion is to the story that Minerva, goddess of wisdom, the arts, and martial prowess, sprang full-grown and in full armor from the brain of Jupiter.

59. Hector Boece (?1465–1536), Scottish historian who wrote a *History of Scotland.*

60. Nor does the sound censured society of learned witnesses sing any other song. [I.e., the scholarly community is of the same opinion.]

61. Former name of the River Camel.

62. Scribes.

63. Located.

64. Level and open.

preserved) declareth that of olde time, there was made a notable
garboile[65] by fighting in that place, but in meane time the truth of
the historie is unknowne unto the common sorte. Many things no
doubt even in this our age are founde out of the same place by
ploughmen and those that delve at the river: such as are these
quoynes[66] which shewe the governments of auncient personages,
ringes, fragments of harnesse and brasen ornaments for bridles
unguilte, for trappers and also saddles for horses. This is my
conjecture, both by reason of the scituation[67] of the place, and also
for the name of the river Alaune, running hard by, yet not far
dissonant[68] (if a man behold it more throughly) from Camblan.
Arthure now draweth neare, and passing over the river of
Tamermouth, by knowne passages, yet otherwise a streame most
violent in many places and most deepe (the enimy fugitive not
being regarded) he pitcheth tents against tents. Behold,
desperation (as oft times it hapneth) restoreth unwonted boldnes to
the overcommed part. And wherupon both partes provoke battle,
burning with hope of spoyle and of victory, as also fearing nothing
lesse then death.

> *Quis cladem illius pugnae, quis funera fando*
> *Explicet: aut possit lachrymis aequare labores.*

> *Who shall that bloodie broyle expresse or the dead corpses name?*
> *Or who can justly tell the toyles, with just teares for the same?*

Mordred the first forman[69] of all mischiefe (this battle being
attempted) and he thrust through with the sword, received a just
rewarde for his breach of faith or perjury. Let him be an example,
and that for ever, to such as for desire of government infringe and
violate their faith. There was slaine together with the tyrant a great
number of noble personages and of old beaten souldiers: But
neither was the victorie without bloodshedde befallen unto Arthure.
For in that broyle and fierce fight, himselfe was either slaine
outright, or wounded past recovery, so that a little while after with
publike lamentation of all Brittaine (but specially of his heavie

---

65. Tumult.
66. Coins.
67. Location.
68. Different.
69. Leader.

hearted chevalyers for the mischance of so noble a prince) he was carried away from thence. And this in deede was the end or death of the most puissant Prince Arthure.

Chapter 15.
King Arthures Tombe Found.

When the Saxones powre grewe to some force after Arthures death, and that the Picts and Scots by and by were put to flight, and chased away beyond the vale of Severne, the same Saxones began not so much to feare, and much lesse to esteeme of, but rather openly to set at nought the remnauntes of those vanquished Brittaines. Wherefore, the glory of them beganne to floorish, but of the Brittaines to decrease and fade away: Yet so, as the Saxones left almost nothing (touching affaires passed betweene them and the Brittaines) at that time perfectly written for the posterytie.

For, those thinges which were written (after Christ was knowne unto them) concerning the first victories of the Saxones, are delivered by the reportes of the common people, and so received, and in writinges so committed: or els the Brittaines being utterly worne away by so many battles, bestowed scarce any just or right dilligence in writing of the historie. Only there are extant certaine fragments of Gildas the moncke of the city Bangor rather flaying alive, dismembring, and wounding to death the Brittaines, then allowing them with any value of vertue, so farre foorth as he seemeth a rethorician thorowly moved to make evyll reporte. By this meanes were the affaires of Brittaine, through calamitie of battles left obscure or unrevayled. The historicall singers only studied to preserve also with musicall meanes the famous memorie of nobles in those daies. They sung the famous facts of noble personages upon the harp. This studie or practise wonderfully profited knowledge, as it were delivered by hand unto posterity. Whereupon in deede it so commeth heere to passe also, that the name, fame, and glory of Arthure might so be preserved after a sorte.

. . . .

William a Norman[70] had conquered the nation of Englishmen by permission of God, and now came the kingdome of

---

70. William the Conqueror, Duke of Normandy, who invaded England in 1066. When his son, William II, died in a hunting accident, Henry I, known as Henry Beauclerk because of the belief that he could read Latin, succeeded to the throne of England. Henry arranged for the marriage of his daughter Matilda to Geoffrey

England, unto Henry the second of that name, nephew by Matildes the daughter of Henry Beuaclercke, and the sonne of Geoffry Plantagenet, Duke of Gaunt. This man endevoring by all meanes to enlarge the limittes of his kingdome, applyed also his minde unto the kingdome of Ireland. Richard of Clare[71] Erle of Chepstowe, (so called by reason of the wanderinge river) a man both most noble by birth, fortune, and vertue, went into Ireland, beeing before requested of Deronutius the ruler of Lagenia, so to do: in which expedition hee behaved him selfe so valiantly, that (they being cast out by heapes put to flight, and vanquished which withstood the ruler) he purchased him selfe fame and immortall glory and (if this also might anything availe to the purpose) he obtayned besides greate riches unto himselfe thereby, taking to wife Eva the daughter of Deronicius, and heire by right nougth.[72] King Henry had understanding of the successe of Richard the Erle of Chepestowe, and whether he envyed his glory, or (which is most like) that hee earnestly sought the pray[73] of this rich kingdome, hee forbad this Richard in the meane time to beare rule in Ireland, not disdayning yet to proffer him reward. He being wise, fully knowing the Princes purpose, gave place unto his right. In the meane season Henry having prepared no small part of an hoast,[74] came into Cambria or Wales, and purposing there to appoynt the residue, he thence straight sayled from Menevia or Sanct Davids into Ireland, with hope of which kingdome to obtaine, hee burned as hote as fire. Whiles he busieth him selfe here aboutes being (for his worthinesse as befitted) receyved of the governoures of Wales, at his banquettes there (using an interpreter) he gave eare not with out pleasure unto the historicall singers, which singe to the harpe famous actes of noble men. Truly there was one amongst the rest most skilfull in knowledge of antiquitie. He so sunge the praises and noble actes of Arthure comparing Henry with him as conquerour in time to come for many respectes, that hee both wonderfully pleased, and also delighted the Kinges eares: at what time also the King learned this

---

Plantagenet. The word "nephew" in this paragraph is used in the archaic sense of "grandson."

71. Richard of Clare formed an alliance with Dermot, King of Leinster (the Deronutius of Lagenia of the text), and married Dermot's daughter.

72. This is a strange phrase, the meaning of which should be "sole heir," the sense of the Latin phrase it translates ("ex asse haerede").

73. Booty.

74. Host, i.e., army.

thing especially of the historical singer, that Arthure was buried at Avalonia in the religiouse place. Whereupon sending away the saide singer as witnesse of such a monument most liberally rewarded, he had conference with Henricus Blesensis, alias Soliacensis his nephew, who even then or a litle after was made of an abbot in the Isle of Bermundsege, cheife magistrate over Glastenbury that he might with most exquisite diligence search out thorowly the tombe or burying place of Arthure within the compasse of that religiouse house. It was assayed by him otherwhiles and at length founde out with greate difficulty, in the last dayes, as some suppose of Henry the Second, King of England: but as others thinke (unto whom I easely assent) in the beginning of the raigne of Richard the First, his sonne.

Touching both this searching for, and finding out of the bones, two persons specially amongst others have written their mindes: of which two one was a moncke of Glastenbury,[75] and by name unknowne to me, but the other was Silvester Giraldus.[76] Furdermore there had beene hereunto added also Gulielmus Meildunensis,[77] as the third witnesse to be conferrred with them both, but that death had taken him away in his aged yeares before the sepulcre or tombe was found. The testimonies of these men will I use especially, and at this instant I will bring hether the wordes of Annonymus the moncke. King Arthure was entombed, like as (by King Henry the Second) Henry the Abbot had learned, whose cosen germaine[78] and familier friend he of late was. But the King had often times heard this out of the actes of the Brittaines, and of their historicall singers, that Arthure was buried neare unto the old church in the religiouse place betweene two pyramedes in times

---

75. The account can be found in John of Glastonbury's *Cronica sive Antiquitates Glastoniensis Ecclesia* (Chronicle of Glastonbury Abbey), which has been edited by James Carley and translated by David Townsend (Woodbridge: The Boydell Press, 1985).

76. Presumably Gerald of Wales (Giraldus Cambrensis) (1146–1223), a British historian who gives an account of the finding of Arthur's tomb in two works, the *De Principis Instructione* and the *Speculum Ecclesiae.*

77. William of Malmesbury died in 1143, almost fifty years before Arthur's tomb was reported to have been found (in 1190 or early 1191). Leland suggests that William would have spoken about Arthur's tomb if he had lived long enough to see its discovery. Perhaps he does this to anticipate the argument that William says in Book III of his *Gesta Regum Anglorum* (History of the Kings of England) that Arthur's tomb is nowhere to be seen.

78. Near relative.

past, nobly engraven, and erected as it is reported for the memory of him.

And King Arthure was buryed verie deeply for feare of the Saxons, whom he had often times vanquished, and whome he had altogether rejected or cast out of the Isle of Brittaine. And whome Mordred his mischeevous nephew had first called backe againe and brought thither against him: least they (should also with mallice of minde raige in crueltie towardes the deade body) which had laboured by tooth and naile even now to possesse againe the whole island after his death. Againe for and in respect of the same feare, he was laide in a certaine broade stone, (as it were at a grave) found of them which digged there, of seaven foote as it were under the earth: when yet notwithstanding Arthures tombe was founde more lower, of nyne foote depth.[79] There was moreover founde a leaden crosse not set into the uppermost but rather neathermost parte of the stone, having thereon these letters engraven.

HIC JACET SEPULTUS INCLITUS REX
ARTHURIUS IN INSULA AVALONIAE.[80]

And the crosse taken out of the stone, (the saide Abbot Henry shewing the same) we have seene with our eyes, and have reade these letters. But like as the crosse was infixed to the neathermost parte of the stone: So that parte of the crosse engraven (to the ende it might be more secrete) was turned towardes the stone. Doubtlesse a wonderfull industrie and exquisite wisdome of the men in that age, who by all endevoures desired to hide in secret manner the body of so greate a personage, and their soveraigne lord, especially the patrone of that place, by reason of the instant troubled state: And who yet had further care that at one or other time afterwardes (when the trouble surceased,[81] by the perfect order of those letters engraven in the crosse and found out other whiles) they might make apparant testimonies of his buriall.

And as the foresaide King Henry had before declared all the matter to the Abbot: so the body of Arthure was found not in a marble tombe (as it befitted so noble a kinge) not in a stony place, or graven out of the white Paris stone, but rather in a wodden tombe made hollow for this purpose, and of sixtene foote deepe in

---

79. I.e., the tomb was sixteen feet down.

80. Here lies buried the famous King Arthur in the Isle of Avalon.

81. Ended.

the earth, more for the hastie then the honourable burying of so puyssant a prince, that time of trouble requyring the same.

Anno Domini. 1189. The King besetting the place, with caldrons, on a certaine day, commanded them to digge there. Herehence the delvers having searched an exceeding depth, and now almost being past hope, beholde yet they found out a wodden tombe of a wonderfull greatnesse fast closed rounde aboute. Which being lift up, and opened, they found therin the Kinges bones of an incredible bignesse, so as the bone of his shinne, might reach from the ground unto the middle of the legge in a tall man. They also found a leaden crosse on the other side. Thus engraven.

> HIC JACET SEPULTUS INCLITUS
> REX ARTHURIUS IN INSULA AVALONIAE.

Herehence they opening the tombe of the Queene buried with Arthure founde a yealow locke of womans heaire, both faire of it selfe, and also twisted together with wonderful curiositie: which when they had touched, mouldred[82] away too nothing. Then the Abbot and his convent, taking up their lyneaments[83] translated the same with joy into the greater church, placing them in a new tombe (nobly engraven and pullished in the inwarde partes) after a twofold fashion: That is to say, the Kinges body by it selfe at the heade of the tombe: The Queene, at the feete of him, namely in the easte parte: where, untill this day present, they honourably take their rest. But this epitaph is engraven upon their tombe.

> *Hic jacet Arthurius flos regum, gloria regni,*
> *Quem, mores, probitas, commendant laude perenni.*

> *Here lyeth Arthure the floure of kinges, and glory of his kingdome,*
> *Whome life and honestie commende with lasting praise to come.*

Thus farre most diligently, and also most faithfully have we converted these things out of the booke at Glastenbury into this present use. . . .

---

82. Crumbled.
83. Remains.

From: The Faerie Queene

by

EDMUND SPENSER

Book I
Canto VII.

The Redcrosse knight is captive made
　　By gyaunt proud opprest,
Prince Arthur meets with Una great-
　　ly with those newes distrest.

What man so wise, what earthly wit so ware,[1]
　　As to descry[2] the crafty cunning traine,
　　By which deceipt doth maske in visour faire,
　　And cast her colours dyed deepe in graine,
　　To seeme like Truth, whose shape she well can faine,
　　And fitting gestures to her purpose frame,
　　The guiltlesse man with guile to entertaine?
　　Great maistresse of her art was that false dame,
The false Duessa, cloked with Fidessaes name.

Who when returning from the drery Night,
　　She fownd not in that perilous house of Pryde,
　　Where she had left, the noble Redcrosse knight,
　　Her hoped pray;[3] she would no lenger bide,
　　But forth she went, to seeke him far and wide.
　　Ere long she fownd, whereas he wearie sate,
　　To rest him selfe, foreby[4] a fountaine side,

---

1. Prudent.
2. Discover.
3. Prey.
4. Close by.

Disarmed all of yron-coted plate,[5]
And by his side his steed the grassy forage ate.

He feedes upon the cooling shade, and bayes[6]
    His sweatie forehead in the breathing wind,
    Which through the trembling leaves full gently playes
    Wherein the cherefull birds of sundry[7] kind
    Do chaunt sweet musick, to delight his mind:
    The witch approching gan[8] him fairely greet,
    And with reproch of carelesnesse unkind
    Upbrayd, for leaving her in place unmeet,[9]
With fowle words tempring faire, soure gall with hony sweet.

Unkindnesse past, they gan of solace treat,
    And bathe in pleasaunce of the joyous shade,
    Which shielded them against the boyling heat,
    And with greene boughes decking a gloomy glade,
    About the fountaine like a girlond made;
    Whose bubbling wave did ever freshly well,
    Ne ever would through fervent sommer fade:
    The sacred Nymph, which therein wont to dwell,
Was out of Dianes[10] favour, as it then befell.

The cause was this: one day when Phoebe fayre
    With all her band was following the chace,
    This Nymph, quite tyr'd with heat of scorching ayre
    Sat downe to rest in middest of the race:
    The goddesse wroth gan fowly her disgrace,[11]
    And bad the waters, which from her did flow,
    Be such as she her selfe was then in place.
    Thenceforth her waters waxed dull and slow,
And all that drunke thereof, did faint and feeble grow.

---

5. Armor.

6. Bathes.

7. Various.

8. "Gan" is an indicator of the past tense; thus "gan . . . greet" = "greeted."

9. Unsuitable.

10. Diana, goddess of the moon. "Phoebe" in the next line is another name for Diana.

11. Disparage.

Hereof this gentle knight unweeting[12] was,
    And lying downe upon the sandie graile,[13]
    Drunke of the streame, as cleare as cristall glas;
    Eftsoones[14] his manly forces gan to faile,
    And mightie strong was turnd to feeble fraile.
    His chaunged powres at first them selves not felt,
    Till crudled[15] cold his corage gan assaile,
    And chearefull bloud in faintnesse chill did melt,
Which like a fever fit through all his body swelt.

Yet goodly court he made still to his dame,
    Pourd out in loosnesse on the grassy grownd,
    Both carelesse of his health, and of his fame:
    Till at the last he heard a dreadfull sownd,
    Which through the wood loud bellowing, did rebownd,
    That all the earth for terrour seemd to shake,
    And trees did tremble. Th'Elfe therewith astownd,[16]
    Upstarted lightly from his looser make,[17]
And his unready weapons gan in hand to take.

But ere he could his armour on him dight,[18]
    Or get his shield, his monstrous enimy
    With sturdie steps came stalking in his sight,
    An hideous geant horrible and hye,
    That with his talnesse seemd to threat the skye,
    The ground eke[19] groned under him for dreed;
    His living like saw never living eye,
    Ne durst[20] behold: his stature did exceed
The hight of three the tallest sonnes of mortall seed.

---

12. Unaware.

13. Gravel. (This word has nothing to do with the Holy Grail.)

14. Soon.

15. Congealed (but the sense seems to be "congealing").

16. The "Elfe" is the Red Cross Knight, who is from the realm of the Fairy Queen. "Astownd" means "astonished."

17. Mate.

18. Put.

19. Also.

20. Nor dared.

The greatest Earth his uncouth mother was,
  And blustring Aeolus[21] his boasted sire,
  Who with his breath, which through the world doth pas,
  Her hollow womb did secretly inspire,
  And fild her hidden caves with stormie yre,
  That she conceiv'd; and trebling the dew time,
  In which the wombes of women do expire,[22]
  Brought forth this monstrous masse of earthly slime,
Puft up with emptie wind, and fild with sinfull crime.

So growen great through arrogant delight
  Of th'high descent, whereof he was yborne,
  And through presumption of his matchlesse might,
  All other powres and knighthood he did scorne.
  Such now he marcheth to this man forlorne,
  And left to losse:[23] his stalking steps are stayde
  Upon a snaggy oke, which he had torne
  Out of his mothers[24] bowelles, and it made
His mortall mace, wherewith his foemen he dismayde.

That when the knight he spide, he gan advance
  With huge force and insupportable mayne,[25]
  And towardes him with dreadfull fury praunce;
  Who haplesse, and eke hopelesse, all in vaine
  Did to him pace, sad battaile to darrayne,[26]
  Disarmd, disgrast, and inwardly dismayde,
  And eke so faint in every joynt and vaine,
  Through that fraile fountaine, which him feeble made,
That scarsely could he weeld his bootlesse single blade.

The geaunt strooke so maynly[27] mercilesse,
  That could have overthrowne a stony towre,
  And were not heavenly grace, that him did blesse,

---

21. God of the winds.
22. Breathe out, i.e., give birth.
23. Ruin.
24. I.e., the Earth's.
25. Might.
26. Engage in.
27. Powerfully.

He had beene pouldred[28] all, as thin as flowre:
But he was wary of that deadly stowre,[29]
And lightly lept from underneath the blow:
Yet so exceeding was the villeins powre,
That with the wind it did him overthrow,
And all his sences stound,[30] that still he lay full low.

As when that divelish yron engin[31] wrought
In deepest Hell, and framd by Furies skill,
With windy nitre[32] and quick sulphur fraught,
And ramd with bullet round, ordaind to kill,
Conceiveth fire, the heavens it doth fill
With thundring noyse, and all the ayre doth choke,
That none can breath, nor see, nor heare at will,
Through smouldry cloud of duskish stincking smoke,
That th'onely breath[33] him daunts, who hath escapt the stroke.

So daunted when the geaunt saw the knight,
His heavie hand he heaved up on hye,
And him to dust thought to have battred quight,
Untill Duessa loud to him gan crye;
O great Orgoglio, greatest under skye,
O hold thy mortall hand for ladies sake,
Hold for my sake, and do him not to dye,
But vanquisht thine eternall bondslave make,
And me thy worthy meed unto thy leman[34] take.

He hearkned, and did stay[35] from further harmes,
To gayne so goodly guerdon,[36] as she spake:
So willingly she came into his armes,
Who her as willingly to grace did take,

---

28. Pulverized.

29. Combat.

30. Stun.

31. The cannon.

32. Potassium nitrate, used in making gunpowder.

33. Just the force of the blast.

34. Reward as your lover.

35. Refrain.

36. Reward.

And was possessed of his new found make.[37]
Then up he tooke the slombred sencelesse corse,
And ere he could out of his swowne awake,
Him to his castle brought with hastie forse,
And in a dongeon deepe him threw without remorse.

From that day forth Duessa was his deare,
And highly honourd in his haughtie eye,
He gave her gold and purple pall[38] to weare,
And triple crowne set on her head full hye,
And her endowd with royall majestye:
Then for to make her dreaded more of men,
And peoples harts with awfull terrour tye,
A monstrous beast ybred in filthy fen
He chose, which he had kept long time in darksome den.

Such one it was, as that renowmed Snake[39]
Which great Alcides in Stremona slew,
Long fostred in the filth of Lerna lake,
Whose many heads out budding ever new,
Did breed him endlesse labour to subdew:
But this same monster much more ugly was;
For seven great heads out of his body grew,
An yron brest, and backe of scaly bras,
And all embrewd[40] in bloud, his eyes did shine as glas.

His tayle was stretched out in wondrous length,
That to the house of heavenly gods it raught,[41]
And with extorted powre, and borrow'd strength,
The ever-burning lamps from thence it brought,
And prowdly threw to ground, as things of nought;
And underneath his filthy feet did tread

---

37. Mate.

38. Rich cloth.

39. One of the Labors of Hercules (here called Alcides, i.e., son of Alcaeus) was to slay the nine-headed serpent, the Hydra of the Lernean marshes. The difficulty of the task lay in the fact that when one head was cut off, two new ones grew up in its place.

40. Stained.

41. Reached.

The sacred things, and holy heasts foretaught.[42]
Upon this dreadfull beast with sevenfold head
He set the false Duessa, for more aw and dread.

The wofull dwarfe, which saw his maisters fall,
 Whiles he had keeping of his grasing steed,
 And valiant knight become a caytive thrall,[43]
 When all was past, tooke up his forlorne weed,[44]
 His mightie armour, missing most at need;
 His silver shield, now idle maisterlesse;
 His poynant[45] speare, that many made to bleed,
 The ruefull moniments of heavinesse,
And with them all departes, to tell his great distresse.

He had not travaild long, when on the way
 He wofull ladie, wofull Una met,
 Fast flying from the paynims greedy pray,
 Whilest Satyrane[46] him from pursuit did let:
 Who when her eyes she on the dwarfe had set,
 And saw the signes, that deadly tydings spake,
 She fell to ground for sorrowfull regret,
 And lively breath her sad brest did forsake,
Yet might her pitteous hart be seene to pant and quake.

The messenger of so unhappie newes,
 Would faine[47] have dyde: dead was his hart within,
 Yet outwardly some little comfort shewes:
 At last recovering hart, he does begin
 To rub her temples, and to chaufe[48] her chin,
 And every tender part does tosse and turne:
 So hardly[49] he the flitted life does win,

---

42. Commandments previously taught.

43. Captive slave.

44. Clothing, i.e., armor.

45. Sharp.

46. Satyrane represents natural virtue. In Canto vi of Book I he helped Una escape from the satyrs and then fought with the "paynim" or pagan Sansloy (the name meaning "without law") while she escaped.

47. Gladly.

48. Rub.

49. With difficulty.

Unto her native prison[50] to retourne:
Then gins her grieved ghost[51] thus to lament and mourne.

Ye dreary instruments of dolefull sight,
 That doe this deadly spectacle behold,
 Why do ye lenger feed on loathed light,
 Or liking find to gaze on earthly mould,
 Sith cruell fates the carefull threeds unfould,[52]
 The which my life and love together tyde?
 Now let the stony dart of senselesse cold
 Perce to my hart, and pas through every side,
And let eternall night so sad sight fro me hide.

O lightsome day, the lampe of highest Jove,[53]
 First made by him, mens wandring wayes to guyde,
 When darkenesse he in deepest dongeon drove,
 Henceforth thy hated face for ever hyde,
 And shut up heavens windowes shyning wyde:
 For earthly sight can nought but sorrow breed,
 And late repentance, which shall long abyde.
 Mine eyes no more on vanitie shall feed,
But seeled up with death, shall have their deadly meed.[54]

Then downe againe she fell unto the ground;
 But he her quickly reared up againe:
 Thrise did she sinke adowne in deadly swownd,
 And thrise he her reviv'd with busie paine:
 At last when life recover'd had the raine,[55]
 And over-wrestled his strong enemie,
 With foltring tong, and trembling every vaine,
 Tell on (quoth she) the wofull tragedie,
The which these reliques sad present unto mine eie.

Tempestuous fortune hath spent all her spight,
 And thrilling sorrow throwne his utmost dart;

---

50. I.e., the body.
51. Spirit.
52. Since cruel Fates unwind the sorrow-filled threads of life.
53. Jove or Jupiter was the god of the sky.
54. Reward.
55. Control.

Thy sad tongue cannot tell more heavy plight,
Then that I feele, and harbour in mine hart:
Who hath endur'd the whole, can beare each part.
If death it be, it is not the first wound,
That launched hath my brest with bleeding smart.
Begin, and end the bitter balefull stound;[56]
If lesse, then that I feare, more favour I have found.

Then gan the dwarfe the whole discourse declare,
The subtill traines of Archimago[57] old;
The wanton loves of false Fidessa faire,
Bought with the bloud of vanquisht paynim bold:
The wretched payre transform'd to treen mould;[58]
The house of Pride, and perils round about;
The combat, which he with Sansjoy did hould;
The lucklesse conflict with the gyant stout,
Wherein captiv'd, of life or death he stood in doubt.

She heard with patience all unto the end,
And strove to maister sorrowfull assay,[59]
Which greater grew, the more she did contend,
And almost rent[60] her tender hart in tway;
And love fresh coles unto her fire did lay:
For greater love, the greater is the losse.
Was never ladie loved dearer day,
Then she did love the knight of the Redcrosse;
For whose deare sake so many troubles her did tosse.

At last when fervent sorrow slaked[61] was,
She up arose, resolving him to find
A live or dead: and forward forth doth pas,

---

56. Pain.

57. Archimago is the hypocritical evil magician who represents the Catholic Church. Earlier in the book he adopted the clothes of the Red Cross Knight. The account of earlier events continues with reference to "Fidessa," one of the guises adopted by Duessa, who represents falsehood; the transformation of Fradubio and Fraelissa into trees by Duessa; Duessa's leading the Red Cross Knight to the house of Pride and his battle with "Sansjoy" (without joy).

58. The form of trees.

59. Tribulation.

60. Tore.

61. Abated.

All as the dwarfe the way to her assynd:[62]
And evermore in constant carefull mind
She fed her wound with fresh renewed bale;[63]
Long tost with stormes, and bet[64] with bitter wind,
High over hils, and low adowne the dale,
She wandred many a wood, and measurd many a vale.

At last she chaunced by good hap[65] to meet
A goodly knight, faire marching by the way
Together with his squire, arayed meet:
His glitterand armour shined farre away,
Like glauncing light of Phoebus[66] brightest ray;
From top to toe no place appeared bare,
That deadly dint of steele endanger may:
Athwart his brest a bauldrick[67] brave he ware,
That shynd, like twinkling stars, with stons most pretious rare.

And in the midst thereof one pretious stone
Of wondrous worth, and eke of wondrous mights,
Shapt like a ladies head, exceeding shone,
Like Hesperus[68] emongst the lesser lights,
And strove for to amaze the weaker sights;
Thereby his mortall blade full comely hong
In yvory sheath, ycarv'd with curious slights;[69]
Whose hilts were burnisht gold, and handle strong
Of mother pearle, and buckled with a golden tong.

His haughtie helmet, horrid[70] all with gold,
Both glorious brightnesse, and great terrour bred;
For all the crest a dragon did enfold
With greedie pawes, and over all did spred
His golden wings: his dreadfull hideous hed

---

62. Pointed out.
63. Torment.
64. Struck.
65. Luck.
66. The sun's.
67. Belt.
68. The evening star.
69. Designs.
70. Bristling, i.e., covered or decorated.

Close couched on the bever,[71] seem'd to throw
From flaming mouth bright sparkles fierie red,
That suddeine horror to faint harts did show;
And scaly tayle was stretcht adowne his backe full low.

Upon the top of all his loftie crest,
    A bunch of haires discolourd diversly,
    With sprincled pearle, and gold full richly drest,
    Did shake, and seem'd to daunce for jollity,
    Like to an almond tree ymounted hye
    On top of greene Selinis[72] all alone,
    With blossomes brave bedecked daintily;
    Whose tender locks do tremble every one
At every little breath, that under heaven is blowne.

His warlike shield all closely cover'd was,
    Ne might of mortall eye be ever seene;
    Not made of steele, nor of enduring bras,
    Such earthly mettals soone consumed bene:
    But all of diamond perfect pure and cleene
    It framed was, one massie entire mould,
    Hewen out of adamant[73] rocke with engines keene,
    That point of speare it never percen could,
Ne dint of direfull sword[74] divide the substance would.

The same to wight he never wont disclose,[75]
    But when as monsters huge he would dismay,
    Or daunt unequall armies of his foes,
    Or when the flying heavens he would affray;
    For so exceeding shone his glistring ray,
    That Phoebus golden face it did attaint,[76]
    As when a cloud his beames doth over-lay;

---

71. Overlaid on the visor.
72. A Greek city on the southwest coast of Sicily.
73. Made of adamant (diamond).
74. Nor blow of terrible sword.
75. To [any] person he was never accustomed to disclose.
76. That it sullied the sun's golden face.

And silver Cynthia[77] wexed pale and faint,
As when her face is staynd with magicke arts constraint.

No magicke arts hereof had any might,
Nor bloudie wordes of bold enchaunters call,
But all that was not such, as seemd in sight,
Before that shield did fade, and suddeine fall:
And when him list the raskall routes[78] appall,
Men into stones therewith he could transmew,[79]
And stones to dust, and dust to nought at all;
And when him list the prouder lookes subdew,
He would them gazing blind, or turne to other hew.

Ne let it seme, that credence this exceedes,
For he that made the same, was knowne right well
To have done much more admirable deedes.
It Merlin was, which whylome did excell
All living wightes in might of magicke spell:
Both shield, and sword, and armour all he wrought
For this young Prince, when first to armes he fell;
But when he dyde, the Faerie Queene it brought
To Faerie lond, where yet it may be seene, if sought.

A gentle youth, his dearely loved squire
His speare of heben[80] wood behind him bare,
Whose harmefull head, thrice heated in the fire,
Had riven many a brest with pikehead[81] square;
A goodly person, and could menage faire
His stubborne steed with curbed canon bit,[82]
Who under him did trample as the aire,

---

77. Diana, goddess of the moon, called Cynthia because she was born on Mount Cynthus in Delos.

78. It pleased him the lower-class mobs.

79. Transform.

80. Ebony.

81. Metal tip, as on a pike.

82. Smooth, round bit.

And chauft,[83] that any on his backe should sit;
The yron rowels[84] into frothy fome he bit.

When as this knight nigh to the ladie drew,
    With lovely court he gan her entertaine;
    But when he heard her answeres loth, he knew
    Some secret sorrow did her heart distraine:[85]
    Which to allay, and calme her storming paine,
    Faire feeling words he wisely gan display,
    And for her humour fitting purpose faine,
    To tempt the cause it selfe for to bewray:[86]
Wherewith emmov'd, these bleeding words she gan to say.

What worlds delight, or joy of living speach
    Can heart, so plung'd in sea of sorrowes deepe,
    And heaped with so huge misfortunes, reach?
    The carefull cold beginneth for to creepe,
    And in my heart his yron arrow steepe,
    Soone as I thinke upon my bitter bale:[87]
    Such helplesse harmes yts better hidden keepe,
    Then rip up griefe, where it may not availe,
My last left comfort is, my woes to weepe and waile.

Ah Ladie deare, quoth then the gentle knight,
    Well may I weene,[88] your griefe is wondrous great;
    For wondrous great griefe groneth in my spright,[89]
    Whiles thus I heare you of your sorrowes treat.
    But wofull Ladie let me you intrete,
    For to unfold the anguish of your hart:
    Mishaps are maistred by advice discrete,
    And counsell mittigates the greatest smart;
Found never helpe, who never would his hurts impart.

---

83. Raged.
84. Knobs on a horse's bit.
85. Constrain.
86. Reveal.
87. Grief.
88. Guess.
89. Spirit.

O but (quoth she) great griefe will not be tould,
    And can more easily be thought, then said.
    Right so; (quoth he) but he, that never would,
    Could never: will to might gives greatest aid.
    But griefe (quoth she) does greater grow displaid,
    If then it find not helpe, and breedes despaire.
    Despaire breedes not (quoth he) where faith is staid.
    No faith so fast (quoth she) but flesh does paire.[90]
Flesh may empaire (quoth he) but reason can repaire.

His goodly reason, and well guided speach
    So deepe did settle in her gratious thought,
    That her perswaded to disclose the breach,
    Which love and fortune in her heart had wrought,
    And said; Faire Sir, I hope good hap[91] hath brought
    You to inquire the secrets of my griefe,
    Or that your wisedome will direct my thought,
    Or that your prowesse can me yield reliefe:
Then heare the storie sad, which I shall tell you briefe.

The forlorne maiden, whom your eyes have seene
    The laughing stocke of fortunes mockeries,
    Am th'only daughter of a King and Queene,
    Whose parents deare, whilest equall destinies
    Did runne about, and their felicities
    The favourable heavens did not envy,
    Did spread their rule through all the territories,
    Which Phison[92] and Euphrates floweth by,
And Gehons golden waves doe wash continually.

Till that their cruell cursed enemy,
    An huge great dragon horrible in sight,
    Bred in the loathly lakes of Tartary,[93]
    With murdrous ravine,[94] and devouring might

---

90. Lessen.

91. Luck.

92. The rivers mentioned here are three of the four rivers of Paradise: the Pison, the Gihon, and the Euphrates. (The fourth river is the Hiddekel.) (Cf. Genesis 2:10-14.)

93. Tartarus, the infernal regions in classical mythology.

94. Voracity.

Their kingdome spoild, and countrey wasted quight:
Themselves, for feare into his jawes to fall,
He forst to castle strong to take their flight,
Where fast embard in mightie brasen wall,
He has them now foure yeres besiegd to make them thrall.

Full many knights adventurous and stout
Have enterprizd[95] that monster to subdew;
From every coast that heaven walks about,
Have thither come the noble martiall crew,
That famous hard atchievements still pursew,
Yet never any could that girlond win,
But all still shronke,[96] and still he greater grew:
All they for want of faith, or guilt of sin,
The pitteous pray[97] of his fierce crueltie have bin.

At last yledd with[98] farre reported praise,
Which flying fame throughout the world had spred,
Of doughtie knights, whom Faery land did raise,
That noble order hight[99] of Maidenhed,
Forthwith to court of Gloriane[100] I sped,
Of Gloriane great Queene of glory bright,
Whose kingdomes seat Cleopolis is red,[101]
There to obtaine some such redoubted knight,
That parents deare from tyrants powre deliver might.

It was my chance (my chance was faire and good)
There for to find a fresh unproved knight,
Whose manly hands imbrew'd[102] in guiltie blood
Had never bene, ne ever by his might
Had throwne to ground the unregarded right:
Yet of his prowesse proofe he since hath made

---

95. Ventured.

96. Failed.

97. Victims.

98. Led by.

99. Named.

100. The Fairy Queen, who represents Elizabeth. The capital of her realm is called Cleopolis.

101. Called.

102. Defiled.

(I witnesse am) in many a cruell fight;
The groning ghosts of many one dismaide
Have felt the bitter dint of his avenging blade.

And ye the forlorne reliques of his powre,
His byting sword, and his devouring speare,
Which have endured many a dreadfull stowre,[103]
Can speake his prowesse, that did earst you beare,
And well could rule: now he hath left you heare,
To be the record of his ruefull losse,
And of my dolefull disaventurous[104] deare:
O heavie record of the good Redcrosse,
Where have you left your lord, that could so well you tosse?

Well hoped I, and faire beginnings had,
That he my captive langour[105] should redeeme,
Till all unweeting,[106] an enchaunter bad
His sence abusd, and made him to misdeeme[107]
My loyalty, not such as it did seeme;
That rather death desire, then such despight.
Be judge ye heavens, that all things right esteeme,
How I him lov'd, and love with all my might,
So thought I eke of him, and thinke I thought aright.

Thenceforth me desolate he quite forsooke,
To wander, where wilde fortune would me lead,
And other bywaies he himselfe betooke,
Where never foot of living wight did tread,
That brought not backe the balefull body dead;
In which him chaunced false Duessa meete,
Mine onely foe, mine onely deadly dread,
Who with her witchcraft and misseeming[108] sweete,
Inveigled him to follow her desires unmeete.

---

103. Combat.
104. Unfortunate.
105. Woeful plight.
106. Unwitting.
107. Misjudge.
108. Deceit.

At last by subtill sleights[109] she him betraid
    Unto his foe, a gyant huge and tall,
    Who him disarmed, dissolute,[110] dismaid,
    Unwares surprised, and with mightie mall[111]
    The monster mercilesse him made to fall,
    Whose fall did never foe before behold;
    And now in darkesome dungeon, wretched thrall,
    Remedilesse, for aie[112] he doth him hold;
This is my cause of griefe, more great, then may be told.

Ere she had ended all, she gan to faint:
    But he her comforted and faire bespake,
    Certes,[113] Madame, ye have great cause of plaint,
    That stoutest heart, I weene, could cause to quake.
    But be of cheare, and comfort to you take:
    For till I have acquit your captive knight,
    Assure your selfe, I will you not forsake.
    His chearefull words reviv'd her chearelesse spright,
So forth they went, the dwarfe them guiding ever right.

Canto VIII

Fair virgin to redeeme her deare
    brings Arthur to the fight:
Who slayes the gyant, wounds the beast,
    and strips Duessa quight.

Ay me, how many perils doe enfold
    The righteous man, to make him daily fall?
    Were not, that heavenly grace doth him uphold,
    And stedfast truth acquite him out of all.
    Her love is firme, her care continuall,
    So oft as he through his owne foolish pride,
    Or weaknesse is to sinfull bands made thrall:

---

109. Tricks.
110. Lax.
111. Club.
112. Forever.
113. Surely.

Else should this Redcrosse knight in bands[114] have dyde,
For whose deliverance she this prince doth thither guide.

They sadly traveild thus, untill they came
    Nigh to a castle builded strong and hie:
    Then cryde the dwarfe, lo yonder is the same,
    In which my lord my liege doth lucklesse lie,
    Thrall to that gyants hatefull tyrannie:
    Therefore, deare Sir, your mightie powres assay.
    The noble knight alighted by and by
    From loftie steede, and bad the ladie stay,
To see what end of fight should him befall that day.

So with the squire, th'admirer of his might,
    He marched forth towards that castle wall;
    Whose gates he found fast shut, ne living wight[115]
    To ward[116] the same, nor answere commers call.
    Then tooke that squire an horne of bugle small,
    Which hong adowne his side in twisted gold,
    And tassels gay. Wyde wonders over all
    Of that same hornes great vertues weren told,
Which had approved bene in uses manifold.

Was never wight, that heard that shrilling sound,
    But trembling feare did feele in every vaine;
    Three miles it might be easie heard around,
    And Ecchoes three answerd it selfe againe:
    No false enchauntment, nor deceiptfull traine
    Might once abide the terror of that blast,
    But presently was voide and wholly vaine:
    No gate so strong, no locke so firme and fast,
But with that percing noise flew open quite, or brast.[117]

The same before the geants gate he blew,
    That all the castle quaked from the ground,
    And every dore of freewill open flew.
    The gyant selfe dismaied with that sownd,

---

114. Bonds.
115. Person.
116. Guard.
117. Burst.

Where he with his Duessa dalliance[118] fownd,
In hast came rushing forth from inner bowre,
With staring countenance sterne, as one astownd,
And staggering steps, to weet, what suddein stowre,
Had wrought that horror strange, and dar'd his dreaded powre.

And after him the proud Duessa came,
High mounted on her manyheaded beast,
And every head with fyrie tongue did flame,
And every head was crowned on his creast,
And bloudie mouthed with late cruell feast.
That when the knight beheld, his mightie shild
Upon his manly arme he soone addrest,
And at him fiercely flew, with courage fild,
And eger greedinesse through every member thrild.

Therewith the gyant buckled him to fight,
Inflam'd with scornefull wrath and high disdaine,
And lifting up his dreadfull club on hight,[119]
All arm'd with ragged snubbes[120] and knottie graine,
Him thought at first encounter to have slaine.
But wise and warie was that noble pere,[121]
And lightly leaping from so monstrous maine,
Did faire avoide the violence him nere;
It booted[122] nought, to thinke, such thunderbolts to beare.

Ne shame he thought to shunne so hideous might:
The idle stroke, enforcing furious way,
Missing the marke of his misaymed sight
Did fall to ground, and with his heavie sway
So deepely dinted in the driven clay,
That three yardes deepe a furrow up did throw:
The sad earth wounded with so sore assay,
Did grone full grievous underneath the blow,
And trembling with strange feare, did like an earthquake show.

---

118. Amorous play.
119. On high.
120. Snags or stubs.
121. Knight.
122. Availed.

As when almightie Jove in wrathfull mood,
>To wreake the guilt of mortall sins is bent,
>Hurles forth his thundring dart with deadly food,
>Enrold in flames, and smouldring dreriment,
>Through riven cloudes and molten firmament;
>The fierce threeforked engin[123] making way,
>Both loftie towres and highest trees hath rent,
>And all that might his angrie passage stay,
And shooting in the earth, casts up a mount of clay.

His boystrous club, so buried in the ground,
>He could not rearen up againe so light,
>But that the knight him at avantage found,
>And whiles he strove his combred clubbe to quight[124]
>Out of the earth, with blade all burning bright
>He smote off his left arme, which like a blocke
>Did fall to ground, depriv'd of native might;
>Large streames of bloud out of the truncked stocke
Forth gushed, like fresh water streame from riven rocke.

Dismaied with so desperate deadly wound,
>And eke impatient of unwonted paine,
>He loudly brayd with beastly yelling sound,
>That all the fields rebellowed[125] againe;
>As great a noyse, as when in Cymbrian plaine[126]
>An heard of bulles, whom kindly rage doth sting,
>Do for the milkie mothers want complaine,
>And fill the fields with troublous bellowing,
The neighbour woods around with hollow murmur ring.

That when his deare Duessa heard, and saw
>The evill stownd, that daungerd her estate,
>Unto his aide she hastily did draw
>Her dreadfull beast, who swolne with bloud of late
>Came ramping forth with proud presumpteous gate,
>And threatned all his heads like flaming brands.
>But him the squire made quickly to retrate,

---

123. Device, i.e., the lightning bolt.

124. His trapped club to set free.

125. Echoed his bellowing.

126. The homeland of the Teutonic tribe known as the Cimbri, now Jutland.

Encountring fierce with single sword in hand,
And twixt him and his lord did like a bulwarke stand.

The proud Duessa full of wrathfull spight,
    And fierce disdaine, to be affronted so,
    Enforst[127] her purple beast with all her might
    That stop out of the way to overthroe,
    Scorning the let[128] of so unequall foe:
    But nathemore would that courageous swayne
    To her yeeld passage, gainst his lord to goe,
But with outrageous strokes did him restraine,
And with his bodie bard the way atwixt them twaine.

Then tooke the angrie witch her golden cup,
    Which still she bore, replete with magick artes;
    Death and despeyre did many thereof sup,
    And secret poyson through their inner parts,
    Th'eternall bale of heavie wounded harts;
    Which after charmes and some enchauntments said,
    She lightly sprinkled on his weaker parts;
    Therewith his sturdie courage soone was quayd,[129]
And all his senses were with suddeine dread dismayd.

So downe he fell before the cruell beast,
    Who on his necke his bloudie clawes did seize,
    That life nigh crusht out of his panting brest:
    No powre he had to stirre, nor will to rize.
    That when the carefull knight gan well avise,
    He lightly left the foe, with whom he fought,
    And to the beast gan turne his enterprise;
    For wondrous anguish in his hart it wrought,
To see his loved squire into such thraldome brought.

And high advauncing his bloud-thirstie blade,
    Stroke one of those deformed heads so sore,
    That of his puissance[130] proud ensample made;
    His monstrous scalpe downe to his teeth it tore,

---

127. Drove on.
128. Hindrance.
129. Daunted.
130. Power.

And that misformed shape mis-shaped more:
A sea of bloud gusht from the gaping wound,
That her gay garments staynd with filthy gore,
And overflowed all the field around;
That over shoes in bloud he waded on the ground.

Thereat he roared for exceeding paine,
That to have heard, great horror would have bred,
And scourging th'emptie ayre with his long traine,
Through great impatience of his grieved hed
His gorgeous ryder from her loftie sted
Would have cast downe, and trod in durtie myre,
Had not the gyant soone her succoured;
Who all enrag'd with smart and franticke yre,
Came hurtling in full fierce, and forst the knight retyre.

The force, which wont[131] in two to be disperst,
In one alone left hand he now unites,
Which is through rage more strong then both were erst;[132]
With which his hideous club aloft he dites,[133]
And at his foe with furious rigour smites,
That strongest oake might seeme to overthrow:
The stroke upon his shield so heavie lites,
That to the ground it doubleth him full low:
What mortall wight could ever beare so monstrous blow?

And in his fall his shield, that covered was,
Did loose his vele[134] by chaunce, and open flew:
The light whereof, that heavens light did pas,
Such blazing brightnesse through the aier threw,
That eye mote not the same endure to vew.
Which when the gyaunt spyde with staring eye,
He downe let fall his arme, and soft withdrew
His weapon huge, that heaved was on hye
For to have slaine the man, that on the ground did lye.

And eke the fruitfull-headed beast, amaz'd

---

131. Was accustomed.
132. Formerly.
133. Raises.
134. Cover.

At flashing beames of that sunshiny shield,
Became starke blind, and all his senses daz'd,
That downe he tumbled on the durtie field,
And seem'd himselfe as conquered to yield.
Whom when his maistresse proud perceiv'd to fall,
Whiles yet his feeble feet for faintnesse reeld,
Unto the gyant loudly she gan call,
O helpe Orgoglio, helpe, or else we perish all.

At her so pitteous cry was much amoov'd,[135]
    Her champion stout, and for to ayde his frend,
    Againe his wonted angry weapon proov'd:
    But all in vaine: for he has read his end
    In that bright shield, and all their forces spend
    Themselves in vaine: for since that glauncing sight,
    He hath no powre to hurt, nor to defend;
    As where th'Almighties lightning brond does light,
It dimmes the dazed eyen,[136] and daunts the senses quight.

Whom when the Prince, to battell new addrest,
    And threatning high his dreadfull stroke did see,
    His sparkling blade about his head he blest,[137]
    And smote off quite his right leg by the knee,
    That downe he tombled; as an aged tree,
    High growing on the top of rocky clift,
    Whose hartstrings[138] with keene steele nigh hewen be,
    The mightie trunck halfe rent, with ragged rift
Doth roll adowne the rocks, and fall with fearefull drift.

Or as a castle reared high and round,
    By subtile engins and malitious slight[139]
    Is undermined from the lowest ground,
    And her foundation forst, and feebled quight,
    At last downe falles, and with her heaped hight
    Her hastie ruine does more heavie make,
    And yields it selfe unto the victours might;

---

135. Troubled.
136. Eyes.
137. Brandished.
138. Tendons or nerves supposed to brace the heart, here figurative.
139. Ingenious machines and malicious trickery.

Such was this gyaunts fall, that seemd to shake
The stedfast globe of earth, as it for feare did quake.

The knight then lightly leaping to the pray,
 With mortall steele him smot againe so sore,
 That headlesse his unweldy bodie lay,
 All wallowd in his owne fowle bloudy gore,
 Which flowed from his wounds in wondrous store.[140]
 But soone as breath out of his breast did pas,
 That huge great body, which the gyaunt bore,
 Was vanisht quite, and of that monstrous mas
Was nothing left, but like an emptie bladder was.

Whose grievous fall, when false Duessa spide,
 Her golden cup she cast unto the ground,
 And crowned mitre rudely threw aside;
 Such percing griefe her stubborne hart did wound,
 That she could not endure that dolefull stound,[141]
 But leaving all behind her, fled away:
 The light-foot squire her quickly turnd around,
 And by hard meanes enforcing her to stay,
So brought unto his lord, as his deserved pray.[142]

The royall virgin, which beheld from farre,
 In pensive plight, and sad perplexitie,
 The whole atchievement[143] of this doubtfull warre,
 Came running fast to greet his victorie,
 With sober gladnesse, and myld modestie,
 And with sweet joyous cheare him thus bespake;
 Faire braunch of noblesse, flowre of chevalrie,
 That with your worth the world amazed make,
How shall I quite[144] the paines, ye suffer for my sake?

And you fresh bud of vertue springing fast,
 Whom these sad eyes saw nigh unto deaths dore,
 What hath poore virgin for such perill past,

---

140. Abundance.
141. Pain.
142. Booty.
143. Action.
144. Repay.

Wherewith you to reward? Accept therefore
My simple selfe, and service evermore;
And he that high does sit, and all things see
With equall eyes, their merites to restore,[145]
Behold what ye this day have done for mee,
And what I cannot quite, requite with usuree.[146]

But sith the heavens, and your faire handeling
Have made you maister of the field this day,
Your fortune maister eke[147] with governing,
And well begun end all so well, I pray,
Ne let that wicked woman scape away;
For she it is, that did my lord bethrall,[148]
My dearest lord, and deepe in dongeon lay,
Where he his better dayes hath wasted all.
O heare, how piteous he to you for ayd does call.

Forthwith he gave in charge unto his squire,
That scarlot whore to keepen carefully;
Whiles he himselfe with greedie great desire
Into the castle entred forcibly,
Where living creature none he did espye;
Then gan he lowdly through the house to call:
But no man car'd to answere to his crye.
There raignd a solemne silence over all,
Nor voice was heard, nor wight was seene in bowre or hall.

At last with creeping crooked pace forth came
An old old man, with beard as white as snow,
That on a staffe his feeble steps did frame,
And guide his wearie gate[149] both too and fro:
For his eye sight him failed long ygo,
And on his arme a bounch of keyes he bore,
The which unused rust did overgrow:

---

145. With impartial eyes, their merits to compensate.
146. And what I cannot pay, repay with interest.
147. Also.
148. Enslave.
149. Step.

Those were the keyes of every inner dore,
But he could not them use, but kept them still in store.[150]

But very uncouth sight was to behold,
How he did fashion his untoward[151] pace,
For as he forward moov'd his footing old,
So backward still was turnd his wrincled face,
Unlike to men, who ever as they trace,
Both feet and face one way are wont to lead.
This was the auncient keeper of that place,
And foster father of the gyant dead;
His name Ignaro did his nature right aread.[152]

His reverend haires and holy gravitie
The knight much honord, as beseemed[153] well,
And gently askt, where all the people bee,
Which in that stately building wont[154] to dwell.
Who answerd him full soft, he could not tell.
Againe he askt, where that same knight was layd,
Whom great Orgoglio with his puissaunce fell[155]
Had made his caytive thrall;[156] againe he sayde,
He could not tell: ne[157] ever other answere made.

Then asked he, which way he in might pas:
He could not tell, againe he answered.
Thereat the curteous knight displeased was,
And said, old sire, it seemes thou hast not red[158]
How ill it sits with that same silver hed
In vaine to mocke, or mockt in vaine to bee:
But if thou be, as thou art pourtrahed

---

150. In reserve.

151. Slow.

152. Declare. I.e., his name, from the Latin word for "ignorant" or "unaware" defines his character.

153. Was fitting.

154. Used.

155. Deadly power.

156. Captive slave.

157. Nor.

158. Perceived.

With natures pen, in ages grave degree,
Aread[159] in graver wise, what I demaund of thee.

His answere likewise was, he could not tell.
    Whose sencelesse speach, and doted ignorance
    When as the noble Prince had marked well,
    He ghest[160] his nature by his countenance,
    And calmd his wrath with goodly temperance.
    Then to him stepping, from his arme did reach
    Those keyes, and made himselfe free enterance.
    Each dore he opened without any breach;
There was no barre to stop, nor foe him to empeach.[161]

There all within full rich arayd he found,
    With royall arras[162] and resplendent gold,
    And did with store of every thing abound,
    That greatest princes presence might behold.
    But all the floore (too filthy to be told)
    With bloud of guiltlesse babes, and innocents trew,
    Which there were slaine, as sheepe out of the fold,
    Defiled was, that dreadfull was to vew,
And sacred ashes over it was strowed[163] new.

And there beside of marble stone was built
    An altare, carv'd with cunning imagery,
    On which true Christians bloud was often spilt,
    And holy martyrs often doen[164] to dye,
    With cruell malice and strong tyranny:
    Whose blessed sprites[165] from underneath the stone
    To God for vengeance cryde continually,
    And with great griefe were often heard to grone,
That hardest heart would bleede, to heare their piteous mone.

---

159. Declare.
160. Guessed.
161. Impede.
162. Rich tapestry.
163. Strewn.
164. Caused.
165. Spirits.

Through every rowme he sought, and every bowr,
But no where could he find that wofull thrall:
At last he came unto an yron doore,
That fast was lockt, but key found not at all
Emongst that bounch, to open it withall;
But in the same a little grate was pight,[166]
Through which he sent his voyce, and lowd did call
With all his powre, to weet,[167] if living wight
Were housed therewithin, whom he enlargen[168] might.

Therewith an hollow, dreary, murmuring voyce
These piteous plaints and dolours did resound;
O who is that, which brings me happy choyce
Of death, that here lye dying every stound,[169]
Yet live perforce in balefull darkenesse bound?
For now three moones have changed thrice their hew,[170]
And have beene thrice hid underneath the ground,
Since I the heavens chearefull face did vew:
O welcome thou, that doest of death bring tydings trew.

Which when that champion heard, with percing point
Of pitty deare his hart was thrilled sore,
And trembling horrour ran through every joynt,
For ruth[171] of gentle knight so fowle forlore:
Which shaking off, he rent[172] that yron dore,
With furious force, and indignation fell;
Where entred in, his foot could find no flore,
But all a deepe descent, as darke as hell,
That breathed ever forth a filthie banefull smell.

But neither darkenesse fowle, nor filthy bands,
Nor noyous[173] smell his purpose could withhold,
(Entire affection hateth nicer hands)

---

166. Set.
167. Know.
168. Free.
169. Moment.
170. Form.
171. Pity.
172. Broke in.
173. Vexing.

But that with constant zeale, and courage bold,
After long paines and labours manifold,
He found the meanes that prisoner up to reare;
Whose feeble thighes, unhable to uphold
His pined corse,[174] him scarse to light could beare,
A ruefull spectacle of death and ghastly drere.[175]

His sad dull eyes deepe sunck in hollow pits,
Could not endure th'unwonted sunne to view;
His bare thin cheekes for want of better bits,
And empty sides deceived of their dew,
Could make a stony hart his hap to rew;[176]
His rawbone armes, whose mighty brawned bowrs[177]
Were wont to rive[178] steele plates, and helmets hew,
Were cleane consum'd, and all his vitall powres
Decayd, and all his flesh shronk up like withered flowres.

Whom when his lady saw, to him she ran
With hasty joy: to see him made her glad,
And sad to view his visage pale and wan,
Who earst[179] in flowres of freshest youth was clad.
Tho when her well of teares she wasted had,
She said, Ah dearest lord, what evill starre
On you hath fround,[180] and pourd his influence bad,
That of your selfe ye thus berobbed arre,
And this misseeming[181] hew your manly looks doth marre?

But welcome now my Lord, in wele or woe,
Whose presence I have lackt too long a day;
And fie on Fortune mine avowed foe,
Whose wrathfull wreakes[182] them selves do now alay.
And for these wrongs shall treble penaunce pay

---

174. Exhausted body.
175. Gloom.
176. His fortune to pity.
177. Well-developed muscles.
178. Split.
179. Formerly.
180. Frowned.
181. Unbecoming.
182. Pains.

Of treble good: good growes of evils priefe.[183]
The chearelesse man, whom sorrow did dismay,
Had no delight to treaten[184] of his griefe;
His long endured famine needed more reliefe.

Faire Lady, then said that victorious knight,
    The things, that grievous were to do, or beare,
    Them to renew, I wote,[185] breeds no delight;
    Best musicke breeds delight in loathing eare:
    But th'onely good, that growes of passed feare,
    Is to be wise, and ware of like agein.
    This dayes ensample[186] hath this lesson deare
    Deepe written in my heart with yron pen,
That blisse may not abide in state of mortall men.

Henceforth sir knight, take to you wonted strength,
    And maister these mishaps with patient might;
    Loe where your foe lyes stretcht in monstrous length,
    And loe that wicked woman in your sight,
    The roote of all your care, and wretched plight,
    Now in your powre, to let her live, or dye.
    To do her dye (quoth Una) were despight,[187]
    And shame t'avenge so weake an enimy;
But spoile her of[188] her scarlot robe, and let her fly.

So as she bad, that witch they disaraid,
    And robd of royall robes, and purple pall,
    And ornaments that richly were displaid;
    Ne spared they to strip her naked all.
    Then when they had despoild her tire and call,[189]
    Such as she was, their eyes might her behold,
    That her misshaped parts did them appall,
    A loathly, wrinckled hag, ill favoured, old,
Whose secret filth good manners biddeth not be told.

---

183. From the experiencing of evil.
184. Speak.
185. Know.
186. Example.
187. To put her to death, said Una, would be shameful.
188. Take from her.
189. Clothing and caul (a netted cap or headdress).

Her craftie head was altogether bald,
 And as in hate of honorable eld,[190]
 Was overgrowne with scurfe and filthy scald;[191]
 Her teeth out of her rotten gummes were feld,
 And her sowre breath abhominably smeld;
 Her dried dugs, like bladders lacking wind,
 Hong downe, and filthy matter from them weld;
 Her wrizled skin as rough, as maple rind,
So scabby was, that would have loathd all womankind.

Her neather parts, the shame of all her kind,
 My chaster Muse for shame doth blush to write;
 But at her rompe she growing had behind
 A foxes taile, with dong all fowly dight;[192]
 And eke her feete most monstrous were in sight;
 For one of them was like an eagles claw,
 With griping talaunts armd to greedy fight,
 The other like a beares uneven paw:
More ugly shape yet never living creature saw.

Which when the knights beheld, amazd they were,
 And wondred at so fowle deformed wight.
 Such then (said Una) as she seemeth here,
 Such is the face of falshood, such the sight
 Of fowle Duessa, when her borrowed light
 Is laid away, and counterfesaunce[193] knowne.
 Thus when they had the witch disrobed quight,
 And all her filthy feature open showne,
They let her goe at will, and wander wayes unknowne.

She flying fast from heavens hated face,
 And from the world that her discovered wide,
 Fled to the wastfull wildernesse apace,
 From living eyes her open shame to hide,

---

190. Age.

191. "Scurfe" is "a morbid condition of the skin, esp. of the head, characterized by the separation of branny scales" (OED); and "scald" is a scaly disease of the skin.

192. Dirtied.

193. Dissimulation.

And lurkt in rocks and caves long unespide.[194]
But that faire crew of knights, and Una faire
Did in that castle afterwards abide,
To rest them selves, and weary powres repaire,
Where store they found of all, that dainty was and rare.

Canto IX

His loves and lignage Arthur tells:
The knights knit friendly bands:
. . . .

O goodly golden chaine, wherewith yfere[195]
The vertues linked are in lovely wize:[196]
And noble minds of yore allyed were,
In brave poursuit of chevalrous emprize,[197]
That none did others safety despize,
Nor aid envy to him, in need that stands,
But friendly each did others prayse devize,
How to advaunce with favourable hands,
As this good prince redeemd the Redcrosse knight from bands.

Who when their powres, empaird through labour long,
With dew repast they had recured[198] well,
And that weake captive wight now wexed[199] strong,
Them list[200] no lenger there at leasure dwell,
But forward fare, as their adventures fell,
But ere they parted, Una faire besought
That straunger knight his name and nation tell;
Least so great good, as he for her had wrought,
Should die unknown, and buried be in thanklesse thought.

---

194. Unseen.
195. Together.
196. Manner.
197. Enterprise.
198. Recovered.
199. Grew.
200. It pleased them.

Faire virgin (said the Prince) ye me require
    A thing without the compas[201] of my wit:
    For both the lignage and the certain sire,
    From which I sprong, from me are hidden yit.
    For all so soone as life did me admit
    Into this world, and shewed heavens light,
    From mothers pap I taken was unfit:
    And streight delivered to a faery knight,
To be upbrought in gentle thewes[202] and martiall might.

Unto old Timon he me brought bylive,[203]
    Old Timon, who in youthly yeares hath beene
    In warlike feates th'expertest man alive,
    And is the wisest now on earth I weene;[204]
    His dwelling is low in a valley greene,
    Under the foot of Rauran[205] mossy hore,
    From whence the river Dee as silver cleene
    His tombling billowes rolls with gentle rore:
There all my dayes he traind me up in vertuous lore.

Thither the great Magicien Merlin came,
    As was his use, ofttimes to visit me:
    For he had charge my discipline to frame,
    And Tutours nouriture to oversee.
    Him oft and oft I askt in privitie,
    Of what loines and what lignage I did spring:
    Whose aunswere bad me still assured bee,
    That I was sonne and heire unto a king,
As time in her just terme the truth to light should bring.

Well worthy impe,[206] said then the lady gent,
    And pupill fit for such a tutours hand.
    But what adventure, or what high intent
    Hath brought you hither into Faery land,

---

201. Beyond the limit.
202. Customs.
203. At once.
204. Suppose.
205. Rauran is a mountain in Wales.
206. Scion.

Aread[207] Prince Arthur, crowne of martiall band?
Full hard it is (quoth he) to read aright
The course of heavenly cause, or understand
The secret meaning of th'eternall might,
That rules mens wayes, and rules the thoughts of living wight.

For whither he through fatall deepe foresight
Me hither sent, for cause to me unghest,
Or that fresh bleeding wound, which day and night
Whilome[208] doth rancle in my riven brest,
With forced fury following his behest,
Me hither brought by wayes yet never found,
You to have helpt I hold my selfe yet blest.
Ah curteous knight (quoth she) what secret wound
Could ever find, to grieve the gentlest hart on ground?

Deare Dame (quoth he) you sleeping sparkes awake,
Which troubled once, into huge flames will grow,
Ne ever will their fervent fury slake,
Till living moysture into smoke do flow,
And wasted life do lye in ashes low.
Yet sithens[209] silence lesseneth not my fire,
But told it flames, and hidden it does glow,
I will revele, what ye so much desire:
Ah Love, lay downe thy bow, the whiles I may respire.[210]

It was in freshest flowre of youthly yeares,
When courage first does creepe in manly chest,
Then first the coale of kindly heat appeares
To kindle love in every living brest;
But me had warnd old Timons wise behest,[211]
Those creeping flames by reason to subdew,
Before their rage grew to so great unrest,

---

207. Declare.
208. At times.
209. Since.
210. Live.
211. Injunction.

As miserable lovers use to rew,
Which still wex[212] old in woe, whiles woe still wexeth new.

That idle name of love, and lovers life,
    As losse of time, and vertues enimy
    I ever scornd, and joyd to stirre up strife,
    In middest of their mournfull tragedy,
    Ay wont to laugh, when them I heard to cry,
    And blow the fire, which them to ashes brent:[213]
    Their God himselfe, griev'd at my libertie,
    Shot many a dart at me with fiers intent,
But I them warded all with wary government.[214]

But all in vaine: no fort can be so strong,
    Ne fleshly brest can armed be so sound,
    But will at last be wonne with battrie long,
    Or unawares at disavantage found;
    Nothing is sure, that growes on earthly ground:
    And who most trustes in arme of fleshly might,
    And boasts, in beauties chaine not to be bound,
    Doth soonest fall in disaventrous[215] fight,
And yeeldes his caytive neck to victours most despight.[216]

Ensample make of him your haplesse joy,
    And of my selfe now mated, as ye see;
    Whose prouder vaunt[217] that proud avenging boy
    Did soone pluck downe, and curbd my libertie.
    For on a day prickt[218] forth with jollitie
    Of looser life, and heat of hardiment,[219]
    Raunging the forest wide on courser free,
    The fields, the floods, the heavens with one consent
Did seeme to laugh on me, and favour mine intent.

---

212. Grow.
213. Burned.
214. Control.
215. Disastrous.
216. Contemptuous.
217. Boast.
218. Rode.
219. Courage.

For-wearied with my sports, I did alight
    From loftie steed, and downe to sleepe me layd;
    The verdant gras my couch did goodly dight,[220]
    And pillow was my helmet faire displayd:
    Whiles every sence the humour sweet embayd,[221]
    And slombring soft my hart did steale away,
    Me seemed, by my side a royall mayd
    Her daintie limbes full softly down did lay:
So faire a creature yet saw never sunny day.

Most goodly glee and lovely blandishment
    She to me made, and bad me love her deare,
    For dearely sure her love was to me bent,
    As when just time expired should appeare.
    But whether dreames delude, or true it were,
    Was never hart so ravisht with delight,
    Ne living man like words did ever heare,
    As she to me delivered all that night;
And at her parting said, She Queene of Faeries hight.[222]

When I awoke, and found her place devoyd,
    And nought but pressed gras, where she had lyen,
    I sorrowed all so much, as earst I joyd,
    And washed all her place with watry eyen.
    From that day forth I lov'd that face divine;
    From that day forth I cast in carefull mind,
    To seeke her out with labour, and long tyne,[223]
    And never vow to rest, till her I find,
Nine monethes I seeke in vaine yet ni'll[224] that vow unbind.

Thus as he spake, his visage wexed pale,
    And chaunge of hew great passion did bewray;[225]
    Yet still he strove to cloke his inward bale,
    And hide the smoke, that did his fire display,
    Till gentle Una thus to him gan say;

---

220. Adorn.
221. Pervaded.
222. Was called.
223. Sorrow.
224. Will not.
225. Betray.

O happy Queene of Faeries, that hast found
Mongst many, one that with his prowesse may
Defend thine honour, and thy foes confound:
True Loves are often sown, but seldom grow on ground.

Thine, O then, said the gentle Redcrosse knight,
Next to that ladies love, shalbe the place,
O fairest virgin, full of heavenly light,
Whose wondrous faith, exceeding earthly race,
Was firmest fixt in mine extremest case.
And you, my Lord, the patrone of my life,
Of that great Queene may well gaine worthy grace:
For onely worthy you through prowes priefe[226]
Yf living man mote worthy be, to be her liefe.[227]

So diversly discoursing of their loves,
The golden Sunne his glistring head gan shew,
And sad remembraunce now the Prince amoves,[228]
With fresh desire his voyage to pursew:
Als Una earnd[229] her traveill to renew.
Then those two knights, fast friendship for to bynd,
And love establish each to other trew,
Gave goodly gifts, the signes of gratefull mynd,
And eke as pledges firme, right hands together joynd.

Prince Arthur gave a boxe of diamond sure,
Embowd with gold and gorgeous ornament,
Wherein were closd few drops of liquor pure,
Of wondrous worth, and vertue excellent,
That any wound could heale incontinent:[230]
Which to requite, the Redcrosse knight him gave
A booke, wherein his Saveours testament
Was writ with golden letters rich and brave;
A worke of wondrous grace, and able soules to save.

---

226. Trial.
227. Beloved.
228. Stirs (the emotions of).
229. Also Una yearned.
230. Immediately.

Thus beene they parted, Arthur on his way
    To seeke his love, and th'other for to fight
    With Unaes foe, that all her realme did pray.[231]
    But she now weighing the decayed plight,
    And shrunken synewes of her chosen knight,
    Would not a while her forward course pursew,
    Ne bring him forth in face of dreadfull fight,
    Till he recovered had his former hew:
For him to be yet weake and wearie well she knew.

. . . .

---

231. Plunder.

The Speeches at Prince Henries Barriers[1]

by

BEN JONSON

THE LADY OF THE LAKE, *first discovered.*

A silence, calme as are my waters, meet
Your raysd attentions, whilst my silver feet
Touch on the richer shore; and to this seat[2]
Vow my new duties and mine old repeat.
    Lest any yet should doubt, or might mistake
What Nymph I am; behold the ample lake
Of which I am stild;[3] and neere it Merlins tombe,
Grave of his cunning, as of mine the wombe.
    By this it will not aske me to proclaime
More of my selfe, whose actions, and whose name
Were so full fam'd in Brittish Arthurs court;
No more then it will fit[4] me to report
What hath before bene trusted to our squire
Of me, my knight, his fate, and my desire
To meet, if not prevent[5] his destiny,
And stile[6] him to the court of Britany;
Now when the Iland hath regain'd her fame
Intire, and perfect, in the ancient name,
And that a monarch æquall good and great,
Wise, temperate, just, and stout, claimes Arthurs seat.
Did I say æquall? O too prodigall wrong

---

    1. The celebration in honor of the investiture of Henry, eldest son of King James, as Prince of Wales in 1610.

    2. Site of a court or government.

    3. After which I am named.

    4. Befit.

    5. Precede.

    6. Name.

Of my o're-thirsty, and unæquall tongue!
How brighter farre, then when our Arthur liv'd
Are all the glories of this place reviv'd!
What riches doe I see; what beauties here!
What awe! what love! what reverence! joy! and feare!
What ornaments of counsaile as of court!
All that is high and great, or can comport[7]
Unto the stile[8] of majesty, that knowes
No rivall, but it selfe, this place here showes.
Onely the house of Chivalrie (how ere
The inner parts and store be full, yet here
In that which gentry should sustaine) decayd
Or rather ruin'd seemes; her buildings layd
Flat with the earth; that were the pride of time
And did the barbarous Memphian[9] heapes out-clime.
Those obelisks and columnes broke, and downe,
That strooke the starres, and raisd the British crowne
To be a constellation: Shields and swords,
Cob-webd, and rusty; not a helme affords
A sparke of lustre, which were wont to [10] give
Light to the world, and made the nation live,
When in a day of honour fire was smit[11]
To have put out Vulcan's[12] and have lasted yet.
O, when this ædifice[13] stood great and high,
That in the carcasse hath such majesty,
Whose very sceleton boasts so much worth,
What grace, what glories did it then send forth?
When to the structure went more noble names
Then the Ephesian temple lost in flames:[14]

---

7. Act.

8. In accordance with the name.

9. Egyptian (from Memphis, the capital of ancient Egypt).

10. Which used to.

11. Struck.

12. God of fire.

13. Building.

14. The grandiose temple of Diana at Ephesus, which had an area of about 80,000 square feet, was one of the seven wonders of the ancient world. It was burned in 356 B.C. by a man named Herostratus, who wanted to acquire lasting fame, even if as the result of a great crime. The rebuilt temple was burned again by the Goths in A.D. 262 .

When every stone was laid by vertuous hands;
And standing so, (O that it yet not stands!)
More truth of architecture there was blaz'd,
Then liv'd in all the ignorant Gothes have raz'd.
There porticos were built, and seats for knights
That watchd for all adventures, dayes and nights,
The nieces[15] filld with statues, to invite
Young valures[16] forth, by their old formes to fight.
With arkes[17] triumphall for their actions done,
Out-striding the Colossus of the sunne.
And trophæs, reard, of spoyled enemies,
Whose toppes pierc'd through the cloudes, and hit the skies.

ARTHUR.
[Discoverd as a starre above.]

And thither hath thy voyce pierc'd. Stand not maz'd,
Thy eyes have here on greater glories gaz'd
And not beene frighted. I, thy Arthur, am
Translated to a starre; and of that frame
Or constellation that was calld of mee
So long before, as showing what I should bee,
Arcturus,[18] once thy king, and now thy starre.
Such the rewards of all good princes are.
Nor let it trouble thy designe, faire dame,
That I am present to it with my flame
And influence; since the times are now devolv'd
That Merlin's misticke prophesies are absolv'd,[19]
In Britain's name, the union of this Ile;
And clayme both of my scepter and my stile.[20]
      Faire fall his vertue, that doth fill that throne

___

15. Niches.

16. Valors.

17. Arches.

18. Arcturus is a star of the first magnitude in the constellation Boötes. Here Arthur is glorified by being presented as a star (punning on Arcturus / Arturus). Classical mythology contains many stories of characters being translated to the heavens as stars or constellations–e.g., Orion and the Pleiades, the Hyades, Cassiopeia, and others.

19. Explained.

20. Name.

In which I joy to find my selfe so'out-shone;
And for the greater, wish, men should him take,
As it is nobler to restore then make.
    Proceed in thy great worke; bring forth thy knight
Preserved for his times, that by the might
And magicke of his arme, he may restore
These ruin'd seates of vertue, and build more.
Let him be famous, as was Tristram, Tor,[21]
Launc'lot, and all our list of knight-hood: or
Who were before, or have beene since. His name
Strike upon heaven, and there sticke his fame.
Beyond the paths, and searches of the sunne
Let him tempt fate; and when a world is wunne,
Submit it duely to this state, and throne,
Till time, and utmost stay make that his owne.
    But first receive this shield; wherein is wrought
The truth that he must follow; and (being taught
The wayes from heaven) ought not be despisd.
It is a piece, was by the fates devisd
To arme his maiden valure;[22] and to show
Defensive armes th'offensive should fore-goe.
Indowe him with it, Lady of the Lake.
And for the other mysteries, here, awake
The learned Merlin; when thou shutst him there,
Thou buriedst valure too, for letters reare
The deeds of honor high, and make them live.
If then thou seeke to restore prowesse, give
His spirit freedome; then present thy knight:
For armes and arts sustaine each others right.

LADY.

    My error I acknowledge, though too late
To expiate it; there's no resisting fate.
Arise, great soule; fame by surreption[23] got
May stead us for the time, but lasteth not.
    O, doe not rise with storme, and rage. Forgive

---

    21. Son of Pellinore by the wife of a cowherd. Tor becomes a knight of the Round Table.

    22. Valor.

    23. Stealth.

Repented wrongs. I'am cause thou now shalt live
Æternally, for being deprest a while,
Want makes us know the price of what we avile.[24]

MERLIN.

[Arising out of the tombe.]

I neither storme, nor rage; 'tis earth; blame her
That feeles these motions when great spirits stirre.
She is affrighted, and now chid by heaven,
Whilst we walke calmely on, upright and even.
Call forth the faire Meliadus,[25] thy knight,
They are his fates that make the elements fight:
And these but usuall throwes, when time sends forth
A wonder or a spectacle of worth.
At common births the world feeles nothing new;
At these she shakes; Mankind lives in a few.

LADY.

The heavens, the fates, and thy peculiar starres,
Meliadus, shew thee; and conclude all jarres.[26]

Meliadus, and his sixe assistants here discovered.

MERLIN.

I,[27] now the spheares are in their tunes againe.[28]
What place is this so bright that doth remaine
Yet undemolishd? or but late built! O
I read it now. St. George's Portico![29]
The supreme head of all the world, where now
Knighthood lives honord with a crowned brow.

---

24. The [true] worth of what we hold in low esteem.

25. The name by which Prince Henry is known in the masque.

26. Dissension.

27. Aye (yes).

28. A reference to the music believed to be made by the revolution of the heavenly bodies (spheres) in their orbits.

29. Saint George is the patron saint of England. One of the scenes designed by Inigo Jones for this masque depicted "St. George's Portico."

A noble scene, and fit to shew him in
That must of all worlds fame the ghirland[30] winne.

LADY.

Do's he not sit like Mars,[31] or one that had
The better of him, in his armor clad?
And those his sixe assistants, as the pride
Of the old Græcian heroes had not died?
Or like Apollo, raisd to the worlds view,
The minute after he the Python[32] slew.

MERLIN.

'Tis all too little, Lady, you can speake.
My thought growes great of him, and faine[33] would breake.
Invite him forth, and guide him to his tent,
That I may read this shield his fates present.

LADY.

Glory of knights, and hope of all the earth,
Come forth; your fostresse[34] bids; who from your birth
Hath bred you to this hower,[35] and for this throne.
This is the field to make your vertue knowne.
    If he were now (he sayes) to vow his fires
Of faith, of love, of service, then his squires
Had uttered nothing for him: But he hopes
In the first tender of himselfe, his scopes[36]
Were so well read, as it were no decor'me,[37]
Where truth is studied, there to practise forme.

---

30. Garland.
31. God of war.
32. A monstrous serpent slain near Delphi by the god Apollo.
33. Gladly.
34. Nurturer.
35. Hour, i.e., time or moment.
36. Intentions.
37. Proper thing.

MERLIN.

No, let his actions speake him; and this shield
Let downe from heaven, that to his youth will yeeld
Such copy of incitement: Not the deedes
Of antique knights, to catch their fellowes steedes,
Or ladies palfreyes[38] rescue from the force
Of a fell gyant, or some score to un-horse.
These were bold stories of our Arthurs age;
But here are other acts; another stage
And scene appeares; it is not since as then:
No gyants, dwarfes, or monsters here, but men.
His arts must be to governe, and give lawes
To peace no lesse then armes. His fate here drawes
An empire with it, and describes each state
Preceding there, that he should imitate.
   First, faire Meliadus, hath shee wroght an Ile,
The happiest of the earth (which to your stile
In time must adde) and in it placed high
Britayne, the only name, made Caesar flie.[39]
Within the neerer parts, as apt, and due
To your first speculation, you may view
The eye of justice shooting through the land,
Like a bright planet strengthned by the hand
Of first, and warlike Edward;[40] then th'increase
Of trades and tillage,[41] under lawes and peace,
Begun by him, but settled and promov'd[42]
By the third heroe of his name, who lov'd
To set his owne aworke, and not to see
The fatnesse of his land a portion bee
For strangers. This was he erected first
The trade of clothing, by which arte were nurst
Whole millions to his service, and releev'd
So many poore, as since they have beleev'd
The golden fleece, and need no forrayne mine,

---

38. Riding horses.

39. Reference to the fact that Julius Caesar was unable to conquer Britain.

40. Edward I (1272–1307).

41. Agriculture.

42. Promoted.

If industrie at home doe not decline.[43]

    To prove which true, observe what treasure here
The wise and seventh Henry[44] heapt each yeere,
To be the strength and sinewes of a warre,
When Mars should thunder, or his peace but jarre.
And here how the eighth Henry,[45] his brave sonne,
Built forts, made generall musters, trayn'd youth on
In exercise of armes, and girt his coast
With strength; to which (whose fame no tongue can boast
Up to her worth, though all best tongues be glad
To name her still) did great Eliza[46] adde
A wall of shipping, and became thereby
The ayde, or feare of all the nations nigh.
These, worthyest Prince, are set you neere to reade,
That civill arts the martiall must precede.
That lawes and trade bring honors in and gayne,
And armes defensive a safe peace maintayne.
But when your fate shall call you forth to'assure
Your vertue more (though not to make secure)
View here, what great examples shee hath plac'd.
    First, two brave Britayne heroes, that were grac'd
To fight their Saviours battailes, and did bring
Destruction on the faithlesse; one a king,
Richard, surnamed with the lyons hart.[47]
The other, Edward,[48] and the first, whose part
(Then being but Prince) it was to lead these warres
In the age after, but with better starres.
For here though Coeur de lion like a storme
Powre on the Saracens, and doth performe
Deedes past an angell, arm'd with wroth and fire,
Ploughing whole armies up, with zealous ire,

---

    43. Edward III (1327–1377) encouraged the wool trade, which remained an important and profitable industry even in the reign of James. Because it freed the country from dependence on foreign ("forrayne") wealth, the wool produced in England is likened to the Golden Fleece that Jason won with the help of Medea.

    44. Henry VII (1457–1509) was the first of the Tudor rulers of England.

    45. Henry VIII (1491–1547) was the son of Henry VII.

    46. Queen Elizabeth I (1533–1603).

    47. Richard I (1157–1199) took part in the Third Crusade.

    48. As Prince, Edward (later Edward I) took part in the Eighth Crusade from 1268 to 1272.

And walled cities, while he doth defend
That cause that should all warres begin and end;
Yet when with pride, and for humane respect
The Austrian cullors[49] he doth here deject
With too much scorne,[50] behold at length how fate
Makes him a wretched prisoner to that state;
And leaves him, as a marke of Fortunes spight,
When Princes tempt their starres beyond their light:
Whilst upright Edward shines no lesse then he,
Under the wings of golden victorie,
Nor lets out no lesse rivers of the bloud
Of infidels, but makes the field a floud,
And marches through it, with S. Georges crosse,[51]
Like Israels host to the Ægyptians losse,
Through the Red Sea:[52] the earth beneath him cold
And quaking such an enemie to behold.
For which, his temper'd zeale, see Providence
Flying in here, and armes him with defence
Against th'assassinate made upon his life
By a foule wretch, from whom he wrests the knife,
And gives him a just hire: which yet remaynes
A warning to great chiefes, to keepe their traynes
About 'hem still, and not, to privacie,
Admit a hand that may use treacherie.
    Neerer then these, not for the same high cause,
Yet for the next (what was his right by lawes
Of nations due) doth fight that Mars of men,
The Black Prince Edward,[53] 'gainst the French who then
At Cressey[54] field had no more yeeres then you.
Here his glad father has him in the view

---

49. Regiments or soldiers.

50. Stephen Orgel says, "The incident occurred in 1191, after the siege of Acre, which had been successful largely because of the efforts of Richard, a fact he chose to emphasize by means of gratuitous insults to his allies" (in his notes to *Ben Jonson: The Complete Masques* [New Haven: Yale University Press, 1969], p. 480).

51. The device of Saint George was a red cross on a white background.

52. The allusion is to Exodus 14:21 and ff. where Moses parts the Red Sea to lead the Israelites out of Egypt.

53. Edward, Prince of Wales (1330–1376) eldest son of Edward III.

54. In the Battle of Crécy (1346) Edward III and the Black Prince defeated a much larger French force by means of superior tactics and the use of the longbow.

As he is entring in the schoole of warre,
And powres all blessings on him from a farre,
That wishes can; whilst he (that close of day)
Like a yong lyon, newly taught to prey,
Invades the herds, so fled the French, and teares
From the Bohemian crowne the plume he weares,
Which after for his crest he did preserve
To his fathers use, with this fit word, I SERVE.[55]
But here at Poictiers[56] he was Mars indeed.
Never did valour with more streame succeed
Then he had there. He flow'd out like a sea
Upon their troupes, and left their armes no way:
Or like a fire carryed with high windes,
Now broad, and spreading, by and by it findes
A vent upright, to looke which way to burne.
Then shootes along againe, or round doth turne,
Till in the circling spoile[57] it hath embrac'd
All that stood nigh, or in the reach to wast:
Such was his rage that day; but then forgot
Soone as his sword was sheath'd, it lasted not,
After the King, the Dauphine,[58] and French Peeres[59]
By yeelding to him, wisely quit their feares,
Whom he did use with such humanitie,
As they complayn'd not of captivitie;
But here to England without shame came in.
To be his captives was the next to win.
    Yet rests the other thunder-bolt of warre,
Harry the Fift, to whom in face you are
So like, as Fate would have you so in worth,

---

55. According to tradition Edward the Black Prince was inspired by the example of one of his adversaries, John the King of Bohemia, who, though blind, insisted on being brought to the battlefield at Crécy so he could wield his sword against the enemy. Edward III is said to have taken three ostrich feathers from the helmet of the dead king and given them to the Black Prince, who then adopted the feathers and the motto of King John of Bohemia, "Ich Dien" (I serve). Though the Black Prince did use the feathers and the motto, there is little evidence to suggest the connection to the King of Bohemia.

56. In the Battle of Poitiers (1356) the English, led by the Black Prince, defeated the French and captured King John II and more than 1000 knights.

57. Ruin.

58. The title given to the heir to the French throne.

59. Nobles.

Illustrious Prince. This vertue ne're came forth,
But Fame flue greater for him, then shee did
For other mortalls; Fate her selfe did bid
To save his life: The time it reach'd unto,
Warre knew not how to give'him enough to doe.
His very name made head against his foes.
And here at Agin-Court[60] where first it rose,
It there hangs still a comet over France,
Striking their malice blind, that dare advance
A thought against it, lightned by your flame
That shall succeed him both in deedes and name.

    I could report more actions yet of weight
Out of this orbe, as here of eightie eight,[61]
Against the proud Armada, stil'd by Spaine
The Invincible, that cover'd all the mayne,
As if whole Ilands had broke loose, and swame;
Or halfe of Norway with her firre-trees came,
To joyne the continents, it was so great;
Yet by the auspice of Eliza beat:
That deare-belov'd of heaven, whom to preserve
The windes were call'd to fight, and stormes to serve.
One tumor[62] drown'd another, billowes strove
To out-swell ambition, water ayre out-drove,
Though shee not wanted on that glorious day,
An ever-honor'd Howard to display
S. Georges ensigne; and of that high race
A second, both which ply'd the fight and chase:
And sent first bullets, then a fleet of fire,
Then shot themselves like ordinance; and a tire
Of ships for pieces,[63] through the enemies moone,
That wan'd before it grew, and now they soone
Are rent, spoild, scatterd, tost with all disease,
And for their thirst of Britayne drinke the seas.

---

60. At the Battle of Agincourt (1415) Henry V defeated the French army.

61. In 1588 the Spanish Armada of 131 ships sailed against England. Admiral Charles Howard of Effingham (mentioned below) led the English fleet against the Spanish. The English sent burning ships among the Spanish vessels to set them on fire. A storm that destroyed many of the Spanish vessels did more than the British fleet to save England.

62. Swelling, i.e., wave.

63. Cannon, used to discharge the "ordinance" or missiles.

The fish were never better fed than then,
Although at first they fear'd the bloud of men
Had chang'd their element; and Neptune shooke
As if the Thunderer had his palace tooke.[64]
    So here in Wales, Low Countries, France, and Spayne,
You may behold both on the land and mayne
The conquests got, the spoiles, the trophæes reard
By British kings, and such as noblest heard
Of all the nation, which may make t'invite
Your valure upon need, but not t'incite
Your neighbour Princes, give them all their due,
And be prepar'd if they will trouble you.
He doth but scourge him selfe, his sword that drawes
Without a purse, a counsaile and a cause.
    But all these spurres to vertue, seedes of praise
Must yeeld to this that comes. Here's one will raise
Your glorie more, and so above the rest,
As if the acts of all mankind were prest
In his example. Here are kingdomes mixt
And nations joyn'd, a strength of empire fixt
Conterminate[65] with heaven; the golden veine
Of Saturnes age[66] is here broke out againe.
Henry but joyn'd the Roses, that ensign'd
Particular families, but this hath joyn'd
The Rose and Thistle,[67] and in them combin'd
A union, that shall never be declin'd.
Ireland that more in title, then in fact
Before was conquer'd, is his Lawrels act.
The wall of shipping by Eliza made,
Decay'd (as all things subject are to fade)

---

64. Neptune is the god of the sea and the Thunderer is Jupiter, god of the sky.

65. Coextensive.

66. Classical writers, such as Hesiod, Horace, and Vergil, described an idyllic time when Saturn (Greek Cronus) rather than his son Jupiter (Greek Zeus) was the ruling god. This golden age degenerated into progressively inferior ones: the silver, bronze, and iron ages.

67. Henry VII united the Lancasters (symbolized by the red rose) and the Yorks (symbolized by the white rose); but Prince Henry, as a member of the Stuart family, joins the rose (representing England) and the thistle (representing Scotland).

He hath new built, or so restor'd, that men
For noble use, preferre it afore then:
Royall, and mightie James,[68] whose name shall set
A goale for all posteritie to sweat,
In running at, by actions hard and high:
This is the height at which your thoughts must fly.
He knowes both how to governe, how to save,
What subjects, what their contraries should have,
What can be done by power, and what by love,
What should to mercie, what to justice move:
All arts he can, and from the hand of Fate
Hath he enforc'd the making his owne date.
Within his proper vertue hath he plac'd
His guards 'gainst Fortune, and there fixed fast
The wheele of chance, about which Kings are hurl'd,
And whose outragious raptures fill the world.

LADY.

I,[69] this is hee, Meliadus, whom you
Must only serve, and give your selfe unto:
And by your diligent practice to obay
So wise a Master learne the arte of sway.
        Merlin, advance the shield upon his tent.
And now prepare, faire Knight, to prove th'event
Of your bold challenge. Bee your vertue steeld,[70]
And let your drumme give note you keepe the field.
Is this the land of Britaine so renownd
For deeds of armes, or are their hearings drownd
That none doe answere?

MERLIN.

        Stay, me thinkes I see
A person in yond' cave. Who should that bee?
I know her ensignes now: 'Tis Chevalrie
Possess'd with sleepe, dead as a lethargie:
If any charme will wake her, 'tis the name

---

68. James I (1566–1625), who was also James VI of Scotland.
69. Aye (yes).
70. Armored.

Of our Meliadus. I'll use his fame.
    Lady, Meliadus, lord of the Iles,
Princely Meliadus, and whom Fate now stiles
The faire Meliadus, hath hung his shield
Upon his tent, and here doth keepe the field,
According to his bold and princely word;
And wants employment for his pike, and sword.

CHEVALRY.

    Were it from death that name would wake mee. Say
Which is the knight? O I could gaze a day
Upon his armour that hath so reviv'd
My spirits, and tels me that I am long liv'd
In his apparance. Breake, you rustie dores,
That have so long beene shut, and from the shores
Of all the world, come knight-hood like a flood
Upon these lists,[71] to make the field, here, good,
And your owne honours, that are now call'd forth
Against the wish of men to prove your worth.

THE BARRIERS.
After which Merlin speakes.

    Nay, stay your valure, 'tis a wisdome high
In Princes to use fortune reverently.
He that in deeds of armes obeyes his blood
Doth often tempt his destinie beyond good.
Looke on this throne, and in his temper view
The light of all that must have grace in you:
His equall Justice, upright Fortitude
And settled Prudence, with that Peace indued
Of face, as minde, alwayes himselfe and even.
So Hercules, and good men beare up heaven.
    I dare not speake his vertues for the feare
Of flattring him, they come so high and neare
To wonders: yet thus much I prophesy
Of him and his. All eares your selves apply.
    You, and your other you, great King and Queene,
Have yet the least of your bright Fortune seene,

---

71. Field for jousting or tournaments.

Which shal rise brighter every houre with Time,
And in your pleasure quite forget the crime
Of change; your ages night shall be her noone.
And this yong Knight, that now puts forth so soone
Into the world, shall in your names atchieve
More ghyrlands[72] for this state, and shall relieve
Your cares in government; while that yong lord
Shall second him in armes, and shake a sword
And launce against the foes of God and you.
Nor shall lesse joy your royall hopes pursue
In that most princely Mayd,[73] whose forme might call
The world to warre, and make it hazard all
His valure for her beautie, she shall bee
Mother of nations, and her Princes see
Rivals almost to these. Whilst you sit high,
And lead by them, behold your Britaine fly
Beyond the line, when what the seas before
Did bound, shall to the sky then stretch his shore.

---

72. Garlands.
73. Elizabeth, daughter of James and sister of Prince Henry.

A Famous Prediction of Merlin,
The British Wizard,
Written Above a Thousand Years Ago,
And Relating to the Year 1709
With Explanatory Notes by T.N. Philomath
Written in the Year 1709

by

JONATHAN SWIFT

Last year was published a paper of predictions, pretended to be written by one Isaac Bickerstaff, Esq; but the true design of it was to ridicule the art of astrology, and expose its professors as ignorant, or impostors. Against this imputation,[1] Dr. Partrige hath learnedly vindicated himself in his Almanack for that year.

For a farther defence of this famous art, I have thought fit to present the world with the following prophecy. The original is said to be of the famous Merlin, who lived about a thousand years ago: And the following translation is two hundred years old; for it seems to be written near the end of Henry the Seventh's reign. I found it in an old edition of Merlin's Prophecies; imprinted at London by Johan Haukyns, in the year 1530. Page 39. I set it down word for word in the old orthography, and shall take leave to subjoin a few explanatory notes.

> SEVEN and TEN addyd to NINE,
> Of Fraunce hir Woe thys is the Sygne,
> Tamys Ryvere twys y-frozen,
> Walke sans wetyng Shoes ne Hosen.[2]
> Then cometh foorthe, Ich[3] understonde,

---

1. Charge.
2. Without wetting shoes or stockings.
3. I.

From Toune of Stoffe to fattyn Londe,
An herdie Chiftan, woe the Morne
To Fraunce, that evere he was borne.
Then shall the Fyshe beweyle his Bosse;
Nor shal grin Berrys make up the Losse.
Yonge Symnele shall again miscarrye:
And Norways Pryd again shall marrey.
And from the Tree where Blosums fele,
Ripe Fruit shall come, and all is wele.
Reaums shall daunce honde in honde,
And it shall be merye in old Inglonde.
Then old Inglonde shall be no more,
And no Man shall be sorie therefore.
Geryon shall have three Hedes agayne,
Till Hapsburge makyth them but twayne.

Explanatory Notes

Seven and Ten. This line describes the year when these events
shall happen. Seven and ten make seventeen, which I explain
seventeen hundred, and this number added to nine makes the year
we are now in; for it must be understood of the natural year, which
begins the first of January.

Tamys Ryvere twys, &c. The River Thames frozen twice in one
year, so as men to walk on it, is a very signal[4] accident; which
perhaps hath not fallen out for several hundred years before; and is
the reason why some astrologers have thought that this prophecy
could never be fulfilled; because they imagined such a thing could
never happen in our climate.

From Toune of Stoffe, &c. This is a plain designation of the
Duke of Marlborough. One kind of stuff used to fatten land is called
Marle, and every body knows, that *Borough* is a name for a town; and
this way of expression is after the usual dark manner of old
astrological predictions.

Then shall the Fyshe, &c. By the *Fish* is understood the
Dauphin[5] of France, as the Kings eldest sons are called: It is here

---

4. Remarkable.

5. "Dauphin" is the hereditary title of the French kings. From the French
word for "dolphin," the title originally applied to the lords of Viennois, France,
whose coat of arms bore three dolphins. It was adopted by the French crown princes
when the Viennois province Dauphiné was ceded to the crown.

said, he shall lament the loss of the Duke of Burgundy, called the *Bosse,* which is an old English word for *Hump-shoulder* or *Crook-back,* as that Duke is known to be: And the prophecy seems to mean, that he should be overcome, or slain. By the *Grin Berrys,* in the next line, is meant the young Duke of Berry, the Dauphin's third son, who shall not have valour or fortune enough to supply the loss of his eldest brother.

Yonge Symnele, &c. By *Symnele* is meant the pretended Prince of Wales; who, if he offers to attempt any thing against England, shall miscarry as he did before. Lambert Symnel is the name of a young man noted in our histories for personating the son (as I remember) of Edward the Fourth.[6]

And Norways Pryd, &c. I cannot guess who is meant by *Norways Pride,*[7] perhaps the reader may, as well as the sense of the two following lines.

Reaums shall, &c. *Reaums,* or as the word is now, *Realms,* is the old name for *Kingdoms:* And this is a very plain prediction of our happy union, with the felicities that shall attend it. It is added, that Old England shall be no more, and yet no man shall be sorry for it. And, indeed, properly speaking, England is now no more; for the whole island is one kingdom, under the name of Britain.

Geryon shall, &c. This prediction, though somewhat obscure is wonderfully adapt. *Geryon*[8] is said to have been a king of Spain, whom Hercules slew. It was a fiction of the poets, that he had three heads, which the author says he shall have again. That is, Spain shall have three kings; which is now wonderfully verified: For, besides the King of Portugal, which properly is part of Spain, there are now two rivals for Spain; Charles and Philip.[9] But Charles being descended from the Count of Hapsburgh, founder of the Austrian family, shall

---

6. In 1486 Lambert Simnel was put forth as the heir to the British throne, first as the son of Edward IV (i.e., as one of the princes murdered in the Tower) but then as his nephew (son of Edward's brother George Duke of Clarence, whose son had been erroneously reported to have died in the Tower). After putting down the rebellion, Henry VII took Simnel into his own service as a scullion.

7. Queen Anne. The prophecy means, that she should marry a second time, and have children that would live [author's, note].

8. Geryon was a three-headed ogre who was robbed of his herd and slain by Hercules on the mythical island of Erytheia.

9. The War of the Spanish Succession (1701–14) was fought when Archduke Charles, second son of the Holy Roman Emperor Leopold I, and Philip, duc d'Anjou and grandson of Louis XIV, claimed the Spanish throne.

soon make those heads but two; by overturning Philip, and driving him out of Spain.

Some of these predictions are already fulfilled; and it is highly probable the rest may be in due time: And, I think, I have not forced the words, by my explication, into any other sense than what they will naturally bear. If this be granted, I am sure it must be also allowed, that the author (whoever he were) was a person of extraordinary sagacity; and that astrology brought to such perfection as this, is, by no means, an art to be despised; whatever Mr. Bickerstaff, or other merry gentlemen are pleased to think. As to the tradition of these lines, having been writ in the original by Merlin; I confess, I lay not much weight upon it: But it is enough to justify their authority, that the book from whence I have transcribed them, was printed 170 years ago, as appears by the title-page. For the satisfaction of any gentleman, who may be either doubtful of the truth, or curious to be informed; I shall give order to have the very book sent to the printer of this paper, with directions to let any body see it that pleases; because I believe it is pretty scarce.

Tom Thumb

by

HENRY FIELDING

Preface

A Preface is become almost as necessary to a play, as a Prologue: It is a word of advice to the reader, as the other to the spectator: And as the business of a Prologue is to commend the play, so that of the Preface is to compliment the actors.

A Preface requires a style entirely different from all other writings; a style for which I can find no name in either the *Sublime* of Longinus,[1] or the *Profund* of Scriblerus:[2] which I shall therefore venture to call the supernatural, after the celebrated author of *Hurlothrumbo*:[3] who, tho' no writer of Prefaces, is a very great master of their style.

As Charon[4] in Lucian suffers none to enter his boat till stripped of every thing they have about them, so should no word by any means enter into a Preface till stripped of all its ideas. Mr. Lock[5] complains of confused ideas in words, which is entirely amended by suffering them to give none at all: This may be done by adding, diminishing, or changing a letter, as instead of *Paraphernalia*, writing *Paraphonalia*: For a man may turn Greek into nonsense, who cannot turn sense into either Greek or Latin.

---

1. Third-century Greek philosopher who wrote *On the Sublime*, a treatise on aesthetics.

2. A pseudonym used by Alexander Pope when he wrote *Peri Bathos: or the Art of Sinking in Poetry*.

3. A burlesque written in 1729 by a Manchester dancing master named Samuel Johnson (1691–1773).

4. In Greek mythology Charon is the ferryman who transports the souls of the dead across the River Styx to the Elysian Fields. He figures in some of the dialogues of the Greek author Lucian of Samosata (c. A.D. 125–c. 200).

5. John Locke (1632–1704), English philosopher who wrote *Essay Concerning Human Understanding*.

A second method of stripping words of their ideas is by putting half a dozen incoherent ones together: Such as *when the people of our age shall be ancestors,* etc. By which means one discordant word, like a surly man in company, spoils the whole sentence, and makes it entirely prefatical.

Some imagine this way of writing to have been originally introduced by Plato, whom Cicero observes to have taken especial pains in wrapping up his sentiments from the understandings of the vulgar. But I can in no wise agree with them in this conjecture, any more than their deriving the word Preface, *quasi Plaface, a Plato:*[6] whereas the original word is *Playface, quasi Players Face:* and sufficiently denotes some player, who was as remarkable for his face, as his prefaces, to have been the inventor of it.

But that the Preface to my Preface be not longer than that to my play: I shall have done with the performances of others, and speak a word or two of my own.

This Preface then was writ at the desire of my bookseller, who told me that some elegant criticks had made three great objections to this tragedy: which I shall handle without any regard to precedence: And therefore I begin to defend the last scene of my play against the third objection of these[7] Kriticks, which is, to the destroying all the Characters in it, this I cannot think so unprecedented as these gentlemen would insinuate, having my-self known it done in the first act of several plays: Nay, it is common in modern tragedy for the characters to drop, like the citizens in the first scene of *Oedipus,*[8] as soon as they come upon the stage.

Secondly, they object to the killing a ghost. This (say they) far exceeds the rules of probability; perhaps it may; but I would desire these gentlemen seriously to recollect, whether they have not seen in several celebrated plays, such expressions as these, *kill my soul, stab my very soul, bleeding soul, dying soul, cum multis aliis,*[9] all which visibly confess that for a soul or ghost to be killed is no impossibility.

---

6. As if [it were from] "Plaface," from Plato.

7. Prefatical language [author's note].

8. In John Dryden's *Oedipus* the opening stage direction is: "The Curtain rises to a plaintive Tune, representing the present condition of Thebes; Dead Bodies appear at a distance in the Streets; Some faintly go over the Stage, others drop."

9. With many others.

As for the first objection which they make, and the last which I answer, *viz.*[10] to the subject, to this I shall only say, that it is in the choice of my subject I have placed my chief merit.

It is with great concern that I have observed several of our (the Grubstreet)[11] tragical writers, to celebrate in their immortal lines the actions of heroes recorded in historians and poets, such as Homer or Virgil, Livy or Plutarch, the propagation of whose works is so apparently against the interest of our society; when the romances, novels, and histories, *vulgo*[12] call'd story-books, of our own people, furnish such abundant and proper themes for their pens, such are *Tom Tram, Hickathrift,*[13] etc.

And here I congratulate my cotemporary writers, for their having enlarged the sphere of tragedy: The ancient tragedy seems to have had only two effects on an audience, *viz.* It either awakened terror and compassion, or composed those and all other uneasy sensations, by lulling the audience in an agreeable slumber. But to provoke the mirth and laughter of the spectators, to join the sock to the buskin,[14] is a praise only due to modern tragedy.

Having spoken thus much of the play, I shall proceed to the performers, amongst whom if any shone brighter than the rest it was Tom Thumb. Indeed such was the excellence thereof, that no one can believe unless they see its representation, to which I shall refer the curious: Nor can I refrain from observing how well one of the Mutes set off his part: So excellent was his performance, that it out-did even my own wishes: I gratefully give him my share of praise, and desire the audience to refer the whole to his beautiful action.

And now I must return my hearty thanks to the musick,[15] who, I believe, played to the best of their skill, because it was for their own reputation, and because they are paid for it: So have I

---

10. That is to say.

11. Grub Street in London was inhabited by impoverished writers and literary hacks.

12. Commonly.

13. Tom Tram, a man who would do only what pleased him, and Thomas Hickathrift, a poor man's son endowed with prodigious strength, were characters in eighteenth-century chapbooks, as was Tom Thumb.

14. The "sock" is a light shoe worn by Greek and Roman comic actors and therefore used to denote comedy, as the "buskin," a boot worn by tragic actors, denotes tragedy. The two combined suggest drama or the theatrical profession as a whole.

15. Musicians.

thrown little *Tom Thumb* on the town, and hope they will be favourable to him, and for an answer to all censures, take these words of Martial,[16]

> Seria cum possim, quod delectantia malim
> Scribere, Tu, Causa es—

Prologue
By no friend of the author's.

With mirth and laughter to delight the mind
The modern tragedy was first design'd:
'Twas this made farce with tragedy unite,
And taught each scribler in the town to write.

The glorious heroes who, in former years,
Dissolv'd all Athens and all Rome in tears;
Who to our stage, have been transplanted too;
Whom Shakespear taught to storm, and Lee[17] to woo,
And could to softness, ev'ry heart subdue,
Grub-Street has turn'd to farce.—Oh glorious lane!
O, may thy authors never write in vain!
May crowded theatres ne'er give applause
To any other than the Grub-Street cause!

Since then, to laugh, to tragedies you come,
What heroe is so proper as Tom Thumb?
Tom Thumb! whose very name must mirth incite,
And fill each merry Briton with delight.

Britons, awake!—Let Greece and Rome no more
Their heroes send to our heroick shore.
Let home-bred subjects grace the modern muse,

---

16. Roman poet (c. A.D. 40–103/4), known for his epigrams. The following lines, from Book V, no. 16, of Martial's *Epigrams,* mean: "That I, who could write what is serious, prefer to write what is entertaining, you are the cause" (translation from the Loeb Classical Library edition, by Walter C. A. Ker).

17. Nathaniel Lee (?1649–1692), author of extravagant tragedies. (He collaborated with Dryden on *Oedipus.*)

And Grub-Street from her self, her heroes chuse:
Her story-books immortalize in fame,
Hickathrift, Jack the Giant-Killer, and Tom Tram.
No Venus shou'd in sign-post painter shine;
No Roman hero in a scribler's line:
The monst'rous dragon to the sign belongs,
And Grub-Street's heroes best adorn her songs.
To-night our bard, spectators, would be true
To farce, to tragedy, Tom Thumb, and you.
May all the hissing audience be struck dumb;
Long live the man who cries, Long live Tom Thumb.

Epilogue
Sent by an unknown hand.

Tom Thumb, twice dead, is a third time reviv'd,
And, by your favour, may be yet long-liv'd.
But, more I fear the snarling critick's brow,
Than Grizzle's dagger, or the throat of cow![18]
Well then—toupees, I warrant you suppose
I'll be exceeding witty on the beaus;
But faith! I come with quite a diff'rent view,
To shew there are Tom Thumbs, as well as you.
Place me upon the awful bench, and try
If any judge can sleep more sound than I.
Or let me o'er a pulpit-cushion peep,
See who can set you in a sounder sleep.
Tom Thumb can feel the pulse, can give the pill;
No doctor's feather shall more surely kill.
I'll be a courtier, give me but a place;
A title makes me equal with his grace:
Lace but my coat, where is a prettier spark?
I'll be a justice—give me but a clerk.
A poet too—when I have learnt to read,
And plunder both the living and the dead:

---

18. The two means by which Tom Thumb died.

Any of these, Tom Thumb with ease can be,
For many such, are nothing more than he.

But, for the ladies, they, I know, despise
The little things of my inferior size.
Their mighty souls are all of them too large
To take so small a heroe to their charge.
Take pity, ladies, on a young beginner;
Faith! I may prove, in time, a thumping sinner.
Let your kind smiles our author's cause defend;
He fears no foes, while Beauty is his friend.

DRAMATIS PERSONAE

MEN

KING ARTHUR
TOM THUMB
LORD GRIZZLE
MR. NOODLE
MR. DOODLE
1 PHYSICIAN
2 PHYSICIAN

WOMEN.

QUEEN DOLLALOLLA
PRINCESS HUNCAMUNCA
CLEORA
MUSTACHA

COURTIERS, SLAVES, BAILIFFS, ETC.

SCENE: *The Court of King Arthur.*

ACT I

SCENE I.

SCENE: *The Palace.*

Mr. Doodle, Mr. Noodle.

DOODLE. Sure, such a day as this was never seen!
The Sun himself, on this auspicious day,

Shines like a beau in a new birth-day suit:
All Nature, O my Noodle! grins for joy.
    NOODLE. This day, O Mr. Doodle! is a day
Indeed, a day we never saw before.
The mighty Thomas Thumb victorious comes;
Millions of giants crowd his chariot wheels,
Who bite their chains, and frown and foam like mad-dogs.
He rides, regardless of their ugly looks.
So some cock-sparrow in a farmer's yard,
Hops at the head of an huge flock of turkeys.
    DOODLE. When Goody[19] Thumb first brought this Thomas
        forth,
The Genius of our Land triumphant reign'd;
Then, then, O Arthur! did thy Genius reign.
    NOODLE. They tell me, it is whisper'd in the books
Of all our sages, that this mighty hero
(By Merlin's art begot) has not a bone
Within his skin, but is a lump of gristle.
    DOODLE. Wou'd Arthur's subjects were such gristle, all!
He then might break the bones of ev'ry foe.
    NOODLE. But hark! these trumpets speak the king's
        approach.
    DOODLE. He comes most luckily for my petition!
Let us retire a little.

SCENE II.

King, Queen, Lord Grizzle, Doodle, Noodle.

    KING. Let nothing but a face of joy appear;
The man who frowns this day, shall lose his head,
That he may have no face to frown again.
Smile, Dollalolla;—Ha! what wrinkled sorrow
Sits, like some Mother Demdike,[20] on thy brow?
Whence flow those tears fast down thy blubber'd cheeks,
Like a swoln gutter, gushing through the streets?

---

19. A shortened form of "Goodwife," the equivalent of "Mrs."

20. Elizabeth Sowthern, a Lancashire woman who confessed to being a witch.
In an account of the Lancashire witches, *The Wonderful Discovery of Witches in the
County of Lancaster* (1613), Thomas Potts calls her the "rankest hag that ever troubled
daylight."

QUEEN. Excess of joy, my lord, I've heard folks say,
Gives tears, as often as excess of grief.
KING. If it be so, let all men cry for joy,
'Till my whole court be drowned with their tears;
Nay, 'till they overflow my utmost land,
And leave me nothing but the sea to rule.
DOODLE. My liege! I've a petition—
KING. Petition me no petitions, sir, to-day;
Let other hours be set apart for bus'ness.
To-day it is our pleasure to be drunk,
And this our queen shall be as drunk as us.
QUEEN. If the capacious goblet overflow
With arrack-punch[21]—'fore George![22] I'll see it out;
Of rum, or brandy, I'll not taste a drop.
KING. Tho' rack, in punch, eight shillings be a quart,
And rum and brandy be no more than six,
Rather than quarrel, you shall have your will.
        Trumpets.
But, ha! the warrior comes; Tom Thumb approaches;
The welcome hero, giant-killing lad,
Preserver of my kingdom, is arrived.

SCENE III.

*Tom Thumb, attended; King, Queen,
Lord Grizzle, Doodle, Noodle.*

KING. O welcome, ever welcome to my arms,
My dear Tom Thumb! How shall I thank thy merit?
TOM THUMB. By not b'ing thank'd at all, I'm thank'd
        enough;
My duty I have done, and done no more.
QUEEN. [*Aside.*] Was ever such a lovely creature seen!
KING. Thy modesty's a candle to thy merit,
It shines itself, and shews thy merit too.
Vain impudence, if it be ever found
With virtue, like the trumpet in a consort,

---

21. Arrack is a beverage of high alcoholic content that tastes like rum. It is
distilled in the Far East from the fermented juice of the coconut palm or from a
fermented mash of rice and molasses.

22. Saint George.

Drowns the sweet musick of the softer flute.
But say, my boy, where didst thou leave the giants?
    TOM THUMB. My liege, without the castle gates they stand,
The castle gates too low for their admittance.
    KING. What look they like?
    TOM THUMB. Like twenty things, my liege;
Like twenty thousand oaks, by winter's hand
Strip'd of their blossoms; like a range of houses,
When fire has burnt their timber all away.
    KING. Enough: The vast idea fills my soul;
I see them, yes, I see them now before me.
The monst'rous, ugly, barb'rous sons of whores,
Which, like as many rav'nous wolves, of late
Frown'd grimly o'er the land, like lambs look now.
O Thumb, what do we to thy valour owe!
The Princess Huncamunca is thy prize.
    QUEEN. Ha! Be still, my soul!
    TOM THUMB. Oh, happy, happy hearing!
Witness, ye stars! cou'd Thumb have ever set
A bound to his ambition—it had been
the Princess Huncamunca, in whose arms
Eternity would seem but half an hour.
    QUEEN. Consider, sir, reward your soldier's merit,
But give not Huncamunca to Tom Thumb.
    KING. Tom Thumb! Odzooks, my wide extended realm
Knows not a name so glorious as Tom Thumb.
Not Alexander,[23] in his highest pride,
Could boast of merits greater than Tom Thumb.
Not Caesar, Scipio, all the flow'rs of Rome,
Deserv'd their triumphs better than Tom Thumb.
    QUEEN. Tho' greater yet his boasted merit was,
He shall not have the Princess, that is pos'.[24]
    KING. Say you so, Madam? We will have a trial.
When I consent, what pow'r has your denyal?
For, when the wife her husband over-reaches,
Give him the petticoat, and her the breeches.
    NOODLE. Long health and happiness attend the general!

---

23. Tom Thumb is said to be a greater hero than Alexander the Great (and below) Julius Caesar and Scipio Africanus (who defeated Hannibal at the battle of Zama in 202 B.C.).

24. Positive.

Long may he live, as now, the publick joy,
While ev'ry voice is burthen'd with his praise.
    TOM THUMB. Whisper, ye winds! that Huncamunca's mine;
Ecchoes repeat, that Huncamunca's mine!
The dreadful bus'ness of the war is over,
And Beauty, heav'nly Beauty! crowns the toil.
I've thrown the bloody garment now aside,
And Hymeneal[25] sweets invite my bride.
    So when some chimney-sweeper, all the day,
Has through dark paths pursu'd the sooty way,
At night, to wash his face and hands he flies,
And in his t'other shirt with his Brickdusta lies.
        Exeunt all but Grizzle.

SCENE IV

Lord Grizzle, solus.

    GRIZZLE. See how the cringing coxcombs[26] fawn upon him!
The sun-shine of a court can, in a day,
Ripen the vilest insect to an eagle:
And ev'ry little wretch, who but an hour
Before had scorn'd, and trod him under feet,
Shall lift his eyes aloft, to gaze at distance,
And flatter what they scorn'd.

SCENE V

Enter Queen, to Lord Grizzle.

    QUEEN. Well met, my lord.
You are the man I sought. Have you not heard
(What ev'ry corner of the court resounds)
That little Thumb will be a great man made.
    GRIZZLE. I heard it, I confess—for who, alas!
Can always stop his ears—but would my teeth,
By grinding knives, had first been set on edge.
    QUEEN. Would I had heard at the still noon of night,
The dreadful cry of fire in ev'ry street!

---

25. Nuptial (from "Hymen," the Greek god of marriage).
26. Conceited dandies.

Odsbobs! I could almost destroy my self,
To think I should a grand-mother be made
By such a rascal.—Sure, the king forgets,
When in a pudding, by his mother put,
The bastard, by a tinker, on a stile[27]
Was drop'd.—O, good Lord Grizzle! can I bear
To see him, from a pudding, mount the throne?
    GRIZZLE. Oh horror! horror! horror! cease my queen,
Thy voice, like twenty screech-owls, wracks my brain.
    QUEEN. Then rouze thy spirit—we may yet prevent
This hated match.—
    GRIZZLE. We will.—Not Fate, itself,
Should it conspire with Thomas Thumb, should cause it.
I'll swim through seas; I'll ride upon the clouds;
I'll dig the earth; I'll blow out ev'ry fire;
I'll rave; I'll rant; I'll rush; I'll rise; I'll roar
Fierce as the man whom smiling dolphins bore,
From the prosaick to poetick shore.[28]
I'll tear the scoundrel into twenty pieces.
    QUEEN. Oh, no! prevent the match, but hurt him not;
For, tho' I would not have him have my daughter,
Yet, can we kill the man who kill'd the giants?
    GRIZZLE. I tell you, madam, it was all a trick,
He made the giants first, and then he kill'd them;
As fox-hunters bring foxes to a wood,
And then with hounds they drive them out again.
    QUEEN. How! Have you seen no giants? Are there not
Now, in the yard, ten thousand proper giants?
    GRIZZLE. Indeed, I cannot positively tell,
But firmly do believe there is not one.
    QUEEN. Hence! from my sight! thou traytor, hie away;

---

27. A series of steps by which one can pass over a fence, which remains a
barrier to livestock. The story is told in the chapbook ballad *The Famous History of
Tom Thumb: Wherein Is Declared His Marvellous Acts of Manhood* (reprinted in abridged
form in *Chap-Books of the Eighteenth Century*, ed. John Ashton [1882; rpt. New York:
Benjamin Blom, 1966]).

28. In the notes to his edition of *Tom Thumb* (Berkeley: University of
California Press, 1970) L. J. Morrissey suggests the allusion to the dolphin refers to
the "tale of the boy and the playful dolphins of Hippo" in Pliny the Younger's
"Epistle" 9.33 and notes that "Edward Young had made reference to it in his 'Naval
Lyrick' put out only a few weeks before this play, and Fielding is ironically playing
with Young's ability to make Pliny into 'poetry.'"

By all my stars! thou enviest Tom Thumb.
Go, sirrah![29] go; hie[30] away! hie!—thou art
A setting-dog[31]—and like one I use thee.
    GRIZZLE. Madam, I go.
Tom Thumb shall feel the vengeance you have rais'd.
So when two dogs are fighting in the streets,
With a third dog, one of the two dogs meets,
With angry teeth, he bites him to the bone,
And this dog smarts for what that dog had done. *Exit.*

SCENE VI

Queen, sola.

    QUEEN. And whither shall I go?—Alack-a-day!
I love Tom Thumb—but must not tell him so;
For what's a woman, when her virtue's gone?
A coat without its lace; wig out of buckle;
A stocking with a hole in't.—I can't live
Without my virtue, or without Tom Thumb.
Then let me weigh them in two equal scales,
In this scale put my virtue, that, Tom Thumb.
Alas! Tom Thumb is heavier than my virtue.
But hold!—Perhaps I may be left a widow:
This match prevented, then Tom Thumb is mine,
In that dear hope, I will forget my pain.
    So when some wench to Tothill-Bridewell's[32] sent,
With beating hemp, and flogging, she's content;
She hopes, in time, to ease her present pain;
At length is free, and walks the streets again. *Exit.*

---

    29. A contemptuous term of address to men or boys.

    30. Hasten.

    31. A dog that sets or indicates game.

    32. I.e., to prison. "Bride's Well" was a holy well in London, near which Henry VII had a lodging, which Edward VI later gave to be used as a hospital that was subsequently converted to a prison. Tothill was a London street where a prison was located.

ACT II

SCENE I

SCENE: *The Street.*

Bailiff, Follower.

BAILIFF. Come on, my trusty follower, inur'd[33]
To ev'ry kind of danger; cudgell'd oft;
Often in blankets toss'd—oft pump'd upon:
Whose virtue in a horse-pond hath been try'd.
Stand here by me.—This way must Noodle pass.
  FOLLOWER. Were he an half-pay officer, a bully,
A highway-man, or prize-fighter, I'd nab him.
  BAILIFF. This day discharge thy duty, and at night
A double mug of beer and beer shall glad thee.
Then in an ale-house may'st thou sit at ease,
And quite forget the labours of the day.
So wearied oxen to their stalls retire,
And rest from all the burthens of the plough.
  FOLLOWER. No more, no more, O Bailiff! ev'ry word
Inspires my soul with virtue.—O! I long
To meet the enemy in the street—and nab him;
To lay arresting hands upon his back,
And drag him trembling to the spunging-house.[34]
  BAILIFF. There, when I have him, I will spunge upon him.
O glorious thought! By the sun, moon, and stars,
I will enjoy it, tho' it be in thought!
Yes, yes, my follower, I will enjoy it.
So lovers, in imagination strong,
Enjoy their absent mistresses in thought,
And hug their pillows, as I now do thee:
And as they squeeze its feathers out—so I
Would from his pockets squeeze the money out.
  FOLLOWER. Alas! too just your simile, I fear,
For courtiers often nothing are but feathers.
  BAILIFF. Oh, my good follower! when I reflect

---

33. Used (to something undesirable).
34. A place used for preliminary confinement of debtors by bailiffs and sheriffs (from "sponge" in the sense of "to press someone for money").

On the big hopes I once had entertain'd,
To see the law, as some devouring wolf,
Eat up the land,—'till, like a garrison,
Its whole provision's gone,—lawyers were forc'd,
For want of food, to feed on one another.
But Oh! fall'n hope. The law will be reduc'd
Again to reason, whence it first arose.
But ha! our prey approaches—let us retire.

SCENE II

Tom Thumb, Noodle, Bailiff, Follower.

TOM THUMB. Trust me, my Noodle, I am wond'rous sick;
For tho' I love the gentle Huncamunca,
Yet at the thought of marriage, I grow pale;
For Oh!—but swear thou'lt keep it ever secret,
I will unfold a tale will make thee stare.
　　　NOODLE. I swear by lovely Huncamunca's charms.
　　　TOM THUMB. Then know—my grand-mamma hath often
　　　　　said—
Tom Thumb, beware of marriage.—
　　　NOODLE. Sir, I blush
To think a warrior great in arms as you,
Should be affrighted by his grand-mamma.
Can an old woman's empty dreams deter
The blooming hero from the virgin's arms?
Think of the joy which will your soul alarm,
When in her fond embraces clasp'd you lie,
While on her panting breast dissolv'd in bliss,
You pour out all Tom Thumb in ev'ry kiss.
　　　TOM THUMB. Oh, Noodle! thou hast fir'd my eager soul;
Spight of[35] my grandmother, she shall be mine;
I'll hug, caress, I'll eat her up with love.
Whole days, and nights, and years shall be too short
For our enjoyment; ev'ry sun shall rise
Blushing, to see us in our bed together.
　　　NOODLE. Oh, sir! this purpose of your soul pursue.
　　　BAILIFF. Oh, sir! I have an action against you.

---

35. Despite.

NOODLE. At whose suit is it?

BAILIFF. At your taylor's, sir.

Your taylor put this warrant in my hands,

And I arrest you, sir, at his commands.

TOM THUMB. Ha! Dogs! Arrest my friend before my face!

Think you Tom Thumb will swallow this disgrace!

But let vain cowards threaten by their word,

Tom Thumb shall show his anger by his sword.

    Kills the Bailiff.

BAILIFF. Oh, I am slain!

FOLLOWER. I'm murdered also,

And to the shades,[36] the dismal shades below,

My Bailiff's faithful follower I go.

TOM THUMB. Thus perish all the bailiffs in the land,

'Till debtors at noon-day shall walk the street,

And no one fear a bailiff, or his writ.

SCENE III

The Princess Huncamunca's Apartment.
Huncamunca, Cleora, Mustacha.

HUNCAMUNCA. Give me some musick to appease my soul:

Gentle Cleora, sing my fav'rite song.

CLEORA [*sings*].

Cupid, ease a love-sick maid,
Bring thy quiver to her aid;
With equal ardor wound the swain:
Beauty should never sigh in vain.
Let him feel the pleasing smart,
Drive thy arrow through his heart;
When one you wound, you then destroy;
When both you kill, you kill with joy.

HUNCAMUNCA. O, Tom Thumb! Tom Thumb! wherefore art
    thou Tom Thumb?

Why had'st thou not been born of royal blood?

Why had not mighty Bantam been thy father?

---

36. Spirits.

Or else the King of Brentford, old or new?[37]

MUSTACHA. I am surprized that your Highness can give your self a moment's uneasiness about that little insignificant fellow, Tom Thumb. One properer for a play-thing than a husband.—Were he my husband, his horns[38] should be as long as his body.—If you had fallen in love with a grenadier,[39] I should not have wondered at it. If you had fallen in love with something; but to fall in love with nothing!

HUNCAMUNCA. Ceace, my Mustacha, on your duty cease.
The Zephyr,[40] when in flowry vales it plays,
Is not so soft, so sweet as Thummy's breath.
The dove is not so gentle to its mate.

MUSTACHA. The dove is every bit as proper for a husband. Alas! Madam, there's not a beau about the court that looks so little like a man. He is a perfect butterfly, a thing without substance, and almost without shadow too.

HUNCAMUNCA. This rudeness is unseasonable; desist,
Or I shall think this railing comes from love.
Tom Thumb's a creature of that charming form,
That no one can abuse, unless they love him.

CLEORA. Madam, the king.

SCENE IV

King, Huncamunca.

KING. Let all but Huncamunca leave the room.
Exit Cleora, and Mustacha.
Daughter, I have of late observ'd some grief

---

37. L. J. Morrissey identifies "Bantam" as "a reference to Fielding's earlier burlesque called *The Author's Farce* (London, 1730), in which the poet Luckless is discovered to be Henry I, King of Bantam, on the death of his father Francis IV"; and the "King of Brentford" as "an allusion to *The Author's Farce*" in the last act of which "Harriet, Luckless' landlady's daughter, is discovered to be Harrietta, Princess of Old Brentford. This fortunate last act discovery allows Fielding to ridicule such fortunate accidents and to allude to Buckingham's *The Rehearsal* (London, 1671), an earlier burlesque of dramatic bombast. In it there are two Kings of Brentford" (106).

38. This refers to the folk belief that when a woman has cuckolded her husband, i.e., been unfaithful to him, horns grow on his head.

39. A soldier, originally one who threw grenades, but by the eighteenth century one of a company of the finest men in the regiment.

40. The west wind.

Unusual in your countenance, your eyes
That, like two open windows, us'd to shew
The lovely beauty of the room within,
Have now two blinds before them—What is the cause?
Say, have you not enough of meat or drink?
We've giv'n strict orders not to have you stinted.
     HUNCAMUNCA. Alas! my lord, a tender maid may want
What she can neither eat nor drink—
     KING. What's that?
     HUNCAMUNCA. Oh! Spare my blushes, but I mean a
       husband.
     KING. If that be all, I have provided one,
A husband great in arms, whose warlike sword
Streams with the yellow blood of slaughter'd giants.
Whose name in *terrâ incognitâ*[41] is known,
Whose valour, wisdom, virtue make a noise,
Great as the kettle drums of twenty armies.
     HUNCAMUNCA. Whom does my royal father mean?
     KING. Tom Thumb.
     HUNCAMUNCA. Is it possible?
     KING. Ha! the window-blinds are gone,
A country dance of joys is in your face,
Your eyes spit fire, your cheeks grow red as beef.
     HUNCAMUNCA. O, there's a magick-musick in that sound,
Enough to turn me into beef indeed.
Yes, I will own, since licens'd[42] by your word,
I'll own Tom Thumb the cause of all my grief.
For him I've sigh'd, I've wept, I've gnaw'd my sheets.

SCENE V

King, Huncamunca, Doodle.

     DOODLE. Oh! fatal news—the great Tom Thumb is dead.
     KING. How dead!
     DOODLE. Alas! as dead as a door-nail.
Help, help, the princess faints!

---

41. Unknown land.
42. Admit, since authorized.

KING. Fetch her a dram.[43]
HUNCAMUNCA. Under my bed you'll find a quart of rum.
Exit Doodle.
KING. How does my pretty daughter?
HUNCAMUNCA. Thank you, papa,
I'm something better now.
Enter Slave.
KING. What slave waits there?
Go order the physicians strait before me,
That did attend Tom Thumb—now by my stars,
Unless they give a full and true account
Of his distemper,[44] they shall all be hang'd.
DOODLE. [*Returns.*] Here is the bottle, and here is the glass.
I found them both together—
KING. Give them me.
Fills the glass.
Drink it all off, it will do you no harm.

SCENE VI

King, Huncamunca, Doodle, Physicians.

1 PHYSICIAN. We here attend your majesty's command.
KING. Of what distemper did Tom Thumb demise?
1 PHYSICIAN. He died, may it please your majesty, of a
distemper which Paracelsus[45] calls the *diaphormane,*[46] Hippocrates
the *catecumen,* Galen the *regon*—He was taken with a dizziness in his
head, for which I bled[47] him, and put on four blisters[48]—he then

---

43. A small draft of cordial or stimulant.

44. Illness.

45. Here and in the following lines famous physicians are cited as authorities.
Paracelsus (1493–1541) was a Swiss alchemist and physician who wrote treatises on
medicine. Hippocrates (460?-370? B.C.) was a Greek physician who is said to have
originated the Hippocratic oath. Galen (A.D. 130?-201?) was a Greek physician and
anatomist.

46. The medical terms in this paragraph (*diaphormane, catecumen,* and *regon*),
like the term below (*peripilusis*), seem to be nonsense terms that contribute to the
general satire of physicians.

47. Bleeding was a common practice in early medicine as a means of
restoring the proper balance of bodily humors.

48. Something applied to raise a blister.

had the gripes,[49] wherefore I thought it proper to apply a glister, a purge, and a vomit.[50]

2 PHYSICIAN. Doctor, you mistake the case; the distemper was not the *diaphormane*, as you vainly imagine; it was the *peripilusis*—and tho' I approve very much of all that you did—let me tell you, you did not do half enough—you know he complained of a pain in his arm, I would immediately have cut off his arm, and have laid open his head, to which I would have applied some *trahifick* plaister;[51] after that I would have proceeded to my catharticks, emeticks, and diureticks.[52]

1 PHYSICIAN. In the *peripilusis* indeed these methods are not only wholesome but necessary: but in the *diaphormane* otherwise.

2 PHYSICIAN. What are the symptoms of the *diaphormane?*

1 PHYSICIAN. They are various—very various and uncertain.

2 PHYSICIAN. Will you tell me that a man died of the *diaphormane* in one hour—when the crisis of that distemper does not rise till the fourth day?

1 PHYSICIAN. The symptoms are various, very various and uncertain.

SCENE VII

To them. Tom Thumb attended.

TOM THUMB. Where is the princess? where's my
    Huncamunca?
Lives she? O happy Thumb! for even now
A murmur humming skips about the court,
That Huncamunca was defunct.
    KING. Bless me!
Ye blazing stars—sure 'tis illusion all.
Are you Tom Thumb, and are you too alive?
    TOM THUMB. Tom Thumb I am, and eke also alive.
    KING. And have you not been dead at all?—

---

49. Spasms of pain.

50. A "glister" is an enema; a "purge" is a medicine that causes evacuation of the bowels; and a "vomit" is a medicine that induces vomiting.

51. A curative application designed to draw out harmful elements from the body.

52. "Catharticks" are laxatives; "emeticks" are medicines or agents that cause vomiting; and "diureticks" are drugs that increase the discharge of urine.

TOM THUMB. Not I.

1 PHYSICIAN. I told you, doctor, that cathartick would do his business.

2 PHYSICIAN. Ay, and I am very much suprized to find it did not.

SCENE VIII

King, Tom Thumb, Huncamunca, Physicians, Doodle, Noodle.

NOODLE. Great news, may it please your majesty, I bring,
A traytor is discover'd, who design'd
To kill Tom Thumb with poison.
KING. Ha! say you?
NOODLE. A girl had dress'd her monkey in his habit,
And that was poisoned by mistake for Thumb.
KING. Here are physicians for you, whose nice art
Can take a dress'd up monkey for a man.
Come to my arms, my dearest son-in-law!
Happy's the wooing, that's not long a doing;
Proceed we to the temple, there to tye
The burning bridegroom to the blushing bride.
And if I guess aright, Tom Thumb this night
Shall give a being to a new Tom Thumb.
TOM THUMB. It shall be my endeavour so to do.
HUNCAMUNCA. O fie upon you, sir, you make me blush.
TOM THUMB. It is the virgin's sign, and suits you well—
I know not where, nor how, nor what I am,
I'm so transported, I have lost my self.
HUNCAMUNCA. Forbid it, all the stars; for you're so small,
That were you lost, you'd find your self no more.
So the unhappy sempstress,[53] once, they say,
Her needle in a pottle,[54] lost, of hay.
In vain she look'd, and look'd, and made her moan;
For ah! the needle was for ever gone.
KING. Long may ye live, and love, and propagate,
'Till the whole land be peopled with Tom Thumbs.
So when the Chesire-cheese a maggot breeds,

---

53. Seamstress.
54. Twelve acres of land.

Another and another still succeeds;
By thousands and ten thousands they encrease,
Till one continu'd maggot fills the rotten cheese.

SCENE IX

Manent Physicians.

1 PHYSICIAN. Pray, Doctor Church-yard, what is your
Peripilusis? I did not care to own my ignorance to the king; but I
never heard of such a distemper before.
2 PHYSICIAN. Truly, Doctor Fillgrave, it is more nearly allied
to the *diaphormane* than you imagine—and when you know the one,
you will not be very far from finding out the other. But it is now past
ten; I must haste to Lord Weekleys, for he'll be dead before eleven,
and so I shall lose my fee.
1 PHYSICIAN. Doctor, your servant.
Exeunt severally.[55]

SCENE X

Enter Queen sola.

QUEEN. How am I forc'd to wander thus alone,
As if I were the phaenix[56] of my kind;
Tom Thumb is lost—yet Hickathrift remains,
And Hickathrift's as great a man as Thumb.
Be he then our gallant—but ha! what noise
Comes trav'ling onward, bellowing as loud
As thunder rumbling through th' ætherial plains?

SCENE XI

King, Queen, Huncamunca, Courtiers.

KING. Open the prisons, set the wretched free,
And bid our treasurer disburse six pounds
To pay their debts.—Let no one weep to-day.

---

55. Separately.
56. The phoenix is a unique bird that consumed itself by fire after five
hundred years and rose renewed from its own ashes.

Come, my fair consort, sit thee down by me.
Here seated, let us view the dancers sport;
Bid them advance.—This is the wedding-day
Of Princess Huncamunca and Tom Thumb.
        Dance, epithalamium,[57] *and sports.*

SCENE THE LAST

Noodle, King, Queen, Huncamunca, Courtiers.

NOODLE. Oh monstrous! dreadful! terrible! Oh! Oh!
Deaf be my ears, for ever blind my eyes,
Dumb be my tongue, feet lame, all senses lost.
        KING. What does the blockhead mean?
        NOODLE. Whilst from my garret
I look'd abroad into the street below,
I saw Tom Thumb attended by the mob,
Twice twenty shoe-boys, twice two dozen links,[58]
Chairmen, and porters, hackney-coachmen, whores;
When on the sudden through the streets there came
A cow, of larger than the usual size,
And in a moment, guess, oh! guess the rest,
And in a moment swallow'd up Tom Thumb.
        KING. Horrible indeed!
        GRIZZLE. Swallowed she him alive?
        NOODLE. Alive, alive, Lord Grizzle; so the boys
Of fishmongers do swallow gudgeons down.[59]
        GRIZZLE. [*Aside.*] Curse on the cow that took my vengeance
                from me.
        KING. Shut up again the prisons, bid my treasurer
Not give three farthings out—hang all the culprits,
Guilty or not—no matter.—Ravish virgins,
Go bid the school-masters whip all their boys;
Let lawyers, parsons, and physicians loose,
To rob, impose on, and to kill the world.
        Ghost of Tom Thumb rises.
        GHOST. Tom Thumb I am—but am not eke alive.

---

57. A nuptial song celebrating the bride and bridegroom.

58. Torchbearers.

59. "Fishmongers" are sellers of fish; "gudgeons" are small fish.

My body's in the cow, my ghost is here.
    GRIZZLE. Thanks, O ye stars, my vengeance is restor'd,
Nor shalt thou fly me—for I'll kill thy ghost.
        Kills the ghost.
    HUNCAMUNCA. O barbarous deed!—I will revenge him so.
        Kills Grizzle.
    DOODLE. Ha! Grizzle kill'd—then murtheress beware.
        Kills Huncamunca.
    QUEEN. O wretch!—have at thee.
        Kills Doodle.
    NOODLE. And have at thee too.
        Kills the queen.
    CLEORA. Thou'st kill'd the queen.
        Kills Noodle.
    MUSTACHA. And thou hast kill'd my lover.
        Kills Cleora.
    KING. Ha! murtheress vile, take that.
        Kills Mustacha.
And take thou this.
        Kills himself, and falls.
So when the child whom nurse from mischief guards,
Sends Jack for mustard[60] with a pack of cards;
Kings, queens, and knaves, throw one another down,
'Till the whole pack lies scatter'd and o'erthrown;
So all our pack upon the floor is cast,
And all I boast is, that I fall the last.
        Dies.
            FINIS.

---

60. L. J. Morrissey identifies "Jack-a-mustard" as "a card game joke in which the cards are sprayed about and the butt must pick them up" (107).

The Marriage of Sir Gawaine

from

BISHOP THOMAS PERCY'S

Reliques of Ancient English Poetry

Part the First

King Arthur lives in merry Carleile,[1]
  And seemely[2] is to see;
And there with him queene Guenever,
  That bride soe bright of blee.[3]

And there with him queene Guenever,
  That bride so bright in bowre:[4]
And all his barons about him stoode,
  That were both stiffe and stowre.[5]

The king a royale Christmasse kept,
  With mirth and princelye cheare;
To him repaired many a knighte,
  That came both farre and neare.

And when they were to dinner sette,
  And cups went freely round;
Before them came a faire damsèlle,
  And knelt upon the ground.

---

1. Carlisle, one of the traditional seats of Arthur's court.
2. Fair.
3. Complexion.
4. Chamber.
5. Bold and strong.

A boone,[6] a boone, O kinge Arthùre,
    I beg a boone of thee;
Avenge me of a carlish[7] knighte,
    Who hath shent[8] my love and me.

At Tearne-Wadling[9] his castle stands,
    Near to that lake so fair,
And proudlye rise the battlements,
    And streamers deck the air.

Noe gentle knighte, nor ladye gay,
    May pass that castle-walle:
But from that foule discurteous knighte,
    Mishappe will them befalle.

Hee's twyce the size of common men,
    Wi' thewes,[10] and sinewes stronge,
And on his backe he bears a clubbe,
    That is both thicke and longe.

This grimme baròne 'twas our harde happe,[11]
    But yester morne to see;
When to his bowre he bare my love,
    And sore misused mee.

And when I told him, king Arthùre
    As lyttle shold him spare;
Goe tell, sayd hee, that cuckold[12] kinge,
    To meete mee if he dare.

Upp then sterted king Arthùre,
    And sware by hille and dale,

---

6. Favor.

7. Villainous.

8. Disgraced.

9. A small tarn or lake in Cumberland (and the setting of the Middle English romance *The Awntyrs off Arthure at the Terne Wathelyne*).

10. Muscles.

11. Bad fortune.

12. A "cuckold" is one whose wife has been untrue to him.

He ne'er wolde quitt that grimme baròne,
    Till he had made him quail.

Goe fetch my sword Excalibar:
    Goe saddle mee my steede;
Nowe, by my faye, that grimme baròne
    Shall rue[13] this ruthfulle deede.

And when he came to Tearne Wadlinge
    Benethe the castle walle:
"Come forth; come forth; thou proude baròne,
    Or yielde thyself my thralle."[14]

On magicke grounde that castle stoode,
    And fenc'd with many a spelle:
Noe valiant knighte could tread thereon,
    But straite[15] his courage felle.

Forth then rush'd that carlish knight,
    King Arthur felte the charme:
His sturdy sinewes lost their strengthe,
    Downe sunke his feeble arme.

Nowe yield thee, yield thee, kinge Arthùre,
    Now yield thee, unto mee:
Or fighte with mee, or lose thy lande,
    Noe better termes maye bee,

Unless thou sweare upon the rood,
    And promise on thy faye,
Here to returne to Tearne-Wadling,
    Upon the new-yeare's daye;

And bringe me worde what thing it is
    All women moste desyre;
This is thy ransome, Arthur, he sayes,
    Ile have noe other hyre.

---

13. Regret.
14. Slave.
15. Immediately.

King Arthur then helde up his hande,
    And sware upon his faye,[16]
Then tooke his leave of the grimme barone
    And faste hee rode awaye.

And he rode east, and he rode west,
    And did of all inquyre,
What thing it is all women crave,
    And what they most desyre.

Some told him riches, pompe, or state;
    Some rayment fine and brighte;
Some told him mirthe; some flatterye;
    And some a jollye knighte.

In letters all king Arthur wrote,
    And seal'd them with his ringe:
But still his minde was helde in doubte,
    Each tolde a different thinge.

As ruthfulle he rode over a more,[17]
    He saw a ladye sette
Betweene an oke, and a greene holléye,
    All clad in red scarlette.

Her nose was crookt and turnd outwàrde,
    Her chin stoode all awrye;
And where as sholde have been her mouthe,
    Lo! there was set her eye:

Her haires, like serpents, clung aboute
    Her cheekes of deadlye hewe:
A worse-form'd ladye than she was,
    No man mote ever viewe.

To hail the king in seemelye sorte
    This ladye was fulle faine;
But king Arthùre all sore amaz'd,
    No aunswere made againe.

---

16. Faith.
17. A broad tract of open land.

What wight[18] art thou, the ladye sayd,
    That wilt not speake to mee;
Sir, I may chance to ease thy paine,
    Though I be foule to see.

If thou wilt ease my paine, he sayd,
    And helpe me in my neede;
Ask what thou wilt, thou grimme ladyè
    And it shall bee thy meede.[19]

O sweare mee this upon the roode,
    And promise on thy faye;
And here the secrette I will telle,
    That shall thy ransome paye.

King Arthur promis'd on his faye,
    And sware upon the roode;
The secrette then the ladye told,
    As lightlye well shee cou'de.

Now this shall be my paye, sir king,
    And this my guerdon[20] bee,
That some yong fair and courtlye knight,
    Thou bringe to marrye mee.

Fast then pricked king Arthùre
    Ore hille, and dale, and downe:
And soone he founde the barone's bowre:
    And soone the grimme[21] baroùne.

He bare his clubbe upon his backe,
    Hee stoode bothe stiffe and stronge;
And, when he had the letters reade,
    Awaye the lettres flunge.

Nowe yielde thee, Arthur, and thy lands,
    All forfeit unto mee;

---

18. Person.
19. Reward.
20. Reward.
21. Fierce.

For this is not thy paye, sir king,
    Nor may thy ransome bee.

Yet hold thy hand, thou proud baròne,
    I praye thee hold thy hand;
And give mee leave to speake once more
    In reskewe of my land.

This morne, as I came over a more,
    I saw a ladye sette
Betwene an oke, and a greene hollèye,
    All clad in red scarlètte.

Shee sayes, all women will have their wille,
    This is their chief desyre;
Now yield, as thou art a barone true,
    That I have payd mine hyre.[22]

An earlye vengeaunce light on her!
    The carlish baron swore:
Shee was my sister tolde thee this,
    And shee's a mishapen whore.

But here I will make mine avowe,
    To do her as ill a turne:
For an[23] ever I may that foule theefe gette,
    In a fyre I will her burne.

Part the Seconde

Homewarde pricked[24] king Arthùre,
    And a wearye man was hee;
And soon he mette queene Guenever,
    That bride so bright of blee.

What newes! what newes! thou noble king,
    Howe, Arthur, hast thou sped?

---

22. Payment.
23. If.
24. Rode.

Where hast thou hung the carlish knighte?
And where bestow'd his head?

The carlish knight is safe for mee,
And free fro mortal harme:
On magicke grounde his castle stands,
And fenc'd with many a charme.

To bowe to him I was fulle faine,
And yielde mee to his hand:
And but for a lothly[25] ladye, there
I sholde have lost my land.

And nowe this fills my hearte with woe,
And sorrowe of my life;
I swore a yonge and courtlye knight,
Sholde marry her to his wife.

Then bespake him sir Gawàine,
That was ever a gentle knighte:
That lothly ladye I will wed;
Therefore be merrye and lighte.

Nowe naye, nowe naye, good sir Gawàine;
My sister's sonne yee bee;
This lothlye ladye's all too grimme,
And all too foule for yee.

Her nose is crookt and turn'd outwàrde;
Her chin stands all awrye;
A worse form'd ladye than shee is
Was never seen with eye.

What though her chin stand all awrye,
And shee be foule to see:
I'll marry her, unkle, for thy sake,
And I'll thy ransome bee.

Nowe thankes, nowe thankes, good sir Gawàine;
And a blessing thee betyde!

---

25. Loathsome.

To-morrow wee'll have knights and squires,
    And wee'll goe fetch thy bride.

And wee'll have hawkes and wee'll have houndes,
    To cover our intent;
And wee'll away to the greene forèst,
    As wee a hunting went.

Sir Lancelot, sir Stephen[26] bolde,
    They rode with them that daye;
And foremoste of the companye
    There rode the stewarde Kaye:

Soe did sir Banier and sir Bore,[27]
    And eke sir Garratte[28] keene;
Sir Tristram too, that gentle knight,
    To the forest freshe and greene.

And when they came to the greene forrèst,
    Beneathe a faire holley tree
There sate that ladye in red scarlètte
    That unseemelye was to see.

Sir Kay beheld that lady's face,
    And looked upon her sweere;[29]
Whoever kisses that ladye, he sayes,
    Of his kisse he stands in feare.

Sir Kay beheld that ladye againe,
    And looked upon her snout;
Whoever kisses that ladye, he sayes,
    Of his kisse he stands in doubt.[30]

Peace, brother Kay, sayde sir Gawàine,
    And amend thee of thy life:

---

26. Sir Stephen is not traditionally one of the knights of Arthur's court.
27. Sir Ban and Sir Bors.
28. Sir Gareth.
29. Neck.
30. Fear.

For there is a knight amongst us all,
    Must marry her to his wife.

What marry this foule queane,[31] quoth Kay,
    I' the devil's name anone;
Gett mee a wife wherever I maye,
    In sooth shee shall be none.

Then some tooke up their hawkes in haste,
    And some took up their houndes;
And sayd they wolde not marry her,
    For cities, nor for townes.

Then bespake him king Arthùre,
    And sware there by this daye;
For a little foule sighte and mislikìnge,
    Yee shall not say her naye.

Peace, lordinges, peace; sir Gawaine sayd;
    Nor make debate and strife;
This lothlye ladye I will take,
    And marry her to my wife.

Nowe thankes, nowe thankes, good sir Gawaine,
    And a blessinge be thy meede!
For as I am thine owne ladyè,
    Thou never shalt rue this deede.

Then up they took that lothly dame,
    And home anone they bringe:
And there sir Gawaine he her wed,
    And married her with a ringe.

And when they were in wed-bed laid,
    And all were done awaye:
"Come turne to mee, mine owne wed-lord
    Come turne to mee I praye."

Sir Gawaine scant could lift his head,
    For sorrowe and for care;

---

31. Base woman.

When, lo! instead of that lothelye dame,
    Hee sawe a young ladye faire.

Sweet blushes stayn'd her rud-red cheeke,
    Her eyen were blacke as sloe:[32]
The ripening cherrye swellde her lippe,
    And all her necke was snowe.

Sir Gawaine kiss'd that lady faire,
    Lying upon the sheete:
And swore, as he was a true knighte,
    The spice was never soe sweete.

Sir Gawaine kiss'd that lady brighte,
    Lying there by his side:
"The fairest flower is not soe faire:
    Thou never can'st bee my bride."

I am thy bride, mine owne deare lorde,
    The same whiche thou didst knowe,
That was soe lothlye, and was wont
    Upon the wild more to goe.

Nowe, gentle Gawaine, chuse, quoth shee,
    And make thy choice with care;
Whether by night, or else by daye,
    Shall I be foule or faire?

"To have thee foule still in the night,
    When I with thee should playe!
I had rather farre, my lady deare,
    To have thee foule by daye."

What when gaye ladyes goe with their lordes
    To drinke the ale and wine;
Alas! then I must hide myself,
    I must not goe with mine?

"My faire ladyè, sir Gawaine sayd,
    I yield me to thy skille;

---

32. A dark-colored, plumlike fruit.

Because thou art mine owne ladyè
    Thou shalt have all thy wille."

Nowe blessed be thou, sweete Gawàine,
    And the daye that I thee see;
For as thou seest mee at this time,
    Soe shall I ever bee.

My father was an aged knighte,
    And yet it chanced soe,
He tooke to wife a false ladyè,
    Whiche broughte me to this woe.

She witch'd[33] mee, being a faire yonge maide,
    In the greene forèst to dwelle;
And there to abide in lothlye shape,
    Most like a fiend of helle.

Midst mores and mosses; woods, and wilds;
    To lead a lonesome life:
Till some yong faire and courtlye knighte
    Wolde marrye me to his wife:

Nor fully to gaine mine owne trewe shape,
    Such was her devilish skille;
Until he wolde yielde to be rul'd by mee,
    And let mee have all my wille.

She witchd my brother to a carlish boore,
    And made him stiffe and stronge;
And built him a bowre on magicke grounde,
    To live by rapine[34] and wronge.

But now the spelle is broken throughe,
    And wronge is turnde to righte;
Henceforth I shall bee a faire ladyè,
    And hee be a gentle knighte.

---

33. Bewitched.
34. Plundering.

The Egyptian Maid
or
The Romance of the Water-Lily

by

WILLIAM WORDSWORTH

[For the names and persons in the following poem, see the "History of the renowned Prince Arthur and his Knights of the Round Table;"[1] for the rest the Author is answerable; only it may be proper to add, that the Lotus, with the bust of the goddess apppearing to rise out of the full-blown flower, was suggested by the beautiful work of ancient art, once included among the Townley Marbles,[2] and now in the British Museum.]

> While Merlin paced the Cornish sands,
> Forth-looking toward the Rocks of Scilly,[3]
> The pleased Enchanter was aware
> Of a bright Ship that seemed to hang in air,
> Yet was she work of mortal hands,
> And took from men her name—THE WATER LILY.
>
> Soft was the wind, that landward blew;
> And, as the Moon, o'er some dark hill ascendant,
> Grows from a little edge of light
> To a full orb, this Pinnace[4] bright,

---

1. This is the title that the earlier of the two 1816 editions of Malory's *Morte Darthur* (the two-volume edition edited by Alexander Chalmers) bore on its title page.

2. Charles Townley (or Towneley) (1737-1805) was an English archaeologist and collector of marbles. His marbles and other artifacts were purchased by the British Museum and form part of its Graeco-Roman collection.

3. The Scilly Islands, off Cornwall at the entrance to the English Channel.

4. A small sailing boat.

As nearer to the Coast she drew,
Appeared more glorious, with spread sail and pendant.

Upon this winged Shape so fair
Sage Merlin gazed with admiration:
Her lineaments,[5] thought he, surpass
Aught that was ever shown in magic glass;
In patience built with subtle care;
Or, at a touch, set forth with wondrous transformation.

Now, though a Mechanist,[6] whose skill
Shames the degenerate grasp of modern science,
Grave Merlin (and belike[7] the more
For practising occult and perilous lore)
Was subject to a freakish will
That sapped good thoughts, or scared them with defiance.

Provoked to envious spleen, he cast
An altered look upon the advancing Stranger
Whom he had hailed with joy, and cried,
"My Art shall help to tame her pride—"
Anon the breeze became a blast,
And the waves rose, and sky portended danger.

With thrilling word, and potent sign
Traced on the beach, his work the Sorcerer urges;
The clouds in blacker clouds are lost,
Like spiteful Fiends that vanish, crossed
By Fiends of aspect more malign;
And the winds roused the Deep with fiercer scourges.

But worthy of the name she bore
Was this Sea-flower, this buoyant Galley;
Supreme in loveliness and grace
Of motion, whether in the embrace
Of trusty anchorage, or scudding o'er
The main flood roughened into hill and valley.

---

5. Shape.

6. Mechanism is the doctrine that all natural phenomena are explicable by material causes and mechanical principles.

7. Probably.

Behold, how wantonly she laves[8]
Her sides, the Wizard's craft confounding;
Like something out of Ocean sprung
To be for ever fresh and young,
Breasts the sea-flashes, and huge waves
Top-gallant high, rebounding and rebounding!

But Ocean under magic heaves,
And cannot spare the Thing he cherished:
Ah! what avails that She was fair,
Luminous, blithe, and debonair?
The storm has stripped her of her leaves;
The Lily floats no longer!—She hath perished.

Grieve for her,—She deserves no less;
So like, yet so unlike, a living Creature!
No heart had she, no busy brain;
Though loved, she could not love again;
Though pitied, *feel* her own distress;
Nor aught that troubles us, the fools of Nature.

Yet is there cause for gushing tears;
So richly was this Galley laden;
A fairer[9] than Herself she bore,
And, in her struggles, cast ashore;
A lovely One, who nothing hears
Of wind or wave—a meek and guileless Maiden.

Into a cave had Merlin fled
From mischief, caused by spells himself had muttered;
And, while repentant all too late,
In moody posture there he sate,[10]
He heard a voice, and saw, with half-raised head,
A Visitant by whom these words were uttered:

"On Christian service this frail Bark
Sailed" (hear me, Merlin!) "under high protection,
Though on her prow a sign of heathen power

---

8. Washes.
9. Fairer [one].
10. Sat.

Was carved—a Goddess with a Lily flower,
The old Egyptian's emblematic mark
Of joy immortal and of pure affection.

"Her course was for the British strand,
Her freight it was a Damsel peerless;
God reigns above, and Spirits strong
May gather to avenge this wrong
Done to the Princess, and her Land
Which she in duty left, though sad not cheerless.

"And to Caerleon's[11] loftiest tower
Soon will the Knights of Arthur's Table
A cry of lamentation send;
And all will weep who there attend,
To grace that Stranger's bridal hour,
For whom the sea was made unnavigable.

"Shame! should a Child of Royal Line
Die through the blindness of thy malice:"
Thus to the Necromancer spake
Nina,[12] the Lady of the Lake,
A gentle Sorceress, and benign,
Who ne'er embittered any good man's chalice.

"What boots,"[13] continued she, "to mourn?
To expiate thy sin endeavour!
From the bleak isle where she is laid,
Fetched by our art, the Egyptian Maid
May yet to Arthur's court be borne
Cold as she is, ere life be fled for ever.

"My pearly Boat, a shining Light,
That brought me down that sunless river,
Will bear me on from wave to wave,
And back with her to this sea-cave;

---

11. Caerleon is a small town in Gwent on the River Usk, often referred to as the site of Arthur's court.

12. A variant of the name Niniane, perhaps deliberately changed because of Nina's function as a teacher rather than a nemesis of Merlin.

13. Avails it.

Then Merlin! for a rapid flight
Through air to thee my charge will I deliver.

"The very swiftest of thy Cars
Must, when my part is done, be ready;
Meanwhile, for further guidance, look
Into thy own prophetic book;
And, if that fail, consult the Stars
To learn thy course;[14] farewell! be prompt and steady."

This scarcely spoken, she again
Was seated in her gleaming Shallop,[15]
That, o'er the yet-distempered Deep,
Pursued its way with bird-like sweep,
Or like a steed, without a rein,
Urged o'er the wilderness in sportive gallop.

Soon did the gentle Nina reach
That Isle without a house or haven;
Landing, she found not what she sought,
Nor saw of wreck or ruin aught
But a carved Lotus cast upon the shore
By the fierce waves, a flower in marble graven.

Sad relique, but how fair the while!
For gently each from each retreating
With backward curve, the leaves revealed
The bosom half, and half concealed,
Of a Divinity, that seemed to smile
On Nina as she passed, with hopeful greeting.

No quest was hers of vague desire,
Of tortured hope and purpose shaken;
Following the margin of a bay,
She spied the lonely Cast-away,
Unmarred, unstripped of her attire,
But with closed eyes,—of breath and bloom forsaken.

---

14. The way you should act.
15. An open boat fitted with oars, sails, or both.

Then Nina, stooping down, embraced,
With tenderness and mild emotion,
The Damsel, in that trance embound;
And, while she raised her from the ground,
And in the pearly shallop placed,
Sleep fell upon the air, and stilled the ocean.

The turmoil hushed, celestial springs
Of music opened, and there came a blending
Of fragrance, underived from earth,
With gleams that owed not to the Sun their birth,
And that soft rustling of invisible wings
Which Angels make, on works of love descending.

And Nina heard a sweeter voice
Than if the Goddess of the Flower had spoken:
"Thou hast achieved, fair Dame! what none
Less pure in spirit could have done;
Go, in thy enterprise rejoice!
Air, earth, sea, sky, and heaven, success betoken."

So cheered she left that Island bleak,
A bare rock of the Scilly cluster;
And, as they traversed the smooth brine,
The self-illumined Brigantine[16]
Shed, on the Slumberer's cold wan cheek
And pallid brow, a melancholy lustre.

Fleet[17] was their course, and when they came
To the dim cavern, whence the river
Issued into the salt-sea flood,
Merlin, as fixed in thought he stood,
Was thus accosted by the Dame:
"Behold to thee my Charge I now deliver!

"But where attends thy chariot—where?"
Quoth Merlin, "Even as I was bidden,
So have I done; as trusty as thy barge
My vehicle shall prove—O precious Charge!

---

16. Technically, a two-masted sailing ship.
17. Swift.

If this be sleep, how soft! if death, how fair!
Much have my books disclosed, but the end is hidden."

He spake, and gliding into view
Forth from the grotto's dimmest chamber
Came two mute Swans, whose plumes of dusky white
Changed, as the pair approached the light,
Drawing an ebon car,[18] their hue
(Like clouds of sunset) into lucid amber.

Once more did gentle Nina lift
The Princess, passive to all changes:
The car received her; then up-went
Into the ethereal element
The Birds with progress smooth and swift
As thought, when through bright regions memory ranges.

Sage Merlin, at the Slumberer's side,
Instructs the Swans their way to measure;[19]
And soon Caerleon's towers appeared,
And notes of minstrelsy were heard
From rich pavilions spreading wide,
For some high day of long-expected pleasure.

Awe-stricken stood both Knights and Dames
Ere on firm ground the car alighted;
Eftsoons[20] astonishment was past,
For in that face they saw the last
Last lingering look of clay, that tames
All pride, by which all happiness is blighted.

Said Merlin, "Mighty King, fair Lords,
Away with feast and tilt and tourney!
Ye saw, throughout this Royal House,
Ye heard, a rocking marvellous
Of turrets, and a clash of swords
Self-shaken, as I closed my airy journey.

---

18. Black chariot.
19. Directs the swans on their course.
20. Soon.

"Lo! by a destiny well known
To mortals, joy is turned to sorrow;
This is the wished-for Bride, the Maid
Of Egypt, from a rock conveyed
Where she by shipwreck had been thrown;
Ill sight! but grief may vanish ere the morrow."

"Though vast thy power, thy words are weak,"
Exclaimed the King, "a mockery hateful;
Dutiful Child! her lot how hard!
Is this her piety's reward?
Those watery locks, that bloodless cheek!
O winds without remorse! O shore ungrateful!

"Rich robes are fretted by the moth;
Towers, temples, fall by stroke of thunder;
Will that, or deeper thoughts, abate
A Father's sorrow for her fate?
He will repent him of his troth;
His brain will burn, his stout heart split asunder.

"Alas! and I have caused this woe;
For, when my prowess from invading Neighbours
Had freed his Realm, he plighted word
That he would turn to Christ our Lord,
And his dear Daughter on a Knight bestow
Whom I should choose for love and matchless labours.

"Her birth was heathen, but a fence
Of holy Angels round her hovered;
A Lady added to my court
So fair, of such divine report
And worship, seemed a recompence
For fifty kingdoms by my sword recovered.

"Ask not for whom, O champions true!
She was reserved by me her life's betrayer;
She who was meant to be a bride
Is now a corse; then put aside
Vain thoughts, and speed ye, with observance due
Of Christian rites, in Christian ground to lay her."

"The tomb," said Merlin, "may not close
Upon her yet, earth hide her beauty;
Not froward[21] to thy sovereign will
Esteem me, Liege! if I, whose skill
Wafted her hither, interpose
To check this pious haste of erring duty.

"My books command me to lay bare
The secret thou art bent on keeping;
Here must a high attest be given,
What Bridegroom was for her ordained by Heaven;
And in my glass significants there are
Of things that may to gladness turn this weeping.

"For this, approaching, One by One,
Thy Knights must touch the cold hand of the Virgin;
So, for the favoured One, the Flower may bloom
Once more; but, if unchangeable her doom,
If life departed be for ever gone,
Some blest assurance, from this cloud emerging,

May teach him to bewail his loss;
Not with a grief that, like a vapour, rises
And melts; but grief devout that shall endure
And a perpetual growth secure
Of purposes which no false thought shall cross
A harvest of high hopes and noble enterprises."

"So be it," said the King;—"anon,
Here, where the Princess lies, begin the trial;
Knights each in order as ye stand
Step forth."—To touch the pallid hand
Sir Agravaine advanced; no sign he won
From Heaven or Earth;—Sir Kaye had like denial.

Abashed, Sir Dinas[22] turned away;
Even for Sir Percival was no disclosure;
Though he, devoutest of all Champions, ere

---

21. Stubbornly disobedient.
22. Sir Dinas is originally King Mark's seneschal and later a knight of Arthur's court.

He reached that ebon car, the bier
Whereon diffused like snow the Damsel lay,
Full thrice had crossed himself in meek composure.

Imagine (but ye Saints! who can?)
How in still air the balance trembled;
The wishes, peradventure the despites[23]
That overcame some not ungenerous Knights;
And all the thoughts that lengthened out a span
Of time to Lords and Ladies thus assembled.

What patient confidence was here!
And there how many bosoms panted!
While drawing toward the Car Sir Gawaine, mailed
For tournament, his Beaver vailed,[24]
And softly touched; but, to his princely cheer
And high expectancy, no sign was granted.

Next, disencumbered of his harp,
Sir Tristram, dear to thousands as a brother,
Came to the proof,[25] nor grieved that there ensued
No change;—the fair Izonda[26] he had wooed
With love too true, a love with pangs too sharp,
From hope too distant, not to dread another.

Not so Sir Launcelot;—from Heaven's grace
A sign he craved, tired slave of vain contrition;
The royal Guinever looked passing glad
When his touch failed.—Next came Sir Galahad;
He paused, and stood entranced by that still face
Whose features he had seen in noontide vision.

For late, as near a murmuring stream
He rested 'mid an arbour green and shady,
Nina, the good Enchantress, shed
A light around his mossy bed;

---

23. Perhaps the ignoble feelings.
24. His visor closed.
25. Undertook the challenge.
26. Isolt.

And, at her call, a waking dream
Prefigured to his sense the Egyptian Lady.

Now, while the bright-haired front he bowed,
And stood, far-kenned[27] by mantle furred with ermine,
As o'er the insensate Body hung
The enrapt, the beautiful, the young,
Belief sank deep into the crowd
That he the solemn issue would determine.

Nor deem it strange; the Youth had worn
That very mantle on a day of glory,
The day when he achieved that matchless feat,
The marvel of the PERILOUS SEAT,
Which whosoe'er approached of strength was shorn,[28]
Though King or Knight the most renowned in story.

He touched with hesitating hand,
And lo! those Birds, far-famed through Love's dominions,
The Swans, in triumph clap their wings;
And their necks play, involved in rings,
Like sinless snakes in Eden's happy land;—
"Mine is she," cried the Knight;—again they clapped their pinions.[29]

"Mine was she—mine she is, though dead,
And to her name my soul shall cleave in sorrow;"
Whereat, a tender twilight streak
Of colour dawned upon the Damsel's cheek;
And her lips, quickening with uncertain red,
Seemed from each other a faint warmth to borrow.

Deep was the awe, the rapture high,
Of love emboldened, hope with dread entwining,
When, to the mouth, relenting Death
Allowed a soft and flower-like breath,
Precursor to a timid sigh,
To lifted eyelids, and a doubtful shining.

---

27. Known from afar.
28. Deprived.
29. Wings.

In silence did King Arthur gaze
Upon the signs that pass away or tarry;
In silence watched the gentle strife
Of Nature leading back to life;
Then eased his Soul at length by praise
Of God, and Heaven's pure Queen—the blissful Mary.

Then said he, "Take her to thy heart
Sir Galahad! a treasure that God giveth
Bound by indissoluble ties to thee
Through mortal change and immortality;
Be happy and unenvied, thou who art
A goodly Knight that hath no Peer that liveth!"

Not long the Nuptials were delayed;
And sage tradition still rehearses
The pomp, the glory of that hour
When toward the Altar from her bower
King Arthur led the Egyptian Maid,
And Angels carolled these far-echoed verses;—

Who shrinks not from alliance
Of evil with good Powers,
To God proclaims defiance,
And mocks whom he adores.

A Ship to Christ devoted
From the Land of Nile did go;
Alas! the bright Ship floated,
An Idol at her Prow.

By magic domination
The Heaven-permitted vent
Of purblind[30] mortal passion,
Was wrought her punishment.

The Flower, the Form within it,
What served they in her need?
Her port she could not win it,
Nor from mishap be freed.

---

30. Totally blind.

The tempest overcame her,
And she was seen no more;
But gently gently blame her,
She cast a Pearl ashore.

The Maid to Jesu hearkened,
And kept to him her faith,
Till sense in death was darkened,
Or sleep akin to death.

But Angels round her pillow
Kept watch, a viewless[31] band;
And, billow favouring billow,
She reached the destined strand.

Blest Pair! whate'er befall you,
Your faith in Him approve
Who from frail earth can call you,
To bowers of endless love!

---

31. Invisible.

II.
THE VICTORIANS

Introduction

The Victorian age saw a renaissance of Arthurian poetry. Among the Victorian poets who looked to Arthurian themes for their subject matter were Thomas Westwood, who published in 1866 *The Sword of Kingship*, which tells of Arthur's youth and his pulling the sword from the anvil, and "The Quest of the Sancgreall" (1868); Robert Stephen Hawker, who wrote "The Quest of the Sangraal" (1864); Edward Bulwer-Lytton, who wrote the epic poem *King Arthur*, which appeared in 1848; Scottish poet John Veitch, who in "Merlin" (1889) treats, as his introductory note explains, "Merlin Caledonius, known also as Merlin Wylt and Silvestris," the earlier of the two Merlins from which the romancers formed "a third or legendary Merlin"; John Davidson, author of "The Last Ballad" (1899); as well as the better-known poets, such as William Morris, Algernon Charles Swinburne, and Matthew Arnold, discussed below. But no author had as much influence on the renewed interest in the Matter of Britain as Alfred, Lord Tennyson (1809–1892).

A central event in Tennyson's life was the death of his beloved friend Arthur Hallam at the age of twenty-two in 1833. This event informed much of Tennyson's poetry for the rest of his life. It led directly to the writing of one of the greatest English elegiac poems, *In Memoriam* (published in 1850 but begun shortly after Hallam's death in 1833). As John D. Rosenberg has so perceptively observed, it is no coincidence that a draft of Tennyson's "Morte d'Arthur," which later became part of the idyll "The Passing of Arthur," "appears in the same notebook that contains the earliest sections of *In Memoriam*. This first-composed but last-in-sequence of the *Idylls* is sandwiched between Section XXX of *In Memoriam*, which commemorates the Tennyson family's first desolate Christmas at Somersby without Hallam, and Section XXXI, which depicts Lazarus rising from the dead. The physical placement of the 'Morte' graphically expresses the poet's longing" (229).

Added to this personal association of King Arthur with Arthur Hallam are larger patterns that make the *Idylls* much more than an idealization of a lost friend. As the *Idylls of the King* grew from the "Morte d'Arthur" to the completed collection, Tennyson maintained a thematic and structural consistency that not only is compelling in its own right but also seems to be a perfect reflection of the Victorian age. In addition to—and probably more essential than—his stated theme of soul at war with sense, Tennyson consistently balances "the true and the false" (which he initially intended to be a subtitle to the 1859 *Idylls of the King*), appearance and reality; and he presents characters who, like all of us, must cope with the fact that things are sometimes better and often worse than they seem. The resulting tensions thus have a universal significance at the same time that they are a metaphor for an age that was itself torn between faith and doubt, hope and despair.

The Victorian age saw in the very scientific, technological and intellectual advances that brought hope of bettering the human condition a darker side, an undermining of faith (expressed so well in Arnold's poem "Dover Beach") and a possibility of exploitation that called into question the notion of progress. This duality, which lasts even to the present day, helps to explain the popularity of Arthurian material among modern poets. The Arthurian world, like the modern world, has great potential for improving the human condition; but it seems that such an ideal is always frustrated by the failings and imperfections that are inherent in the world and those who inhabit it. Tennyson captures this duality and expresses it in a form perfectly suited to it.

The writing of the *Idylls* occupied Tennyson for most of his creative life. The poem that began with the notebook version of "Morte d'Arthur" in 1833 was virtually finished in 1885 with the publication of the "Balin and Balan" idyll in *Tiresias and Other Poems* (although he was still making small changes as late as 1891). In between, the poems that make up the finished epic appeared in various stages. The first was in 1859 with the publication of *Idylls of the King*, a volume containing four idylls: "Enid," "Vivien," "Elaine," and "Guinevere." Later the names were changed ("Elaine" becoming "Lancelot and Elaine," for example); and "Enid" was divided into two idylls, as Tennyson strove for the twelve parts conventional in an epic. The 1859 volume was followed in 1869 by the publication of "The Coming of Arthur," "The Holy Grail," "Pelleas and Ettarre," and "The Passing of Arthur"; then in 1872 by "Gareth and Lynette" and "The Last Tournament"; and finally in 1885 by "Balin and Balan."

The first installment in 1859 captured the Victorian imagination and was often reprinted and illustrated. Indeed, the image of the Lily Maid of Astolat in her barge is one of the most commonly depicted scenes in all Arthurian literature. The same basic story is at the root of another of Tennyson's poems. However, the Elaine of the idyll is a vastly different figure from the title character in "The Lady of Shalott" (1832, reprinted in a revised form in 1842), who represents the artist, destined to be lonely and unappreciated. As Jerome Buckley has pointed out, "The curse upon her is the endowment of sensibility that commits her to a vicarious life. Confined to her island and her high tower, she must perceive actuality always at two removes, at a sanctifying distance and then only in the mirror that catches the pictures framed by her narrow casement" (49).

The Lady of Shalott has an almost allegorical quality, as does another early creation, the title character of "Sir Galahad" (1842, but written in 1834). Tennyson's Galahad, who says of himself, "My strength is as the strength of ten, / Because my heart is pure," is moral perfection personified. He is also a character who, like the Arthur of the *Idylls,* is beyond human passion because "all my heart is drawn above."

In "Merlin and the Gleam" (1889) Tennyson again returns to an exploration of the life of the artist. Merlin represents Tennyson himself and the Gleam he follows is the artist's imagination. Thus this last published of Tennyson's Arthurian poems has a more mature sense of the importance of art and of the role of the poet than "The Lady of Shalott," his first published Arthurian piece (though "Sir Launcelot and Queen Guinevere" was actually his first Arthurian effort—written, at least in part, in 1830, but not published until 1842).

The popularity of Tennyson's *Idylls* was tremendous. The poems went through many editions both in England and in America; and they inspired other works of art, including book illustrations, paintings, tiles, and literary parodies. But other Victorian poets also contributed to the development of Arthurian literature in this period. Perhaps the most important Arthurian poem of the age besides the *Idylls* was William Morris's "The Defence of Guenevere" (1858). The 1859 *Idylls* gave women a central place in the Arthurian stories, but Morris's poem let

Guenevere speak for herself and in her own defense and thus is at the beginning of a tradition that extends to Parke Godwin's *Beloved Exile* (1980) and Wendy Mnookin's *Guenever Speaks* (1991).

In "The Defence of Guenevere" the Queen uses various rhetorical strategies to explain her actions and to defend them and herself. As she describes the birth of the passionate attraction between herself and Launcelot and reminds Gauwaine of the fatal outcome of his own mother's passion, she both links herself to Morgawse as a device for evoking sympathy and suggests the disastrous results of an inability to accept human nature or to pity a wrongdoer. In addition, early in the poem Morris puts into her mouth a revealing metaphor. The comparison of her decision to a choice offered by an angel between two cloths, one representing heaven and one hell, shows how difficult and arbitrary life's choices sometimes are and how momentous an apparently small decision can be. When she speaks of the accusations made by Mellyagraunce, Guenevere is issuing a warning and a threat to those who would accuse the woman championed by Launcelot.

There is some doubt as to what Guenevere actually believes to be true and what she says for effect. Is she sincere when she tells Gauwaine that he lies in his accusation of her? If so, perhaps she means that she never intended to be treasonous, to undermine Arthur and his realm. Perhaps she is suggesting that on the night she and Launcelot were surprised in her chamber they had not slept together. Or perhaps she is merely denying the accusation to buy time until Launcelot comes to her rescue, as she knows he will. However the ambiguity is resolved, it is clear that Morris's Guenevere is in sharp contrast to the grief-stricken queen who grovels at Arthur's feet in Tennyson's *Idylls.* She is a proud woman who "never shrunk, / But spoke on bravely, glorious lady fair."

In "King Arthur's Tomb" Morris shows first Launcelot's and then Guenevere's perspective on their relationship before bringing them together for a final meeting at Arthur's tomb. In addition to the poignance he attains in this last encounter, Morris uses imagery skillfully to convey meaning, as when he describes an arras on which "the wind set the silken kings a-sway," an image that recalls the instability and ultimate collapse of Arthur's realm.

Matthew Arnold had neither Tennyson's nor Morris's knowledge of or empathy for the characters of the Arthurian legend. Yet he wrote one poem, "Tristram and Iseult," that is a significant addition to the Matter of Britain. Arnold's plot begins with a dying Tristram who waits for a last visit from Iseult of Ireland. The lovers do enjoy a final moment together, but then both die. Arnold's Iseult has not come with the power to cure, merely to join him in death, which cools the heat of their passion. Very soon they are "cold as those who lived and loved / A thousand years ago." There is a nice play of imagery of heat and cold in the death scene. The "air of the December night / steals coldly" around the chamber where the lifeless lovers lie and flaps the tapestry on which is depicted a huntsman in "a fresh forest scene." He seems to stare at the pitiful lovers "with heated cheeks and flurried air" as he wonders who they might be. The hunter in the tapestry is a variation on the "cold pastoral" of Keats's "Ode on a Grecian Urn." He is warmer than the real lovers because he represents life. And the confusion ascribed to him as he seems to ponder the scene before him suggests that art, like life, is not an escape from reality. Only death cools the fires of "the gradual furnace of the world."

This imagery suggests that there is something ominous in what might otherwise be a touching portrayal of Iseult and her children "warm in their mantles" in the final section of the poem, "Iseult of Brittany," wherein Arnold portrays a saddened Iseult of Brittany who "seems one dying in a mask of youth." The picture of a woman who has grown old before her time is heightened by the fact that she watches over her own children, whose vitality has not yet been dried up by the world's sorrow. And yet their very warmth (their cheeks were "flush'd" and their brows "hot" even before being wrapped in the mantles) implies that they too are subject to "the gradual furnace of the world" that has already robbed Iseult of joy.

Another original touch that Arnold adds to his plot is its ending: Iseult tells her children the story of Merlin and Vivian, an ironically appropriate tale. It underscores the plight of Iseult, who wanted her lover beside her, by describing a Vivian who "grew passing weary of her love." Iseult is actually more like Merlin than Vivian. She is trapped in a life that holds little joy for her and that is very limited, trapped because she was rejected by a lover who did not desire her attentions.

Algernon Charles Swinburne also took up the Tristram legend in "Tristram of Lyonesse," which focuses on the passion of the lovers. This poem offers a view of the Arthurian world that contrasts sharply with Tennyson's. It is rich in natural imagery that emphasizes the natural force of the love shared by Tristram and Iseult and presents a view of their love far different from that of Tennyson, who turns the great passion into a sordid affair.

As in Swinburne's retelling of the Tristram story, so too in his *Tale of Balen* is fate an overpowering force. The author did not have to alter Malory's version of Balin's story very much to show how destiny governs human life. Even in Malory, Balin is buffeted by fortune as harshly and as clearly as Oedipus, and there is something of the feel of a Greek play about the tale. But whereas in Malory Balin's story is preparatory to subtler tragedies that follow and dissipate its effect, in Swinburne's version this is not the case, and the reader feels the full power of fate.

Among Swinburne's shorter poems are two that are analogous to Morris's "Defence of Guenevere" and "King Arthur's Tomb." "The Day Before the Trial" and "Lancelot" form a diptych depicting the relationship between Arthur and Guenevere in one panel and between Lancelot and Guenevere in the other. In both poems there is a play between the Grail and Guenevere. In the former Arthur's monologue is virtually framed by the thought of "My wife that loves not me." In addition to watching her love turn toward another, he was precluded by his marriage to her from the vision of the Grail. He says, "No maid was I, to see / The white Sangreal borne up in air . . . ." He speaks ironically of his "honours," which were to be found at Camelot, not Carbonek: "I had the name of king to bear, / And watch the eyes of Guenevere, / My wife, who loves not me."

In the "Lancelot" frame of the diptych, which presents a dream of a dialogue with an angel, a vision of the Grail is adumbrated by "a shadow on my sight." The shadow that blots out the light of the Grail is Guenevere. The intensity of Lancelot's passion for her is conveyed in pictures reminiscent of the Pre-Raphaelite painters:

> Always sate I, watching her,
> By her carven gilded chair,
> Full of wonder and great fear
> If one long lock of her hair
> In the soft wind sink or stir,
>   Fallen to her knee.
> All about her face and head

The flat sunset overspread
Like an aureole of red
Stained as drops from wounds that bled
In some bitter fight.

Though Lancelot has intimations of the Grail, he, like Arthur, fails in his quest because of Guenevere. And in his vision Lancelot speaks lines that echo Arthur's from "The Day Before the Trial," an echo that makes clear the intentional diptych nature of the pair of poems. Lancelot says, "All my love avails not her, / And she loves not me." The two poems are very different in form and content, but they combine like frames of a diptych depicting thematically related scenes to reveal the tragedy of Camelot as experienced by Arthur and by Lancelot.

Because of writers like Tennyson, Morris, Arnold and Swinburne, in the Victorian age poetry was the preeminent and most popular form for treating Arthurian themes. But a play produced late in Victoria's reign led to a shift in emphasis so that drama became the preferred form for treating the legends in the first part of the twentieth century.

J. Comyns Carr's *King Arthur* (1895) was the type of spectacular production that could not help but capture the attention of the public—and of other writers. Not only did it star two of the most famous actors of the day (Ellen Terry as Guinevere and Henry Irving as Arthur), but its sets and costumes were designed by Burne-Jones and its music scored by Sir Arthur Sullivan. As Jennifer Goodman noted in her article on the production, "The contemporary verdict on Irving's *King Arthur* was manifestly approving. The play ran for a hundred nights, toured the United States and Canada successfully, and might well have been revived if the 1898 fire had not destroyed the scenery" (255).

Carr's play employed dramatic spectacle in a manner consistent with the other "blockbuster" elements of the production. In the prologue Excalibur rises magically from the lake; in the first act the Holy Grail appears brilliantly: from its center "a red light strikes like a star through the transparent veil that covers it"; later, in the third act, a solemn procession carries the bier of Elaine of Astolat into Camelot; and in the last act, after Arthur is reported dead, he returns and reveals himself before his single combat with Mordred.

The scope of the play, which treats Arthur's career from the time he receives Excalibur until his death, requires considerable condensing of the traditional material; but Carr manages to maintain the unity of his piece by focusing attention on a few principal characters. His primary interest seems to be in Arthur, Guinevere, and Mordred, the last of whom is at times Iago-like in his deceit and manipulation. Carr's Lancelot is less interesting and less heroic than is usual. Because he fears that Mordred will tell Arthur of the love between him and the Queen, Lancelot delays telling the King of a threat to the Kingdom. But, in a dramatic touch lacking in Malory or Tennyson, Lancelot redeems himself by slaying Mordred after the villain has given Arthur his fatal wound. Carr blends elements from Malory, Tennyson, and Shakespeare and from his own imagination to create a spectacular new version of the Arthurian story.

In the following years, really through the first half of the twentieth century, drama gained unprecedented importance as a medium for treating Arthurian subjects. Even many of the Arthurian poems in this period, like Robinson's *Merlin, Lancelot,* and *Tristram,* were decidedly dramatic in nature.

Though Victorian fiction virtually ignored the Arthurian legends, one relatively unknown work is nevertheless a fascinating Arthurian document. *The Feasts of Camelot,* written in 1863 by "Mrs. T. K. Hervey" (Eleanora Louisa Montagu Hervey), a series of tales told by various members of Arthur's court, was influenced by Chaucer's *Canterbury Tales,* the Gothic novel, and Malory's *Morte Darthur. The Feasts of Camelot* is among the earliest works of Arthurian fiction and the first to be written by a woman. Though the point could be debated, it might also be considered the first feminist Arthurian novel. And, despite the fact that the form seems well suited to the Matter of Britain, Hervey's book remains one of the very few unified collections of short Arthurian tales to be written in the modern period.

One of the more interesting aspects of this book is what Hervey does with the legend of Tristram, Isond (as she calls Isolt), and Mark. Their stories are told in the course of three tales that seem designed to redeem not only the lovers but even King Mark. Though Hervey clearly draws on traditional material, her account is unconventional in almost every way. In Chapter III of the *Feasts,* Tristram tells the tale of "Mad King Mark." In this chapter, which seems to present a typically evil Mark in an atypical way, Tristram is called upon to fight for Mark's sovereignty, which he objects to doing because Mark calls himself a king. Tristram recognizes Arthur as the sole ruler in all of Britain. Nevertheless, Tristram is goaded into combat with Sir Maurice of Ireland, who taunts him with false stories spread by Mark that Tristram is afraid to meet him in battle. This, of course, is in contrast to the traditional story, in which Tristram is eager to fight to end the allegiance owed by Cornwall to Ireland. After defeating, but not killing, Maurice, Tristram is sent to Ireland with a sealed message that contains a request that Tristram be watched as one who has plotted to usurp Mark's land and also a request for Isond's hand.

Hervey's redemption of the lovers is found in this chapter. After Tristram escapes from Ireland through a bizarre plot devised by Isond, he goes, as instructed by her, to her namesake (who resides not in Brittany but in Wales) to have an old wound that has reopened cured. He marries Isond of Wales, who is still his wife as the tales are being told at Camelot.

The desire of Hervey to redeem even the most wicked of her traditional characters is seen in an exchange that takes place at the end of this chapter. Merlin has harsh words for the bards who speak of Camelot not so much because they have declared him to be a wizard but because "they have even dared to call our gracious lady Morgana, the 'Fay-lady.'" In response Guenever tells him the reason is that Merlin "taught her so many learned things that women seldom know of, that rumour has fixed upon her the blame of dealing with unlawful magic." Merlin has taken steps to set things right by recording the true story in books that are "fast locked in the great pyx in the church of St. Stephen." He adds, "Heaven grant they never be lost; or a sorry history will be given of us all in the ages to come!" These comments are a digression from the main concern of the chapter but are thematically linked to it. The sorry history is obviously the traditional account of Merlin and Morgan but also of Tristram and Isond and Mark. And it is such an account that the tales in *The Feasts of Camelot* are trying to correct (in more than one sense of that term).

Later in the book, in Chapter XI, Isond tells of Mark's "One Good Deed." Most of her account does not concern Mark at all but rather the deeds and misdeeds of two brothers. Although a love interest is introduced, elements of the tale are reminiscent of Malory's treatment of Balin and Balan. One brother, Bertrand, is responsible for the death of the other, Walter, and, at least in part because of the guilt he feels, dies shortly thereafter. Mark's good deed is to have the body of Walter brought back to his castle to be buried beside the woman he loved and to have prayers said for them. Of course, as Arthur says, "It could be wished that the living rather than the dead had been so humanely dealt with."

The redemption of Mark is not completed until Chapter XII, the last in the *Feasts*, which contains a tale told by Alisaunder, the Alysaundir the Orphelyn who is "slayne by the treson of kynge Marke" in Malory. But here he is not slain. In fact, he responds to Arthur's request for a tale revealing that someone of Mark's "blood and race" has done "acts of nobleness and generosity, whence we may infer that nature is not all in fault, but that circumstance has wrought in him some of the ill that he has done."

Alisaunder tells of the young Tristram's forgiveness of his stepmother, who twice tried to poison him. Tristram's pleading saved her from the death to which his father, Meliodus, had condemned her and even transformed her from a wicked to a devoted stepmother who "loved him tenderly ever after" and a penitent who "scourged herself and wore sackcloth for her sin." As a result of the story Arthur is forced to admit that Tristram, Alisaunder's father (Mark's brother), and Alisaunder himself show that there are "traits of nobleness and self-denial in the blood of King Mark's line."

Since Mark's misdeeds are not a fault of nature, the explanation can then be found in the realm of nurture. Merlin recounts a rumor that he had prophesized that "one near akin" to Mark would "usurp his power, and hold him captive till his death-day." The prophecy kept him "ever in dread" and caused him to wage "unnatural war with all his race." Even his wife claims that "King Mark has ever been kind and tender to me" and only cruel or unjust when "led to suspect treachery through a foolish rumour." Mark, now rightly understood, is led in and allowed to join in the feasting and fellowship, and "many a pleasant tale and touching song wiled away the last trace of care from the softened heart of King Mark."

It would be easy to see this story merely as a naive and unsophisticated retelling that tries to give a happy ending to a tragic story. But it might be more fruitful to look on it as an indication of how deeply the Arthurian legend had entered the Victorian popular consciousness and how variously it could be molded by that age. Hervey's redemption of the characters of the Tristan legend is as much an expression of the values of the Victorian age as Tennyson's condemnation of them. For a complete understanding of the use of the Tristan legend in the nineteenth century, because of the female perspective it provides and because of the intriguing blend of sources, Hervey's account of Tristram and Isond and the book in which it appears are worthy of further study.

The Lady of Shalott

by

ALFRED, LORD TENNYSON

Part I

On either side the river lie
Long fields of barley and of rye,
That clothe the wold[1] and meet the sky;
And thro' the field the road runs by
    To many-tower'd Camelot;
And up and down the people go,
Gazing where the lilies blow
Round an island there below,
    The island of Shalott.

Willows whiten, aspens quiver,
Little breezes dusk and shiver
Thro' the wave that runs for ever
By the island in the river
    Flowing down to Camelot.
Four gray walls, and four gray towers,
Overlook a space of flowers,
And the silent isle imbowers[2]
    The Lady of Shalott.

By the margin, willow-veil'd,
Slide the heavy barges trail'd
By slow horses; and unhail'd
The shallop[3] flitteth silken-sail'd
    Skimming down to Camelot:
But who hath seen her wave her hand?

---

1. Plain.
2. Encloses, as in a bower or shady recess.
3. An open boat fitted with oars, sails, or both.

Or at the casement seen her stand?
Or is she known in all the land,
        The Lady of Shalott?

Only reapers, reaping early
In among the bearded[4] barley,
Hear a song that echoes cheerly
From the river winding clearly,
        Down to tower'd Camelot;
And by the moon the reaper weary,
Piling sheaves in uplands airy,
Listening, whispers "'T is the fairy
        Lady of Shalott."

Part II

There she weaves by night and day
A magic web with colors gay.
She has heard a whisper say,
A curse is on her if she stay
        To look down to Camelot.
She knows not what the curse may be,
And so she weaveth steadily,
And little other care hath she,
        The Lady of Shalott.

And moving thro' a mirror clear
That hangs before her all the year,
Shadows of the world appear.
There she sees the highway near
        Winding down to Camelot;
There the river eddy whirls,
And there the surly village-churls,
And the red cloaks of market girls,
        Pass onward from Shalott.

Sometimes a troop of damsels glad,
An abbot on an ambling pad,[5]
Sometimes a curly shepherd-lad,

---

4. Having bristles or hairy tufts.
5. A horse that moves at an easy pace.

Or long-hair'd page in crimson clad,
    Goes by to tower'd Camelot;
And sometimes thro' the mirror blue
The knights come riding two and two:
She hath no loyal knight and true,
    The Lady of Shalott.

But in her web she still delights
To weave the mirror's magic sights,
For often thro' the silent nights
A funeral, with plumes and lights
    And music, went to Camelot;
Or when the moon was overhead,
Came two young lovers lately wed:
"I am half sick of shadows," said
    The Lady of Shalott.

Part III

A bow-shot from her bower-eaves,
He rode between the barley-sheaves.
The sun came dazzling thro' the leaves,
And flamed upon the brazen greaves[6]
    Of bold Sir Lancelot.
A red-cross knight for ever kneel'd
To a lady in his shield,
That sparkled on the yellow field,
    Beside remote Shalott.

The gemmy bridle glitter'd free,
Like to some branch of stars we see
Hung in the golden Galaxy.
The bridle bells rang merrily
    As he rode down to Camelot;
And from his blazon'd baldric[7] slung
A mighty silver bugle hung,
And as he rode his armor rung,
    Beside remote Shalott.

---

6. Brass leg armor.

7. A "baldric" is a belt worn across the chest to support a sword or bugle. This one is "blazon'd" or adorned, as if with heraldic devices.

All in the blue unclouded weather
Thick-jewell'd shone the saddle-leather,
The helmet and the helmet-feather
Burn'd like one burning flame together,
    As he rode down to Camelot;
As often thro' the purple night,
Below the starry clusters bright,
Some bearded meteor, trailing light,
    Moves over still Shalott.

His broad clear brow in sunlight glow'd;
On burnish'd hooves his war-horse trode;
From underneath his helmet flow'd
His coal-black curls as on he rode,
    As he rode down to Camelot.
From the bank and from the river
He flash'd into the crystal mirror,
"Tirra lirra," by the river
    Sang Sir Lancelot.

She left the web, she left the loom,
She made three paces thro' the room,
She saw the water-lily bloom,
She saw the helmet and the plume,
    She look'd down to Camelot.
Out flew the web and floated wide;
The mirror crack'd from side to side;
"The curse is come upon me," cried
    The Lady of Shalott.

Part IV

In the stormy east-wind straining,
The pale yellow woods were waning,
The broad stream in his banks complaining,
Heavily the low sky raining
    Over tower'd Camelot;
Down she came and found a boat
Beneath a willow left afloat,
And round about the prow she wrote
    The Lady of Shalott.

And down the river's dim expanse
Like some bold seër in a trance,
Seeing all his own mischance—
With a glassy countenance
     Did she look to Camelot.
And at the closing of the day
She loosed the chain, and down she lay;
The broad stream bore her far away,
     The Lady of Shalott.

Lying, robed in snowy white
That loosely flew to left and right—
The leaves upon her falling light—
Thro' the noises of the night
     She floated down to Camelot;
And as the boat-head wound along
The willowy hills and fields among,
They heard her singing her last song,
     The Lady of Shalott.

Heard a carol, mournful, holy,
Chanted loudly, chanted lowly,
Till her blood was frozen slowly,
And her eyes were darken'd wholly,
     Turn'd to tower'd Camelot.
For ere she reach'd upon the tide
The first house by the water-side,
Singing in her song she died,
     The Lady of Shalott.

Under tower and balcony,
By garden-wall and gallery,
A gleaming shape she floated by,
Dead-pale between the houses high,
     Silent into Camelot.
Out upon the wharfs they came,
Knight and burgher,[8] lord and dame,
And round the prow they read her name,
     The Lady of Shalott.

---

8. Merchant.

Who is this? and what is here?
And in the lighted palace near
Died the sound of royal cheer;
And they cross'd themselves for fear,
    All the knights at Camelot:
But Lancelot mused a little space;
He said, "She has a lovely face;
God in his mercy lend her grace,
    The Lady of Shalott."

Sir Galahad

by

ALFRED, LORD TENNYSON

My good blade carves the casques[1] of men,
    My tough lance thrusteth sure,
My strength is as the strength of ten,
    Because my heart is pure.
The shattering trumpet shrilleth high,
    The hard brands[2] shiver on the steel,
The splinter'd spear-shafts crack and fly,
    The horse and rider reel:
They reel, they roll in clanging lists,[3]
    And when the tide of combat stands,
Perfume and flowers fall in showers,
    That lightly rain from ladies' hands.

How sweet are looks that ladies bend
    On whom their favours fall!
For them I battle till the end,
    To save from shame and thrall:
But all my heart is drawn above,
    My knees are bow'd in crypt and shrine:
I never felt the kiss of love,
    Nor maiden's hand in mine.
More bounteous aspects on me beam,
    Me mightier transports move and thrill;
So keep I fair thro' faith and prayer
    A virgin heart in work and will.

---

1. Helmets.
2. Swords.
3. Field for jousting or tournaments.

When down the stormy crescent goes,
 A light before me swims,
Between dark stems the forest glows,
 I hear a noise of hymns:
Then by some secret shrine I ride;
 I hear a voice but none are there;
The stalls are void,[4] the doors are wide,
 The tapers burning fair.
Fair gleams the snowy altar-cloth,
 The silver vessels sparkle clean,
The shrill bell rings, the censer[5] swings,
 And solemn chaunts resound between.

Sometimes on lonely mountain-meres[6]
 I find a magic bark;
I leap on board: no helmsman steers:
 I float till all is dark.
A gentle sound, an awful[7] light!
 Three angels bear the holy Grail:
With folded feet, in stoles of white,
 On sleeping wings they sail.
Ah, blessed vision! blood of God!
 My spirit beats her mortal bars,
As down dark tides the glory slides,
 And star-like mingles with the stars.

When on my goodly charger borne
 Thro' dreaming towns I go,
The cock crows ere the Christmas morn,
 The streets are dumb with snow.
The tempest crackles on the leads,
 And, ringing, springs from brand and mail;
But o'er the dark a glory spreads,
 And gilds the driving hail.
I leave the plain, I climb the height;
 No branchy thicket shelter yields;

---

4. The seats are empty.

5. A vessel in which incense is burned.

6. Mountain-lakes.

7. Awe-inspiring.

But blessed forms in whistling storms
    Fly o'er waste fens and windy fields.

A maiden knight—to me is given
    Such hope, I know not fear;
I yearn to breathe the airs of heaven
    That often meet me here.
I muse on joy that will not cease,
    Pure spaces clothed in living beams,
Pure lilies of eternal peace,
    Whose odours haunt my dreams;
And, stricken by an angel's hand,
    This mortal armour that I wear,
This weight and size, this heart and eyes,
    Are touch'd, are turn'd to finest air.

The clouds are broken in the sky,
    And thro' the mountain-walls
A rolling organ-harmony
    Swells up, and shakes and falls.
Then move the trees, the copses nod,
    Wings flutter, voices hover clear:
"O just and faithful knight of God!
    Ride on! the prize is near."
So pass I hostel,[8] hall, and grange;[9]
    By bridge and ford, by park and pale,[10]
All-arm'd I ride, whate'er betide,
    Until I find the holy Grail.

---

8. Inn.

9. Farmhouse.

10. A "pale" is a fence or the area enclosed by a fence.

Merlin and the Gleam

by

ALFRED, LORD TENNYSON

I

O young Mariner,
You from the haven
Under the sea-cliff,
You that are watching
The gray Magician
With eyes of wonder,
I am Merlin,
And *I* am dying,
I am Merlin
Who follow The Gleam.

II

Mighty the Wizard
Who found me at sunrise
Sleeping, and woke me
And learn'd'd[1] me Magic!
Great the Master,
And sweet the Magic,
When over the valley,
In early summers,
Over the mountain,
On human faces,
And all around me,
Moving to melody,
Floated The Gleam.

---

1. Taught.

III

Once at the croak of a Raven who crost it,
A barbarous people,
Blind to the magic,
And deaf to the melody,
Snarl'd at and cursed me.
A demon vext me,
The light retreated,
The landskip[2] darken'd,
The melody deaden'd,
The Master whisper'd
"Follow The Gleam."

IV

Then to the melody,
Over a wilderness
Gliding, and glancing at
Elf of the woodland,
Gnome of the cavern,
Griffin and Giant,
And dancing of Fairies
In desolate hollows,
And wraiths[3] of the mountain,
And rolling of dragons
By warble of water,
Or cataract music
Of falling torrents,
Flitted The Gleam.

V

Down from the mountain
And over the level,
And streaming and shining on
Silent river,
Silvery willow,
Pasture and plowland,

---

2. An archaic form of "landscape."
3. Phantoms.

Horses and oxen,
Innocent maidens,
Garrulous children,
Homestead and harvest,
Reaper and gleaner,
And rough-ruddy faces
Of lowly labour,
Slided The Gleam.—

VI

Then, with a melody
Stronger and statelier,
Led me at length
To the city and palace
Of Arthur the king;
Touch'd at the golden
Cross of the churches,
Flash'd on the Tournament,
Flicker'd and bicker'd
From helmet to helmet,
And last on the forehead
Of Arthur the blameless
Rested The Gleam.

VII

Clouds and darkness
Closed upon Camelot;
Arthur had vanish'd
I knew not whither,
The king who loved me,
And cannot die;
For out of the darkness
Silent and slowly
The Gleam, that had waned to a wintry glimmer
On icy fallow
And faded forest,
Drew to the valley

Named of the shadow,[4]
And slowly brightening
Out of the glimmer,
And slowly moving again to a melody
Yearningly tender,
Fell on the shadow,
No longer a shadow,
But clothed with The Gleam.

VIII

And broader and brighter
The Gleam flying onward,
Wed to the melody,
Sang thro' the world;
And slower and fainter,
Old and weary,
But eager to follow,
I saw, whenever
In passing it glanced upon
Hamlet[5] or city,
That under the Crosses
The dead man's garden,
The mortal hillock,[6]
Would break into blossom;
And so to the land's
Last limit I came—
And can no longer,
But die rejoicing,
For thro' the Magic
Of Him the Mighty,
Who taught me in childhood,
There on the border
Of boundless Ocean,
And all but in Heaven
Hovers The Gleam.

---

4. The line alludes to Psalms 23:4 ("Though I walk through the valley of the shadow of death, I will fear no evil").

5. Small village.

6. Small hill, i.e., grave mound.

IX

Not of the sunlight,
Not of the moonlight,
Not of the starlight!
O young Mariner,
Down to the haven,
Call your companions,
Launch your vessel,
And crowd your canvas,[7]
And, ere it vanishes
Over the margin,
After it, follow it,
Follow The Gleam.

---

7. To put on sail in excess of the usual for greater speed.

The Defence of Guenevere

by

WILLIAM MORRIS

But, knowing now that they would have her speak,
She threw her wet hair backward from her brow,
Her hand close to her mouth touching her cheek,

As though she had had there a shameful blow,
And feeling it shameful to feel ought but shame
All through her heart, yet felt her cheek burned so,

She must a little touch it; like one lame
She walked away from Gauwaine, with her head
Still lifted up; and on her cheek of flame

The tears dried quick; she stopped at last and said:
"O knights and lords, it seems but little skill
To talk of well-known things past now and dead.

"God wot[1] I ought to say, I have done ill,
And pray you all forgiveness heartily!
Because you must be right, such great lords; still

"Listen, suppose your time were come to die,
And you were quite alone and very weak;
Yea, laid a dying while very mightily

"The wind was ruffling up the narrow streak
Of river through your broad lands running well:
Suppose a hush should come, then some one speak:

"'One of these cloths is heaven, and one is hell,
Now choose one cloth for ever; which they be,

---

1. Knows.

I will not tell you, you must somehow tell

"'Of your own strength and mightiness; here, see!'
Yea, yea, my lord, and you to ope[2] your eyes,
At foot of your familiar bed to see

"A great God's angel standing, with such dyes,
Not known on earth, on his great wings, and hands,
Held out two ways, light from the inner skies

"Showing him well, and making his commands
Seem to be God's commands, moreover, too,
Holding within his hands the cloths on wands;[3]

"And one of these strange choosing cloths was blue,
Wavy and long, and one cut short and red;
No man could tell the better of the two.

"After a shivering half-hour you said:
'God help! heaven's colour, the blue;' and he said, 'hell.'
Perhaps you then would roll upon your bed,

"And cry to all good men that loved you well,
'Ah Christ! if only I had known, known, known;'
Launcelot went away, then I could tell,

"Like wisest man how all things would be, moan,
And roll and hurt myself, and long to die,
And yet fear much to die for what was sown.

"Nevertheless you, O Sir Gauwaine, lie,
Whatever may have happened through these years,
God knows I speak truth, saying that you lie."

Her voice was low at first, being full of tears,
But as it cleared, it grew full loud and shrill,
Growing a windy shriek in all men's ears,

A ringing in their startled brains, until
She said that Gauwaine lied, then her voice sunk,

---

2. Open.
3. Sticks.

And her great eyes began again to fill,

Though still she stood right up, and never shrunk,
But spoke on bravely, glorious lady fair!
Whatever tears her full lips may have drunk,

She stood, and seemed to think, and wrung her hair,
Spoke out at last with no more trace of shame,
With passionate twisting of her body there:

"It chanced upon a day that Launcelot came
To dwell at Arthur's court: at Christmas-time
This happened; when the heralds sung his name,

"'Son of King Ban of Benwick,' seemed to chime
Along with all the bells that rang that day,
O'er the white roofs, with little change of rhyme.

"Christmas and whitened winter passed away,
And over me the April sunshine came,
Made very awful with black hail-clouds, yea

"And in the Summer I grew white with flame,
And bowed my head down: Autumn, and the sick
Sure knowledge things would never be the same,

"However often Spring might be most thick
Of blossoms and buds, smote on me, and I grew
Careless of most things, let the clock tick, tick,

"To my unhappy pulse, that beat right through
My eager body; while I laughed out loud,
And let my lips curl up at false or true,

"Seemed cold and shallow without any cloud.
Behold my judges, then the cloths were brought;
While I was dizzied thus, old thoughts would crowd,

"Belonging to the time ere I was bought
By Arthur's great name and his little love;
Must I give up for ever then, I thought,

"That which I deemed would ever round me move
Glorifying all things; for a little word,
Scarce ever meant at all, must I now prove

"Stone-cold for ever? Pray you, does the Lord
Will that all folks should be quite happy and good?
I love God now a little, if this cord

"Were broken, once for all what striving could
Make me love anything in earth or heaven?
So day by day it grew, as if one should

"Slip slowly down some path worn smooth and even,
Down to a cool sea on a summer day;
Yet still in slipping there was some small leaven

"Of stretched hands catching small stones by the way,
Until one surely reached the sea at last,
And felt strange new joy as the worn head lay

"Back, with the hair like sea-weed; yea all past
Sweat of the forehead, dryness of the lips,
Washed utterly out by the dear waves o'ercast,

"In the lone sea, far off from any ships!
Do I not know now of a day in Spring?
No minute of the wild day ever slips

"From out my memory; I hear thrushes sing,
And wheresoever I may be, straightway
Thoughts of it all come up with most fresh sting:

"I was half mad with beauty on that day,
And went without my ladies all alone,
In a quiet garden walled round every way;

"I was right joyful of that wall of stone,
That shut the flowers and trees up with the sky,
And trebled all the beauty: to the bone,

"Yea right through to my heart, grown very shy
With weary thoughts, it pierced, and made me glad;
Exceedingly glad, and I knew verily,

"A little thing just then had made me mad;
I dared not think, as I was wont[4] to do,
Sometimes, upon my beauty; if I had

"Held out my long hand up against the blue,
And, looking on the tenderly darken'd fingers,
Thought that by rights one ought to see quite through,

"There, see you, where the soft still light yet lingers,
Round by the edges; what should I have done,
If this had joined with yellow spotted singers,

"And startling green drawn upward by the sun?
But shouting, loosed out, see now! all my hair,
And trancedly stood watching the west wind run

"With faintest half-heard breathing sound: why there
I lose my head e'en now in doing this;
But shortly listen: In that garden fair

"Came Launcelot walking; this is true, the kiss
Wherewith we kissed in meeting that spring day,
I scarce dare talk of the remember'd bliss,

"When both our mouths went wandering in one way,
And aching sorely, met among the leaves;
Our hands being left behind strained far away.

"Never within a yard of my bright sleeves
Had Launcelot come before: and now so nigh!
After that day why is it Guenevere grieves?

"Nevertheless you, O Sir Gauwaine, lie,
Whatever happened on through all those years,
God knows I speak truth, saying that you lie.

"Being such a lady could I weep these tears
If this were true? A great queen such as I
Having sinn'd this way, straight her conscience sears;

---

4. Accustomed.

"And afterwards she liveth hatefully,
Slaying and poisoning, certes[5] never weeps:
Gauwaine be friends now, speak me lovingly.

"Do I not see how God's dear pity creeps
All through your frame, and trembles in your mouth?
Remember in what grave your mother sleeps,[6]

"Buried in some place far down in the south,
Men are forgetting as I speak to you;
By her head sever'd in that awful drouth

"Of pity that drew Agravaine's fell blow,
I pray your pity! let me not scream out
For ever after, when the shrill winds blow

"Through half your castle-locks! let me not shout
For ever after in the winter night
When you ride out alone! in battle-rout

"Let not my rusting tears make your sword light!
Ah! God of mercy, how he turns away!
So, ever must I dress me to the fight,

"So: let God's justice work! Gauwaine, I say,
See me hew down your proofs: yea all men know
Even as you said how Mellyagraunce[7] one day,

"One bitter day in *la Fausse Garde*, for so
All good knights held it after, saw:
Yea, sirs, by cursed unknightly outrage; though

"You, Gauwaine, held his word without a flaw,
This Mellyagraunce saw blood upon my bed:
Whose blood then pray you? is there any law

---

5. Surely.

6. In the following lines Guenevere reminds Gauwaine that his own mother, Morgawse, was slain by his brother Agravaine when he found her in bed with Lamorak.

7. The knight who abducts Guenevere and, after her rescue by Launcelot, accuses her of adultery. In a trial by combat Mellyagraunce is killed by Launcelot.

"To make a queen say why some spots of red
Lie on her coverlet? or will you say:
'Your hands are white, lady, as when you wed,

"'Where did you bleed?' and must I stammer out, 'Nay,
I blush indeed, fair lord, only to rend
My sleeve up to my shoulder, where there lay

"'A knife-point last night:' so must I defend
The honour of the Lady Guenevere?
Not so, fair lords, even if the world should end

"This very day, and you were judges here
Instead of God. Did you see Mellyagraunce
When Launcelot stood by him? what white fear

"Curdled his blood, and how his teeth did dance,
His side sink in? as my knight cried and said:
'Slayer of unarm'd men, here is a chance!

"'Setter of traps, I pray you guard your head,
By God I am so glad to fight with you,
Stripper of ladies, that my hand feels lead

"'For driving weight; hurrah now! draw and do,
For all my wounds are moving in my breast,
And I am getting mad with waiting so.'

"He struck his hands together o'er the beast,
Who fell down flat, and grovell'd at his feet,
And groan'd at being slain so young: 'At least,'

"My knight said, 'rise you, sir, who are so fleet[8]
At catching ladies, half-arm'd will I fight,
My left side all uncovered!' Then I weet,[9]

"Up sprang Sir Mellyagraunce with great delight
Upon his knave's face; not until just then
Did I quite hate him, as I saw my knight

---

8. Quick.
9. Know.

"Along the lists look to my stake and pen
With such a joyous smile, it made me sigh
From agony beneath my waist-chain, when

"The fight began, and to me they drew nigh;
Ever Sir Launcelot kept him on the right,
And traversed warily, and ever high

"And fast leapt caitiff's[10] sword, until my knight
Sudden threw up his sword to his left hand,
Caught it, and swung it; that was all the fight,

"Except a spout of blood on the hot land;
For it was hottest summer; and I know
I wonder'd how the fire, while I should stand,

"And burn, against the heat, would quiver so,
Yards above my head; thus these matters went;
Which things were only warnings of the woe

"That fell on me. Yet Mellyagraunce was shent,[11]
For Mellyagraunce had fought against the Lord;
Therefore, my lords, take heed lest you be blent[12]

"With all this wickedness; say no rash word
Against me, being so beautiful; my eyes,
Wept all away to grey, may bring some sword

"To drown you in your blood; see my breast rise,
Like waves of purple sea, as here I stand;
And how my arms are moved in wonderful wise,

"Yea also at my full heart's strong command,
See through my long throat how the words go up
In ripples to my mouth; how in my hand

"The shadow lies like wine within a cup
Of marvellously colour'd gold; yea now
This little wind is rising, look you up,

---

10. [The] coward's.
11. Destroyed.
12. Deceived.

"And wonder how the light is falling so
Within my moving tresses: will you dare,
When you have looked a little on my brow,

"To say this thing is vile? or will you care
For any plausible lies of cunning woof,[13]
When you can see my face with no lie there

"For ever? am I not a gracious proof:
'But in your chamber Launcelot was found:'
Is there a good knight then would stand aloof,

"When a queen says with gentle queenly sound:
'O true as steel come now and talk with me,
I love to see your step upon the ground

"'Unwavering, also well I love to see
That gracious smile light up your face, and hear
Your wonderful words, that all mean verily

"'The thing they seem to mean: good friend, so dear
To me in everything, come here to-night,
Or else the hours will pass most dull and drear;

"'If you come not, I fear this time I might
Get thinking over much of times gone by,
When I was young, and green hope was in sight:

"'For no man cares now to know why I sigh;
And no man comes to sing me pleasant songs,
Nor any brings me the sweet flowers that lie

"'So thick in the gardens; therefore one so longs
To see you, Launcelot; that we may be
Like children once again, free from all wrongs

"'Just for one night.' Did he not come to me?
What thing could keep true Launcelot away
If I said, 'Come'? there was one less than three

---

13. Texture.

"In my quiet room that night, and we were gay;
Till sudden I rose up, weak, pale, and sick,
Because a bawling broke our dream up, yea

"I looked at Launcelot's face and could not speak,
For he looked helpless too, for a little while;
Then I remember how I tried to shriek,

"And could not, but fell down; from tile to tile
The stones they threw up rattled o'er my head
And made me dizzier; till within a while

"My maids were all about me, and my head
On Launcelot's breast was being soothed away
From its white chattering, until Launcelot said:

"By God! I will not tell you more to-day,
Judge any way you will: what matters it?
You know quite well the story of that fray,

"How Launcelot still'd their bawling, the mad fit
That caught up Gauwaine: all, all, verily,
But just that which would save me; these things flit.

"Nevertheless you, O Sir Gauwaine, lie,
Whatever may have happen'd these long years,
God knows I speak truth, saying that you lie!

"All I have said is truth, by Christ's dear tears."
She would not speak another word, but stood
Turn'd sideways; listening, like a man who hears

His brother's trumpet sounding through the wood
Of his foes' lances. She lean'd eagerly,
And gave a slight spring sometimes, as she could

At last hear something really; joyfully
Her cheek grew crimson, as the headlong speed
Of the roan charger drew all men to see,
The knight who came was Launcelot at good need.

King Arthur's Tomb

by

WILLIAM MORRIS

Hot August noon: already on that day
    Since sunrise through the Wiltshire downs,[1] most sad
Of mouth and eye, he had gone leagues of way;
    Ay and by night, till whether good or bad

He was, he knew not, though he knew perchance
    That he was Launcelot, the bravest knight
Of all who since the world was, have borne lance,
    Or swung their swords in wrong cause or in right.

Nay, he knew nothing now, except that where
    The Glastonbury[2] gilded towers shine,
A lady dwelt, whose name was Guenevere;
    This he knew also; that some fingers twine,

Not only in a man's hair, even his heart,
    (Making him good or bad I mean,) but in his life,
Skies, earth, men's looks and deeds, all that has part,
    Not being ourselves, in that half-sleep, half-strife,

(Strange sleep, strange strife,) that men call living; so
    Was Launcelot most glad when the moon rose,
Because it brought new memories of her. "Lo,
    Between the trees a large moon, the wind lows

"Not loud, but as a cow begins to low,
    Wishing for strength to make the herdsman hear:
The ripe corn gathereth dew; yea, long ago,
    In the old garden life, my Guenevere

---

1. Hills.
2. Legendary site of Arthur's burial (see *The Assertion of King Arthur*).

"Loved to sit still among the flowers, till night
      Had quite come on, hair loosen'd, for she said,
Smiling like heaven, that its fairness might
      Draw up the wind sooner to cool her head.

"Now while I ride how quick the moon gets small,
      As it did then: I tell myself a tale
That will not last beyond the whitewashed wall,
      Thoughts of some joust must help me through the vale,

"Keep this till after: How Sir Gareth ran
      A good course that day under my Queen's eyes,
And how she sway'd laughing at Dinadan.[3]
      No. Back again, the other thoughts will rise,

"And yet I think so fast 'twill end right soon:
      Verily then I think, that Guenevere,
Made sad by dew and wind, and tree-barred moon,
      Did love me more than ever, was more dear

"To me than ever, she would let me lie
      And kiss her feet, or, if I sat behind,
Would drop her hand and arm most tenderly,
      And touch my mouth. And she would let me wind

"Her hair around my neck, so that it fell
      Upon my red robe, strange in the twilight
With many unnamed colours, till the bell
      Of her mouth on my cheek sent a delight

"Through all my ways of being; like the stroke
      Wherewith God threw all men upon the face
When he took Enoch, and when Enoch woke
      With a changed body in the happy place.[4]

"Once, I remember, as I sat beside,
      She turn'd a little, and laid back her head,

---

3. A knight known as a jester and satirist.

4. Genesis 5:23-24 observes that after Enoch lived 365 years, "he was not; for God took him." Later tradition has it that Enoch was "translated" into heaven by God (cf. Hebrews 11:5).

And slept upon my breast; I almost died
    In those night-watches with my love and dread.

"There lily-like she bow'd her head and slept,
    And I breathed low, and did not dare to move,
But sat and quiver'd inwardly, thoughts crept,
    And frighten'd me with pulses of my Love.

"The stars shone out above the doubtful green
    Of her bodice, in the green sky overhead;
Pale in the green sky were the stars I ween,[5]
    Because the moon shone like a star she shed

"When she dwelt up in heaven a while ago,
    And ruled all things but God: the night went on,
The wind grew cold, and the white moon grew low,
    One hand had fallen down, and now lay on

"My cold stiff palm; there were no colours then
    For near an hour, and I fell asleep
In spite of all my striving, even when
    I held her whose name-letters make me leap.

"I did not sleep long, feeling that in sleep
    I did some loved one wrong, so that the sun
Had only just arisen from the deep
    Still land of colours, when before me one

"Stood whom I knew, but scarcely dared to touch,
    She seemed to have changed so in the night;
Moreover she held scarlet lilies, such
    As Maiden Margaret bears upon the light

"Of the great church walls, natheless did I walk
    Through the fresh wet woods, and the wheat that morn,
Touching her hair and hand and mouth, and talk
    Of love we held, nigh hid among the corn.

"Back to the palace, ere the sun grew high,
    We went, and in a cool green room all day

---

5. Suppose.

I gazed upon the arras[6] giddily,
　　Where the wind set the silken kings a-sway.

"I could not hold her hand, or see her face;
　　For which may God forgive me! but I think,
Howsoever, that she was not in that place."
　　These memories Launcelot was quick to drink;

And when these fell, some paces past the wall,
　　There rose yet others, but they wearied more,
And tasted not so sweet; they did not fall
　　So soon, but vaguely wrenched his strained heart sore

In shadowy slipping from his grasp: these gone,
　　A longing followed; if he might but touch
That Guenevere at once! Still night, the lone
　　Grey horse's head before him vex'd him much,

In steady nodding over the grey road:
　　Still night, and night, and night, and emptied heart
Of any stories; what a dismal load
　　Time grew at last, yea, when the night did part,

And let the sun flame over all, still there
　　The horse's grey ears turn'd this way and that,
And still he watch'd them twitching in the glare
　　Of the morning sun, behind them still he sat,

Quite wearied out with all the wretched night,
　　Until about the dustiest of the day,
On the last down's brow he drew his rein in sight
　　Of the Glastonbury roofs that choke the way.

And he was now quite giddy as before,
　　When she slept by him, tired out, and her hair
Was mingled with the rushes on the floor,
　　And he, being tired too, was scarce aware

Of her presence; yet as he sat and gazed,
　　A shiver ran throughout him, and his breath

---

6. Tapestry.

Came slower, he seem'd suddenly amazed,
    As though he had not heard of Arthur's death.

This for a moment only, presently
    He rode on giddy still, until he reach'd
A place of apple-trees, by the thorn-tree
    Wherefrom St. Joseph[7] in the days past preached.

Dazed there he laid his head upon a tomb,
    Not knowing it was Arthur's, at which sight
One of her maidens told her, "He is come,"
    And she went forth to meet him; yet a blight

Had settled on her, all her robes were black,
    With a long white veil only; she went slow,
As one walks to be slain, her eyes did lack
    Half her old glory, yea, alas! the glow

Had left her face and hands; this was because
    As she lay last night on her purple bed,
Wishing for morning, grudging every pause
    Of the palace clocks, until that Launcelot's head

Should lie on her breast, with all her golden hair
    Each side: when suddenly the thing grew drear,
In morning twilight, when the grey downs bare
    Grew into lumps of sin to Guenevere.

At first she said no word, but lay quite still,
    Only her mouth was open, and her eyes
Gazed wretchedly about from hill to hill;
    As though she asked, not with so much surprise

As tired disgust, what made them stand up there
    So cold and grey. After, a spasm took
Her face, and all her frame, she caught her hair,
    All her hair, in both hands, terribly she shook,

And rose till she was sitting in the bed,
    Set her teeth hard, and shut her eyes and seem'd

---

7. Joseph of Arimathea, from whose staff the first thorn tree at Glastonbury is said to have grown.

As though she would have torn it from her head,
    Natheless she dropp'd it, lay down, as she deem'd

It matter'd not whatever she might do:
    O Lord Christ! pity on her ghastly face!
Those dismal hours while the cloudless blue
    Drew the sun higher: He did give her grace;

Because at last she rose up from her bed,
    And put her raiment on, and knelt before
The blessed rood,[8] and with her dry lips said,
    Muttering the words against the marble floor:

"Unless you pardon, what shall I do, Lord,
    But go to hell? and there see day by day
Foul deed on deed, hear foulest word on word,
    For ever and ever, such as on the way

"To Camelot I heard once from a churl,
    That curled me up upon my jennet's[9] neck
With bitter shame; how then, Lord, should I curl
    For ages and for ages? dost thou reck[10]

"That I am beautiful, Lord, even as you
    And your dear mother? why did I forget
You were so beautiful, and good, and true,
    That you loved me so, Guenevere? O yet

"If even I go to hell, I cannot choose
    But love you, Christ, yea, though I cannot keep
From loving Launcelot; O Christ! must I lose
    My own heart's love? see, though I cannot weep,

"Yet am I very sorry for my sin;
    Moreover, Christ, I cannot bear that hell,
I am most fain[11] to love you, and to win
    A place in heaven some time: I cannot tell:

---

8. Crucifix.

9. A jennet is a small Spanish horse.

10. Consider.

11. Glad.

"Speak to me, Christ! I kiss, kiss, kiss your feet;
    Ah! now I weep!" The maid said, "By the tomb
He waiteth for you, lady," coming fleet,[12]
    Not knowing what woe filled up all the room.

So Guenevere rose and went to meet him there,
    He did not hear her coming, as he lay
On Arthur's head, till some of her long hair
    Brush'd on the new-cut stone: "Well done! to pray

"For Arthur, my dear Lord, the greatest king
    That ever lived." "Guenevere! Guenevere!
Do you not know me, are you gone mad? fling
    Your arms and hair about me, lest I fear

"You are not Guenevere, but some other thing."
    "Pray you forgive me, fair lord Launcelot!
I am not mad, but I am sick; they cling,
    God's curses, unto such as I am; not

"Ever again shall we twine arms and lips."
    "Yea, she is mad: thy heavy law, O Lord,
Is very tight about her now, and grips
    Her poor heart, so that no right word

"Can reach her mouth; so, Lord, forgive her now,
    That she not knowing what she does, being mad,
Kills me in this way: Guenevere, bend low
    And kiss me once! for God's love kiss me! sad

"Though your face is, you look much kinder now;
    Yea once, once for the last time kiss me, lest I die."
"Christ! my hot lips are very near his brow,
    Help me to save his soul! Yea, verily,

"Across my husband's head, fair Launcelot!
    Fair serpent mark'd with V upon the head!
This thing we did while yet he was alive,
    Why not, O twisting knight, now he is dead?

---

12. Quickly.

"Yea, shake! shake now and shiver! if you can
        Remember anything for agony,
Pray you remember how when the wind ran
        One cool spring evening through fair aspen-tree,

"And elm and oak about the palace there
        The king came back from battle, and I stood
To meet him, with my ladies, on the stair,
        My face made beautiful with my young blood."

"Will she lie now, Lord God?" "Remember too,
        Wrung heart, how first before the knights there came
A royal bier, hung round with green and blue,
        About it shone great tapers with sick flame.

"And thereupon Lucius, the Emperor,[13]
        Lay royal-robed, but stone-cold now and dead,
Not able to hold sword or sceptre more,
        But not quite grim; because his cloven head

"Bore no marks now of Launcelot's bitter sword,
        Being by embalmers deftly solder'd up;
So still it seem'd the face of a great lord,
        Being mended as a craftsman mends a cup.

"Also the heralds sung rejoicingly
        To their long trumpets; 'Fallen under shield,
Here lieth Lucius, King of Italy,
        Slain by Lord Launcelot in open field.'

"Thereat the people shouted: 'Launcelot!'
        And through the spears I saw you drawing nigh,
You and Lord Arthur: nay, I saw you not,
        But rather Arthur, God would not let die,

"I hoped, these many years; he should grow great,
        And in his great arms still encircle me,
Kissing my face, half blinded with the heat
        Of king's love for the queen I used to be.

---

13. The Emperor of Rome, who demands tribute from Arthur and is slain (in
Morris's poem) by Launcelot in the ensuing battle.

"Launcelot, Launcelot, why did he take your hand,
    When he had kissed me in his kingly way?
Saying: 'This is the knight whom all the land
    Calls Arthur's banner, sword, and shield to-day;

"'Cherish him, love.' Why did your long lips cleave
    In such strange way unto my fingers then?
So eagerly glad to kiss, so loath to leave
    When you rose up? Why among helmed men

"Could I always tell you by your long strong arms,
    And sway like an angel's in your saddle there?
Why sicken'd I so often with alarms
    Over the tilt-yard?[14] Why were you more fair

"Than aspens in the autumn at their best?
    Why did you fill all lands with your great fame,
So that Breuse[15] even, as he rode, fear'd lest
    At turning of the way your shield should flame?

"Was it nought then, my agony and strife?
    When as day passed by day, year after year,
I found I could not live a righteous life!
    Didst ever think queens held their truth for dear?

"O, but your lips say: 'Yea, but she was cold
    Sometimes, always uncertain as the spring;
When I was sad she would be overbold,
    Longing for kisses.' When war-bells did ring,

"The back-toll'd bells of noisy Camelot."
    "Now, Lord God, listen! listen, Guenevere,
Though I am weak just now, I think there's not
    A man who dares to say: 'You hated her,

"'And left her moaning while you fought your fill
    In the daisied meadows!' lo you her thin hand,
That on the carven stone can not keep still,
    Because she loves me against God's command,

---

14. Jousting field.
15. A wicked knight and an enemy of Arthur who did not observe the laws of
chivalry. He was known as Breuse Sans Pitie (without pity).

"Has often been quite wet with tear on tear,
  Tears Launcelot keeps somewhere, surely not
In his own heart, perhaps in Heaven, where
  He will not be these ages." "Launcelot!

"Loud lips, wrung heart! I say when the bells rang,
  The noisy back-toll'd bells of Camelot,
There were two spots on earth, the thrushes sang
  In the lonely gardens where my love was not,

"Where I was almost weeping; I dared not
  Weep quite in those days, lest one maid should say,
In tittering whispers: 'Where is Launcelot
  To wipe with some kerchief those tears away?'

"Another answer sharply with brows knit,
  And warning hand up, scarcely lower though:
'You speak too loud, see you, she heareth it,
  This tigress fair has claws, as I well know,

"'As Launcelot knows too, the poor knight! well-a-day!
  Why met he not with Iseult from the West,
Or better still, Iseult of Brittany?
  Perchance indeed quite ladyless were best.'

"Alas, my maids, you loved not overmuch
  Queen Guenevere, uncertain as sunshine
In March; forgive me! for my sin being such,
  About my whole life, all my deeds did twine,

"Made me quite wicked; as I found out then,
  I think; in the lonely palace where each morn
We went, my maids and I, to say prayers when
  They sang mass in the chapel on the lawn.

"And every morn I scarce could pray at all,
  For Launcelot's red-golden hair would play,
Instead of sunlight, on the painted wall,
  Mingled with dreams of what the priest did say;

"Grim curses out of Peter and of Paul;
    Judging of strange sins in Leviticus;[16]
Another sort of writing on the wall,[17]
    Scored deep across the painted heads of us.

"Christ sitting with the woman at the well,[18]
    And Mary Magdalen[19] repenting there,
Her dimmed eyes scorch'd and red at sight of hell
    So hardly 'scaped, no gold light on her hair.

"And if the priest said anything that seemed
    To touch upon the sin they said we did,
(This in their teeth) they looked as if they deem'd
    That I was spying what thoughts might be hid

"Under green-cover'd bosoms, heaving quick
    Beneath quick thoughts; while they grew red with shame,
And gazed down at their feet: while I felt sick,
    And almost shriek'd if one should call my name.

"The thrushes sang in the lone garden there:
    But where you were the birds were scared I trow:
Clanging of arms about pavilions fair,
    Mixed with the knights' laughs; there, as I well know,

"Rode Launcelot, the king of all the band,
    And scowling Gauwaine, like the night in day,
And handsome Gareth, with his great white hand
    Curl'd round the helm-crest, ere he join'd the fray;

---

16. Leviticus, the third book of the Bible, contains laws relating to the priests and Levites and ceremonial observances. It talks of such things as the distinction between clean and unclean animals, the purification of women after childbirth, unnatural lusts, etc.

17. In Daniel 5, at Belshazzar's sinful feast, a hand appears and writes on the wall words that Daniel interpreted as predicting the downfall of Belshazzar and his kingdom. That night Belshazzar died.

18. Cf. John 4:6-29, in which Jesus tells the woman at the well that she has had five husbands and that the one she has now is not her husband.

19. A woman in the New Testament from whom Jesus drove out evil spirits, considered identical with the repentant prostitute in Luke 7:36-50.

"And merry Dinadan with sharp dark face,
      All true knights loved to see; and in the fight
Great Tristram, and though helmed you could trace
      In all his bearing the frank noble knight;

"And by him Palomydes,[20] helmet off,
      He fought, his face brush'd by his hair,
Red heavy swinging hair; he fear'd a scoff
      So overmuch, though what true knight would dare

"To mock that face, fretted with useless care,
      And bitter useless striving after love?
O Palomydes, with much honour bear
      Beast Glatysaunt[21] upon your shield, above

"Your helm that hides the swinging of your hair,
      And think of Iseult, as your sword drives through
Much mail and plate: O God, let me be there
      A little time, as I was long ago!

"Because stout Gareth lets his spear fall low,
      Gauwaine and Launcelot, and Dinadan
Are helm'd and waiting; let the trumpets go!
      Bend over, ladies, to see all you can!

"Clench teeth, dames, yea, clasp hands, for Gareth's spear
      Throws Kay from out his saddle, like a stone
From a castle-window when the foe draws near:
      'Iseult!' Sir Dinadan rolleth overthrown.

"'Iseult!' again: the pieces of each spear
      Fly fathoms up, and both the great steeds reel;
'Tristram for Iseult!' 'Iseult!' and 'Guenevere!'
      The ladies' names bite verily like steel.

"They bite: bite me, Lord God! I shall go mad,
      Or else die kissing him, he is so pale,
He thinks me mad already, O bad! bad!
      Let me lie down a little while and wail."

---

20. A Saracen knight who loves Iseult and thus is a rival of Tristan's.
21. The Questing Beast pursued by Palomydes.

"No longer so, rise up, I pray you, love,
    And slay me really, then we shall be heal'd,
Perchance, in the aftertime by God above."
    "Banner of Arthur, with black-bended shield

"Sinister-wise across the fair gold ground!
    Here let me tell you what a knight you are,
O sword and shield of Arthur! you are found
    A crooked sword, I think, that leaves a scar

"On the bearer's arm, so be he thinks it straight,
    Twisted Malay's crease[22] beautiful blue-grey,
Poison'd with sweet fruit; as he found too late,
    My husband Arthur, on some bitter day!

"O sickle cutting hemlock the day long!
    That the husbandman across his shoulder hangs,
And, going homeward about evensong,
    Dies the next morning, struck through by the fangs!

"Banner, and sword, and shield, you dare not die,
    Lest you meet Arthur in the other world,
And, knowing who you are, he pass you by,
    Taking short turns that he may watch you curl'd,

"Body and face and limbs in agony,
    Lest he weep presently and go away,
Saying: 'I loved him once,' with a sad sigh,
    Now I have slain him, Lord, let me go too, I pray.
        [Launcelot *falls.*

"Alas! alas! I know not what to do,
    If I run fast it is perchance that I
May fall and stun myself, much better so,
    Never, never again! not even when I die."

        LAUNCELOT, *on awaking.*
"I stretch'd my hands towards her and fell down,
    How long I lay in swoon I cannot tell:

---

22. A Malay dagger with a wavy blade.

My head and hands were bleeding from the stone,
When I rose up, also I heard a bell."

The Day before the Trial

by

ALGERNON CHARLES SWINBURNE

King Arthur says being alone.
>Now the day comes near and near
>I feel its hot breath, and see it clear,
>How strange it is and full of fear;
>And I grow old waiting here,
>Grow sick with pain of Guenevere,
>>My wife, that loves not me.
>So strange it seems to me, so new
>To have such shame between us two,
>I dare not hold this Mador true
>Nor false, because his words ran thro'
>My blood with all the shame they drew
>And burnt me to the bone; I knew
>>That some such tale would be
>For all these years she grew more fair,
>More sweet her low sweet speeches were,
>More long and heavy grew her hair,
>Not such as other women wear;
>But ever as I looked on her
>>Her face seemed fierce and thin.
>I felt half sick, and on my head
>The gold crown seemed not gold but lead;
>Strange words I heard that no man said,
>Strange noises where all noise was dead;
>Was it pure blood that made her red
>>From brows to rounded chin?
>Sometimes I knew she loved me not;
>Down to my hands the blood went hot
>In a dull hate of Launcelot
>For all the praise of her he got,
>>Being so pure of sin.

For he was clean as any maid,
And on his head God's hand was laid
As on a maiden's; so men said;
But I, a woman's hands there weighed
Instead of God's upon my head,
    No maid was I, to see
The white Sangreal borne up in air,
To touch at last God's body fair,
To feel strange terror stir my hair
As a slow light went past; but here
I had to my honours year by year,
I had the name of king to bear,
And watch the eyes of Guenevere,
    My wife, who loves not me.

Lancelot

by

ALGERNON CHARLES SWINBURNE

LANCELOT

Very long and hot it was,
The dry light on the dry grass,
The set noon on lakes of glass,
    All that summer time;
And the great woods burnt and brown,
With dry tendrils dropping down,
And the sky's white rampart thrown
On the bare wall of a town,
    Round breadths of oak and lime.
Thro' the woods I rode and rode,
No prayer of mine clomb[1] up to God;
Sharp leaves crackled on the road
Where my horse the heaviest trode,
    Over leaves and grass.
Thro' the sad boughs rent on high
Naked burnt the great blind sky;
Yet I did not pray to die,
    For no pain that was.
Here and there some colour was
Hidden in the muffled grass,
Some late flower that one might pass,
Or else a brown, smooth beech-mast was,
    Or carven acorn cup.
And birds sang, and could not long,
For a trouble in their song:

---

1. Climbed.

All things there did suffer wrong,
    All but I who rode along.
Now I grow so tired of this,
I would give much gold to kiss
One leaf of those primroses
That grow here when the green spring is
    Whereof their life is made.
Under moon and under star
I have ridden fast and far
Where the deep leaves thickest are
    In the huddled shade.

I cannot see what I shall do.

Now the day drops angrily,
Leaves a red stain on the sea,
And fierce light on field and tree,
    Red as any brand.
A great slumber takes me round
In this place of sleepy sound;
Surely now the gift is found
    And ready to my hand.
For there is left me nothing new
And none rides with me riding through
These brown wood walks so straight and few
    For many nights and days.
And men say that I shall not win,
Tho' the chosen for all my sin;
The sleepy beams crawl out and in
Under the branches rare and thin
    Where thro' I ride always.

                       (He sleeps.)

THE ANGEL

Lo, the air begins to move
Like a heart that beats with love
All about thee and above,
For the hope it whispers of

But a little while.
A great love has healed his heart,
The shut eyelids move and start,
The shut lips are breathed apart
    In a sleepy smile.

LANCELOT

Ah! dear Christ, this thing I see
Is too wonderful for me,
If I think indeed to be
    In Thy very grace.
Clear flame shivers all about,
But the bright ark alters not,
Borne upright where angels doubt;
The blessed maiden looketh out
White, with barèd face and throat
    Leaned into the dark.
On her hair's faint light and shade
A large aureole[2] is laid,
All about the tresses weighed.

THE ANGEL

This is what thou wert to find.
Lo, the thin flames blown behind
Tremble in the blowing wind
As loose hair that girls unbind
    In a woody place.

LANCELOT

Ah, sweet Lord that art my Lord,
Thy light is sharp as any sword;
My heart is strainèd as a cord
    That a child may break.
Evenwise each side her head

---

2. Halo.

So they stand, the blessed maid,
      The angels and the ark.

It were strange if I should see
Sweet new things for love of Thee;
For such hope was not to be;
Yet hast Thou had ruth[3] on me
      For my sorrow's sake.
I tremble, but I cannot weep,
I fear so much I am asleep;
Round the faces ranged and steep
A thin splendour seems to creep
Thro' the night so dear and deep,
Seems to stir as leaves that dip
      In a lilied lake.

Ah, sweet Lord that died on rood,[4]
Of old time Thy word hath stood
And we saw it very good;
Yet is this Thy happy blood
      I was not to see.

THE ANGEL

Where she standeth in the night
Clasped about with solemn light,
Clothed upon with samite[5] bright,
The blessed maiden very white,
This is all the happy sight
      That I may bring for thee.

LANCELOT

Over me the glory smites,
Sharp and level as the lights
Spear-shap'd on solemn winter nights

---

3. Pity.
4. On the cross.
5. Rich silk.

That strike from shade to shade;
Only all the inner place
(Ah, my Lord, is this Thy grace?)
Shineth as a happy face
In a clear and golden space
    That itself hath made.
Is this love that I may win,
Love of mine for all my sin?
The straight flames flicker out and in,
    Tho' they never fade.
But the light of that strange place
(Lord, I thank Thee for Thy grace!)
Thro' the lights of moving space
Trembles like a living face
    Whereon some pain is laid.

THE ANGEL

Turn thine eyes against the light,
Where the spearèd splendours smite
Round the ark, most close and white;
This is given me to-night
    For the love of thee.

LANCELOT

All the wonder shown above
(Lord, I praise Thee for Thy love!)
Thro' the lights that mix and move
Like blown feathers of a dove
    Stirreth, strange to see;
And midway the solemn place
(As my soul were full of grace)
Leaning hither, the clear Face
    Seemeth to bless me.

THE ANGEL

Points of sharp light star the ground;
Thro' the wind is blown a sound
As of singing voices round
    Over the dark land.
Christ the Lord is fair and crowned,
Whose pure blood, in bitter swound,[6]
Droppèd from the holy wound;
Surely now the gift is found
    And ready to thy hand.

LANCELOT

Lo, between me and the light
Grows a shadow on my sight,
A soft shade to left and right,
    Branchèd as a tree.
Green the leaves that stir between,
And the buds are lithe and green,
And against it seems to lean
One in stature as the Queen
    That I prayed to see.
Ah, what evil thing is this?
For she hath no lips to kiss,
And no brows of balm and bliss
    Bended over me.
For between me and the shine
Grows a face that is not mine,
On each curve and tender line
And each tress drawn straight and fine
    As it used to be.

THE ANGEL

This is Guenevere the Queen.

---

6. Swoon.

LANCELOT

For the face that comes between
Is like one that I have seen
    In the days that were.
Nay, this new thing shall not be.
Is it her own face I see
Thro' the smooth leaves of the tree,
    Sad and very fair?
All the wonder that I see
Fades and flutters over me
Till I know not what things be
    As I seemed to know.
But I see so fair she is,
I repent me not in this;
And to kiss her but one kiss
I would count it for my bliss
    To be troubled so,
For she leans against it straight,
Leans against it all her weight,
All her shapeliness and state;
And the apples golden-great
    Shine about her there.
Light creeps round her as she stands,
Round her face and round her hands,
Fainter light than dying brands
When day fills the eastern lands
    And the moon is low.
And her eyes in some old dream
Woven thro' with shade and gleam
Stare against me till I seem
To be hidden in a dream,
To be drowned in a deep stream
    Of her dropping hair.
That is Guenevere the Queen.
Now I know not what they mean,
Those close leaves that grow so green,
Those large fruits that burn between,
    Each a laugh new lit.

Now I know not what they were,
The light fires that trembled there
Sharp and thin in the soft air,
Nor the faces dumb and fair,
Nor the happy singing near;
But I seem to see her hair
      And the light on it.
Day by day and hour by hour
Grew her white face like a flower,
Palest where the day grew lower
      On the fiery sea.
Always sate I, watching her,
By her carven gilded chair,
Full of wonder and great fear
If one long lock of her hair
In the soft wind sink or stir,
      Fallen to her knee.
All about her face and head
The flat sunset overspread
Like an aureole of red,
Stained as drops from wounds that bled
      In some bitter fight.
All the tender shapen head
Dimly blurred with golden red,
And the thin face, as I said,
Drawn and white as snows wind-shed
On the green place of the dead
      In a windy night.
Coloured flakes of stormy fire
Clomb the rent[7] clouds high and higher,
And the wind like a great lyre
      Sounded vague and loud.
And the sunset lines that flee
On the flats of fiery sea
Far below us, her and me,
Were as golden red to see

---

7. Torn or split.

As the heaped hair on her knee
        Or as the coloured cloud.
So we sat in love and fear,
And no faces came anear,
And no voices touched our ear
But of angels singing clear
Out of all the sunset drear
        Round us and above.
And she listened; and a light
Shivered upward in my sight
Thro' her set face, sad and white;
Till I hid mine eyes for fright
        And for very love.
Drear and void the sunset was
On stained flats of fire and glass
Where she saw the angels pass
        That I could not see:
For none eyes but hers might pierce
Thro' the colours vague and fierce
That a sunset weaves and wears;
Downward slipt the long thin tears
As she turned and sang this verse
        That she made for me.

"*Eastward under skies that dip*
As to touch the water's lip,
Pass, my ship, with sails that drip
        Not with dew, nor with rain.
Thro' the morning float and pass
From the shores of flower and grass,
Thro' a space of golden glass
        Stained with a blood-red stain.
Evil ship on evil sea,
Bear him back again to me
Till I see what secrets be
        Hidden in all this pain."

Then she spake not, neither stirred,
But I shook for that one word

With the pain of that I heard
    That she spake of me.
For the ship that seemed to pass
Thro' the sea of fiery glass,
That strange ship mine own soul was
    And my life the sea.
And the sin that I had done
In the fierce time that was gone
When I slew her knight alone
Face to face with the red sun
    Setting in the west.
And my soul began to see
All the ill she had of me
When I bore her to the sea
    From her place of rest.
Yet I loved her long and well;
Yea, my tongue would tire to tell
All the love that her befell,
And the slow speech faint and fail
    Ere the love was told.
Now she dwelleth by me here,
In my castle builded fair;
But no crown of mine will wear
That I thought to keep for her,
And on her beloved hair
    Lay the royal gold.
And her face grows grey and long
And harsh breaths come thro' her song
And her heart is worn with wrong,
    As is plain to see.
Should I die, no help it were
Now men say she is not fair,
For the pain she seems to wear
In grey cheeks and waning hair;
All my love avails not her,
    And she loves not me.
Vain was the prayer I prayed alway,
Where in evil case I lay,

That she might love me one day
    As the manner is;
Vain the prayer that I have prayed,
That, lying between light and shade,
I that loved her as I said,
I that never kissed a maid,
    I might have her kiss.

Tristram and Iseult

by

MATTHEW ARNOLD

I
TRISTRAM

Tristram

Is she not come? The messenger was sure.
Prop me upon the pillows once again—
Raise me, my page! this cannot long endure.
—Christ, what a night! how the sleet whips the pane!
What lights will those out to the northward be?

The Page

The lanterns of the fishing-boats at sea.

Tristram

Soft—who is that, stands by the dying fire?

The Page

Iseult.

Tristram

Ah! not the Iseult I desire.

*   *   *   *

What Knight is this so weak and pale,
Though the locks are yet brown on his noble head,
Propt on pillows in his bed,
Gazing seaward for the light
Of some ship that fights the gale
On this wild December night?
Over the sick man's feet is spread
A dark green forest-dress;
A gold harp leans against the bed,

Ruddy in the fire's light.
I know him by his harp of gold,
Famous in Arthur's court of old;
I know him by his forest-dress—
The peerless hunter, harper, knight,
Tristram of Lyoness.

What Lady is this, whose silk attire
Gleams so rich in the light of the fire?
The ringlets on her shoulders lying
In their flitting lustre vying
With the clasp of burnish'd gold
Which her heavy robe doth hold.
Her looks are mild, her fingers slight
As the driven snow are white;
But her cheeks are sunk and pale.
Is it that the bleak sea-gale
Beating from the Atlantic sea
On this coast of Brittany,
Nips too keenly the sweet flower?
Is it that a deep fatigue
Hath come on her, a chilly fear,
Passing all her youthful hour
Spinning with her maidens here,
Listlessly through the window-bars
Gazing seawards many a league,
From her lonely shore-built tower,
While the knights are at the wars?
Or, perhaps, has her young heart
Felt already some deeper smart,
Of those that in secret the heart-strings rive,[1]
Leaving her sunk and pale, though fair?
Who is this snowdrop by the sea?—
I know her by her mildness rare,
Her snow-white hands, her golden hair;
I know her by her rich silk dress,
And her fragile loveliness—
The sweetest Christian soul alive,
Iseult of Brittany.

---

1. Tear.

Iseult of Brittany?—but where
Is that other Iseult fair,
That proud, first Iseult, Cornwall's queen?
She, whom Tristram's ship of yore
From Ireland to Cornwall bore,
To Tyntagel, to the side
Of King Marc, to be his bride?
She who, as they voyaged, quaff'd
With Tristram that spiced magic draught,
Which since then for ever rolls
Through their blood, and binds their souls,
Working love, but working teen?—[2]
There were two Iseults who did sway
Each her hour of Tristram's day;
But one possess'd his waning time,
The other his resplendent prime.
Behold her here, the patient flower,
Who possess'd his darker hour!
Iseult of the Snow-White Hand
Watches pale by Tristram's bed.
She is here who had his gloom,
Where art thou who hadst his bloom?
One such kiss as those of yore
Might thy dying knight restore!
Does the love-draught work no more?
Art thou cold, or false, or dead,
Iseult of Ireland?

            *   *   *   *

Loud howls the wind, sharp patters the rain,
And the knight sinks back on his pillows again.
He is weak with fever and pain,
And his spirit is not clear.
Hark! he mutters in his sleep,
As he wanders far from here,
Changes place and time of year,
And his closéd eye doth sweep
O'er some fair unwintry sea,

---

2. Grief.

Not this fierce Atlantic deep,
While he mutters brokenly:—

Tristram

The calm sea shines, loose hang the vessel's sails;
Before us are the sweet green fields of Wales,
And overhead the cloudless sky of May.—
"Ah, would I were in those green fields at play,
Not pent on ship-board this delicious day!
Tristram, I pray thee, of thy courtesy,
Reach me my golden phial stands by thee,
But pledge me in it first for courtesy.—"
Ha! dost thou start? are thy lips blanch'd like mine?
Child, 'tis no true draught this, 'tis poison'd wine!
Iseult! . . . .

                    *   *   *   *

Ah, sweet angels, let him dream!
Keep his eyelids! let him seem
Not this fever-wasted wight[3]
Thinn'd and paled before his time,
But the brilliant youthful knight
In the glory of his prime,
Sitting in the gilded barge,
At thy side, thou lovely charge,
Bending gaily o'er thy hand,
Iseult of Ireland!
And she too, that princess fair,
If her bloom be now less rare,
Let her have her youth again—
Let her be as she was then!
Let her have her proud dark eyes,
And her petulant quick replies—
Let her sweep her dazzling hand
With its gesture of command,
And shake back her raven hair
With the old imperious air!
As of old, so let her be,
That first Iseult, princess bright,

---

3. Person.

Chatting with her youthful knight
As he steers her o'er the sea,
Quitting at her father's will
The green isle where she was bred,
And her bower in Ireland,
For the surge-beat Cornish strand;
Where the prince whom she must wed
Dwells on loud Tyntagel's hill
High above the sounding sea.
And that potion rare her mother
Gave her, that her future lord,
Gave her, that King Marc and she,
Might drink it on their marriage-day,
And for ever love each other—
Let her, as she sits on board,
Ah, sweet saints, unwittingly!
See it shine, and take it up,
And to Tristram laughing say:
"Sir Tristram, of thy courtesy,
Pledge me in my golden cup!"
Let them drink it—let their hands
Tremble, and their cheeks be flame,
As they feel the fatal bands
Of a love they dare not name,
With a wild delicious pain,
Twine about their hearts again!
Let the early summer be
Once more round them, and the sea
Blue, and o'er its mirror kind
Let the breath of the May-wind,
Wandering through their drooping sails,
Die on the green fields of Wales!
Let a dream like this restore
What his eye must see no more!

Tristram

Chill blows the wind, the pleasaunce-walks are drear—
Madcap, what jest was this, to meet me here?
Were feet like those made for so wild a way?

The southern winter-parlour, by my fay,[4]
Had been the likeliest trysting-place to-day!
"Tristram!—nay, nay—thou must not take my hand!—
Tristram!—sweet love!—we are betray'd—out-plann'd.
Fly—save thyself—save me!—I dare not stay."—
One last kiss first!—*"Tis vain—to horse—away!"*

              *   *   *   *

Ah! sweet saints, his dream doth move
Faster surely than it should,
From the fever in his blood!
All the spring-time of his love
Is already gone and past,
And instead thereof is seen
Its winter, which endureth still—
Tyntagel on its surge-beat hill,
The pleasaunce-walks, the weeping queen,
The flying leaves, the straining blast,
And that long, wild kiss—their last.
And this rough December-night,
And his burning fever-pain,
Mingle with his hurrying dream,
Till they rule it, till he seem
The press'd fugitive again,
The love-desperate banish'd knight
With a fire in his brain
Flying o'er the stormy main.
—Whither does he wander now?
Haply in his dreams the wind
Wafts him here, and lets him find
The lovely orphan child again
In her castle by the coast;
The youngest, fairest chatelaine,[5]
Whom this realm of France can boast,
Our snowdrop by the Atlantic sea,
Iseult of Brittany.
And—for through the haggard air,
The stain'd arms, the matted hair

---

4. Faith.
5. Mistress of a castle.

Of that stranger-knight ill-starr'd,
There gleam'd something, which recall'd
The Tristram who in better days
Was Launcelot's guest at Joyous Gard—
Welcomed here, and here install'd,
Tended of his fever here,
Haply he seems again to move
His young guardian's heart with love;
In his exiled loneliness,
In his stately, deep distress,
Without a word, without a tear.
—Ah! 'tis well he should retrace
His tranquil life in this lone place;
His gentle bearing at the side
Of his timid youthful bride;
His long rambles by the shore
On winter-evenings, when the roar
Of the near waves came, sadly grand,
Through the dark, up the drown'd sand,
Or his endless reveries
In the woods, where the gleams play
On the grass under the trees,
Passing the long summer's day
Idle as a mossy stone
In the forest-depths alone,
The chase neglected, and his hound
Couch'd beside him on the ground.
—Ah! what trouble's on his brow?
Hither let him wander now;
Hither, to the quiet hours
Pass'd among these heaths of ours
By the grey Atlantic sea;
Hours, if not of ecstasy,
From violent anguish surely free!

Tristram

All red with blood the whirling river flows,
The wide plain rings, the dazed air throbs with blows.
Upon us are the chivalry of Rome—
Their spears are down, their steeds are bathed in foam.
"Up, Tristram, up," men cry, "thou moonstruck knight!
What foul fiend rides thee? On into the fight!"

—Above the din her voice is in my ears;
I see her form glide through the crossing spears.—
Iseult! . . . .

*   *   *   *

Ah! he wanders forth again;
We cannot keep him; now, as then,
There's a secret in his breast
Which will never let him rest.
These musing fits in the green wood
They cloud the brain, they dull the blood!
—His sword is sharp, his horse is good;
Beyond the mountains will he see
The famous towns of Italy,
And label with the blessed sign
The heathen Saxons on the Rhine.
At Arthur's side he fights once more
With the Roman Emperor.
There's many a gay knight where he goes
Will help him to forget his care;
The march, the leaguer, Heaven's blithe air,
The neighing steeds, the ringing blows—
Sick pining comes not where these are.
Ah! what boots it, that the jest
Lightens every other brow,
What, that every other breast
Dances as the trumpets blow,
If one's own heart beats not light
On the waves of the toss'd fight,
If oneself cannot get free
From the clog of misery?
Thy lovely youthful wife grows pale
Watching by the salt sea-tide
With her children at her side
For the gleam of thy white sail.
Home, Tristram, to thy halls again!
To our lonely sea complain,
To our forests tell thy pain!

Tristram

All round the forest sweeps off, black in shade,
But it is moonlight in the open glade;
And in the bottom of the glade shine clear
The forest-chapel and the fountain near.
—I think, I have a fever in my blood;
Come, let me leave the shadow of this wood,
Ride down, and bathe my hot brow in the flood.
—Mild shines the cold spring in the moon's clear light;
God! 'tis *her* face plays in the waters bright.
"Fair love," she says, "canst thou forget so soon,
At this soft hour, under this sweet moon?"—
Iseult! . . .

*   *   *   *

Ah, poor soul! if this be so,
Only death can balm thy woe.
The solitudes of the green wood
Had no medicine for thy mood;
The rushing battle clear'd thy blood
As little as did solitude.
—Ah! his eyelids slowly break
Their hot seals, and let him wake;
What new change shall we now see?
A happier? Worse it cannot be.

Tristram

Is my page here? Come, turn me to the fire!
Upon the window-panes the moon shines bright;
The wind is down—but she'll not come to-night.
Ah no! she is asleep in Cornwall now,
Far hence; her dreams are fair—smooth is her brow.
Of me she recks not, nor my vain desire.
—I have had dreams, I have had dreams, my page,
Would take a score years from a strong man's age;
And with a blood like mine, will leave, I fear,
Scant leisure for a second messenger.
—My princess, art thou there? Sweet, do not wait!
To bed, and sleep! my fever is gone by;
To-night my page shall keep me company.
Where do the children sleep? kiss them for me!

Poor child, thou art almost as pale as I;
This comes of nursing long and watching late.
To bed—good night!

            *   *   *   *

She left the gleam-lit fireplace,
She came to the bed-side;
She took his hands in hers—her tears
Down on his wasted fingers rain'd.
She raised her eyes upon his face—
Not with a look of wounded pride,
A look as if the heart complained—
Her look was like a sad embrace;
The gaze of one who can divine
A grief, and sympathise.
Sweet flower! thy children's eyes
Are not more innocent than thine.
      But they sleep in shelter'd rest,
Like helpless birds in the warm nest,
On the castle's southern side;
Where feebly comes the mournful roar
Of buffeting wind and surging tide
Through many a room and corridor.
—Full on their window the moon's ray
Makes their chamber as bright as day.
It shines upon the blank white walls,
And on the snowy pillow falls,
And on two angel-heads doth play
Turn'd to each other—the eyes closed,
The lashes on the cheeks reposed.
Round each sweet brow the cap close-set
Hardly lets peep the golden hair;
Through the soft-open'd lips the air
Scarcely moves the coverlet.
One little wandering arm is thrown
At random on the counterpane,
And often the fingers close in haste
As if their baby-owner chased
The butterflies again.
This stir they have, and this alone;
But else they are so still!

—Ah, tired madcaps! you lie still;
But were you at the window now,
To look forth on the fairy sight
Of your illumined haunts by night,
To see the park-glades where you play
Far lovelier than they are by day,
To see the sparkle on the eaves,
And upon every giant-bough
Of those old oaks, whose wet red leaves
Are jewell'd with bright drops of rain—
How would your voices run again!
And far beyond the sparkling trees
Of the castle-park one sees
The bare heaths spreading, clear as day,
Moor behind moor, far, far away,
Into the heart of Brittany.
And here and there, lock'd by the land,
Long inlets of smooth glittering sea,
And many a stretch of watery sand
All shining in the white moon-beams—
But you see fairer in your dreams!

What voices are these on the clear night-air?
What lights in the court—what steps on the stair?

II
ISEULT OF IRELAND

Tristram
Raise the light, my page! that I may see her.—
    Thou art come at last, then, haughty Queen!
Long I've waited, long I've fought my fever;
    Late thou comest, cruel thou hast been.

Iseult
Blame me not, poor sufferer! that I tarried;
    Bound I was, I could not break the band.
Chide not with the past, but feel the present!
    I am here—we meet—I hold thy hand.

Tristram

Thou art come, indeed—thou hast rejoin'd me;
    Thou hast dared it—but too late to save.
Fear not now that men should tax thine honour!
    I am dying: build—(thou may'st)—my grave!

Iseult

Tristram, ah, for love of Heaven, speak kindly!
    What, I hear these bitter words from thee?
Sick with grief I am, and faint with travel—
    Take my hand—dear Tristram, look on me!

Tristram

I forget, thou cómest from thy voyage—
    Yes, the spray is on thy cloak and hair.
But thy dark eyes are not dimm'd, proud Iseult!
    And thy beauty never was more fair.

Iseult

Ah, harsh flatterer! let alone my beauty!
    I, like thee, have left my youth afar.
Take my hand, and touch these wasted fingers—
    See my cheek and lips, how white they are!

Tristram

Thou art paler—but thy sweet charm, Iseult!
    Would not fade with the dull years away.
Ah, how fair thou standest in the moonlight!
    I forgive thee, Iseult!—thou wilt stay?

Iseult

Fear me not, I will be always with thee;
    I will watch thee, tend thee, soothe thy pain;
Sing thee tales of true, long-parted lovers,
    Join'd at evening of their days again.

Tristram

No, thou shalt not speak! I should be finding
    Something alter'd in thy courtly tone.
Sit—sit by me! I will think, we've lived so
    In the green wood, all our lives, alone.

Iseult

Alter'd, Tristram? Not in courts, believe me,
    Love like mine is alter'd in the breast;
Courtly life is light and cannot reach it—
    Ah! it lives, because so deep-suppress'd!

What, thou think'st men speak in courtly chambers
    Words by which the wretched are consoled?
What, thou think'st this aching brow was cooler,
    Circled, Tristram, by a band of gold?

Royal state with Marc, my deep-wrong'd husband—
    That was bliss to make my sorrows flee!
Silken courtiers whispering honied nothings—
    Those were friends to make me false to thee!

Ah, on which, if both our lots were balanced,
    Was indeed the heaviest burden thrown—
Thee, a pining exile in thy forest,
    Me, a smiling queen upon my throne?

Vain and strange debate, where both have suffer'd,
    Both have pass'd a youth consumed and sad,
Both have brought their anxious day to evening,
    And have now short space for being glad!

Join'd we are henceforth; nor will thy people,
    Nor thy younger Iseult take it ill,
That a former rival shares her office,
    When she sees her humbled, pale, and still.

I, a faded watcher by thy pillow,
    I, a statue on thy chapel-floor,
Pour'd in prayer before the Virgin-Mother,
    Rouse no anger, make no rivals more.

She will cry: "Is this the foe I dreaded?
    This his idol? this that royal bride?
Ah, an hour of health would purge his eyesight!
    Stay, pale queen! for ever by my side."

Hush, no words! that smile, I see, forgives me.
    I am now thy nurse, I bid thee sleep.

Close thine eyes—this flooding moonlight blinds them!—
    Nay, all's well again! thou must not weep.

Tristram

I am happy! yet I feel, there's something
    Swells my heart, and takes my breath away.
Through a mist I see thee; near—come nearer!
    Bend—bend down!—I yet have much to say.

Iseult

Heaven! his head sinks back upon the pillow—
    Tristram! Tristram! let thy heart not fail!
Call on God and on the holy angels!
    What, love, courage!—Christ! he is so pale.

Tristram

Hush, 'tis vain, I feel my end approaching!
    This is what my mother said should be,
When the fierce pains took her in the forest,
    The deep draughts of death, in bearing me.

"Son," she said, "thy name shall be of sorrow;
    Tristram art thou call'd for my death's sake."
So she said, and died in the drear forest.
    Grief since then his home with me doth make.

I am dying.—Start not, nor look wildly!
    Me, thy living friend, thou canst not save.
But, since living we were ununited,
    Go not far, O Iseult! from my grave.

Close mine eyes, then seek the princess Iseult;
    Speak her fair, she is of royal blood!
Say, I will'd so, that thou stay beside me—
    She will grant it; she is kind and good.

Now to sail the seas of death I leave thee—
    One last kiss upon the living shore!

Iseult

Tristram!—Tristram!—stay—receive me with thee!
    Iseult leaves thee, Tristram! never more.

      *   *   *   *

You see them clear—the moon shines bright.
Slow, slow and softly, where she stood,
She sinks upon the ground;—her hood
Had fallen back; her arms outspread
Still hold her lover's hand; her head
Is bow'd, half-buried, on the bed.
O'er the blanch'd sheet her raven hair
Lies in disorder'd streams; and there,
Strung like white stars, the pearls still are,
And the golden bracelets, heavy and rare,
Flash on her white arms still.
The very same which yesternight
Flash'd in the silver sconces' light,
When the feast was gay and the laughter loud
In Tyntagel's palace proud.
But then they deck'd a restless ghost
With hot-flush'd cheeks and brilliant eyes,
And quivering lips on which the tide
Of courtly speech abruptly died,
And a glance which over the crowded floor,
The dancers, and the festive host,
Flew ever to the door.
That the knights eyed her in surprise,
And the dames whispered scoffingly:
"Her moods, good lack, they pass like showers!
But yesternight and she would be
As pale and still as wither'd flowers,
And now to-night she laughs and speaks
And has a colour in her cheeks;
Christ keep us form such fantasy!"—

Yes, now the longing is o'erpast,
Which, dogg'd by fear and fought by shame,
Shook her weak bosom day and night,
Consumed her beauty like a flame,
And dimm'd it like the desert-blast.
And though the bed-clothes hide her face,
Yet were it lifted to the light,
The sweet expression of her brow
Would charm the gazer, till his thought
Erased the ravages of time,
Fill'd up the hollow cheek, and brought

A freshness back as of her prime—
So healing is her quiet now.
So perfectly the lines express
A tranquil, settled loveliness,
Her younger rival's purest grace.

The air of the December-night
Steals coldly around the chamber bright,
Where those lifeless lovers be;
Swinging with it, in the light
Flaps the ghostlike tapestry.
And on the arras wrought you see
A stately Huntsman, clad in green,
And round him a fresh forest-scene.
On that clear forest-knoll he stays,
With his pack round him, and delays.
He stares and stares, with troubled face,
At this huge, gleam-lit fireplace,
At that bright, iron-figured door,
And those blown rushes on the floor.
He gazes down into the room
With heated cheeks and flurried air,
And to himself he seems to say:
"What place is this, and who are they?
Who is that kneeling Lady fair?
And on his pillows that pale Knight
Who seems of marble on a tomb?
How comes it here, this chamber bright,
Through whose mullion'd[6] *windows clear*
The castle-court all wet with rain,
The drawbridge and the moat appear,
And then the beach, and, mark'd with spray,
The sunken reefs, and far away
The unquiet bright Atlantic plain?
—What, has some glamour made me sleep,
And sent me with my dogs to sweep,
By night, with boisterous bugle-peal,
Through some old, sea-side, knightly hall,
Not in the free green wood at all?

---

6. Having vertical bars dividing the panes.

That Knight's asleep, and at her prayer
That Lady by the bed doth kneel—
Then hush, thou boisterous bugle-peal!"
—The wild boar rustles in his lair;
The fierce hounds snuff the tainted air;
But lord and hounds keep rooted there.

Cheer, cheer thy dogs into the brake,
O Hunter! and without a fear
Thy golden-tassell'd bugle blow,
And through the glades thy pastime take—
For thou wilt rouse no sleepers here!
For these thou seest are unmoved;
Cold, cold as those who lived and loved
A thousand years ago.

III
ISEULT OF BRITTANY

A year had flown, and o'er the sea away,
In Cornwall, Tristram and Queen Iseult lay;
In King Marc's chapel, in Tyntagel old—
There in a ship they bore those lovers cold.

The young surviving Iseult, one bright day,
Had wander'd forth. Her children were at play
In a green circular hollow in the heath
Which borders the sea-shore—a country path
Creeps over it from the till'd fields behind.
The hollow's grassy banks are soft-inclined,
And to one standing on them, far and near
The lone unbroken view spreads bright and clear
Over the waste. This cirque[7] of open ground
Is light and green; the heather, which all round
Creeps thickly, grows not here; but the pale grass
Is strewn with rocks, and many a shiver'd mass
Of vein'd white-gleaming quartz, and here and there
Dotted with holly-trees and juniper.
In the smooth centre of the opening stood

---

7. Circle.

Three hollies side by side, and made a screen,
Warm with the winter-sun, of burnish'd green
With scarlet berries gemm'd, the fell-fare's[8] food.
Under the glittering hollies Iseult stands,
Watching her children play; their little hands
Are busy gathering spars[9] of quartz, and streams
Of stagshorn[10] for their hats; anon, with screams
Of mad delight they drop their spoils, and bound
Among the holly-clumps and broken ground,
Racing full speed, and startling in their rush
The fell-fares and the speckled missel-thrush
Out of their glossy coverts;—but when now
Their cheeks were flush'd, and over each hot brow,
Under the feather'd hats of the sweet pair,
In blinding masses shower'd the golden hair—
Then Iseult call'd them to her, and the three
Cluster'd under the holly-screen, and she
Told them an old-world Breton history.

Warm in their mantles wrapt the three stood there,
Under the hollies, in the clear still air—
Mantles with those rich furs deep glistering
Which Venice ships do from swart[11] Egypt bring.
Long they stay'd still—then, pacing at their ease,
Moved up and down under the glossy trees.
But still, as they pursued their warm dry road,
From Iseult's lips the unbroken story flow'd,
And still the children listen'd, their blue eyes
Fix'd on their mother's face in wide surprise;
Nor did their looks stray once to the sea-side,
Nor to the brown heaths round them, bright and wide,
Nor to the snow, which, though 't was all away
From the open heath, still by the hedgerows lay,
Nor to the shining sea-fowl, that with screams
Bore up from where the bright Atlantic gleams,
Swooping to landward; nor to where, quite clear,

---

8. A species of thrush.

9. Fragments of crystalline mineral.

10. A fern.

11. Dark.

The fell-fares settled on the thickets near.
And they would still have listen'd, till dark night
Came keen and chill down on the heather bright;
But, when the red glow on the sea grew cold,
And the grey turrets of the castle old
Look'd sternly through the frosty evening-air,
Then Iseult took by the hand those children fair,
And brought her tale to an end, and found the path,
And led them home over the darkening heath.

And is she happy? Does she see unmoved
The days in which she might have lived and loved
Slip without bringing bliss slowly away,
One after one, to-morrow like to-day?
Joy has not found her yet, nor ever will—
Is it this thought which makes her mien so still,
Her features so fatigued, her eyes, though sweet,
So sunk, so rarely lifted save to meet
Her children's? She moves slow; her voice alone
Hath yet an infantine and silver tone,
But even that comes languidly; in truth,
She seems one dying in a mask of youth.
And now she will go home, and softly lay
Her laughing children in their beds, and play
Awhile with them before they sleep; and then
She'll light her silver lamp, which fishermen
Dragging their nets through the rough waves, afar,
Along this iron coast, know like a star,
And take her broidery-frame, and there she'll sit
Hour after hour, her gold curls sweeping it;
Lifting her soft-bent head only to mind
Her children, or to listen to the wind.
And when the clock peals midnight, she will move
Her work away, and let her fingers rove
Across the shaggy brows of Tristram's hound
Who lies, guarding her feet, along the ground;
Or else she will fall musing, her blue eyes
Fixt, her slight hands clasp'd on her lap; then rise,
And at her prie-dieu[12] kneel, until she have told

---

12. A small kneeling-bench designed for use by a person at prayer and with a
raised shelf on which elbows or a book may be rested.

Her rosary-beads of ebony tipp'd with gold,
Then to her soft sleep—and to-morrow 'll be
To-day's exact repeated effigy.

Yes, it is lonely for her in her hall.
The children, and the grey-hair'd seneschal,
Her women, and Sir Tristram's aged hound,
Are there the sole companions to be found.
But these she loves; and noisier life than this
She would find ill to bear, weak as she is.
She has her children, too, and night and day
Is with them; and the wide heaths where they play,
The hollies, and the cliff, and the sea-shore,
The sand, the sea-birds, and the distant sails,
These are to her dear as to them; the tales
With which this day the children she beguiled
She gleaned from Breton grandames, when a child,
In every hut along this sea-coast wild.
She herself loves them still, and, when they are told,
Can forget all to hear them, as of old.

Dear saints, it is not sorrow, as I hear,
Not suffering, which shuts up eye and ear
To all that has delighted them before,
And lets us be what we were once no more.
No, we may suffer deeply, yet retain
Power to be moved and soothed, for all our pain,
By what of old pleased us, and will again.
No, 'tis the gradual furnace of the world,
In whose hot air our spirits are upcurl'd
Until they crumble, or else grow like steel—
Which kills in us the bloom, the youth, the spring—
Which leaves the fierce necessity to feel,
But takes away the power—this can avail,
By drying up our joy in everything,
To make our former pleasures all seem stale.
This, or some tyrannous single thought, some fit
Of passion, which subdues our souls to it,
Till for its sake alone we live and move—
Call it ambition, or remorse, or love—
This too can change us wholly, and make seem
All which we did before, shadow and dream.

And yet, I swear, it angers me to see
How this fool passion gulls men potently;
Being, in truth, but a diseased unrest,
And an unnatural overheat at best.
How they are full of languor and distress
Not having it; which when they do possess,
They straightway are burnt up with fume and care,
And spend their lives in posting here and there
Where this plague drives them; and have little ease,
Are furious with themselves, and hard to please.
Like that bald Caesar, the famed Roman wight,
Who wept at reading of a Grecian knight
Who made a name at younger years than he;[13]
Or that renown'd mirror of chivalry,
Prince Alexander, Philip's peerless son,
Who carried the great war from Macedon
Into the Soudan's realm, and thundered on
To die at thirty-five in Babylon.

What tale did Iseult to the children say,
Under the hollies, that bright winter's day?

She told them of the fairy-haunted land
Away the other side of Brittany,
Beyond the heaths, edged by the lonely sea;
Of the deep forest-glades of Broce-liande,
Through whose green boughs the golden sunshine creeps,
Where Merlin by the enchanted thorn-tree sleeps.
For here he came with the fay Vivian,
One April, when the warm days first began.
He was on foot, and that false fay, his friend,
On her white palfrey;[14] here he met his end,
In these lone sylvan glades, that April-day.
This tale of Merlin and the lovely fay
Was the one Iseult chose, and she brought clear
Before the children's fancy him and her.

Blowing between the stems, the forest-air

---

13. At the age of thirty-four, according to legend, Julius Caesar grieved because Alexander the Great had conquered the world at a younger age.

14. Riding horse.

Had loosen'd the brown locks of Vivian's hair,
Which play'd on her flush'd cheek, and her blue eyes
Sparkled with mocking glee and exercise.
Her palfrey's flanks were mired and bathed in sweat,
For they had travell'd far and not stopp'd yet.
A brier in that tangled wilderness
Had scored her white right hand, which she allows
To rest ungloved on her green riding-dress;
The other warded off the drooping boughs.
But still she chatted on, with her blue eyes
Fix'd full on Merlin's face, her stately prize.
Her 'haviour had the morning's fresh clear grace,
The spirit of the woods was in her face.
She look'd so witching fair, that learned wight
Forgot his craft, and his best wits took flight;
And he grew fond, and eager to obey
His mistress, use her empire as she may.

They came to where the brushwood ceased, and day
Peer'd 'twixt the stems; and the ground broke away,
In a sloped sward[15] down to a brawling brook;
And up as high as where they stood to look
On the brook's farther side was clear, but then
The underwood and trees began again.
This open glen was studded thick with thorns
Then white with blossom; and you saw the horns,
Through last year's fern, of the shy fallow-deer
Who come at noon down to the water here.
You saw the bright-eyed squirrels dart along
Under the thorns on the green sward; and strong
The blackbird whistled from the dingles near,
And the weird chipping of the woodpecker
Rang lonelily and sharp; the sky was fair,
And a fresh breath of spring stirr'd everywhere.
Merlin and Vivian stopp'd on the slope's brow,
To gaze on the light sea of leaf and bough
Which glistering plays all round them, lone and mild,
As if to itself the quiet forest smiled.
Upon the brow-top grew a thorn, and here

---

15. Grassy area.

The grass was dry and moss'd, and you saw clear
Across the hollow; white anemonies
Starr'd the cool turf, and clumps of primroses
Ran out from the dark underwood behind.
No fairer resting-place a man could find.
"Here let us halt," said Merlin then; and she
Nodded, and tied her palfrey to a tree.

They sate them down together, and a sleep
Fell upon Merlin, more like death, so deep.
Her finger on her lips, then Vivian rose,
And from her brown-lock'd head the wimple throws,
And takes it in her hand, and waves it over
The blossom'd thorn-tree and her sleeping lover.
Nine times she waved the fluttering wimple round,
And made a little plot of magic ground.
And in that daisied circle, as men say,
Is Merlin prisoner till the judgment-day;
But she herself whither she will can rove—
For she was passing weary of his love.

From: *The Feasts of Camelot*

by

MRS. T. K. HERVEY

Chapter III.
Sir Tristram's Tale of Mad King Mark

Never in all the world, I think, was there knight or king so mad as my uncle King Mark. While I was yet but a young squire I was sent into Cornwall to receive knighthood from my uncle; and sorry am I that I received it not rather from any man living; for there was neither honour nor courtesy to be learned from him. Though he calls himself King Mark he is really no king at all, save only by the sufferance of my lord King Arthur, who has forborne[1] him these many years only for my sake, and because of his being kin also to dead Gorlois, Duke of Cornwall. Because of the mystery of King Arthur's early fostering, and the rebellion that came out of it, he seized that corner of land to himself, with all the estates thereto belonging, and would have all men call him king. And there he reigns and raves; and what he cannot do by the strong hand he will do by sleight and cunning; and for that cause has Sir Launcelot of the Lake ever called him "King Fox."

While I was yet but a new-made knight, my uncle's right of kingship was called in question by one Sir Maurice of Ireland, brother to the queen of that country. To end the dispute it was agreed that the matter should be decided by single combat, between Sir Maurice of Ireland and that knight of King Mark's court who should be of the best lineage. Thereupon, my uncle called me to him, and broke the affair to me.

"Fair nephew," said he, "this encounter falls to you by right of birth, and you must have to do with this knight of Ireland whether you be so minded or no."

---

1. Had patience with.

"With your leave, Sir Mark," said I, for I never would call him king, "I must forbear to do battle in this cause."

Then my uncle looked at me askance from under his brows, and, said he, "Fair nephew, why so?"

"Because," I answered, "no true knight will fight but in a just cause; and well you know there is no king in all Logris but only my lord King Arthur."

"Say you so?" said King Mark; "we shall see!"

He said no more at that time; and I thought I was well out of the risk of shedding innocent blood in a wrong cause. But I was young then; and King Mark was more than a match for me.

It was soon spread abroad that I was afraid of Sir Maurice, who was a noble and approved knight; and that I had refused to meet him in single combat. For this cause Sir Maurice took occasion to taunt me as recreant[2] from my vows of knighthood, perjured, and false. My blood was hot; and I threw down my glove, and dared him to meet me in mortal fight. So here were we two come to be deadly foes for no cause save an evil mind and a lying tongue.

We met full savagely. Twice I broke spear on Sir Maurice's hauberk,[3] and twice he hurled at me, so that I had all but been unhorsed. But to make a long story short, I overcame him in the end; and though he never cried me mercy, yet I gave him his life; as Heaven forbid I should not, both because of the just cause he had come to do battle for, and because I began to see that I had been slandered to the knight. He now confessed me to be a worthy foe; and we embraced as friends and brothers, though we were both sorely wounded, and might not bear harness for many a day to come.

From that time my uncle seemed to grow all at once very kind to me. He gave it out that I had fought for his right of kingship; and made it be understood of all men that henceforward none should question it. It was in vain that I denied the tale; I was in the mesh, and I could not get out of it.

Disgusted and sick at heart, I resolved to leave Cornwall, and to set out, in company with Sir Maurice, for the court of King Anguish, of Ireland. My uncle did not oppose me; but as I was on the point of setting foot on shipboard, who should ride up to me, as

---

2. Cowardly.

3. A tunic of chain mail.

I stood on the shore with Sir Maurice, but my uncle, mad King Mark!

"Fair nephew," said he, for so was ever his way of speech when he had some end of his own to serve, "I would that you should take this packet, bound with silken cord, to my brother-king, Anguish, of Ireland, and greet him well from me."

I took the packet, bound with silken cord, and making, as may be guessed, light leave-taking, went on shipboard with Sir Maurice. As I mounted to the deck I heard a low chuckle behind me, and, looking back, saw cunning King Mark go smiling away.

We made good voyage, and soon reached the domains of King Anguish. There I first saw the beautiful Isond. But little did I think what sorrow was in store for me through the crooked dealings of sly King Mark.

At first I was courteously received by all; and was especially happy in the kindness and favour of the beautiful Isond, to whom, the first day of my coming, I began to teach the music of the harp, in which from my earliest youth I had delighted, even more than in hunting. But full soon I saw and felt a change. King Anguish looked askance at me; even Sir Maurice began to slacken in his friendship; and it became clear that the letter I had borne from King Mark was at the root of it all.

Still, though all others looked coldly and suspiciously upon me, Isond remained kind and gentle as ever. So one day I thought I would take courage and ask her the cause why I had grown in such disfavour. Then she told me how King Mark had written to her father to bid him keep me closely watched that I should never return into his country of Cornwall, for that I had plotted to usurp from him his lawful lands; and that when I had pretended to do battle in his cause it was only done to prove his right to possess them, in order that I might, as his nephew, claim them in turn, as he had no sons to come after him. But this was not all. He had the cunning to give some colour to his falsehood by saying that my object in seeking the court of King Anguish was to ask the aid of that king to dispossess him at once of his crown.

For all this I cared little; the worst was to come. King Mark had asked for the hand of the beautiful Isond in marriage, and her father had consented to give her to the ruthless man. This was the greatest misfortune that could have happened to me, as I thought then,—for I was beginning to love, with all the devotion of knighthood, that gentle lady.

Sorrowfully did the beautiful Isond weep as she told me of her father's mistaken pledge to King Mark. But she was dutiful as she was fair; and I, as a good and true knight, was bound in honour henceforth to regard her as the promised wife of my uncle.

Bitterly grieving over her probable fate, I at once determined to depart from that court. By the advice of Isond I arranged to steal secretly from Ireland, lest, in any attempt to detain me, I might be forced to come to open war with her father; and this, with many tears, she earnestly entreated me by all means to avoid.

Just then it so happened that the distress I endured at hearing of my uncle's new treachery against me, together with the sorrow of losing Isond, caused an old wound to break out afresh. What gentle and good thoughts for my happiness were then in her mind I knew not at that time, though I did later; but the kind Isond, though skilled in surgery beyond most of her degree, yet said she was quite unable to attempt my cure.

"Sir Tristram," she said, "your wound has been made with a poisoned arrow; it can only be cured in that country where you received it. The shaft that struck you flew from the bow of one of a band of heathen marauders among the mountains of Wales; so at least a minstrel sang the tale to me. I pray you go now into that country, to the court of the good King Howell, who is my kinsman. His daughter, my cousin and namesake, the gracious Isond, is well skilled in leechcraft. Greet her well from me, and say I would that she would set herself to cure you of your wound. We two are so closely likened to each other, save that my cousin Isond is the fairer, that it may be you shall think the fair hands of Isond of Wales are the hands of the poor Isond which you have taught so well to draw forth the sweet music of the harp. Go now, Sir Tristram," she added, as I would fain have lingered over that sad leave-taking, "and God speed you for a good knight and true!"

Whether our secret talk had been overheard, I know not, but that very night I was seized while asleep, and hurried, bound, to a dungeon below the castle keep.[4] There, for some days, I lay without hope of release; but the gentle Isond was busy devising means for my escape.

The first thing she did was to desire her damsels to spread abroad a report that I was greatly learned in magic arts, so as to put

---

4. The strongest and securest part of a castle.

my gaolers[5] in bodily fear of me. Next, she ordered that her harp should be wrapped in cloth of cloth,[6] and borne with great care into my dungeon to while away the hours of my captivity.

There were at that time in Ireland, as there still are in this land, many people curiously fond of keeping dwarfs, who were brought over from the East. One of these frightful creatures, the smallest and most hideous of his kind, Isond procured. She caused him to coil himself up within the framework of the harp, for which purpose she took care to have the strings removed; that done, the harp, carefully swathed and bound, was brought into my cell, and there left; the dwarf having his orders what to do.

When next the gaoler brought me food and water for the night, I hid myself behind the harp; while the hideous dwarf rushed forward, and soundly rated the gaoler for coming so late with my supper, howling out in his ears, "If you do not go to the foul fiend for this, my name's not Sir Tristram!"

Horror-struck at what he conceived to be my abominable transforming of myself into an imp of Satan, the gaoler rushed out, at his wits' end, leaving the cell door open. Through it I slipped like lightning; and, aided by the dwarf who held the key of the postern gate, where my horse and good sword awaited me, I soon found myself in perfect safety.

Glad enough was I to reach the shores of Wales. There all fell out as I truly believe the virtuous Isond intended that it should. In the court of King Howell my happiest days were passed. His daughter, the gracious Isond, as she was called to distinguish her from her cousin and namesake of Ireland, was the sweetest lady in all the world. Under her loving care all my wounds, both of body and mind, were indeed cured; and here at my side she sits, King Howell's daughter, and the good wife of a poor knight, by name Sir Tristram.

*   *   *   *   *

"And now, Merlin," said Sir Tristram, when he had ended his tale, "I want to know why you smiled when I told of the poisoned arrow? I verily believe you put faith in nothing but God and knighthood."

---

5. Jailers.

6. The phrase "cloth of cloth" appears in the original edition but must be a typographical error.

"Truly," answered Merlin; "I am not so simple as to believe the story of a poisoned wound being only to be cured in the country where the wound was *dealt*; though there is a sort of truth at the bottom of that foolish saying, doubtless. Perhaps he might be nearer the mark who should say, that it would be most likely of cure in the land the poison came from; since it has been said that the wise men among the Saracens, which people make much use of such unknightly weapons, ceased not in their search till they had found out an antidote to the poison with which they tipped their arrows. Be that as it may; as to your bodily wound, Sir Tristram, depend on it there was no poison at all in the case, let the foolish minstrels sing what they may. Mischief take the bards! They will leave nothing as they find it; but are for ever stringing of rhymes and twanging of strings, to the utter confusion of all true history. It matters little that they have set me down for a wizard; but they have even dared to call our gracious lady Morgana, the 'Fay-lady.'"

"Nay, Merlin," said Queen Guenever, who was wife to King Arthur, "blame not the bards so greatly; you yourself are half the cause that my lord King Arthur's sister is accounted more than mortal wise. You found her apt, and taught her so many learned things that women seldom know of, that rumour has fixed upon her the blame of dealing with unlawful magic."

"Right, honoured lady," replied Merlin; "but that all men may know truly in the end, I keep the books of my uncle Bleise, as well as all that I have written down myself, fast locked in the great pyx[7] in the church of St. Stephen. Heaven grant they never be lost; or a sorry history will be given of us all in the ages to come!"

. . . .

Chapter XI.
Queen Isond's Tale of the One Good Deed.

In a castle, built on a strong rock looking over the broad waters that wash the Cornish shores, there lived an old knight who had two sons. When these two youths were yet but unbearded squires, not yet admitted into knighthood, there came to dwell there a young maiden passing fair, the orphan child of the old knight's brother, who had just then been newly slain in the wars.

---

7. A container usually used for holding the host in a church.

The old knight loved her as if she had been a child of his own; and
secretly determined that he would in due time wed her to one or
other of his two sons, if it should turn out that either of them grew
into the young maid's liking.

The two youths were as different in all things as light is from
dark. Bertrand, the elder, was bold and strong of limb, impatient of
control, passionate and revengeful. Walter, the younger, was of a
softer nature, reserved and quiet, but of deep affections; and he
was, to the full, as brave as his brother, though few gave him credit
for the force that was in him.

As time drew on, it happened that the liking of the young
maid, Lenora, fell on the elder, Bertrand. And, as soon as the old
knight noted that his elder son grew to be marvellously fond of the
orphan child, he settled it all as he would have it, and the two were
betrothed.

But when the two young squires had passed their noviciate,
and came to receive knighthood at their father's hands, nothing
would stay Bertrand, the elder, but he would away to the wars,
where a neighbouring country was struggling to free itself from a
foreign yoke. He could not rest, he said, in the old hall of his
fathers, while the world's work was doing outside; but he would go
forth and win for himself renown; and then he should come back
more worthy of his betrothed lady, Lenora, and they would be
wedded with great joy in the old castle of the rock.

With many tears Lenora parted with her lover; and, folding
across his shoulders a scarf of blue samite,[8] richly embroidered by
her own hands, saw him mount and ride away.

Time went on. The wars were over. A year had passed by with
lagging foot; and yet the bridegroom came not. When the autumn
leaves began to fall, the old knight died. With his last breath he
committed the young Lenora to the care of his son, Walter, till
Bertrand, the elder, should return to claim his bride; appointing
him guardian over her person and lands, and bidding him be a
gentle and loving brother to one so forlorn. For, by this time, there
had crept a misgiving into the knight's mind that all was not well
with his son Bertrand, who came not home to the fulfilling of his
pledge.

So the old knight died, and was buried by torchlight. And
now, save for the ancient servitors and men-at-arms who had

---

8. Rich silk.

belonged to his following, there remained in the rock-castle only
the youth, Walter, and Lenora the maiden betrothed.

As a miser guards his hoarded treasure, so did Walter guard
the promised bride of his brother Bertrand. His task was a hard one.
He loved the maid with a better love than his light-minded brother
had done; and as time wore away, and he saw her deserted and
drooping, his heart bled within him, and was sore for her sorrow.
Yet he never spoke of his love to her; but held her in all honour,
and kept his knightly faith unbroken.

At length, over the seas came Bertrand once more. But he
came not alone. He brought with him a bride from a strange land,
one light-minded like himself, who, in after days, brought a just
retribution on his head; for she forsook him as he had forsaken his
once love, Lenora, and broke her wedded vows to flee away in
shameful flight with a knight of her own land.

Now, when Bertrand brought home his light lady, and set her
in the home of his fathers, the just wrath of the good Walter was
roused against him for Lenora's sake; and, mindless for the
moment that he was of his own blood and kin, he challenged him to
the combat as recreant[9] and false, perjured lover and faithless
knight.

The hot blood of Bertrand was up. He fell savagely on his
brother; and, as he was the stronger and hardier of the two, it might
have ended ill for the true Walter, but that the maid, Lenora,
looking down from the rampart, saw the unnatural encounter, and
came swiftly down to part the brothers. She rushed between the
uplifted swords, and fell, wounded to death, beneath the stroke of
Bertrand.

The sight of her innocent blood recalled them to themselves.
Bertrand, aghast and bewildered at the issue of the foul wrong he
had done, stood by, pale, and leaning on his sword; but Walter, all
whose true soul was with the lost Lenora, knelt at her side, and
strove in vain to stanch the wound dealt by the betrayer.

Her life was passing. To Bertrand she only said, "Be happy
with your chosen bride." But to Walter she turned now with tender
trust, crying, "Oh, true heart! well hast thou loved in silent love; and
noble life hast thou lived. Live still, and remember me to the grave,
where we two shall meet and go wedded souls to heaven. Bear with
thy brother, for the sake of the old love that was between him and

---

9. Cowardly.

me. Never again, I charge you, cross sword with Bertrand, your
brother. His I was once: yours am I now for ever." So saying, and
yielding, for the first and last time, her dying lips to the pure kiss of
Walter, Lenora quietly breathed away her life.

The brothers, mindful of her words, fell to battle no more.
But the unruly spirit of Bertrand was hard to bear. He seemed now
to hate his brother, whose virtues were a silent reproach to him. So
Walter sorrowfully departed out of his old father's castle, and went
forth to seek adventure wherein he might forget the tragic ending
of his love. Many years he wandered, and many good deeds are
recorded of him, in helping the oppressed, even to the shedding of
his blood for them in numerous perilous encounters.

In one of his wanderings, it happened that he reached the
skirts of a wood, near which many knights were gathered together,
as if about to set out on some new quest. He turned his horse's head
and joined them company, questioning them of their intent. They
told him of a fierce combat which had just then come about, in
which one knight had slain another unjustly, and against all fair and
honourable laws of chivalry. By the account they gave of the slain
knight and of the bearings on his shield, Sir Walter knew that it
must be his brother Bertrand, who had fallen thus ingloriously; and
he vowed to avenge his fall with the best might that he could. But
when he came to put question as to the false knight he sought, it
was told him that in those parts he was known as the Invisible
Knight, because he ever wore his visor closed, so that no man knew
his face. Out of this, strange tales had arisen of many having got
hard blows at his hand, while none could see who dealt them. Sir
Walter could sift the true from the false; and he well divined that he
should not have far to seek.

Having parted company with the rest, he chose such a path
through the wood as showed, by some broken branches strewed in
the way, that a mounted knight had but newly cleft his way through
the thick-grown trees. His course lay alone for some length; but at a
clearing in the wood, he espied, resting beside a fountain, his arms
soiled and stained with newly-shed blood, a knight of good stature,
whose face he could not see. He doubted not that this was the
Invisible Knight, since he answered in all points to the description
that was given of him.

As the knight Walter looked on the supposed slayer of his
brother Bertrand, the playmate of his youth, and the once-beloved
of his own loved and lost Lenora, something of the fierce passion of
his brother for a moment stirred his blood; and, hurling a bold

defiance at the Invisible Knight, he challenged him to combat.
Nothing loath, the latter mounted, and met his challenger in full
career. Furious were the blows that hailed thick and fast on either
helm. The Invisible Knight, especially, seemed moved by more than
human hate, and fell upon Sir Walter like one possessed by a fiend.

Long and doubtful was the strife. And now, as both paused
for one brief moment to gather breath to renew the fight, the
Invisible Knight, forgetful of all disguise, raised has barred visor,
and gazed fiercely on his foe.

Suddenly the sword dropped from Sir Walter's grasp. "Oh,
Bertrand, my brother!" he cried, "stay thy hand. Pardon, oh pardon!
I knew thee not. Oh my brother, how nearly had I slain thee, or
thou me; and then would all the wide world have been a blank to
one of us two for evermore!" But the frantic Bertrand fell on him
once again. And, as Sir Walter would no more lift his sword against
his brother's life, he fell, wounded, to the earth.

Then, first, a touch of remorse struck to the heart of the
guilty Bertrand; and he repented him of the fatal disguise he had
put on, in exchanging arms with the knight he had waylaid and
slain in the wood.

Walter, seeing what was working in his brother's mind, gave
him what comfort he could, saying, "Bertrand, my brother, if you
were to know for a surety that I died by your own sword-stroke, you
would find peace on this earth never more. See, then, I will wound
myself with a stroke that shall go deeper than thine, that my blood
may not be upon thy head." So speaking, he took his own sword and
fell upon it; and spoke word never more.

Sir Bertrand, deserted by his evil wife, whose paramour he
had set upon and slain in the wood, and now despoiled of his noble
brother and sole of his kin, went mad, and lived but a short while
after.

And now I come to the good deed of my lord King Mark. He
caused the body of Sir Walter to be borne back to his own castle of
the rock, and there to be buried in the chapel, beside the lady
Lenora, in one grave with her. And he caused prayers and blessings
and spousal rites to be read over them, that these two noble and
true souls might go, as Lenora had said, "wedded souls to heaven."
And my lord King Mark caused also to be raised over the sleeping
dead a costly tomb of pure white marble, and on it were written
these words:—

"HERE LYETH THE NOBLE KNIGHT,
WALTER OF THE ROCK:
AND BESIDE HIM
HIS SWEETEST LADY, LENORA;
CRUELLY SLAIN ON EARTH,
BUT WEDDED TO HIM IN HEAVEN."

*   *   *   *   *

When the tale was ended, King Arthur said, "Truly, fairest queen, your tale is a lovely tale; and though sad, yet full of such true nobleness as touches finer chords in the heart than tales of mirth and pleasantry, and leaves a sweeter ring in the soul. As for the good deed of your lord King Mark, it was well done, and showed indeed some ruth and pity, and a feeling for what is truly great; yet it could be wished that the living rather than the dead had been so humanely dealt with. But let us take the deed for what it is worth. Perhaps it may be yet further shown that some of his blood and race have done acts of nobleness and generosity, whence we may infer that nature is not all in fault, but that circumstance has wrought in him some of the ill that he has done. I would some innocent child, unmoved by passion, could speak for him. Young Alisaunder," continued the king, "among all the tales which children devour so eagerly, heard you ever a tale of one of King Mark's line, which might plead for your worst foe? King Mark has been your enemy more than any, for he forgot against your father Sir Baldwin the brother-ties and virtues which yet he honoured in Sir Walter of the Rock. Speak one good word for him, child, if thou canst."

"Gladly would I, my good lord King Arthur," answered the boy; "but indeed I never heard any tale that I remember about the false king's line.—Yet, stay, one strange tale I do remember; but that was not very long ago. Shall I tell it, King Arthur?"

"Do so, child," said the king. And Alisaunder began.

Chapter XII.
The Boy Alisaunder's Tale of the Forgiving Heart

I can't tell where it happened, nor what was the name of the king; but I remember that he had married a sister of King Mark's; and he had a little son who was born in a forest, and who grew up to be a great hunter of beasts, and a minstrel besides. People said it was because he had been born in a forest among the wild deer, and that the first music he ever heard was the loud wind playing amongst the branches of the huge forest trees. Do you think that was so, King Arthur? Ah! you smile: and I see Merlin lifts up his eyebrows and looks at Sir Tristram. But Sir Tristram looks grave, and does not laugh at me; so I will go on.

I don't know what was the name of the little son of the sister of King Mark; but I know his mother died, and his father took a new wife; and she was not like King Mark's sister, not by much so good and so true a lady. She treated her little stepson cruelly, and did him all the harm that she could. She had children of her own; and she hated him because his father loved him best, and often told her that his little son would inherit all his lands, and King Mark's besides; for the boy's uncle, King Mark, had no sons of his own.

One day she sent him out in a wild, wild storm, to gather herbs a long way off. When he came back he was weary and athirst; but she would let him have no drink; for she said he was hot, and he must wait till night, for it was better for him, and more wholesome, to drink the last thing before he lay down to sleep, as the cattle do.

Well, all that day she was brewing and brewing the herbs.—O, now I remember, the name of the king was Meliodus; yes, that was it, King Meliodus.

His little son, when night came, went into the sleeping-room where all the children lay. All were in bed and asleep but he. Before he lay down he bethought him of the drink he had been promised, for he was now more athirst than ever. He saw a cup standing on a settle[10] beside his bed; but he could not believe that it was put there for him, for his stepmother was not used to be so careful of him, or so thoughtful of what he might want. So he said to himself,— "Perhaps it is not meant for me. I will go to bed and lie awake awhile, and see if my stepmother will come and give it me, as I know my own mother would have done if she had been living." With that he laid him down, and soon forgot all about the drink, and fell fast asleep,—he was so very, very weary.

Next day, one of the queen's own children, a little girl, fell sick; and do what the queen could, she might give her no ease. At last a sudden fear came into her mind, and she asked quickly,— "Child, did you take any drink last night?"

---

10. Ledge.

"Yes," said the little girl; "I woke up all hot and dry, and I got up and drank some of my brother's drink that stood by his bedside."

Then the queen fell down in a swoon; and before she could be got round again, her little girl was dead.

King Meliodus was away at this time. When he came home, he was sorely troubled at what had fallen out. Yet, whatever he might think, he said nothing. But one day, when again some drink was set near his little son, which he had seen the queen set there with her own hands, though she saw not that he was watching her, he went into the room where it stood, when the queen and his own little son were there, and none besides; and he took up the cup, and made believe as if he were going to drink; and he watched the queen's face all the while. Very white she grew, and whiter and whiter every moment, as he slowly raised the cup to drink from it. At last, just as it reached his mouth, she suddenly started forward with a great cry, and struck the cup out of his hand, so that it fell on the floor.

Then the king, without a word, took her by the hand and led her away. Across the great hall he led her, and right away to the castle-keep, where all the dungeons were. His little son followed, trembling and afraid, though he knew not what it meant; and begged the king to bring back his stepmother; or only to speak, and not to look so fearful and stern. But his father heeded nothing. Only, when he had gone down the great stone steps to the horrible prison beneath, dragging the queen after him,—and when he had thrust her into a stone cell, and locked and barred the door fast upon her,—then he came back and took his little son by the hand, just as he had taken the queen, speaking no word all the time, and so led him back into the castle, and left him alone.

After that King Meliodus summoned his men-at-arms, and all those that belonged to his following,—for he would do all openly; and he bade a great fire to be kindled with huge logs and hurdles in the middle of the courtyard for the burning of a wicked witch; for he told them how he had by chance found out that his little girl had died through evil practices, and that justice should be done at once, before the sun was two days older.

But the sun was only one day older when his little son came and knelt at his feet, and prayed of his father that he would give him the dungeon key; and let him go and take his stepmother out of the cold, damp stone cell, and bring her back into the hall to the warm log-fire. But his father would not hear him. Three times that day he prayed his father's mercy for the queen, though he knew not as yet the worse fate that was in store for her. But it was all no use.

The next day, when he came with the same pleading, that he might be let go and bring his stepmother indoors to the warm log-fire, his father, King Meliodus, answered him frightfully.

"She shall have logs enough and fire enough, child, be sure," said he. And as he said it the red blood mounted up into his face with fierce anger; and he looked again just as he had looked when the queen grew whiter and whiter, and struck the drinking-cup out of his hand.

Seeing the boy all amazed, he drew him to the window, and showed him where men were busy piling up great dry tree-branches, all in a wide circle round one long, stiff, upright stake that was set up in the midst, with a great iron ring in it, and a chain of iron fastened to the ring.

"See, boy!" said the stern king, "yonder is the fire to be kindled, and there stand the logs ready; think you there will be fire enough there to warm a cold heart—a heart cold and desperately wicked?"

The boy wrung his hands, for he had heard of such things, and he knew what was meant.

"Oh, father!" he cried, "dear father! you never will be so cruel. Forgive her—pray forgive her! What has she done?"

"I will tell you," said his father. "She made a hellish drink, and poisoned her own child with it."

"Oh! never," cried the boy; "never, never—it cannot be!"

"I tell thee, boy, it is so," said his father; "would you save her now?"

"Surely, father," he answered; "if she had killed me, too, she should not be burnt."

"Now, listen to me," said his fierce father; "it was you, boy, yourself that she meant to kill. She put the poison-cup at your own bedside; but my little girl drank of it, and she died."

The boy well remembered about the cup, and he was obliged to believe it now. But it made no difference to him. Still he said, "Spare her, dear father; she must be sorry!"

"Shall I tell you how she showed her sorrow?" said the king. "When her little girl was dead she brewed another hellish cup, and put it in your way. You saw me lift it to my lips; you saw the white witch strike it from my hand: would you spare her now?"

"She shall not suffer—indeed, indeed, she must not!" persisted the boy. "Why, dear, dear father, she saved your life—think how she loves you! Only spare her this once, and I will answer for it she will do this horrid thing never again."

While he spoke, a fearful shriek burst on their ears. Looking out, they saw the queen being led between two men, who were bringing her to the stake, to which they were just going to fasten her with the iron chain.

The boy said no more. He burst through the hall, and out away into the courtyard; and, clasping his arms round her, began to drag his stepmother away from the logs.

The king could resist no longer. He made a sign to the men, and they loosed their hold of her; and the boy, still clasping her closely round, dragged her safely away.

The king's little son was right. His stepmother never did him harm any more, but loved him tenderly ever after; and scourged herself and wore sackcloth for her sin.

*   *   *   *   *

"That is all I know of the story," said Alisaunder. "The king's little son was right to do as he did,—was he not, King Arthur? I know I would have done the same, whatever had come of it. Would not you, Sir Tristram? I am sure you would.—Why, your eyes look as if there were tears in them! Oh, Sir Tristram, *you* are nephew to King Mark! Ah! I know now; it must be your story I have been telling."

King Arthur looked on the boy with a kindly smile. "Child," he said, "thou reprovest me. This story thou hast told so well is indeed the story of thy cousin's, Sir Tristram's, youth, though thou knewest it not. Methinks we have not far to seek for traits of nobleness and self-denial in the blood of King Mark's line, while we have before us this very Sir Tristram, and thy father, Sir Baldwin, that unhappy king's brother. Even in thee, too, my boy, young as thou art, I perceive a strain of true nobleness that will one day make the world ring with thy renown. Be the sins of King Mark, then, freely forgiven, for the virtues' sake of these that are of his kin. In good time, doubtless, we shall know how he has been beguiled to his undoing."

"I believe," said Merlin, "I hold the clue to some of his misdeeds. There went a rumour long ago that I, who—heaven only knows why!—am accounted a prophet, had foretold that one near akin to him should usurp his power, and hold him captive till his death-day. Thus, ever in dread, and knowing not from which hand his doom is to come, he wages an unnatural war with all his race."

"Merlin is ever wise and right," added Queen Isond. "No wonder that his study of the stars and planets has made people account him gifted beyond common men—as indeed he is, though neither wizard nor prophet. My lord King Mark has ever been kind and tender to me; and I think none can lay to his charge any act of cruelty or injustice where he has not been led to suspect treachery through a foolish rumour. When I protected and aided Angelides[11] to withdraw her son from his pursuit, his anger against me was but for a time; and he told me afterwards that he thought it was womanly and well done."

"It is enough," said King Arthur. "When a good wife pleads for her erring lord, who shall deny her? Indeed, it seems to me that all are for him and none against him. Is there yet another voice to plead for King Mark?"

Then spoke the mother of King Arthur, the aged Igerna.

"There is mine, my son," she said. "King Mark is of kin to my first lord, Gorlois, the lover and wedded husband of my youth, before I was wife to Uther Pendragon, thy sire."

Thereupon, King Arthur said no more. But he rose up from his place, and slowly departed out of the hall.

After but a little delay, caused doubtless by a dislike to meet the many eyes that would be bent on him, at the lower end of the hall appeared King Mark: not as a captive, bound by chains; but led forward by no other hand than that of Arthur, the Most Christian King.

As soon as King Mark was seated in the place of greatest honour, next to Igerna, King Arthur spoke.

"In honour of our new guest," said he, "let the tale and the song go round."

Then the great beakers were filled anew: guest pledged guest as if a great conquest had been won in the land; and many a pleasant tale and touching song wiled away the last trace of care from the softened heart of King Mark.

But enough for the present hour. The chronicler of these will—God willing—at a fitting time record other tales of other Feasts of Camelot.

---

11. Mother of Alisaunder the Orphan.

King Arthur
A Drama in a Prologue and Four Acts

by

J. COMYNS CARR

DRAMATIS PERSONAE

KING ARTHUR
SIR LANCELOT
SIR MORDRED
SIR KAY
SIR GAWAINE
SIR BEDEVERE
SIR AGRAVAINE
SIR PERCIVAL
SIR LAVAINE
SIR DAGONET
MERLIN
MESSENGER
GAOLER

GUINEVERE
ELAINE
MORGAN LE FAY
CLARISSANT
SPIRIT OF THE LAKE

KNIGHTS, SQUIRES, LADIES OF THE COURT, ETC., ETC.

SYNOPSIS OF SCENERY

PROLOGUE
EXCALIBUR.
SCENE—THE MAGIC MERE.

ACT I
THE HOLY GRAIL.
SCENE—THE GREAT HALL AT CAMELOT.

ACT II
THE QUEEN'S MAYING.
SCENE—THE WHITETHORN WOOD.

ACT III
THE BLACK BARGE.
SCENE—THE TOWER ABOVE THE RIVER AT CAMELOT.

ACT IV
THE PASSING OF ARTHUR.
SCENE 1—THE QUEEN'S PRISON AT CAMELOT.
SCENE 2—THE GREAT HALL AT CAMELOT.

THE PROLOGUE

EXCALIBUR

SCENE:—*The magic Mere. A wide lake with a rocky path descending to the shore. As the curtain rises there is a faint glimmer on the horizon, which gradually spreads over the water to an effect of dawn.*

CHORUS OF LAKE SPIRITS [*singing*].

Dawn and daytime turn to night,
Darkness wakes to morning light;
All the uncounted hours go by
Swift as clouds across the sky,
While we maidens of the mere,
Heedless of the changing year,
Guard the sword Excalibur.

During the concluding bars of the chorus, Arthur, accompanied by Merlin, appears on the summit of the rocky path.

ARTHUR. What shore is this, haunted by mystic sounds
That are not earthly?
MERLIN.   'Tis no earthly shore,
Nor, till this hour, have mortal eyes beheld
These fairy sands.

ARTHUR. Then thou shalt go alone;
For here, perchance, thy magic arts have power
To lure my soul.
MERLIN. Nay, Arthur, have no fear.
A mightier power than mine had led thy feet
There where I found thee sleeping by the lake:
For whilst I watched a star fell in the sky,
And from the vacant space of Heaven, there came
A voice that cried, "Awake! the hour hath struck:
Now guide him, Merlin, to that caverned home
Where dwells the sacred sword Excalibur."
ARTHUR. What is this sword?
MERLIN. Look well and thou shalt see.
As he speaks an arm rises from the Lake holding aloft a jewelled sword set in its scabbard, which gleams with supernatural light.

CHORUS OF LAKE SPIRITS

Sword, no mortal shall withstand,
Fashioned by no mortal hand,
Long we wait the hour shall bring
England's sword to England's King;
He shall wield Excalibur.

MERLIN. What think'st thou, Arthur?
ARTHUR. Nay, I have no word.
Whence comes this sword?
MERLIN. Long time, ere Time began,
'Twas forged beneath the sea; its glittering blade,
Was tempered by the waves; sea-maidens wrought
Its jewelled scabbard, and that warrior king
Whose arm is strong to wield it in the fight,
Shall rule a kingdom that shall rule the sea.
ARTHUR [*musing*]. For such a sword 'twere well to give the
world,
With such a sword 'twere well to rule the world.
Who is this king?
MERLIN. Nay, list, and thou shalt hear.

CHORUS OF LAKE SPIRITS

Warrior knight, into thy hand,
Monarch of a mighty land

That, in unborn years, shall be
Monarch of the mightier sea;
Great Pendragon's son, to thee
We shall yield Excalibur.
The sword again slowly sinks into the Lake.

ARTHUR. Who is Pendragon's son?
MERLIN.   Thou art the man;
Pendragon's son, albeit thou know'st it not;
For at thy birth I took thee from the Court.
Deep in the woods—a flower amid the flowers—
I watched beside thee, heard thine infant tongue
First lisp responsive to the woodland birds,
And by thy cradle, swung beneath the stars,
Taught thee the wisdom that should fit a throne.
Now art thou called! Stand forth and take thy sword,
Whose might alone can stay these wasting wars,
Whose might alone shall bring the realm of peace.
        ARTHUR [*rising*]. Then was my dream no dream; for while I
                slept
I heard the noise of battle, and I saw
The flashing of innumerable spears
Lightening the dark of Heaven; then I rose
And rode into the strife, and, where I led,
The mightiest fell before me, and men cried,
"It is the King!" Yet did I heed them not,
For in mine ears there rang a clarion voice
Which said, "Nay, stay not till the end is won!
Fight on, thine arm is mightier than theirs,
Fight on, an unborn empire claims thy sword,
Fight on, they strike for glory, thou for peace!"
Long time the battle lasted, and the end
Seemed afar off; yet at the end it came,
And, ere my arm grew weary, I could hear
A hush upon the thunder; and the noise
And cry of war grew fainter, till it fell
To echoing silence. Then far off I saw,
Set in a redd'ning sky of blood and fire,
A face most fair that wore an angel smile;
And down the unending avenue of spears
It drew towards me, seeming as it came
Like a white rose leaf borne upon the tide

Of crimson war. Whereat I knelt and said,
"I have fought for thee, thou hast the smile of peace;"
Yet answer made she none, and I awoke.
Ah, thou who know'st the secrets of the stars,
Tell me whose face I saw!—
    MERLIN.   Nay, ask not that.
    ARTHUR. I will be answered! all the world to me
Dwells in that smile.
    MERLIN.   Then look upon thy fate.
    As he speaks a vision of Guinevere appears. Arthur kneels.
    ARTHUR. Who art thou? Speak!
    MERLIN.   Listen, and thou shalt hear.
    At this a chorus of unseen spirits is heard.

CHORUS

Fairest form of all the earth!
Joy and sorrow at one birth;
Love and beauty, hope and fear,
Wait for thee in Guinevere.

MERLIN.
    Love and beauty, hope and fear,
    Wait for thee in Guinevere.
Thou hearest, Arthur?
    ARTHUR.   Nay, I do but see
A form too fair for this rough world's embrace,
Fit for a kingdom that no sword can win;
Yet would I win thee, take thee for my Queen.
Ah, say she shall be mine!
    MERLIN.   Fate answers thee,
Yet in that gift of beauty lurks thy doom.

ECHOING CHORUS

Love and beauty, hope and fear,
Wait for thee in Guinevere.

    ARTHUR. These fairy tongues are false, for, see, she bears
The emblems of the spring: all the new world
Leaps into flower about her; and the may
Trails its white blossom round those stainless brows.
    MERLIN. Yet thou shouldst know full many a poisonous weed
Grows rank amid the blossoms of the may.

CHORUS

Love and Hate are born in May;
Love, the bird upon the wing,
Hate, the worm devouring
All Love's flowers of yesterday,
    Wait for thee in Guinevere.
The vision fades.

MERLIN.
    All Love's flowers of yesterday,
        Wait for thee in Guinevere.
    ARTHUR. Thou wilt not stay! then I will seek for thee,
And through the world, if thou art of the world,
I'll find thee, crown thee, Guinevere, my Queen!

ECHOING CHORUS

All Love's flowers of yesterday,
    Wait for thee in Guinevere.

    ARTHUR. And yet those mystic voices chaunt of doom!
Ah, thou whose vision spans futurity,
Hath not thy magic art all power to stay
The hand of Fate?
    MERLIN. Our knowledge is not power.
Who knows the end of Life hath reached the end.
His wisdom is but Death; while ye, who stand
Eager to thread the winding maze o' the world,
Led on by faith, do more than angels dare.
Such destiny is thine: for thy right arm
Out of this mound of earth shall raise a throne
Whose glory echoes through unacted time—
Wherefore I charge thee ask no more of fate.
The hand of doom is patient, and the sword
That flashes in the glimmering light of dawn
Falls not till night-fall: thou shalt rule thy day.
    ARTHUR. I'll ask no more; I do but crave my sword.

> *The Spirit of the Lake appears, and at the same time the sword rises
> again from the Lake.*

MERLIN. Thy prayer is answered, she will give it thee.

THE SPIRIT OF THE LAKE

Arthur, England's chosen lord,
Fear not Fate but take thy sword;
Thou the first whose mortal hand
E'er hath touched that mystic brand.
Sword and scabbard both are thine,
Sword and scabbard both divine:
Guard them well and use them well,
So that aftertime shall tell
Of thy kingdom in the sea,
Blazoned on whose shield shall be,
"Right and Might and Liberty."
[Arthur makes a movement toward the sword.]
Yet beware! Time's beating wing,
Restless and untiring,
Speeds along Time's endless way.
Bravely thou shalt rule thy day,
And at last, when Day is done,
Those three Queens of Avalon,
Rulers of the night, who keep
In their charge the keys of sleep,
Far across this mystic mere
Silently thy barge shall steer,
Till thy wearied eyes have won
Endless sleep in Avalon.

ARTHUR. He who would rule the day must greet the dawn.
There is no hour to lose; give me my sword,
For, echoing through the night, I too can hear
The voice of England, like a sobbing child
That longs for day; and, gathering in night's sky,
I see that throng of England's unborn sons,
Whose glory is her glory: prisoned souls
With faces pressed against the bars of Time,
Waiting their destined hour. Give me my sword,
That I may loose Time's bonds and set them free.
     *The chorus is heard, and the picture is held till the fall of the
     curtain.*

CHORUS
Great Pendragon's greater son,
Arthur, ere thy race be run,
Thou shalt rule from sea to sea
England that is yet to be:
Great Pendragon's son, to thee
Here we yield Excalibur.

ACT I

THE HOLY GRAIL.

SCENE:—*The Great Hall at Camelot. A wide opening breast high at the
back, flanked by marble columns, through which is seen a view of blue hills
against a sunset sky.*

Sir Kay, Sir Agravaine, and Sir Bedevere, to whom enters Sir Lancelot.

KAY. Sir Lancelot, this falls well: of late our King
Hath ofttimes asked for thee, and thou shalt learn
The noise of thy great deeds hath far outstripped
Thy good steed's swiftest course, waiting thee here
To swell love's welcome home. What news from Wales?
    LANCELOT. In Wales men speak in whispers; yet 'tis known
That Ryons,[1] lately joined in secret league
With Mark of Cornwall, doth but wait the hour
To strike at Arthur's throne.
    AGRAVAINE.   This news comes pat,[2]
Not three days past, deep in the belt of wood
That circles round Caerleon's clustering towers,
Sir Gawaine's huntsmen chanced upon two spies,
Who now lie fast in chains.
    KAY.   And at this hour
The King holds council, and shall straight declare
If they may live or die.
    AGRAVAINE. Should Gawaine speak
And Arthur listen they were dead ere night.
    GAWAINE. That is most sure.

---

1. Traditionally, a king of Ireland who demands Arthur's beard as a sign of
subservience.

2. Opportunely.

LANCELOT.   Which way doth Mordred tend?

AGRAVAINE. Truth, that were hard to tell! his subtle tongue
Still weaves a web to catch the thought of others,
And hide his own.

LANCELOT. And what then saith the King?

KAY. He waits upon the word of Guinevere.

GAWAINE. I dare be sworn this thing hath troubled him.

KAY. What should he fear though Mark and Ryons, joined
With all the hosts of Cornwall and of Wales,
Knocked at our gates.

LANCELOT. Nay, sirs, he knows not fear,
Whose warrior heart was bred where spears have grown
Thick as the river reeds. Yet in that heart
Dwells a fond nursling hope this news will slay;
For since the coming of Queen Guinevere
The sword Excalibur hath hung at rest
Within its jewelled scabbard, and he dreamed
The lust of blood was past.

KAY.   Would that were all!
King Arthur grieves, but 'tis with graver cause.

LANCELOT. What cause?

KAY.   What cause!

GAWAINE.   In truth we do forget.
Sir Lancelot knows not that at vesper[3] time
A hundred knights of Arthur's fellowship
Take a long leave of Camelot and the King.

LANCELOT. Bound on what quest?

KAY.   No earthly quest is theirs
Who've ta'en a vow to seek the Holy Grail.

LANCELOT. To seek the Grail! Now, sirs, you mock at me!
For who, of mortal born, shall hope to find,
Searching through all the world, that holy cup
Charged with Christ's blood? That cup no eye hath seen
Since long ago to this White Isle 'twas borne
By Joseph, who had filled it at the Cross.[4]
What Heaven hath hid no man may dare to seek,
Save by a sign from Heaven.

---

3. Evening (from the canonical hour of vespers, when evening prayers were said).

4. According to legend, Joseph of Arimathea caught the blood of the crucified Christ in a cup. This sacred vessel became the Holy Grail.

KAY.   Heaven's sign hath come
In miracle and wonder: three nights past—
When all our company were sat at meat—
Above the murmur of the feast there leapt
The crack and cry of thunder, and the roof
Was cloven as with a sword: then down the hall,
Aslant upon a bar of light that gleamed
As though the sun were turned to molten gold,
Passed a white angel, bearing in her hands
The sacred vision of the cup of Christ.
LANCELOT. What like was it to see?
During the following speech the hall darkens.
KAY.   That none may tell,
For, dimly veilèd in a cloth of white,
It went as it had come, unseen of all.
Yet while it passed it left, though none knew how,
The witness of its presence in men's eyes;
And, dumbly gazing, each in other found
The stamp of some new glory; then uprose
Our youngest knight, Sir Percival, and cried:
"Now thanks for what hath been and what shall be!
For here I vow to rest not till these eyes
Have openly beheld the cup itself!"
And, as one note at dawn will wake the woods,
Voice after voice re-echoed Percival's,
Till, one by one, a hundred of our knights
Had joined themselves unto this holy quest.
LANCELOT. If this be so—
GAWAINE.   Why, sir, 'twas in this hall!
KAY. And close upon this hour.
A peal of thunder is heard, followed by a lightning flash.
LANCELOT.   What cry was that?
KAY. Nay, see, 'tis here again.
*As he speaks, a slanting ray of light falls through the hall,
enfolding the form of a maiden bearing the cup, from the centre
of which a red light strikes like a star through the transparent
veil that covers it. Sir Lancelot kneels as the vision passes and
disappears.*
LANCELOT.   Ah, go not yet!
'Tis gone! and did mine eyes not vouch 'twas here,
I'd say it was a dream; for never yet
Hath mortal vision gazed on aught so fair!

Didst thou not note how all the air was filled
With sweetest odours?
      GAWAINE.   So it was before.
      KAY. Said we not truth?
      LANCELOT [*rising*]. Ay, and by this I know
That age of marvels, long ago foretold
By Merlin, when he built our Table Round,
Hath come at last; and we who live to-day
Shall witness wonders great and terrible
Shaking the earth, until that happier hour
When he whom God hath chosen of us all
With mortal eyes shall pierce Heaven's mystery,
And see the Grail itself.
      GAWAINE.   'Twas said last night,
That he alone shall win this saving grace
Whose heart stands clear of sin.
      LANCELOT.   Ay, sir, 'tis so.
And he alone who wills it so can pierce
The secrets of our hearts! Not all may win,
Yet straining at the goal there's none can lose
The grace that comes of strife.

      Mordred has entered unseen during the last speech, carrying a
      scroll in his hand.

      MORDRED.   How now, Sir Knights,
Ye do forget the hour! Have ye not heard
That they whose names are duly here enrolled,
Bound by their vows to seek the Holy Grail,
Within a breathing space shall take their leave
Of Arthur and his Court?
      LANCELOT.   I pray you, sir,
Of your good grace add my name to the roll.
      MORDRED. Hast thou considered well?
      LANCELOT.   My lord, I have,
And shall be ready when the list is called.
      Exit Lancelot.
      MORDRED [*half to himself*]. So Lancelot goes!
      KAY.   I dare be
      sworn he will not,
Nay, though his oath were loudest of them all,
Yet Arthur's love will hold him.

MORDRED [*turning fiercely upon Kay*]. Who dares speak
So gross a treason 'gainst our lord the King?
In truth, Sir Kay, I thought thee worthier
Of Arthur's love.
      KAY.   Nay, sir, I did but think
That Lancelot, who is worthier than us all,
Would go or stay as that same love commands.
      MORDRED. And thou! and thou! yet think ye that the King,
Who loves him best and knows him worthiest,
Would bid him break his vow? Now, hark'e, sirs:
Ye know not him ye worship, and your praise
Is but a vapour that doth hide the sun,
But ye shall know him! Nay, sirs, tarry not,
But see that all is ready for the King.
      KAY. Be sure, my lord, we shall not fail the King.
      Exeunt Kay and other Knights.
      MORDRED [*alone*]. Yea, Arthur's love would hold him, but it
      shall not.
Lancelot shall go, and, in that vacant seat
Where now his heart sits guardian to the King,
Envenomed hate shall keep a closer watch.
Lancelot shall go.

      Enter Morgan.

Ah! mother, thou art here.
What saith the Queen?
      MORGAN.   She doth attend the council.
      MORDRED. And her voice?
      MORGAN.   Is tuned to plead for mercy.
      MORDRED. 'Tis well, for Arthur heeds no voice save hers.
These dogs whose tongues I feared will now go free.
      MORGAN. Then tell me, boy, what tidings did they bear?
      MORDRED. The gathered hosts of Cornwall and of Wales
Wait but my sign.
      MORGAN. They shall not wait for long.
The year grows green, and May-day comes again—
Day of thy birth, and day of Arthur's doom.
      MORDRED. Of Arthur's doom?
      MORGAN.   Ay, for 'twas so foretold,
Ere yet thine eyes had opened on the world,
That he whose hand should strike at Arthur's heart

On May-day must be born. And thou art he,
For in thy veins an avenging poison flows,
Distilled in that dark hour when Merlin's lips
Hailed Arthur as Pendragon's rightful heir,
And left me bastard.
   MORDRED. Ay, yet one thing lacks:
Think you, will Lancelot join this holy quest?
   MORGAN. What should you fear, though Lancelot go or stay?
   MORDRED. I fear, yet know not what—his loyal love
Twines around Arthur like a coil of steel
That turns the keenest edge. Yea, well I know
That while Sir Lancelot stays, the King is safe.
   MORGAN. Thou fool! the King were safer if he went.
   MORDRED. What dost thou say?
   MORGAN.   I say what thou shouldst know:
The King doth love Sir Lancelot?
   MORDRED.   Ay, too well!
   MORGAN. Too well, in truth, for next the King stands one
Who loves him more than well.
   MORDRED.   Not Guinevere?
   MORGAN. Ay, she!
   MORDRED.   This is thy malice.
   MORGAN.   Think'st thou so?
Trust me, 'tis true—a woman hath no wiles
To hide her secret from a woman's gaze,
Whose eyes are never blindfold. Dost forget
When the news came of Lancelot's heavy wound
How she did weep and wail?
   MORDRED.   So did the King.
   MORGAN. Ay, truth, so did the King; yet that's not all;
For later, when the happier tidings came
That, tended by Elaine, his wound was whole,
Hadst thou but seen her then! The King made glad,
But Guinevere's white lips could shape no smile.
Her jealous heart was torn.
   MORDRED.   If this be so,
And Lancelot loves her too, then all are trapped!
   MORGAN. Nay, take it not from me, look for thyself.
   Herald's trumpet heard without.
But see she comes, take heed and guard thy tongue.

  Enter Guinevere.

MORDRED. Madam, what saith the King?
GUINEVERE.   Hast thou not heard?
Thy mother's prayer for mercy hath prevailed.
The spies are pardoned.
MORDRED. Why then, 'tis to thee
They owe their right to live.
GUINEVERE.   Nay, to the King!
Who knowing naught of fear, fears naught to spare
Where weaker hearts would slay. To-day at eve
Our knights ride forth upon a Holy Quest;
At such a season then it was not fit
That on their spotless banners there should rest
The smirch of hireling[5] blood.
MORGAN.   Madam, the King!

Enter Arthur, with Knights attending.

ARTHUR. Our faithful knights do know th' appointed hour.
MORDRED. My lord, they wait your call.
ARTHUR.   Give me the roll.
   Mordred hands scroll to the King.
Is all complete?
MORDRED. Nay, truth, I had forgot:
One name is lacking there.
ARTHUR.   Whose name is that?
Stand there not here enough of goodly knights
That I must lose from our great fellowship,
But ye would cry for more?
MORDRED.   Your pardon, Sire,
I did but learn it now, within the hour:
Sir Lancelot hath returned.
ARTHUR.   Well, sir, what then?
GUINEVERE [*starting*]. Sir Lancelot home!
MORGAN [*approaching her*].   Ay, madam, he is
   here.
ARTHUR. Lancelot is welcome home.
MORDRED.   Yet 'tis to fear
He comes but to depart.
ARTHUR.   What mean you, sir?
MORDRED. He, too, my lord, would join this Holy Quest.

_____

5. Mercenary.

ARTHUR. Sir Lancelot? Nay, you jest! this shall not be.
Go straight and send him here.

MORDRED.   My lord, I will. [*Exit Mordred.*

GUINEVERE. Morgan, thou hast our leave.
    Exeunt Morgan, Ladies of the Court, and Knights.

                                              Nay, good my lord,
This troubles thee.

ARTHUR. It would an[6] it were true;
For, as each added name summed up the list,
Methought though all should go, yet one remains;
Flower of all knighthood, Lancelot, thou at least
Shalt stand beside thy King!

GUINEVERE.   Yet should he go
Thou still hast that which serves thee more than all,
Thy sword Excalibur, whose mystic blade
Hath carved this Island Empire from the sea,—
Thou hast thy goodly sword.

ARTHUR.   Ay, and my Queen,
Whose dear commands are set as Heaven's high voice,
Lifting me nearer Heaven.

GUINEVERE.   Trust thy sword,
'Twill serve thee better far.

ARTHUR.   Long time gone by,
When this same sword by magic hands was given,
Old Merlin said, Take heed and guard it well;
Yet guard the scabbard too, for that is more
E'en than the blade it sheathes. I knew not then
If he spoke false or true: I know it now.
For at thy coming, Guinevere, my Queen,
The havoc turned to harvest at thy feet;
From out the bellowing throat of war there came
A sweeter, softer music, and the earth,
New christened by thy smile, broke forth in flower.
Thou art our scabbard, and in thy pure soul,
Where only peace may dwell, our sword lies sheathed!
Yet that rich dower thy father gave with thee,
That image of the world, our Table Round,
A kingdom's heart set in a rim of steel
Forged of the spears of all the goodliest knights

---

6. If.

Of all the earth; that too must count for much,
And if he now should fail that out of all
Hath shown himself the mightiest, then I think
Our day draws to its end.

Enter Lancelot.

                           Most welcome home!
It was but now I learned from Mordred's lips
Thou too wouldst join this quest.
        LANCELOT.   'Tis so, my lord.
        ARTHUR. If that same word by other lips were spoken
I'd say 'twas false. Dost thou so lightly count
Our long-tried love, that, without word or sign,
Thou'dst quit our side? Nay, but I wrong thee there,
For we are one, and haply thou hast told
Thy purpose to the Queen.
        GUINEVERE.   Not so, indeed.
I heard it not till now.
        LANCELOT.   Nay, hear me, Arthur.
I have no life, no soul that is not thine,
No heart but waits some fitting hour to bleed
In thy great cause; yet, couldst thou see that heart
And know its present sickness, thou wouldst say:
Lancelot, ride forth, thou hast our willing leave.
        ARTHUR. Thinkest thou so? We'll speak of this again.
        LANCELOT. Thy voice alone shall bid me go or stay.
        Exit Lancelot.
        ARTHUR. And thou shalt stay, for now I do divine
This sickness at thy heart. [*Turning to Guinevere.*] Canst thou not
        guess?
        GUINEVERE. Indeed I cannot.
        ARTHUR.   'Tis some cause of love
That bids him go.
        GUINEVERE [*starting*]. Of love?
        ARTHUR.   Ay, dear, of love!
Didst think that our two hearts had drained love's springs?
Thou hast not heard, but, ere thy coming hither,
'Twas known that Lancelot wooed the fair Elaine.
        GUINEVERE. 'Twas she that nursed him when his wound was
        sore?

ARTHUR. Ay, true, 'twas she; but even then their loves
Had drifted wide asunder, and of late
He has not breathed her name.
      GUINEVERE.   Why then 'tis sure
He loves her not.
      ARTHUR. In love there's naught that's sure.
Yet is he framed in such a constant mould
That truly I believe he loves her still.
Some little knot hath ravelled up the skein
That links their hearts. There needs a woman's wit
To set the tangle straight.
      GUINEVERE.   A woman's wit?
      ARTHUR. Ay, dear, and thine.
      GUINEVERE.   Indeed, I think not so.
      ARTHUR. Indeed 'tis so: bid Lancelot come to thee;
Thy tongue will find a charm that may unlock
The guarded secret of his chafing heart.
         Guinevere does not move.
Nay, thou wilt do 't? if our all happy love
Hath known no jar, then must we search the more
To find the missing note for those whose souls
Are not so finely tuned.
      GUINEVERE.   Then thou art sure
Thou art all happy?
      ARTHUR.   Nay, how canst thou ask?
      GUINEVERE. A little field-flower, lighted by a star,
Stands but a tiny speck beneath that lamp
Which shines o'er half the world; yet once it dreamed
That this great beacon light was all its own.
'Tis long since thou hast spoken of thy love,
Dost know how long?
      ARTHUR.   That is the fate of kings,
Whose lives are as a picture for the world,
Not for their own content. When we were wed,
I dreamed of many an hour when we would sit,
Thy hand in mine, recalling that sweet day
When, like a flash of sunlight through the trees,
I saw thy face at Cameliard; but now
The busy hours slip by, each new day brings
Its burden of new duty, and our loves
Are too long silent. Yet full well thou know'st—
      Approaching her.

GUINEVERE [*interrupting him and making away*]. Yes, yes, I
    know; heed not my idle words.
It was a foolish thought that slipped my tongue.
I'll do thy bidding straight.

    Enter Morgan.

MORGAN. Your pardon, madam, but the fair Elaine
Is newly come from Astolat, and craves
An audience with the Queen.
    ARTHUR.   Now this falls well.
So you shall plead for both.
    GUINEVERE [*to Morgan*]. I'll see her here.
Go tell Sir Lancelot I would speak with him.
    Exit Morgan.
    ARTHUR. And later, when Sir Lancelot's name is called,
'Tis thou shalt bid him stay. Till then, farewell!
    Exit Arthur.
    GUINEVERE. Farewell! [*Guinevere is left alone.*
Am I so weak that every random word
Can shake my heart? When Arthur said but now,
"It is some cause of love bids Lancelot go,"
I trembled like a thief that's trapped at night.
For, in his god-like gaze, I thought I saw
The searching eyes of God; piercing my soul,
Where lurks the shameful secret of my love
That none must know. Ah me, if Lancelot knew!
How he would spurn me! But he shall not know.
Wherefore 'twere better he should go away;
For while he was away, within my heart
His image dwelt securely, like a star
Hung high above me in a stainless sky,—
A lamp illumined with a fireless flame
That wrought no ill,—but now, when he is by,
The light grows blinding, and its fiercer rays
Consume my very soul.

    She stands wrapt in thought as enter Elaine.

ELAINE. Thy pardon, madam. Morgan bade me come.
    She kneels as Guinevere turns to her.

GUINEVERE [*aside*]. Indeed, but she is fair! [*Aloud.*] Nay, do
    not kneel.   [*Elaine rises.*
What wouldst thou with me?
    ELAINE.   'Twas but yester eve,
Within thy garden by the castle wall,
For the first time I saw thee with thy maids,
Where, 'midst them all, thy prouder beauty seemed
To wear the gentlest smile; 'twas then I thought:
"Could I but see the Queen, I'd tell my heart
And win her favour." Now methinks I erred.
    GUINEVERE. Has, then, my face so changed?
    ELAINE.   Sweet lady, no.
Yet in thy presence my poor lips are dumb.
    GUINEVERE. Then I must speak for thee: sit near me here.
    Elaine sits at her feet.
So, thou art she our great Sir Lancelot loves?
I do not wonder.
    ELAINE. I did think so once.
    GUINEVERE. Be sure he loves thee still.
    ELAINE.   Ah, would 'twere so!
    GUINEVERE. Was then his love so sweet? tell me how sweet.
    ELAINE. I scarce knew then; for all the uncounted joys
Of that brief time seemed but an earnest paid
From Love's unbounded store. Now, when all's lost,
Remembrance feeds my grief and, drowned in tears,
Brings back each little token of his love
That passed unheeded then.
    GUINEVERE.   There's joy in that—
He loved thee once; methinks I know some hearts
Would take thy sorrow's burden but to win
What thou dost still possess: but tell me more.
Such love, if love it were, could not so end
Without a cause—perchance the fault was thine.
    ELAINE. I think so too, and yet I know not how.
The end came all so swiftly: on that day
When he rode forth I do remember well
I scarce was sad, our parting was so sweet.
But, when he came again, it was as though
The night had fallen at noontide; all was changed.
    GUINEVERE. What time was that?
    ELAINE.   Ah, madam, thou canst date
My sorrow with thy joy.

GUINEVERE [*rising suddenly*]. What dost thou say?

ELAINE. Nay, be not angered: so it chanced to fall,
In that same hour when thou, new crowned a Queen,
Didst come from Cameliard as Arthur's bride—
My love was lost. 'Twas Lancelot brought thee here.

GUINEVERE. Ay, was it so? In truth I had forgot.
Yes, sure, 'twas he. And now thou think'st that I
Can win thy love again! How shall that be?

ELAINE. Hold Lancelot to thy side, I ask but that!
Let him not go to-day upon this quest,
Whence none, perchance, shall live to win his way
Back to King Arthur's court. Ah, bind him here,
That so my love, by some sweet chance, may find
The path it missed before, and creep again
Back to that heart that once did seem its home!
Thou dost not answer?

GUINEVERE.   Hush, what sound is that?

CHAUNT OF THE KNIGHTS [*WITHOUT*]

Look not to thy sword,
     Fame is but a breath,
That, for all reward,
     Brings thee only death.
Rise, and go forth with us who seek the Grail,
     Winning for reward
     Fame that shall not fail.

ELAINE [*who has gone to the back*]. It is the chaunt of those who
     seek the Grail.
See, they make ready. Lancelot is not there!

GUINEVERE. Go, leave me now, for I must speak with him,
And think what I may do to serve thee best.

ELAINE [*kissing her hand*]. Ah, would I owned thy crown that
     may command,
Or thou my love, that so he needs must yield!
     Exit Elaine.

GUINEVERE. And would I ne'er had seen thee, for thy words
Have set my heart on fire! Can it be so?
That then when first we met his love did change?
It is not so, and his own lips shall speak
And say 'tis false, or else I shall go mad.

Enter Lancelot.

Ah, thou art here. Why is thy mind so bent
To leave the court? The King would know the cause.
Think'st thou, because thy favour stands so high
In fame of earthly deeds, that thou shalt win
This heavenly crown?
      LANCELOT. Indeed, I think not so.
His eyes alone shall see that holy cup,
Whose soul stands clear of sin.
      GUINEVERE.   What boots it then
To adventure all upon a hopeless quest?
      LANCELOT. Ay, hopeless, for I may not touch the goal.
Yet once, when I lay stricken nigh to death,
By this same vessel of the Sangrael
My hurt was cured; now, when my heart is pierced,
Though by no mortal stroke of sword or spear,
Perchance again that same sweet miracle
May heal my deeper wound.
      GUINEVERE.   I know thy wound.
      LANCELOT. If that were so I should be shamed indeed!
      GUINEVERE. Indeed, 'tis so. Elaine was here but now.
I did not dream that all the world could show
So fair a maid. No marvel that thy heart
Is sick with love.
      LANCELOT. Madam, I love her not!
      GUINEVERE. Nay, that is false: think it no shame to own
What, in some angry fit, thy tongue denied.
      LANCELOT. My shame lies deeper, seeing I once vowed
A love that now lies dead.
      GUINEVERE.   Elaine's soft eyes
Will find Love's tomb, and charm it back to life.
Go to her now, and plead thy suit again;
I'll warrant you will find her not too hard,
Your wooing is half done.
      LANCELOT.   Urge me no more,
For here, by Heaven, I swear I love her not.
      GUINEVERE. Then wherefore wouldst thou enter on this
          quest?
      LANCELOT. Nay, madam, in thy pity, spare me that!
      GUINEVERE. I will be answered. Am I not thy Queen?

LANCELOT. Thou art indeed, and therefore hast thy will!
I had thought to pass away and leave behind
The dear remembrance of thy loyal love
I once deserved. But now that too has gone,
For thou wouldst wring the secret from my lips,
That brands me traitor.

GUINEVERE.   Traitor!

LANCELOT.   Aye! 'Tis true,
And thou hast known it, else thy gracious heart
Were not so pitiless: 'twas for this I've seen
Those veiled eyes cloak the hate they scorned to tell,
When, by some evil chance, their gaze met mine;
For this thy gentle smile took sudden flight
When I passed by.

GUINEVERE. No! no! no more, no more!

LANCELOT. Nay, madam, drink thy vengeance to the fill.
I leave the court because I love its Queen!

Flings himself at her feet.

GUINEVERE. I did not hear thee; speak that word again.

LANCELOT. Ay, once again, I love thee; all my shame
Lies naked at thy feet; I do but crave
That here my life may end.

GUINEVERE.   Nay, do not rise.
There's something I would say, yet know not how;
For if thy life must end, then so must mine.
You cannot guess my shame.

LANCELOT.   Thou hast no shame,
Save that which my base love hath laid on thee!

GUINEVERE. Indeed, I have. Oft when we kneel and pray
Before God's image bleeding on the Cross,
We cheat our souls, for our vain hearts still seek
The manhood, not the God: 'twas so with me.
That hour when Arthur came, it seemed as though
Christ's hand had beckoned, and I knelt to him,
And, in the mist of worship, thought I saw,
The wingèd heart of love. But when you came,
His great ambassador from Camelot,
I saw Love's heart indeed, and knew I loved—
But not the King.

LANCELOT. What say'st thou? Not the King?
Wouldst make me mad?

GUINEVERE.   Ah me, that home-coming

When we two rode in silence side by side,
And all my heart was hungry for a word!
The blossoms of the springtime turned to flame—
And yet you spoke not; now it is too late.
> *She moves away.*

LANCELOT [*rising*]. No, not too late, unless those lips are
> false.
Ah! hear me now—thou wouldst have heard me then.
My lonely love I could have borne alone,
Counting this mortal life too short a term
Of exile for my sin; but now that's past,
And, through the darkness, like a sudden star,
Thy heart stands clear, lighting our sweeter way.
Nay, do not turn thy face, thou knowest 'tis so.
Love speaks at last—and Love will be obeyed.
> *He moves towards her, and she turns as if to yield to his embrace*
> *when the chaunt of the Knights breaks forth again, and the*
> *movement is arrested.*

> Look not to thy love,
>> Love that lives an hour;
> Heaven's voice above
>> Calls thee from her bower.
> Rise, and go forth, with us who seek the Grail,
>> Winning from above
>> Love that shall not fail.

GUINEVERE. Yea, truth, 'tis love that speaks! But not our love,
The love of Heaven, of honour, and of—him.

> Rise, and go forth, with us who seek the Grail,
>> Winning from above
>> Love that shall not fail.

It is their voice that calls, and thou wilt go.
I thought to hold thee here—I may not now.
> LANCELOT. My shame is dumb; yet, in thy purer heart,
I may find grace to save what still remains
Of my wrecked soul: my trust stands all in thee.
> GUINEVERE. Nay, trust thyself.
> LANCELOT. Thy word must be my law.
> GUINEVERE. Wait not for that; a woman is too weak

To guard what's best in what she loves the best.
We shall not speak again. [*Exit Guinevere.*
     LANCELOT.   Ay, once again,
When from thy lips shall come the dread command
That sends me hence; and like a flaming sword
Love bars the gate of this new paradise
Which love hath won; yet through the desert night
Of life's long pilgrimage, one star shall stay,
And when death comes at last, to end our quest,
My fainting heart shall quicken at the thought,
'Twas thou didst bid me go.

     Enter a Squire.

                        Ah, thou art here.
Put on my sword.

     The trumpet sounds as Arthur enters, preceded by a procession of
     Priests and Choristers chaunting the song of the Grail, while
     the hall fills with a throng of Knights. Arthur and Guinevere
     take their places on the throne, on the steps of which stands
     Elaine next the Queen.

          THE CHAUNT OF THE GRAIL

     Look not to thy sword,
          Fame is but a breath,
     That, for all reward,
          Brings thee only death.
Rise, and go forth with us who seek the Grail,
          Winning for reward
     Fame that shall not fail.

     At the close of the chaunt Percival comes forward from the group of
          the Knights of the Grail and kneels before Arthur.
     PERCIVAL. Here, at thy feet, for all whose vows are sworn,
I kneel and crave thy favour ere we go.
What strange new ways our wandering feet will press,
What dread adventures wait us, none can tell.
Yet this we know, our fealty to thee
Shall stand unbroken, and through all the world
We bear the spotless blazon of thy fame!
     ARTHUR. Rise, Percival, and ye who kneel with him,

Take your new way; ye have our leave to go;
Which yet, if that might be, we could withhold.
The magic circle of our Table Round,
Is broken here: wherefore, in truth, my heart
Is sore within me, and my lips hold back
The message of Farewell. Yet must it be;
For well I know your vows are sworn to Him
Whose voice outbids the mandate of a king.
Therefore ride forth—we wait your glad return!

> *Percival passes out, followed by the other Knights of the Grail, who
> kneel as they pass the throne. At the last comes Lancelot.
> Arthur stops him.*

 ARTHUR. Nay, Lancelot, what is this?
 LANCELOT.   My lord, I too
Would take those vows that bind me to this quest.
 ARTHUR [*to Guinevere*]. Didst thou not speak with him?
 GUINEVERE.   I did,
  my lord.
 ARTHUR. Then had thy voice no power?
 GUINEVERE.   In truth, I think
Some mightier voice than mine doth bid him go.
 ARTHUR. Then I must speak: this quest is not for thee.
For thy rich manhood hath a holier task—
Here, by thy King, to fight for this poor world
Till that last call which sheathes our swords in sleep.
 LANCELOT. My lord, thou knowest me not. I am not fit
To stand by thee.
 ARTHUR. Nay, Lancelot, it is thou
That dost not know thyself for what thou art!
This crippled realm, how shall it find the goal,
If thou, the strongest, who hast been our staff,
If thou, the mightiest, who hast been our shield,
And thou, the gentlest, that art now our guide,
Seek thine own way towards Heaven; and so dost steal
The sun's bright rays wherewith to seek the sun,
Leaving this lonely world to grope its way
In darkness to the end? Thou shalt not go!
 LANCELOT. My lord, did I but know myself as strong
As is the weakest of these knights whose vows
Were sworn but now, it would not need thy voice
To bid me stay.

ARTHUR. Still thy resolve stands firm?
Then thou shalt hear a sager voice than ours.
Old Merlin, by whose mystic craft we read
The unturned page of Time, stand forth and speak!
     Merlin steps forward.
MERLIN.
        All shall seek the Holy Grail,
        All and all save one shall fail.
ARTHUR. Nay, leave thy riddles; shall he go or stay?
MERLIN.
        Fate doth not answer yea or nay.
        Love shall bid him go or stay!
        Love the best, or love the worst,
        Holiest love, or love accurst.
ARTHUR. Say on. What is this love that bids him go?
MERLIN. I can but read the words that Fate hath writ.
ARTHUR. Then we have done with Fate. Go, get thee hence,
And never more shall that dark face of thine
Pass, like a withered shadow, through these halls!
MERLIN.
        I go hence, yet Fate shall stay,
        Till the dawn of that dread day;
        He Pendragon's son shall slay
        That is born with the May!
     As Merlin goes out the hall grows darker, and the sunset at the back
        gleams more brightly.
GUINEVERE. My lord, I pray you call him back again!
ARTHUR. Nay, heed him not, my Queen—nor, Lancelot,
        thou!
For if indeed Love speaks with double voice,
One base, one noble, then be sure my lips
Do bear the nobler message; for the world
Tells of no higher, purer love than that
Of brother unto brother; such in truth
Is my great love for thee, that bids thee stay!
     LANCELOT. I know not how to answer for myself!
Yet, once before, when we were at debate
The verdict of our Queen did end all strife.
I crave it now, her word shall be my law!
     ARTHUR. Then thou shalt stay: for she and I are one,
With but one voice, one tongue, one heart, one soul!
Now, Guinevere, declare thy will.

GUINEVERE. My lord,
A woman is too weak to rule men's hearts.
ARTHUR. Not so, my Queen. Hath not thy purer heart,
Sole ruler over him who rules this realm,
Won, from rude wars, that sweeter crown of peace
That smiles upon our land from sea to sea?
And wouldst thou fail me now? when on thy word
The welfare of a kingdom waits in doubt—
Wouldst thou be dumb?
GUINEVERE.   Indeed, indeed I would.
ARTHUR. Nay, I command thee—speak as I would speak!
ELAINE. Ay, madam, speak! My life lies in thy word.
GUINEVERE [*after a pause, and without looking at Lancelot*]. My
lord, I do thy bidding—Lancelot, stay!

The Knights of the Grail file past, singing as they go.

Ere those lips be dumb
    That would bid thee stay;
Ere the night be come,
    Rise, and come away!
We, who go forth to seek the Holy Grail,
Win, ere night be come,
Light that shall not fail.

ACT II

THE QUEEN'S MAYING.[7]

SCENE:—*The slope of a hill in spring-time studded with bushes of
whitethorn. A company of Maidens, garlanded with white may, descend the
slope. They are followed by Guinevere and her Ladies.*

THE MAY SONG

Ere upon its snowy bed
    Lies the firstborn of the spring,
Ere the crocus lifts its head,
    Or the swallow finds its wing,
        Love is here:
Say ye then Earth's flowers shall fade?
        We shall tell ye nay:

---

7. Festivities celebrating May-Day.

> Love, the first of all flowers made,
>   Lives from May to May.
>
> He beneath whose sun-kissed feet
>   Daisies rise to kiss the sun,
> Lily, rose, and meadow-sweet,—
>   Love, that is all flowers in one,
>   Love is here.
> Heed not then the blooms that fall,
>   Dying with the day,
> Love, the sweetest flower of all,
>   Lives from May to May.

GUINEVERE. Here, on the verge of this untravelled wood,
Beneath Love's flowering banner, we have set
Our camp of war. For, know ye, ladies all,
That dread adventure whereunto ye are called
Is no poor mockery of a tournament
Such as our lords love, jousting for a prize!
Our cause is mortal; and those unseen swords
We women wield are forged to pierce men's hearts.
Whereat, if any cheek grow white with fear,
Let its poor owner straightway quit the field.
Nay, all are brave? 'tis well. Ere day had dawned
Our scouts and spies, which are the wingèd birds,
Reported that a band of swaggering knights
Did challenge our approach; 'gainst them we war.
Yet hear me—not like timorous men who find
Their courage grow from fellowship in fear,
Wherefore in serried ranks they face their foe.
Our greater strength hath ever best been proved
In single combat: so we fight to-day;
Nor need these fairer faces be encased
In casques of steel; that never was our plan—
For so indeed we should but hide from view
All Love's bright armoury that lodges there.
But, truth, I waste my breath where all are skilled
In these same arts of war. Therefore set forth,
Each on her chosen way, for in this wood
Lurks many a pleasant bower o'er-roofed with green,

Where moss and harebells[8] weave a patterned floor
With shifting tracery of added gold,
Shot from the sun's eyes, peeping through the boughs
Of flowering thorn. There should each lady lead
Her conquered knight, that so, by gentler arts,
Her love may cure the wounds that Love hath made.
So, fare we all till sunset. Haste, away!

> *As they move towards the wood Dagonet rushes in and falls on his knees before the Queen. He bears a large rough garland of flowers hanging about his neck like a horse-collar.*

DAGONET [*who is trembling with mock fear*]. Sweet ladies, save
me though ye love me not!
I am sore pressed.

GUINEVERE. What, hath some beast pursued thee?

DAGONET. Ay, truth, a most sweet beast, yet fearsome, too.

CLARISSANT. I pray you, madam, let us call these knights.
We are in danger else.

GUINEVERE. Is this your valour,
That so you quake at shadows? Shame on ye!

DAGONET. Ay, shame, for here is a beast that will harm no
lady, though at this budding season 'tis very fatal to man.

GUINEVERE. I would hear more of this beast. What form hath
it?

DAGONET. Well, to be plain yet modest withal, and not too
curious, it is in all things shaped like a woman.

GUINEVERE. Truly, a very monstrous woman that would so
pursue a fool.

DAGONET. Faith, there be many such, though 'tis only your
sage fool that fears them.

GUINEVERE. Rise, Dagonet, and tell us how it chanced.

DAGONET. Then stiffen your sinews, for 'tis a heart-shaking
legend. Hither came I through the wood, thinking of naught, and
so counting myself wise beyond my years, when of a sudden I espied
a maid who tended a herd of swine; whereat, I do confess it, I fell a-
weeping bitterly, for surely never was mortal woman so fitly
employed.

CLARISSANT. You hear him, madam.

GUINEVERE. Nay, let him run on.

---

8. A slender blue-flowered herb.

DAGONET. Ay, 'tis the finish that will cause ye to quake. For this same maid, not content with her most righteous calling, and haply moved by my tears, most artfully flung this halter about my neck, and swore a most villainous oath that she loved me well. Whereat I, being, as 'tis known, only half a fool, slipped from her embrace, and fled incontinently.

GUINEVERE. Now thou art half a man, and therefore a most complete fool, that could so dread to be loved.

DAGONET. Wherein thou art wrong, for I have a leaning that way, being very tenderly fashioned, and with a taste for red lips. But alack, I am troubled with a most constant heart that goes not with love!

GUINEVERE. How say you? Is it so wise to rail against constancy?

DAGONET. Nay, I would question thee. Canst tell me now what is most like to a river that drains to the sea?

GUINEVERE. Faith, I cannot.

DAGONET. Why, a maiden who weeps in the rain.

GUINEVERE. Where hast thou seen that?

DAGONET. Last night, where I sheltered from the storm, there passed a lady sobbing as she rode, and with her tears the rain kept even tune; 'twas a sweet contest, yet I'll warrant her eyes outstayed the drippings of the sky.

GUINEVERE. Knew you her face?

DAGONET. 'Twas laid so low upon her palfrey's neck I saw it not.

GUINEVERE. Go, fool, on your way.

DAGONET. Ay, madam, by your leave, for I must seek the King, who comes from hunting. In May-time your King and your fool were ever very prettily assorted.

He goes up the hill singing.

> The cuckoo's note doth haunt the May,
> > And some are glad,
> > And some grow mad,
> But the fool goes singing on his way.

Exit Dagonet. As he goes the Queen stands wrapt in thought.

CLARISSANT. Nay, madam, see, 'tis noon; we waste our day.
GUINEVERE [*rousing herself*]. Truly; lift up your voices: let us
    on.

MAY SONG

Dreaming 'neath a whitened thorn,
    Like a rose-leaf on the snow,
Lovers! ere the day be worn,
    Ye shall find him and shall know,
        Love is here.
And, at nightfall when ye part,
    Whispering shall say:
Love is lord of every heart,
    Love is lord of May.

The Ladies wander off through the wood preceded by the company of singing maidens, whose voices grow gradually fainter as they are lost in the distance, and at the last Guinevere follows slowly, and as she goes off, Morgan enters, and stands gazing after her, while at the same time Merlin appears on the rising path above.

MORGAN. March on, my Queen, in all thy bravery!
He that is lord of May and of thy heart,
Blind leader of the blind, shall draw thee on,
Where Lancelot waits for thee, love's slave and ours.
    MERLIN.
        The scabbard's gone, but England's lord
        Holds till death the naked sword.
    MORGAN [*seeing him*]. What wouldst thou now whose work is
        wellnigh done?
May-day is here, and we, thy ministers,
Need no fresh spur to hasten Fate's decree.
    MERLIN [*approaching her*]. At dawn I heard the splashing of
            the mere,
And saw that jewelled scabbard sink and sink
Till, like a glittering rainbow, down the deep
It vanished, and the shuddering tide grew still.
Dost thou know aught of this?
    MORGAN.   Not I, forsooth!
    MERLIN. Thou liest, for I tracked thee in thy theft,
And saw thee creep beside the sleeping King,
Whose hand held fast that naked blade which gleamed,
A bar of quivering moonlight, by his side.
Thou hast stol'n the scabbard, but no mortal hand
Shall take the sword.

MORGAN.   What then? thyself didst say—
The scabbard's worth doth far outweigh the sword.
   MERLIN. To him, but not to thee. 'Tis naught to thee:
Who steals the scabbard doth but draw the sword;
Who holds the sword, holds all save life, and wins,
Though life be spent, a deathless crown from death.
   MORGAN. Whose hand shall take it then, when death draws
     near?
   MERLIN.
     When those Queens of Night shall steer
     Arthur's barge across the mere,
     She who long ago did bring
     England's sword to England's King,
      She shall claim Excalibur!
  Exit Merlin.
   MORGAN. Croak on, let Death but come; we'll chance the
     rest!

  Enter Mordred.

   MORDRED. Whose voice was that?
   MORGAN.   'Twas Merlin's, who grows
     old,
And babbles like a child. What is thy news?
   MORDRED. Beyond our hope; Ryons and Mark are joined
In equal strength of war, and, by this hour,
Their glittering squadrons, like a serpent, coil
Around Caerleon's walls.
   MORGAN.   Whence got you this?
   MORDRED. Sir Morys from Caerleon rode post haste
To warn our Master. He will ride no more. [*Touching his sword.*
   MORGAN. 'Tis well; your men keep watch on every road?
   MORDRED. Ay, all are guarded; let but this day pass
With no unwelcome note to wake the King,
Then war may shriek its loudest; all is sure.
   MORGAN. Hast thou forgotten Lancelot?
   MORDRED [*in alarm*].   What of him?
   MORGAN. Nay, track him through the wood, and thou shalt
     learn.
Come hither, see where, trembling, hand to hand,
With speechless answering eyes, they woo the spring.
Love sets the snare, but the caged bird is ours.

For ere night's dusky arms enfold the sun,
Lancelot shall be thy partner and thy slave.

> *Exeunt Morgan and Mordred. The May Song is heard faintly in
> the distance.*

> *Enter Sir Lavaine and Clarissant.*

LAVAINE. Dost think our love will live from May to May?
CLARISSANT. Nay, ask me that when May-day comes again.
LAVAINE. Ah, tell me now!
CLARISSANT.   I'll tell thee all I know.
If thou dost woo me well, I'll love thee well,—
Should no one woo me better!
LAVAINE.   Wouldst thou be wooed
That art already won?
CLARISSANT. Most surely, sir!
Who holds my heart must win it every day;
And when 'tis won, 'tis then it must be wooed
And won again.
LAVAINE. Why, 'twas but yesterday
That thou didst swear thy love would last till death.
CLARISSANT. Ay, that was yesterday.
LAVAINE.   And shall thine oath
Live but an hour?
CLARISSANT. What is there in these oaths
That you poor men so fondly cherish them?
Perchance they fit your duller brains, which seek,
With empty words, to bind the unborn hours.
But we do wrong to humour you in this.
We should not swear at all, knowing full well
There's no to-morrow in a woman's heart,
Which hath its yesterday of joy or pain,
Whose savour, lingering on our lips to-day,
Makes all the present half a memory—
The future all a blank. Then ask me not
If I shall love thee when the year is worn;
I loved thee yesterday: so be content.
LAVAINE. Ah, but thou lovest to-day?
CLARISSANT.   To-day is young;
Ask me at sundown, I will tell thee then.

> *Exit laughing, and he following her.*

Enter Guinevere and Lancelot.

GUINEVERE. The wood is dark. Let us be in the sun.
LANCELOT. 'Twas dark ere yet the glory of thy face
Came, like a golden message from the sun.
And now, beneath this open vault of day,
'Twould change again to night wert thou not here.
GUINEVERE. I had a foolish fear I should not find thee.
LANCELOT. Nay, Guinevere, thou knowest that could not be.
GUINEVERE. Indeed, 'tis true, for wandering alone
Across the leafy screen that hedged my way,
From every side I heard the echoing laugh
Of Love's encounter. Then the wood grew still,
And, softer than the silence, came the sound
Of whispered vows from lips but newly met;
And then, beneath an opening arch of green,
Two lovers passed, with hand in hand locked close.
Ah, Lancelot! I was lonely as a child
Locked in a darkened room. I called thee then;
Didst thou not hear me?
LANCELOT.   Ay, and saw thee, too.
GUINEVERE. Thou didst not answer?
LANCELOT.   Nay, forgive me, sweet!
I could but watch thee.
GUINEVERE. That was cruel, sir.
LANCELOT. 'Twas but an instant.
GUINEVERE.   No, it was a year!
And in that year a thousand thronging fears
With devil faces perched amid the boughs.
LANCELOT. What were thy fears?
GUINEVERE.   So many all in one:
That I should lose thee.
    Lancelot putting his arms round her.
LANCELOT.   Never, until death.
GUINEVERE. Ah, speak not so of death! I have seen a face
That frighted me like death.
LANCELOT [*starting*]. Whose face and where?
GUINEVERE. Within the wood. 'Twas Merlin's, but so old,
Lancelot, so old and worn I knew it not.
LANCELOT. Those empty words of his do haunt thee still.
I wonder at thy fears.

GUINEVERE. Nay, scold me not.
There's nothing haunts me when I have thee near.
Love shuts the door on all things save itself,
On all that's past and all that is to come
When thou art by! Tell me, 'tis so with thee?
        LANCELOT. Ay, sweet, 'tis so.
        GUINEVERE.   Ah, say it once again!
I could not live, Lancelot, if in thy heart
There lurked the tiniest little ache or pain
Love might not cure.
        LANCELOT. Thou knowest all my heart;
And in my love, which knows no law but love,
The future and the past are drowning straws
Caught in the full tide of our present joy,
That neither ebbs nor flows.

> *He holds her in a close embrace as Morgan and Mordred enter*
> *stealthily; at the same time is heard the sound of distant*
> *thunder, and the scene darkens.*

MORGAN.   Dost mark them well?
LANCELOT. Ambition, honour, duty, all that life
Once held most dear, by thy sweet will subdued,
Now wear Love's livery[9] and would serve Love's Queen.

> *The thunder is heard again and nearer.*

        GUINEVERE [*starting*]. What sound was that? See, it grows
                dark again!
        LANCELOT. 'Tis but a cloud.
        GUINEVERE.   It came like sudden night.
Let us go in. [*Thunder again.*] Ah, 'tis the thunder's bolt
That cracks the sky!
        LANCELOT. Nay, tremble not; 'twill pass,
And leave Heaven's deeper blue. What shouldst thou fear?
        GUINEVERE. I know not. Hold me closer, closer still,
That so my heart may catch the fearless tune
Of thy heart's steadfast music. Now I am brave,
And could be always, wert thou always here.
So let us on. Yet tell me o'er again—
Ah, I do tease thee; 'tis but this once more—
Tell me, whate'er befall, that thou art mine!
        LANCELOT. For ever and for ever I am thine.

---

9. Distinctive clothing worn by the servants of a person of rank.

A crash of thunder and a lightning flash.

MORDRED [*looking after them*]. He lies, my Queen; not thine,
    but mine till death!

ACT III

THE BLACK BARGE.

SCENE:—*A vaulted chamber opening on to the river.*

*As the curtain draws up enter Sir Lancelot, followed by Sir Kay, Sir
Gawaine, and Sir Agravaine.*

LANCELOT. Sir Morys slain?

GAWAINE.   Ay, murdered.

LANCELOT.   But by whom?

KAY. That's still to find. Know you from whence he came?

LANCELOT. Straight from Caerleon, whither, as I heard,
He rode with sealed advices for the King.

KAY. Said I not well? Arthur hath been forestalled.

LANCELOT. Why, 'twas but yesterday the King did note
His long delay.

GAWAINE. It was but yesternight
We found him murdered.

LANCELOT.   Sirs, if this be so,
There's something more than murder.

KAY.   More, in truth!
Lancelot, some traitor lurking near the throne,
In secret league with Arthur's enemies,
By this same villainous act now stands possessed
Of what the King should know.

AGRAVAINE.   What must be done?

GAWAINE. Let Lancelot speak.

LANCELOT.   I'll straightway to the King
And tell him all. Then, should we win his leave,
At nightfall we'll to horse, nor draw the rein
Until Caerleon's towers cut the sky.

    Exeunt Kay, Agravaine, and Gawaine.

    During the next speech Mordred enters.

Whose hand is here? Of all our knights but one

In my most secret heart dare stand accused
Of this foul deed. [*Turns and sees Mordred.*] Mordred! Morys is slain!

      MORDRED. Sir Morys slain! Nay, 'tis some idle jest.

      LANCELOT. That is not all; the advices that he bore—
Are stolen.

      MORDRED. Stolen? Is it possible?

      LANCELOT. Ay, sir, and true; which news must to the King.

      MORDRED. Most surely: yet not now; he is fatigued,
And would not be disturbed. To-morrow, sir.

      LANCELOT. Nay, sir, to-day; an hour's delay may risk
The safety of his throne, perchance his life.

      MORDRED. Well, sir, what then?

      LANCELOT [*in amazement*].   What then?

      MORDRED.   Nay, spare thy skill;
'Tis aptly feigned; in faith, I'd say 'twas true
Did I not hold a key that locks thy heart.

      LANCELOT. What dost thou mean?

      MORDRED.   I mean, should Arthur pass
He leaves behind a kingdom, and a Queen
Who loves him not.

      LANCELOT. Who says so foully lies!

      MORDRED. Lancelot, throw off this mask, it fits thee not;
Be what thou art, nor fear what thou wouldst be.
Let candour answer candour. It was I
Who slew this messenger. His papers here
Bring the rich news that ere a week be past
Caerleon's gates must yield to the assault
Of Ryons' siege, whose vengeance stays not there;
The King himself is doomed; and, the King dead,
His throne is mine, and thine his widowed Queen.

      LANCELOT. Traitor! I knew it. Thou shalt to the King,
In whose dread presence, from that villain's throat,
I'll force those words again.

      MORDRED.   I dare thy worst!
Yet breathe one word and I will tell a tale
Shall make thee cower like a beaten hound.

      LANCELOT. Thou'st naught to tell.

      MORDRED.   What! are her kisses
        naught?
Fie, sir, for shame! So then thou didst not guess
I lurked so near, and saw thee lip to lip,
Cuddling beneath the may; that is love's trick,

Who blindfold deems that all the world is blind.
Now to the King! See, sir, the way is clear.
What! Wouldst thou pause? Hast thou no heart to win
That sweet reward that waits thy loyal zeal—
A traitor's death?

> LANCELOT. What were that death to me?
> MORDRED. True! but the Queen?
> LANCELOT.   Vile wretch!
> *Movement towards Mordred.*
> MORDRED.   Look where she
>   comes;

Take thought with her, she will advise thee well.
We men are rash, a woman's subtler wit
Serves better in such case. Truth, but she's fair—
So fair,—why, Lancelot, I repent me now
I kept not this sweet morsel for mine own.

> LANCELOT. Out of my sight!
> MORDRED [*aside*].   His tongue is safely gagged;

Yet he's but half corrupt, I'll trust him not. [*Exit.*

Lancelot stands in despair as Guinevere enters.

> GUINEVERE. Who went from thee?
> LANCELOT.   'Twas Mordred.
> GUINEVERE [*approaching him*].   Lancelot,

Some evil hath befallen!

> LANCELOT.   'Tis naught. [*He turns away.*
> GUINEVERE.   'Tis much

Can make thee turn from me; ah, but I'll know it!
Didst thou not swear our love should cure all ill?
Then tell me all.

> LANCELOT.   Caerleon is besieged;

Should succour fail 'twill yield to Ryons' arms.

> GUINEVERE. Who brings these tidings?
> LANCELOT.   Mordred.
> GUINEVERE.   And the King?
> LANCELOT. Knows naught.
> GUINEVERE [*with sudden horror*]. Knows naught? Lancelot, ah
>   no! ah no!

Sure thou wouldst tell the King.

> LANCELOT.   Indeed I would.
> GUINEVERE. Then wherefore pause?

LANCELOT. Oh, had I died but then,
In that sweet hour when first I learned thy love,
I had been happy!
GUINEVERE. *What* is in thy heart?
LANCELOT. Mordred is false.
GUINEVERE. False?
LANCELOT. Ay, 'tis he that's hatched
This plot against the King, whereby he thinks
To seize the throne.
GUINEVERE. Then thou shalt prove him false
And save the King.
LANCELOT. I dare not.
GUINEVERE. Dare not?
LANCELOT. No:
All, all is known.
GUINEVERE. To whom?
LANCELOT. To him; he was there
Beside us in the may; his trait'rous hand
Grips at my throat and makes me traitor too.
GUINEVERE. No, no, that cannot be. Ah, look not so!
What wouldst thou do?
LANCELOT. Nay, ask what have I done?
Was there no lamp in Heaven to stay our feet?
Was the night starless, that we needs must wait
Till love's torch, setting all the world ablaze,
Lights up love's ruinous way? Ah, Guinevere,
I'd die a hundred deaths but now to win
One hour of life that's past; ay, one short hour,
So I might drag this devil to the throne
And shout his villainies in every ear.
GUINEVERE. Then do it now.
LANCELOT. I cannot.
GUINEVERE. Yea, thou canst!
Who is there that should stay[10] thee, 'tis not I!
Let love go down the wind, what boots[11] it now?
Look to thyself; think not of all that is lost.
That is all mine: for thee there still remains
Thy soldier's honour, take it, keep it pure.

---

10. Stop.
11. Avails.

LANCELOT. What have I said?
GUINEVERE.   Ah, go! [*Throws herself on couch.*
LANCELOT [*throwing himself at her feet*]. My Queen! My
        Queen!
There's nothing in the world to win or lose
Can count beside thy love. I lied but now;
King, honour, country, all that knighthood boasts
Of faith and loyalty in life or death
Weighs not against the memory of one kiss
From thy dear lips.
GUINEVERE. Then thou art mine again.
To hear thee say that all the world was naught
Against our love hath made me mad for joy.
Yet stay not now; I have a thought to think,
And needs must be alone.
LANCELOT.   Yet, ere I go,
Hear this one word: all that is left of life
Is thine to keep or thine to fling away,
So I may have thy love. [*Exit Lancelot.*
GUINEVERE.   Thou hast, indeed!
So all is won again, and all is lost!
So do we strive that we may have the more
To cast away: and now, when at my feet
He lays his sword, his life, ay, and his soul,
I do but long to find some better way
To give him all again; ay, all again! [*Looks off.*
It is the King. How may I find that way?

        Enter Arthur.

ARTHUR. Ah, thou art here. I bring thee such sad news
As needs must wring thy heart.
GUINEVERE.   What news, my lord?
ARTHUR. Elaine is dead!
GUINEVERE.   Dead! Who hath told thee this?
ARTHUR. There, yonder by the shore, her body lies
Who, while she lived, was named the Fair Elaine.
Canst thou not weep?
GUINEVERE. Truly, my lord, I think
I've lost the use of tears.
ARTHUR.   Thou wouldst have wept
Hadst thou been there when down the vacant stream

That black barge floated, like a speck of night,
Blown on the winds of dawn; and on its deck,
Fallen as a feather from a white dove's wing,
Lay this new prize of Death; whose cunning hands
Had wrought in such fair mimicry of life
That on her parted lips there lingered yet
The memory of a smile.
   GUINEVERE. Why then, perchance,
She's happier far than some who needs must live
And smile no more.
   ARTHUR. It may be; for that brow
Had caught from Death some secret of content
It knew not here, and, looking in those eyes,
Whose tears had ceased their traffic, I dared think,
If aught of sin was there, 'tis pardoned now.
   GUINEVERE. Of sin? What sin?
   ARTHUR.   Ay, for it must be so:
Some sin there was though unrecorded here;
Some stain that smirched her seeming purity,
Which Lancelot, all too noble, could not urge;
Else were it not in nature to refuse
So sweet a gift.
   GUINEVERE. If that indeed be true,
Were it enough to shut the doors of love?
   ARTHUR. Enough? What wouldst thou ask?
   GUINEVERE.   Ay! Ay! enough,
Enough and more! Yet, in some greater heart,
As his, or thine, methought that love might find
Forgiveness e'en for that.
   ARTHUR.   Nay, wrong him not,
Whose upward gaze, set level with the stars,
Would lift from earth the soul he crowns with love,
Making her more than woman; whence if she fall—
Like some lost planet hurled from highest Heaven—
She falls to endless night.
   During Arthur's speech the distant throb of a mournful march is
    heard slowly approaching.
   GUINEVERE. Most like 'tis so,
And death the only way. What sound is that?
   ARTHUR. Up from the stream they bear her body hither,
Where it shall rest beneath this royal roof,
Till, with such liberal honours as befit

So fair a flower, 'tis set again in earth.

> *The procession enters, headed by Mordred and Morgan. Four Knights bear Elaine and are followed by a company of Maidens.*

MORGAN [*aside to Mordred*]. Her cheek grows pale; she will betray herself.

> *She passes across the stage and takes her place behind the Queen. At a sign from Mordred the Knights move forward till they come to where Guinevere is standing rigid and motionless. Then they stop in silence till Guinevere, without turning, cries in agony.*

GUINEVERE. Go on! and set it down!

MORDRED [*coming forward*].   Madam, by your leave,
In that white hand of death a letter lies,
Whose seal we dared not break, for 'tis inscribed
"To Guinevere, the Queen."

ARTHUR [*to Guinevere*]. Then break the seal,
Which hides perchance some secret of her love
We know not yet.

> *Guinevere tries to approach the bier, but cannot touch the body; then with a despairing appeal she turns to Arthur.*

GUINEVERE. I cannot! Give it me.

> *Arthur takes the letter which Guinevere opens and lets fall, staggering back into the arms of Morgan, whose eyes gleam in triumph.*

MORGAN. Nay, madam, nay; what is it moves thee thus?

> *Mordred picks up the letter and gives it to the King.*

ARTHUR [*reading*]. "I that was named Elaine of Astolat,
Whose mortal love for Lancelot passed all measure,
Seeing he loves another, choose to die."
We knew not this. Go, call Sir Lancelot here.

GUINEVERE. My lord, my lord—

> *She struggles forward as though to stop the King's command and then swoons into Morgan's arms.*

ARTHUR. Look to the Queen.

> *Morgan and her Women support her from the stage, and at the same time the Knights lay the body of Elaine under the alcove, and then exeunt, leaving Arthur and Mordred alone.*

MORDRED [*aside*].   Ere Lancelot's blow can fall
I'll strike him to the heart.

ARTHUR [*holding the letter*]. If this be true,
'Tis strange that none had known.

MORDRED.   What's that, my lord?

ARTHUR. What's here set down of Lancelot's later love.

MORDRED. Now would to Heaven those words had ne'er
      been writ
Or ne'er been read.

ARTHUR. Why so?

MORDRED.   Didst thou not note
How the Queen's soul was stirred?

ARTHUR.   She is not used
To look on death; which, coming in such guise,
Might move our soldier hearts.

MORDRED.   Ay, but methought
It was Death's message and not Death itself
That turned those red lips white.

ARTHUR.   Mordred, what's this?
Think you the Queen hath known of this same love?

MORDRED. Nay, I'll not answer that.

ARTHUR.   Nay, but thou shalt.
What is to fear?

MORDRED. My lord, thou art my King;
My sword is thine, and with that sword my life;
But with that life my loyal service ends,
And what is left thou wilt not ask of me.

ARTHUR. Who is it that he loves?

MORDRED.   In sooth, I thought
What all the world had known was known to thee;
Were it not so these lips had still been dumb.
But now 'tis best 'twere said—he loves the Queen! [*A pause.*

ARTHUR. Who forged this lie? Nay, Mordred, 'tis not thou;
And yet I wonder, too, to find thee duped
By this poor tale bred in some baser soul
That loves not Lancelot.

MORDRED.   What! thou think'st 'tis false?
Why then, my lord, 'tis false. I'll think so, too,
We'll speak of it no more.

ARTHUR.   Ay, but we will,
And track this running poison to its source,
Which else should turn all the pure springs of life
To pools of festering filth.

    Enter Morgan hurriedly.

MORGAN.   My lord, the Queen—
Why thou art pale! Nay, do not take it so;
'Twas but a sudden fit and soon will pass.

    ARTHUR. Morgan, come hither: know'st thou aught of this?

    MORGAN. Of what, my lord?

    ARTHUR.   Of Lancelot's love for her—
The Queen?

    MORGAN. The Queen? Now who hath told thee this?
[*Turning to Mordred.*] Shame on thee, shame! I pray you heed him
         not.
I would have cut my tongue out ere I'd spoken
Such evil of our mistress!

    ARTHUR.   Let him be;
He doth but hint what every hawker[12] cries.

    MORGAN. But he did wrong to speak, and thou to hear.
So sweet a lady, and at such an hour!
Were I a man, for all he is my child,
My sword should answer him.

    MORDRED [*with assumed anger*]. Now this is more
Than I have will to bear! Why 'twas thyself
Didst tell how yesternight Sir Lancelot
Went to her bower alone.

    ARTHUR.   Didst thou say so?

    MORGAN. In truth 'twas so; and hath been so before;
Yet did I think no wrong; and now I'm sure
He bore some message from the King himself.

    ARTHUR. No, he did not.

    MORGAN.   Well, then be sure 'twas naught,
And she shall prove it naught.

    MORDRED.   Nay, mother, nay,
Let us be honest! Thou wouldst serve the Queen,
And so would I; yet may we not be false
To him whom Heaven hath made her lord and ours.
How canst thou say 'twas naught? Why, thou wast there
Beside me, when they kissed beneath the may.

    ARTHUR [*turns slowly towards Morgan*]. Tell him he lies.

    MORGAN. My lord, my lord, I cannot. [*A pause.*

    ARTHUR. There'll come a time when I shall know full well
This is a dream; but now I'll play it out

---

12. One who travels about selling goods with a horse and cart.

As though 'twere true. Go, get thee to the Queen.
> MORGAN. Think not too ill of her.
> ARTHUR.   Nay, nor of thee. [*Exit*
> *Morgan.*
[*To Mordred.*] Go on, there's more to come. Think you he knows
You lurked so near and saw him?
> MORDRED.   Ay, most sure,
For now, with lying tongue, he goes about
Whispering that I have hatched some treacherous plot
Against thy throne and thee.
> ARTHUR.   Why, then I think
This is some other Lancelot ye have met
And this some other King! He whom I knew
Was of all knights the bravest and the truest,
Serving a lord who could not have stood dumb
To hear his name befouled.

> *Lancelot enters and approaches the King, who does not turn to*
> *him.*

> LANCELOT. My lord, I am here.
Didst thou not send for me?
> ARTHUR.   Ay, so I did.
Lancelot, the scabbard of Excalibur
Is stolen.
> LANCELOT. Who is the thief?
> ARTHUR.   'Tis thou shalt say.
Dost think 'tis Mordred?
> LANCELOT [*starting*]. Why should I think so?
> ARTHUR. Why not? I have heard there is some grosser charge
That thou wouldst bring against him.
> MORDRED [*with assumed indignation*]. Nay, my good lord—
> ARTHUR. Let Lancelot speak.
> LANCELOT [*after a pause*]. My lord, I bring no charge.
> ARTHUR. Lancelot, think well; art sure thou know'st of
>   naught
That should disturb our peace?
> LANCELOT [*after a pause*]. Of naught, my lord.
> ARTHUR. 'Tis well, 'tis well; then both of ye are true.
> LANCELOT. Was it for this that thou didst send for me?
> ARTHUR. Not so. Come hither, that thine eyes may feast
On this sweet picture.

Lancelot turns and starts at the sight of Elaine.
                    Nay, sir, note it well!
Death too hath gone a-maying, and hath plucked
Life's fairest flower—Elaine.
          LANCELOT.   Methought she slept.
          ARTHUR. Ay, past all waking; and wouldst know the cause?
          LANCELOT. The cause?
          ARTHUR.   Why she doth sleep; 'tis written here.
          He gives Lancelot the letter; as the King watches him he reads it,
                and then falls on his knees before the bier.
Yet squander not thy grief; she heeds thee not.
The dead are dead; we give them ne'er a thought
Whose care is for the living; and, of all,
The most for thee. Wherever she may dwell,
This new-found beauty that hath lured thy heart,
We shall command her love. Nay, but we shall;
For thou art known the courtliest, truest knight
That ever served a king. Then speak her name.
          LANCELOT. My lord, in truth—
          ARTHUR.   Nay, sir, who is this maid?
          LANCELOT. There is no maid.
          ARTHUR.   Lancelot, thou sayest well;
It is the Queen.
          LANCELOT. Ah, no!
          ARTHUR.   Thou knowest 'tis so!
Thou art the thief who so hast stolen away
That scabbard that was worth a hundred swords.
          LANCELOT. Whose tongue hath told thee this? here on my
                    life
I'll answer him who dares accuse her honour.
          MORDRED. Then answer me.
          LANCELOT.   Liar! and so I will!
Yet first I'd have thee known for what thou art.
Traitor—I charge thee now.
          MORDRED [*with a sneer*]. Said I not well?

          Guinevere enters unseen.

          ARTHUR. If *he* be traitor, what art thou whose sword
Strikes at my heart, yet would defend my throne?
Prove this is false, and I'll believe him false;
Prove that he lies, and I'll believe thee true.

LANCELOT. Again I swear 'tis false.

GUINEVERE [*coming between them*]. Nay, nay, 'tis true.

LANCELOT. What hast thou done?

GUINEVERE.   All that was left to do.

ARTHUR. Ay, all; there is no more to do or say;
Death's banner floats above the blackened field,
The fight is ended and our day is done,
If this be so. But I'll not think 'tis so;
Take back that word, and none shall know 'twas said!
Ah! call it back again, and lift the pall
Death spreads upon my heart; so shall I kneel
And bless thee, and this sword shall strike him dumb
That dares to whisper aught against my Queen. [*She stands
              immovable.*
Is this so much to ask? Ay, all too much!
There is no might can give back to the Spring
Its lowliest flower dead under changing skies;
Then how should I, with winter at my heart,
Plead with the ruined summer for its rose?
Thou hast no word?

GUINEVERE. No word to cure what's done.

ARTHUR [*to Lancelot*]. Then arm thyself; my sword shall find
              its sheath
Deep in thy heart.

LANCELOT. Strike on! Strike on! I say,
For death is all I crave.

ARTHUR.   Then take it now.
     *Arthur runs on Lancelot, but the uplifted sword drops from his
         hand.*
I cannot kill thee;
Some sudden palsy doth beat down this arm:
Its strength is gone. Yet think not 'tis the love
I bore thee once; that's clean forgotten now.
Nor is it mercy; for, had this same wrong
Chanced to the meanest hind[13] that calls me King,
My sword had leapt in vengeance, and my soul
Had straight approved the deed. Yet here I stand
That cannot strike a blow in mine own cause.
Is this a curse that Heaven hath set on kings,

---

13. Peasant.

Who may not love nor hate like common men?
Or is there some rank poison in a crown
That stamps the brand of coward on the brows
Of him who wears it? Go, then, get thee hence!
Join with some foe that dares assault our throne;
With Ryons, or with Mark, who hunger still
For open war. Ay, league thyself with them;
And, in that hour, the hand that falters now,
In England's cause shall find its force again,
And strike thee to the earth. Till then live on.
   Lancelot goes out as Arthur turns to Mordred.
Leave us alone. There's something left to say,
Mordred, that's not for thee. [*Exit Mordred.*
  GUINEVERE.   And must I live?
  ARTHUR. It is too late to die.
  GUINEVERE.   Too late! too late!
  ARTHUR. Ay; would Death's marble finger had been laid
On those sweet lips when first they linked with mine! [*Pointing to
  Elaine.*
For, locked in Death's white arms, Love lies secure,
In changeless sleep that knows no dream of change.
'Tis Life, not Death, that is Love's sepulchre;
Where each day tells of passionate hearts grown strange,
And perjured vows chime with the answering bell
That tolls Love's funeral. If thou wouldst boast
Of this new sway a woman's wile hath won,
Go, tell the world thy heart hath slain a heart
That once had been a king's. Yet that's not all,
Thou too hast been a Queen whose soul shone clear,
A star for all men's worship, and a lamp
Set high in Heaven, whereby all frailer hearts
Should steer their course towards God; then, 'tis not I
Whose life lies broken here, for at thy fall
A shattered kingdom bleeds.
   *At the end of this speech a sound of warlike music is heard, and the
   stage fills with Knights headed by Gawaine and Agravaine.*
  GAWAINE.   My lord! my lord!
Caerleon is besieged.

  Enter Mordred.

KAY.   And we thy knights,
Here armed and ready, do but wait to know
Our King's command.
        MORDRED.   Then let me lead them forth.
The chance is desperate, and thy greater life
Is England's, not thine own!
        ARTHUR.   Nay, thou shalt stay;
Thou art the one thing left my soul dare trust.
For, in this wreck of love, truth stands for all.
Sound out for war. [*Pointing to Guinevere.*] Yet, pray you, use her
        well;
We do not roughly trample down the flower
That grows upon a grave. Then use her well,
For there entombed lies one who was my Queen.
Gawaine, I come. Thy King shall lead thee forth;
My sword is drawn, I want no scabbard now.

        *Arthur holds up his naked sword, and all the Knights raise their
        swords in answer as the curtain falls.*

ACT IV

THE PASSING OF ARTHUR.

SCENE I:—*The Queen's prison in the Castle at Camelot. Door leading to the
Queen's chamber. Another door heavily barred. Window at back.*

Gaoler discovered keeping guard. As the scene opens knocking at outer door.

        GAOLER. Who knocks without?
        MESSENGER [*without*].   One who bears a message for
        the Queen.
Gaoler opens door and admits the Messenger.
        GAOLER. What saith Sir Modred? May she see her fool?
        MESSENGER. Ay, I have brought him hither.
        GAOLER. That will content her much; she hath cried often
        for her fool.
        MESSENGER. Yet methinks she shall suck but poor entertain-
ment from the fellow now: his wits are clean gone. And, faith, he is
not like to smile again.
        GAOLER. What mean you, sir?

MESSENGER. The news of Arthur's death is now made sure;
and what is worse, 'tis said 'twas Lancelot's sword that struck him
down.
GAOLER. Who shall tell this to the Queen?
MESSENGER. Within the hour Sir Mordred comes himself
To bear the news. Think you 'twill stir her heart?
GAOLER. Indeed I think not so, look where she comes,
Her white face like the head-stone at a grave,
O'er-lettered with the story of a day
That ended long ago.

Enter Guinevere. She holds a bird in her hands.

GUINEVERE. See what I've trapped: it fluttered at the bars
And fell there at my feet. I'd have it caged,
That I, its gaoler, may have leave to dream
That I am free; and then, perchance, one day
This little bird will come and pray to me,
Who, being a Queen, must needs be merciful
And break its wicker walls.
GAOLER [*taking the bird*]. I'll cage it now.
He goes towards the door, and she sees the Messenger.
GUINEVERE. Ah, sir, you're from the Court. Where is my fool,
Sir Dagonet? Is that denied me too?
'Twas not so much to ask.
MESSENGER.   Madam, he's here,
And yet so changed I fear he will not know thee.

Opens door, and Dagonet enters.

GUINEVERE. That counts for naught. I scarce do know myself.
Come hither, Dagonet. Sirs, by your leave. [*Gaoler and Messenger
    exeunt.*
GUINEVERE. Dost thou not know thy Queen?
DAGONET. Ay, very well, there were two of them: for there
was one, look you, that came with the Spring from Cameliard, and
she had a face that touched Heaven; and there was one that kept a
poison on her lip for Lancelot's kissing. And hark'e, last night
beneath the moon I saw them both kneeling beside a grave.
GUINEVERE. Whose grave?
DAGONET.   I know not, for the stone was bare,
And they did naught but weep.

GUINEVERE. I'll tell thee, then:
This grave I think was Guinevere's who died
That hour when she was born; and these two Queens
Who through the night keep watch beside her tomb,
Are but her shadows fashioned for the masque
Which men call life; poor puppets that must dance
While unseen fingers touch the trembling strings;
But whence that music comes, from Heaven or Hell,
There's none shall say, till all life's lamps burn out
And Death stands forth to claim the harper's fee.

Enter Gaoler.

GAOLER. Make room, Sir Mordred comes.

Enter Mordred.

Exeunt Gaoler and Dagonet.
MORDRED. Great Queen, I bear thee news that sets thee free.
GUINEVERE. What news is that?
MORDRED.   Thy lord, the King, is dead.
GUINEVERE. Dead! art thou sure? Why then, sir, *he* is free,
And I that was his gaoler may not weep;
Yet count not that against me, for I think
Tears are not all.
MORDRED. Truth, thou wert wrong to weep.
Dost thou not know 'twas Arthur's cruel will
That set thee in this prison?
GUINEVERE.   Ay, I know,
That thou hast said 'twas so.
MORDRED.   And so it is:
But now I've come to break these prison bars,
And so give back unto our desert world
Life's sweetest rose that hungers for the sun.
GUINEVERE. And who art thou whose new-found sovereignty
Rides o'er the King's decree?
MORDRED.   I am thy King.
GUINEVERE. There is no King save one, and he is dead.
Yet if it was his will to leave me here,
Why, here I'll stay.
MORDRED. Nay, then thou dost not guess
The gift I bear thee! Guinevere, those lips,

Moulded by Love's own hand, are not yet doomed
For Death's embrace: their kiss is for a king;
Yet not like that dead lord whose bloodless soul
Wings to a frozen heaven: who wooes thee now
Is man, not god, and in his brimming veins
Run longings like thine own.

      GUINEVERE.   I thought till now
That I had suffered all; but here I see
My shame doth but begin. 'Twas not enough
That through my sin, for all succeeding time,
Hell's mocking laugh shall haunt the voice of spring,
And plant its poisoned echo in each bower,
Where lovers' vows are sworn! Nay, this is more;
That she, whom love doth once make false to love,
Must henceforth bear the common brand of lust,
Seeming the painted toy that every man
May purchase at his price.

      MORDRED.   Why, thou dost dream!
Here at thy feet I lay an empire's throne,
Where thou in equal majesty shalt reign
Once more a Queen.

      GUINEVERE. A wanton, not a Queen!
Who for this piece of gold thou call'st a crown
Would take thy murderer's kiss.

      MORDRED.   Nay, have a care!
My love lies near to hate.

      GUINEVERE.   I fear thy love;
Thy hate is naught.

      MORDRED. Truth, thou shalt find it more
Than thou hast ever dreamed.

        Shouts without, "Long live the King."
      MORDRED.   Dost hear that cry?
It is the echoing voice of England's knights,
Who hail me king.

      GUINEVERE. And they were Arthur's knights?

      MORDRED. Ay, they loved Arthur well! Yet when they learn;—
As so they shall, for I will vouch it true—
'Twas Lancelot's sword did pierce him to the heart,
Their eyes will turn on her whose shameful sin
Made Lancelot false. See then, thy fate stands clear,
Thou art Death's bride, or mine—thy choice is free.

GUINEVERE. Why then I choose to die. Yea, though my soul
Slipped down to Hell, Hell were a paradise
Whilst thou art here. [*Exit Guinevere.*
MORDRED.   By Heaven, then thou shalt die!

Enter Morgan.

MORGAN. Ryons is trapped, and dying hath confessed
His treason and thine own.
MORDRED.   Then Arthur lives,
And all is lost.
MORGAN. Nay, all is left to win;
This news is secret, and long ere 'tis known
Thy sword shall pierce his heart.
MORDRED.   Or his sword mine.
MORGAN. What, wouldst thou question Fate?

        He Pendragon's son shall slay,
        That is born with the May.
                        So Fate decreed:
His blood is thine and mine.
        Shouts "Long live King Mordred! Death to Guinevere!" grow
        louder to the end.
                Go, take thy crown,
And none shall dare to question what is done,
Or what remains to do. [*Exit.*
MORDRED.   So Fate take all!
To halt were death, and that on-coming flood
Of Time's uplifted wave can hold no more. [*Exit.*

SCENE 2:—*The Great Hall at Camelot.*

As the scene is disclosed the Hall is filled with armed Knights. Mordred is on
the throne, accompanied by Morgan, and surrounded by the retinue of the
court.

Guinevere stands before the throne. Mordred turns to her.

MORDRED. By England's knights in council thou dost stand
Condemned of treason 'gainst thy lord the King,
Whose death lies at thy charge. Yet we, who bear

The crown that Arthur wore, now give thee leave
To plead in thy defence. If there be aught
Which thou canst urge why judgment should be stayed,
Stand forth and speak.

     AGRAVAINE. We pray you hear her not.

     GUINEVERE [*turning with a look of scorn towards Mordred*]. What
        still is left to say is not for thee!

     MORDRED. Then let the sentence go. Queen Guinevere,
Daughter of Leodograunce of Cornwall,
Now hear thy judgment as the law decrees:
That first, despoilèd of thy royal robes,
Thou shalt be fastened to an iron stake
Until thy mortal body be consumed
In fiery flames.

     GUINEVERE. And saith the law no more?

     MORDRED. Ay, this it adds: that if thy prayer may win
Some champion for thy cause, then this same knight
Shall claim due right of battle 'gainst that lord
Whose charge hath brought thee here.

     GUINEVERE.   And who is that?

     MORDRED. 'Tis I who charge thee now.

     GUINEVERE.   Why then, sir knights,
I'll kneel and pray to you, if haply one
Find heart to serve his Queen. Think not I plead
For this poor gift of life. Nay, could I choose,
These hands should bear fresh faggots to the blaze
That lights me to a tomb. Yet hear me all:
Who stands my knight to-day shall wrest from Time
A crown of glory. Not, sirs, that he fought
For one whose sin knows no desert save death,
That were but shame: yet whoso dares that shame
His sword shall win the right, denied him else,
To slay that crawling thing upon the throne—
Wherefore I cry a champion for my cause!

     Mordred, who has descended from the throne, whispers aside.

     MORDRED. Too late, my Queen! too late! What wouldst thou
        give
To win a king's kiss now? Doth no one speak?
Then, herald, let the trumpet's tongue bray out!
Her knight is gone a-hawking, or perchance
He sleeps too late!

*The trumpet sounds, and at the third call Sir Bedevere breaks
through the throng and stands before Mordred.*

BEDEVERE. Hold there, sir herald, hither comes a knight
To answer for the Queen.
    MORDRED.   Who is this knight?
    BEDEVERE. Sir, by your leave that shall be better told
When all is done.

The Knights give way, and Arthur stands alone with lowered helm.

MORDRED. See, madam, where he stands,
Thy champion, who must needs have come from far
To answer in such cause.
    Guinevere kneels at Arthur's feet.
    GUINEVERE.   I thank thee, sir;
Yet now I do repent me of what's done,
And fain would set thee free. Put up thy sword!
I am not worthy that a true knight's blood
Should flow for me. See, I will tell thee all:
I had a champion once, the mightiest knight,
The bravest and the truest in the world.
He was my lord, and I his chosen Queen
Brought him to shame. Then wherefore praise him now?
Nay, sir, I must: for that is life's hard law,
Which will not yield its secret till the close.
When Arthur went the sun shot scarlet-red,
And all the past lay bare. Then pray thee, sir,
Put up thy sword that waits a worthier cause.
    A pause, but Arthur makes no sign.
    GUINEVERE [*to Arthur*]. Thou wilt not? Then I'll ask this
           much of thee:
When death shall call thee home, it so may chance
That thou shalt meet my lord; if that should be,
Give him this word,—that at the end, his Queen
Knew him for what he was, true lord of all.
    MORDRED. Go, lead her hence.
    AGRAVAINE.   So God defend our King.
    *Exit Guinevere, followed by Agravaine and Knights. Mordred
    turns to Arthur, who remains motionless, Morgan watching
    him intently from the steps of the throne. Sir Bedevere stands by
    Arthur.*

MORDRED. And now I'm thine: yet first, by Heaven, I'll know
The face beneath that mask.

ARTHUR.   'Twas kept for thee.
As he lifts his helm Mordred starts back.

MORDRED. The King.

ARTHUR.   Ay, sir, the King, who but to win
This little hour from out the wreck of time,
Would take life's wearied hand and travel back
Across the ruined past, should fate declare
That only so his sword might claim the right
To slay thee now.

MORDRED. Prate on, I fear thee not.

MORGAN. Thou hast forgot the message of the May;
Then hear it now.

ARTHUR. Enough; 'twas thou, false witch,
That stole the scabbard of Excalibur!
Yet see, the blade remains whose every stroke
Is winged by Death.

MORGAN.   Not so! Not so, my lord!
That fickle steel shall splinter as it falls
On one twice armed by fate—

> "He Pendragon's son shall slay
> That is born with the May."

                    See! there he stands!

ARTHUR. Why then the end is here: set on, Sir Knight,
Death stands betwixt us twain, and Death shall choose.
[*They fight and Arthur is wounded.*
Traitor, that blow ends all. [*He falls to the earth.*

MORGAN. Long live the King!
The trumpet is heard without.
Dost hear that sound? Nay, look not on what's done,
There's more to do: her soul shall join with his
To wing its way across night's starless sky.
        *Exeunt Morgan and Mordred, and as they go they are greeted by
                cries from without.*

VOICES [*without*]. Long live the King!

ARTHUR.   Nay, sirs, 'tis not for
    long.
I'm dying, Bedevere. Where is my sword?

BEDEVERE. There, in thy hand.

ARTHUR. Poor hand, that knew it not.
Go quickly, Bedevere, and bear it hence
Unto that little bay hid in the cliff,
Then cast it in the sea, to wait that day
When upward from the shrieking waves shall spring
A vast sea-brood of mightier strain than ours,
Bearing across the world from end to end
One cry to all, "Our sword is in the sea!"
BEDEVERE. Why, then, 'tis done. [*He takes sword, and goes off.*
ARTHUR. Life's tide is ebbing fast.

Gawaine enters hurriedly.

GAWAINE. Nay, what is here? The wreck of all the world!
ARTHUR. Peace, sir! I know thy news: the Queen is dead.
GAWAINE. Not so; she lives, and thou art well avenged
By one who, dying, struck thy murderer down.
ARTHUR. Didst know him, Gawaine?
GAWAINE. Ay, I knew him once.
The courtliest knight that ever bare a shield,
The sternest soldier to his mortal foe,
Yet gentlest of us all.
ARTHUR. Nay, sir, his name?
GAWAINE. His name, my lord, was Lancelot.
ARTHUR. Lancelot. Ah!
So life's long night is breaking at the last.

*Guinevere enters, while the figure of Merlin appears standing above
the recumbent form of Arthur.*

GUINEVERE. Where is that knight who died that I might live?
GAWAINE. Hush, lady! he is here.
She sees the face of Arthur and falls at his feet.
GUINEVERE. My lord! my lord!
ARTHUR. Whose face was there? I pray you, some one say,
For all grows dark: I know not where I am.
GUINEVERE. Her name was Guinevere.
ARTHUR. What, sirs? why then,
This should be Cameliard. [*Rousing himself with sudden energy.*] See,
'tis the spring!
Down in the vale the blossoms of the May
Are swinging in the sun! and there she stands

That shall be England's Queen!
                        Far up I hear
The ceaseless beating of Death's restless wing,
And round mine eyes the circling veil of night
Grows deeper as it falls. Henceforth my sword
Rests in its scabbard. What remains is peace. [*He falls back dead.*
        GUINEVERE. He's gone, the light of all the world lies dead.
            The stage darkens, leaving a light only on the face of Merlin.
        MERLIN. Not so; he doth but pass who cannot die,
The King that was, the King that yet shall be;
Whose spirit, borne along from age to age,
Is England's to the end. Look where the dawn
Sweeps through a wider heaven, and on its wings
By those three Queens of night his barge is borne
To that sweet Isle of Avalon whose sleep
Can heal all earthly wounds.
            During this speech the stage grows darker, and as the vision
                appears, at the back, of Arthur borne in the barge, with the
                three Queens bending over his body, the chorus breaks out, and
                continues till the end.

CHORUS

        Sleep! oh sleep! till night outworn
        Wakens to the echoing horn
        That shall greet thee King new-born,
            King that was, and is to be.
        And a voice from shore to shore
        Cries, "Arise, and sleep no more;
        Greet the dawn, the night is o'er,
            England's sword is in the sea!"

III.
America

Introduction

Victorian England is justifiably credited with producing some of the most significant Arthurian literature ever written. Perhaps because of this, relatively little attention has been given to the fascinating uses of the legends in America in the nineteenth and early twentieth centuries. It is surprising that Arthurian themes occur at all during this period, when many American authors were asserting their cultural independence from Britain. Indeed, at any time in America's history the approach of Mark Twain, who criticizes a world where advancement is based on birth and inherited wealth rather than on natural ability, seems more in keeping with American values than praise of the hierarchic system operating at Camelot. But American authors repeatedly find ways to make the legends their own, sometimes by Americanizing or democratizing them, sometimes by radically altering the traditional stories.

Of course, not all American authors accepted Arthurian material as appropriate. In fact, Nathaniel Hawthorne's short story "The Antique Ring" seems to argue against the use of such material. Hawthorne's tale tells of a minor writer named Edward Caryl, who gives an antique ring to his fiancée, Clara Pemberton. She asks him to create a legend to accompany the ring, a romantic story that need not be "too scrupulous about facts." The ring, according to Caryl's legend, had once been the property of Merlin, who gave it to the lady he loved. Merlin's "art had made [its] diamond the abiding-place of a spirit, which, though of a fiendish nature, was bound to work only good, so long as the ring was an unviolated pledge of love and faith, both of the giver and receiver. But should love prove false, and faith be broken, then the evil spirit would work his own devilish will, until the ring were purified by becoming the medium of some good and holy act, and again the pledge of faithful love."

The ring was handed down to Queen Elizabeth through her Tudor ancestors, and she gave it to the Earl of Essex, who, now in the Tower awaiting execution, asks the Countess of Shrewsbury to convey it to the Queen as a reminder of her former affection. But the Countess betrays Essex and the ring never reaches Elizabeth. Later, one of Cromwell's soldiers steals it from the ancestral vaults of the Shrewsburys. (The story Caryl uses is based on an apocryphal tradition, first reported many years after the death of Essex. In that tradition the ring is mistakenly given not by Essex himself but by a page boy to the Countess of Nottingham, wife of one of Essex's enemies.)

After being used as a pledge in a series of faithless relationships, the ring reaches the New World: "the legend now crosses the Atlantic," as Caryl tells his audience. It turns up in a collection box in a New England church, where the charity of the giver purifies it and makes it once again a symbol of "faithful and devoted love," and so a fitting engagement ring for Edward Caryl to give to Clara.

Through the device of a story within a story, Hawthorne distances himself from the legend of Merlin's ring. It is important to keep this in mind lest one make the mistake of thinking that Caryl's story is Hawthorne's, when the point is really that it is very different from what Hawthorne usually writes. "The Antique Ring" has received very little critical attention, perhaps because it is not perceived as fitting into the schemes critics generally use to discuss Hawthorne's work.

Edward Caryl is "somewhat of a carpet knight in literature," that is, one who has not entered the fray or undertaken the quest for a truly original (one might say a truly native) literature. He has written "stanzas of Tennysonian sweetness, tales imbued with German mysticism, versions from Jean Paul, criticisms of the old English poets, and essays smacking of Dialistic philosophy." His lack of depth and focus can be seen in the fact that when Clara first proposes his making a legend for the ring, he says, "Shall it be a ballad?—a tale in verse? . . . Enchanted rings often glisten in old English poetry." Thus he proposes imitating the very old English poets that he has criticized. Clara steers him away from this notion, insisting that he "tell the legend in simple prose." But the legend he tells is merely a prosaic version of the sort of story he referred to.

Clara, who is a better critic than Edward, passes final judgment on the tale of Merlin's ring: "Believe me, whatever the world may say of the story, I prize it far above the diamond which enkindled your imagination." It is as if she is saying the world will not think much of it, that it is a story only a fiancée could love. What is wrong is that it does not embody any truth to the human heart, as Hawthorne would use the phrase. As Clara says, "It is really a pretty tale, and very proper for any of the Annuals. But, Edward, your moral does not satisfy me. What thought did you embody in the ring?" Edward replies that he "can never separate the idea from the symbol in which it manifests itself" and then goes on to do just that by explaining that the gem is the human heart, and the Evil Spirit is Falsehood.

As interesting as it may be that Hawthorne writes about Merlin, the structure of his tale implies that he is rejecting such material. Like Chaucer's "Tale of Sir Thopas," Hawthorne's "The Antique Ring" is deliberately flawed in order to comment on the teller of the tale. The fantastic legends of the old English poets, legends like those about Merlin, Hawthorne seems to be suggesting, are not a fruitful area for those who, like Edward Caryl, are seeking to assist in "the growth of American Literature."

Hawthorne, then, brings an Arthurian legend to the New World in order to turn it against itself. He shows the danger of the use of an old English legend by a young American writer trying to define himself and his young country in literature. In a sense "The Antique Ring" is analogous to Hawthorne's "My Kinsman, Major Molineux," a story that depicts a young American whose coming of age requires him to reject, on a personal and political level, the dominance of his kinsman, who is a colonial governor appointed by the King of England. Just as Robin must learn to make his own way in the world, so must Edward Caryl learn to make his own way in literature, free from the dominance of British authors.

Other American authors, however, discover ways to make Arthurian material compatible with New World concerns. James Russell Lowell, for example, used the Grail legend as the basis for *The Vision of Sir Launfal.* Though modern critics find it poorly structured and disorganized and accuse it of simplistic moralizing, the poem was extremely popular in its day. Perhaps that popularity is due to Lowell's changes in the Grail story, changes which make his version more suited to his American audience.

The Vision of Sir Launfal can be understood only as a dream vision. And dream visions are poems in which lessons are learned— whether about love as in Chaucer's *Book of the Duchess,* or about spiritual happiness as in *Pearl,* or about charity as in Lowell's poem. Launfal falls asleep in the first stanza of Part One. All of the action, including the entire quest and the learning of the true meaning of the Grail, takes place in the vision that comes to him as he sleeps. The poem is not a narrative and not a romance in the medieval sense. The reader sees Launfal setting out on the quest and sees him after he has returned. Were it a romance, it would be quite deficient and quite poorly constructed: it would be like *Sir Gawain and the Green Knight* without the temptations and the hunts and the beheading contest.

But even when the poem is seen as a dream vision, structural problems remain. This is because it is an American version of the medieval form. It combines the style and description of an American romantic nature poem with the dream vision. Of course, as a number of critics have pointed out, the countryside described in the poem is more like New England than old England. Yet this Americanizing of the Arthurian world may be one of the reasons for the popularity of the poem in the nineteenth century—just as the anachronisms in Chaucer and other medieval writers made their poems more accessible to contemporary readers.

The use of such natural description is more than a superficial updating. As it does so often in nineteenth-century America, Nature becomes a teacher. The charity and generosity that Launfal must learn are paralleled by the freely given bounty of Nature and Nature's God. The point is made early in the prologue to the first part:

> Earth gets its price for what Earth gives us;
> The beggar is taxed for a corner to die in,
> The priest hath his fee who comes and shrives us,
> We bargain for the graves we lie in;
> At the devil's booth are all things sold,
> Each ounce of dross costs its ounce of gold;
> For a cap and bells our lives we pay,
> Bubbles we buy with a whole soul's tasking:
> 'Tis heaven alone that is given away,
> 'Tis only God may be had for the asking;
> No price is set on the lavish summer;
> June may be had by the poorest comer.

The following line—"And what is so rare as a day in June?"—has become such a cliché that its original importance to the poem is easily overlooked. The rarest and therefore the most valuable thing, the glory of a June day, is freely bestowed. Launfal must learn to bestow his charity as freely and lovingly on his fellow human beings.

But the Americanizing of the story goes beyond the natural description and the moral. Lowell prefaces his poem with a note that deliberately distances his material from Arthur and Camelot.

He writes: "The plot (if I may give that name to any thing so slight) of the following poem is my own, and, to serve its purposes, I have enlarged the circle of competition in search of the miraculous cup in such a manner as to include, not only other persons than the heroes of the Round Table, but also a period of time subsequent to the date of King Arthur's reign." This statement is significant not only because its comment on the slightness of the plot recognizes that the poem is different from traditional narratives, but also—and perhaps especially—because it divorces the Grail legend from Arthur's reign. This is all the more important since there is nothing in the poem that could be used to date it outside of Arthur's time. So Lowell has prefaced his poem with a comment saying it is not set in Arthur's time—though there is no narrative imperative for saying such a thing and though Grail stories are traditionally Arthurian. Even the choice of Launfal as the Grail knight emphasizes this distancing. Lowell might have chosen a more traditional name. He considered changing his own name to Perceval Lowell because of his fascination with the character, and surely "The Vision of Sir Perceval" would have been as acceptable a title as "The Vision of Sir Launfal"—unless Lowell were deliberately attempting to distance himself from the traditional Arthurian legends. In fact, the prefatory note to the poem must make one wonder if Lowell is even thinking of the medieval Launfal who is associated with Arthur's court. At any rate, his Grail story is clearly a non-Arthurian Arthurian poem. By disassociating the Grail from royalty, even the admirable royalty of Arthur, Lowell makes the north country where Launfal's castle is located a world unto itself, a world that can be transformed into a sort of new Eden by the natural charity that Launfal learns from his vision. In addition, the achieving of the Grail—that is, the learning and practicing of this transforming charity—is not something limited to Arthur's time and place and to the few good men that he gathered about him. Rather the achieving of the Grail comes within the reach of all people, certainly a democratic notion appropriate to an American poem.

Another unprecedented use of the Grail theme can be found in the poem "Kathanal" by Katrina Trask. This poem is from *Under King Constantine*, a collection of three poems set in the reign of Constantine, who, according to Malory, became king of Britain after Arthur's passing. Like Lowell, who says that the plot of *The Vision of Sir Launfal* is his own, Trask claims that her tales "have no legendary warrant." Both authors emphasize the originality, the newness, of their Grail stories.

Trask's narrative, however, is far different from Lowell's. In her poem the achieving of the Grail is a way of sublimating the love between Kathanal and Leorre, the wife of his "patron knight." Kathanal's quest is not something he is led to by divine vision or inspiration. It is imposed upon him by Leorre as a way of dealing with the forbidden love they feel for each other.

From the beginning the poem cries out for a Freudian interpretation. Frustrated by his as yet unspoken love for Leorre, Kathanal tears the plume from his helmet and tosses it into the sea. With his "knightly symbol lost" he feels dishonored as a knight, and his boyhood dream of being "a knight like Galahad, pure and true" seems unattainable. Having forgotten "loyalty / And truth and honour for the fair Leorre," Kathanal fears that if he stays near her "tempting charm"

> I shall, through some wild impulse, wantonly
> Fling my unsullied knighthood to the winds,
> As now I flung the plume from out my helm.

The poem becomes an orgy of sexual repression. Kathanal struggles between "deep yearning for some touch of love" and "brave endeavour for self-mastery." He confesses his love to her and she admits she reciprocates it but refuses to let him touch her even though she confesses "my senses thrill / If you but touch the border of my robe. . . ." When her confession prompts him to say he will remain with her, she replies "now, if ever, you will surely go." Lest their love become "inglorious" like that of Tristram and Isoud or Launcelot and Guenever, she asks him to undertake the quest for the Grail. To replace the purple plume from his helmet, Leorre gives him "this spotless scarf, the girdle from my robe," though she admits that her "longing gaze" often watched his plume in tournaments. He wavers but does resist temptation and so ultimately achieves the Grail.

Like Lowell's poem, Trask's has a lesson, not about charity but about love: "All love should be a glory, not a doom; / Love for love's sake, albeit bliss-denied." Kathanal has achieved the Grail, and Leorre's knowledge that love for her made this possible lifts her spirit "Beyond her sorrow and her daily want / Of Kathanal" and leads to a "calm, triumphant peace." In Trask's reinterpretation of the Grail story, as in Lowell's, the sacred vessel becomes attainable not because of supernatural predetermination but by strength of character. Trask and Lowell demonstrate the kinds of liberties some authors will take with the traditional Arthurian material in order to make the legends of Camelot meaningful to American readers.

A rather different approach to the material is taken in the play *The New King Arthur* by Edgar Fawcett. Quite a few plays by American authors of the nineteenth and early twentieth centuries treat Arthurian themes. In fact, the first Arthurian work in America was a play called *Merlin* by Lambert Wilmer (1827). Other early dramatic works include Richard Hovey's sequence of plays collectively called *Launcelot and Guenevere: A Poem in Dramas* (1891-98) and Ralph Adam Cram's *Excalibur* (written in 1893 but not published until 1909). Fawcett's play, however, is different from all of these and indeed from most Arthurian drama in that it is a comic or rather a burlesque play.

The New King Arthur is also a forerunner of Twain's deliberate mockery of the chivalric ideals of Tennyson's Camelot. In Fawcett's mock dedication of the play to Tennyson he says:

> Take, Alfred, this mellifluous verse of mine,
> Nor rank too high the honor I bestow,
> Howe'er it thrill thy soul with grateful pride.
> For thou hast sung of Arthur and his knights,
> And thou hast told of deeds that they have done,
> And thou hast told of loves that they have loved,
> And thou hast told of sins that they have sinned,
> And I have sung in my way, thou in thine.
> I think my way superior to thine,
> Yes, Alfred, yes, in loyal faith I do . . .

Fawcett has removed all of the grandeur, heroic or tragic, from Tennyson's characters. Though Merlin is described as one who "has lived ten spans / Of usual life, and dies but when he wills," his primary power lies in the belief that he possesses two products described by Lancelot in terms that might be suitable for the billboards carried by Twain's knights, who use their errantry to advertise. One is a "face-wash that shall lend those blooming cheeks / A pearlier beauty than of mortal tint"; and the other is a "hair-dye that shall stain each silken strand / Of those rich tresses into sunnier sheen."

In the general chorus that closes the play, Fawcett notes that "no King Arthur / One bit of authenticity may hold / In his apocryphal and mythic mould." Thus he deliberately creates a New King Arthur, one who, like Merlin and Galahad and almost all the other denizens of his Camelot, has human failings. In the new Camelot—one might say the New World Camelot—people are motivated by something as simple as a hair-dye. Thus Fawcett's play foreshadows Twain's *Connecticut Yankee* not only by departing radically from earlier versions of the Arthurian legends but also by introducing some everyday reality and some everyday morality into Camelot.

But the ideal morality often associated with some of the inhabitants of Arthur's realm is a force that influences not only British writers in the tradition of Tennyson but many in America as well. Retellings, such as Sidney Lanier's *The Boy's King Arthur,* are based on the premise that the Arthurian tales provide models of behavior for children, especially for young boys. Of course, the premise is valid only if the tales are bowdlerized, as Lanier's are. This premise extends beyond literature. William Byron Forbush, a minister concerned about "the boy problem," founded an organization known as the Knights of King Arthur, which was designed as a way of channeling the energies of boys. The members of these clubs, or castles as they were called, modeled themselves on a knight of Arthur's court or some other hero and were guided in wholesome and helpful activities by a Merlin.

Largely because of the association of the Arthurian legends with the education of youth, one of America's best-known illustrators, Howard Pyle, wrote and illustrated four books that retold the Arthurian stories from Arthur's birth to his death: *The Story of King Arthur and His Knights* (1903), *The Story of the Champions of the Round Table* (1905), *The Story of Sir Launcelot and His Companions* (1907), and *The Story of the Grail and the Passing of Arthur* (1910). The first of these is clearly in the didactic tradition represented by Lanier and by Forbush's movement: Pyle points out morals based on the tales he tells, a practice that virtually disappears in the later books.

In providing a model for behavior, Pyle Americanizes—or at least democratizes—the medieval legends by suggesting that anyone can achieve the moral equivalent of knighthood or kinghood. Thus his retelling is reminiscent of Lowell's *Vision of Sir Launfal.* In Pyle's stories not the Grail but nobility itself is democratized. Early in *The Story of King Arthur,* just after Arthur has drawn the sword from the anvil, Pyle writes:

Thus Arthur achieved the adventure of the sword that day and
entered into his birthright of royalty. Wherefore, may God grant
His Grace unto you all that ye too may likewise succeed in your
undertakings. For any man may be a king in that life in which he
is placed if so he may draw forth the sword of success from out of
the iron of circumstance. Wherefore when your time of assay
cometh, I do hope it may be with you as it was with Arthur that
day, and that ye too may achieve success with entire satisfaction
unto yourself and to your great glory and perfect happiness.

Later, when Arthur, acting as the champion of Leodegrance of
Cameliard, defeats the Duke of Umber and rides off without waiting
for the gratitude of the King or his people, Pyle notes that

when a man is a king among men, as was King Arthur, then is he
of such a calm and equal temper that neither victory nor defeat
may cause him to become either unduly exalted in his own
opinion or so troubled in spirit as to be altogether cast down into
despair. So if you would become like to King Arthur, then you
shall take all your triumphs as he took this victory, for you will not
be turned aside from your final purposes by the great applause
that many men may give you, but you will first finish your work
that you have set yourself to perform, ere you give yourself ease to
sit you down and to enjoy the fruits of your victory.

Yea, he who is a true king of men, will not say to himself,
"Lo! I am worthy to be crowned with laurels;" but rather will he
say to himself, "What more is there that I may do to make the
world the better because of my endeavors?

The final adventure in *The Story of King Arthur* is a reworking
of the tale of Gawaine and the loathly lady (with additions from *Sir
Gawain and the Green Knight* and Pyle's imagination). Pyle's tale is
based on the ballad "The Marriage of Sir Gawain" from Bishop
Percy's *Reliques of Ancient English Poetry*, but as with all his sources
Pyle feels free to change the traditional material considerably. Pyle
also uses the story to make another link between the reader and the
knights of Camelot. Gawain is willing to marry a woman whose "ears
were very huge and flapped, and her hair hung down over her head
like to snakes, and her face was covered all over with
wrinkles . . . and her eyes were bleared and covered over with a film,
and the eyelids were red as with the continual weeping of her eyes,
and she had but one tooth in her mouth, and her hands . . . were
like claws of bone." He agrees to wed her because Arthur has

promised, as a condition for receiving the answer to the riddle needed to save his life, that she can choose one of his knights for a husband. In the end the enchantment on the lady is broken and she turns into a beautiful bride for Gawaine, although he did not know this would happen when he married her. Pyle advises his readers that they can be like Gawaine if they willingly accept their "duty" even when it appears ugly to them. He adds:

> When you shall have become entirely wedded unto your duty, then shall you become equally worthy with that good knight and gentleman Sir Gawaine; for it needs not that a man shall wear armor for to be a true knight, but only that he shall do his best endeavor with all patience and humility as it hath been ordained for him to do. Wherefore, when your time cometh unto you to display your knightness by assuming your duty, I do pray that you also may approve yourself as worthy as Sir Gawaine approved himself in this story which I have told you of as above written.

For Pyle, Arthur and his knights were not ideals from another time and place for which there were no contemporary parallels. They were examples of certain virtues that could be translated into the modern world, not by the writer but by the reader in his or her personal life.

Though many of the retellings of the Arthurian stories were aimed at boys, several female poets (Sara Teasdale, Edna St. Vincent Millay, Dorothy Parker) writing in the early decades of the twentieth century produced poems that focus on Arthurian women. Perhaps the best of these is Teasdale's "Guenevere," a monologue in the tradition of Morris's "Defence of Guenevere." The Queen complains of being "branded for a single fault." She vividly describes her meeting with Lancelot, and in so doing reveals the deep emotion that caused her to frustrate the expectations of those who wanted her to play a role, to "be right fair, / A little kind, and gownèd wondrously." In fact, the poem might be read as a woman's complaint that she is expected to conform to the standards of others who frown on her strong feelings. This interest in Arthurian women foreshadows the attention they are given by contemporary novelists who see in their stories a way to vitalize the familiar tales of Arthur's realm.

More extended poetic treatment of the Arthurian legends is found in the works of Edwin Arlington Robinson. Robinson's three book-length Arthurian poems—*Merlin* (1917), *Lancelot* (1920), and *Tristram* (1927)—are obviously influenced by the tendency of his age to treat Arthurian themes in plays. All the poems are dramatic, the highpoints usually coming in dialogues between the principal characters. It is also clear that the poems are, on one level, very much a product of their times. In one of his letters Robinson said that "there is a certain amount [of symbolic significance] in *Merlin* and *Lancelot,* which were suggested by the world war—Camelot representing in a way the going of a world that is now pretty much gone."

Robinson's *Lancelot* follows Malory fairly closely as it chronicles the destructive results of the fatal love between Arthur's queen and his greatest knight. But it is more than a verse retelling because of its treatment of psychological motivations and responses. *Tristram,* which won the Pulitzer Prize in 1927, demonstrates Robinson's skill at characterization, particularly through his depiction of the quiet strength and unwavering love of Isolt of Brittany. But the poem is not as good as *Merlin.*

Both *Tristram* and *Merlin* present the tragic loss of an idyllic world that the characters can imagine but cannot attain for more than a moment. In *Merlin* there is a double loss, as Merlin's conscience forces him to leave the Edenic world of Broceliande that he shares with Vivian and to return to Camelot, which he knows he can not save from its impending doom.

The Broceliande to which Robinson's Merlin retreats is not a place where he is held by magic spell. Rather he goes there willingly and leaves when he wishes. It is a place where Merlin forgets, for a time, "that any town alive / had ever such a name as Camelot" and a place that "Fate made . . . a paradise" until Arthur sends Dagonet to ask Merlin to return.

The intrusion of the real world into what Merlin calls an "elysian wilderness" is inevitable despite Vivian's attempt to keep it at bay. She convinces Merlin to shave off his beard, a symbol of change and the passing of time. Her desire to live in a perfect present that never changes is reflected in the recurring references to "specks." When Vivian fills Merlin's goblet with wine, she says she fears that in the bottom of the bottle "there may be specks." The specks she fears are symbolic of imperfection, and Merlin's response that "there are specks everywhere" is true. But that is only more of a reason for fear, not less as Merlin suggests. In fact, she dislikes Arthur because "There are specks / Almost all over him." That is, he is surrounded by imperfection.

Though Vivian feels there is no "fitter name than Eden" for Broceliande, Merlin is able to glimpse perfection in Arthur and his realm. Vivian observes that Merlin made Arthur king because he saw in him "a mirror for the millions," an example for all to follow in order to achieve a better world. Toward the end of the poem, when Merlin realizes he will neither save Arthur's realm nor return to Vivian, he imagines her saying:

> . . . Time called him home,
> And that was as it was; for much is lost
> Between Broceliande and Camelot.

These lines might be seen as thematic. The real world, the world of time and change and tragedy, ever intrudes on the visions of perfection that people can imagine but not actualize. Broceliande and Camelot represent two aspects of that vision: the former, an attempt at escape from the real world to an idyllic place of personal happiness; the latter, an attempt to transform the real world into a Utopia, a place where social justice is the norm. Between the two all our dreams of justice, peace, and happiness are lost. Robinson's Merlin becomes a type of American Adam, who is prevented by historical forces and personal obligations from being successful in creating either of these two Edens he envisions.

The poem ends on a somber note. The last line is: "And there was darkness over Camelot." Yet Robinson said in a letter to Edith Brower (24 June 1917), who had written him about the sadness of the ending, that "there is nothing especially sad about the end of kings and the redemption of the world, and that is what Merlin seems to be driving at." Thus Robinson suggests, as Merlin says, that Arthur's "deeds are wrought for those who are to come." In addition, the darkness is brightened by another vision, that of "two fires that are to light the world." These two fires are "the torch of woman" and "the light that Galahad found," which "together" are "yet to light the world." Galahad's light, the Grail, represents spiritual and moral values. The torch of woman is a less clearcut symbol, perhaps representing the feminine side of people, the side that does not resort to war and violence to solve problems.

Robinson looks forward to many of the concerns and techniques of authors of the modern period. He transforms Vivian into a real woman who is trying to create a world of personal happiness in the midst of the chaos that descends on Camelot; he focuses on the emotions and psychological motivations of his characters; and he relates the action in Arthur's realm to contemporary political and moral concerns. These are traits found in some of the most interesting of the modern treatments of the legends. And yet his Edenic theme, his demystification of the Arthurian characters, and his willingness to reshape Arthurian story place him clearly in the American Arthurian tradition.

The Vision of Sir Launfal

by

JAMES RUSSELL LOWELL

Author's Note: According to the mythology of the Romancers, the San Greal, or Holy Grail, was the cup out of which Jesus partook of the last supper with his disciples. It was brought into England by Joseph of Arimathea, and remained there, an object of pilgrimage and adoration, for many years in the keeping of his lineal descendants. It was incumbent upon those who had charge of it to be chaste in thought, word, and deed; but one of the keepers having broken this condition, the Holy Grail disappeared. From that time it was a favorite enterprise of the knights of Arthur's court to go in search of it. Sir Galahad was at last successful in finding it, as may be read in the seventeenth book of the Romance of King Arthur.[1] Tennyson has made Sir Galahad the subject of one of the most exquisite of his poems.

The plot (if I may give that name to any thing so slight) of the following poem is my own, and, to serve its purposes, I have enlarged the circle of competition in search of the miraculous cup in such a manner as to include, not only other persons than the heroes of the Round Table, but also a period of time subsequent to the date of King Arthur's reign.

Prelude to Part First

Over his keys the musing organist,
    Beginning doubtfully and far away,
First lets his fingers wander as they list,
    And builds a bridge from Dreamland for his lay:
Then, as the touch of his loved instrument
    Gives hopes and fervor, nearer draws his theme,

---

1. In Caxton's edition of Malory the achieving of the Grail is recounted in the seventeenth book.

First guessed by faint auroral flushes sent
Along the wavering vista of his dream.

Not only around our infancy
Doth heaven with all its splendors lie;
Daily, with souls that cringe and plot,
We Sinais[2] climb and know it not;
Over our manhood bend the skies;
Against our fallen and traitor lives
The great winds utter prophecies;
With our faint hearts the mountain strives;
Its arms outstretched, the druid wood
Waits with its benedicite;[3]
And to our age's drowsy blood
Still shouts the inspiring sea.

Earth gets its price for what Earth gives us;
The beggar is taxed for a corner to die in,
The priest hath his fee who comes and shrives us,[4]
We bargain for the graves we lie in;
At the Devil's booth are all things sold
Each ounce of dross costs its ounce of gold;
For a cap and bells[5] our lives we pay,
Bubbles we earn with a whole soul's tasking:
'T is heaven alone that is given away,
'T is only God may be had for the asking;
There is no price set on the lavish summer,
And June may be had by the poorest comer.

And what is so rare as a day in June?
Then, if ever, come perfect days;
Then Heaven tries the earth if it be in tune,
And over it softly her warm ear lays:
Whether we look, or whether we listen,
We hear life murmur, or see it glisten;
Every clod feels a stir of might,

---

2. Sinai is the mountain on which Moses received the law from God (cf.
Exodus 19).

3. Blessing.

4. Hears our confessions.

5. The cap and bells were traditionally worn by a jester or fool.

An instinct within it that reaches and towers,
And, grasping blindly above it for light,
    Climbs to a soul in grass and flowers;
The flush of life may well be seen
    Thrilling back over hills and valleys;
The cowslip startles in meadows green,
    The buttercup catches the sun in its chalice,
And there 's never a leaf or a blade too mean
    To be some happy creature's palace;
The little bird sits at his door in the sun,
    Atilt like a blossom among the leaves,
And lets his illumined being o'errun
    With the deluge of summer it receives;
His mate feels the eggs beneath her wings,
And the heart in her dumb breast flutters and sings;
He sings to the wide world, and she to her nest,—
In the nice ear of Nature which song is the best?

Now is the high-tide of the year,
    And whatever of life hath ebbed away
Comes flooding back, with a ripply cheer,
    Into every bare inlet and creek and bay;
Now the heart is so full that a drop overfills it,
We are happy now because God so wills it;
No matter how barren the past may have been,
'T is enough for us now that the leaves are green;
We sit in the warm shade and feel right well
How the sap creeps up and the blossoms swell;
We may shut our eyes, but we cannot help knowing
That skies are clear and grass is growing;
The breeze comes whispering in our ear,
That dandelions are blossoming near,
    That maize has sprouted, that streams are flowing,
That the river is bluer than the sky,
That the robin is plastering his house hard by;
And if the breeze kept the good news back,
For other couriers we should not lack;
    We could guess it all by yon heifer's lowing,[6]—
And hark! how clear bold chanticleer,[7]

---

6. Mooing.

7. "Chanticleer" is a rooster.

Warmed with the new wine of the year,
    Tells all in his lusty crowing!

Joy comes, grief goes, we know not how;
Every thing is happy now,
    Every thing is upward striving;
'T is as easy now for the heart to be true
As for grass to be green or skies to be blue,—
    'T is the natural way of living:
Who knows whither the clouds have fled?
    In the unscarred heaven they leave no wake;
And the eyes forget the tears they have shed,
    The heart forgets its sorrow and ache;
The soul partakes the season's youth,
    And the sulphurous rifts of passion and woe
Lie deep 'neath a silence pure and smooth,
    Like burnt-out craters healed with snow.
What wonder if Sir Launfal now
Remembered the keeping of his vow?

Part First
I

"My golden spurs now bring to me,
    And bring to me my richest mail,
For to-morrow I go over land and sea
    In search of the Holy Grail;
Shall never a bed for me be spread,
Nor shall a pillow be under my head,
Till I begin my vow to keep;
Here on the rushes will I sleep,
And perchance there may come a vision true
Ere day create the world anew."
    Slowly Sir Launfal's eyes grew dim,
    Slumber fell like a cloud on him,
And into his soul the vision flew.

II

The crows flapped over by twos and threes,
In the pool drowsed the cattle up to their knees,
    The little birds sang as if it were
    The one day of summer in all the year,

And the very leaves seemed to sing on the trees:
The castle alone in the landscape lay
Like an outpost of winter, dull and gray;
'T was the proudest hall in the North Countree,
And never its gates might opened be,
Save to lord or lady of high degree;
Summer besieged it on every side,
But the churlish stone her assaults defied;
She could not scale the chilly wall,
Though round it for leagues her pavilions tall
Stretched left and right,
Over the hills and out of sight;
  Green and broad was every tent,
  And out of each a murmur went
Till the breeze fell off at night.

III

The drawbridge dropped with a surly clang,
And through the dark arch a charger sprang,
Bearing Sir Launfal, the maiden knight,
In his gilded mail, that flamed so bright
It seemed the dark castle had gathered all
Those shafts the fierce sun had shot over its wall
  In his siege of three hundred summers long,
And, binding them all in one blazing sheaf,
  Had cast them forth: so, young and strong,
And lightsome as a locust-leaf,
Sir Launfal flashed forth in his unscarred mail,
To seek in all climes for the Holy Grail.

IV

It was morning on hill and stream and tree,
  And morning in the young knight's heart;
Only the castle moodily
Rebuffed the gifts of the sunshine free,
  And gloomed by itself apart;

The season brimmed all other things up
Full as the rain fills the pitcher-plant's cup.[8]

V

As Sir Launfal made morn through the darksome gate,
　　He was ware of a leper, crouched by the same,
Who begged with his hand and moaned as he sate;
　　And a loathing over Sir Launfal came,
The sunshine went out of his soul with a thrill,
　　The flesh 'neath his armor did shrink and crawl,
And midway its leap his heart stood still
　　Like a frozen waterfall;
For this man, so foul and bent of stature,
Rasped harshly against his dainty nature,
And seemed the one blot on the summer morn,—
So he tossed him a piece of gold in scorn.

VI

The leper raised not the gold from the dust:
"Better to me the poor man's crust,
Better the blessing of the poor,
Though I turn me empty from his door;
That is no true alms which the hand can hold;
He gives nothing but worthless gold
　　Who gives from a sense of duty;
But he who gives a slender mite,
And gives to that which is out of sight,
　　That thread of the all-sustaining Beauty
Which runs through all and doth all unite,—
The hand cannot clasp the whole of his alms,
The heart outstretches its eager palms,
For a god goes with it and makes it store
To the soul that was starving in darkness before."

Prelude to Part Second

Down swept the chill wind from the mountain peak,
　　From the snow five thousand summers old;

---

8. A pitcher-plant is a plant with pitcherlike leaves that attract and trap insects.

On open wold[9] and hill-top bleak
  It had gathered all the cold,
And whirled it like sleet on the wanderer's cheek;
It carried a shiver everywhere
From the unleafed boughs and pastures bare;
The little brook heard it and built a roof
'Neath which he could house him, winter-proof;
All night by the white stars' frosty gleams
He groined his arches[10] and matched his beams;
Slender and clear were his crystal spars
As the lashes of light that trim the stars;
He sculptured every summer delight
In his halls and chambers out of sight;
Sometimes his tinkling waters slipt
Down through a frost-leaved forest-crypt,
Long, sparkling aisles of steel-stemmed trees
Bending to counterfeit a breeze;
Sometimes the roof no fretwork[11] knew
But silvery mosses that downward grew;
Sometimes it was carved in sharp relief
With quaint arabesques of ice-fern leaf;
Sometimes it was simply smooth and clear
For the gladness of heaven to shine through, and here
He had caught the nodding bulrush-tops
And hung them thickly with diamond drops,
Which crystalled the beams of moon and sun,
And made a star of every one:
No mortal builder's most rare device
Could match this winter-palace of ice;
'T was as if every image that mirrored lay
In his depths serene through the summer day,
Each flitting shadow of earth and sky,
  Lest the happy model should be lost,
Had been mimicked in fairy masonry
  By the elfin builders of the frost.

---

  9. Plain.

  10. A "groin" is the curved line or edge formed by the intersection of two vaults.

  11. Ornamental work with repeated symmetrical figures within a border.

Within the hall are song and laughter,
     The cheeks of Christmas glow red and jolly,
And sprouting is every corbel[12] and rafter
     With the lightsome green of ivy and holly;
Through the deep gulf of the chimney wide
Wallows the Yule-log's roaring tide;
The broad flame-pennons[13] droop and flap
     And belly and tug as a flag in the wind;
Like a locust shrills the imprisoned sap,
     Hunted to death in its galleries blind;
And swift little troops of silent sparks,
     Now pausing, now scattering away as in fear,
Go threading the soot-forest's tangled darks
     Like herds of startled deer.

But the wind without was eager and sharp,
Of Sir Launfal's gray hair it makes a harp,
     And rattles and wrings
     The icy strings,
Singing, in dreary monotone,
A Christmas carol of its own,
Whose burden[14] still, as he might guess,
Was—"Shelterless, shelterless, shelterless!"

The voice of the seneschal flared like a torch
As he shouted the wanderer away from the porch,
And he sat in the gateway and saw all night
     The great hall-fire, so cheery and bold,
     Through the window-slits of the castle old,
Build out its piers of ruddy light
     Against the drift of the cold.

Part Second
I

There was never a leaf on bush or tree,
The bare boughs rattled shudderingly;

---

12. A bracket projecting from the face of a wall and used to support a cornice
or arch.

13. Banners.

14. Refrain.

The river was dumb and could not speak,
     For the frost's swift shuttles its shroud had spun;
A single crow on the tree-top bleak
     From his shining feathers shed off the cold sun;
Again it was morning, but shrunk and cold,
As if her veins were sapless and old,
And she rose up decrepitly
For a last dim look at earth and sea.

II

Sir Launfal turned from his own hard gate,
For another heir in his earldom sate;
An old, bent man, worn out and frail,
He came back from seeking the Holy Grail;
Little he recked of[15] his earldom's loss,
No more on his surcoat[16] was blazoned the cross,
But deep in his soul the sign he wore,
The badge of the suffering and the poor.

III

Sir Launfal's raiment thin and spare
Was idle mail 'gainst the barbed air,
For it was just at the Christmas time;
So he mused, as he sat, of a sunnier clime,
And sought for a shelter from cold and snow
In the light and warmth of long ago;
He sees the snake-like caravan crawl
O'er the edge of the desert, black and small,
Then nearer and nearer, till, one by one,
He can count the camels in the sun,
As over the red-hot sands they pass
To where, in its slender necklace of grass,
The little spring laughed and leapt in the shade,
And with its own self like an infant played,
And waved its signal of palms.

---

15. Cared about.
16. A tunic worn over armor.

IV

"For Christ's sweet sake, I beg an alms";—
The happy camels may reach the spring,
But Sir Launfal sees naught save the grewsome thing,
The leper, lank as the rain-blanched bone,
That cowered beside him, a thing as lone
And white as the ice-isles of Northern seas
In the desolate horror of his disease.

V

And Sir Launfal said,—"I behold in thee
An image of Him who died on the tree;
Thou also hast had thy crown of thorns,—
Thou also hast had the world's buffets and scorns,—
And to thy life were not denied
The wounds in the hands and feet and side:
Mild Mary's Son, acknowledge me;
Behold, through him, I give to thee!"

VI

Then the soul of the leper stood up in his eyes
      And looked at Sir Launfal, and straightway he
Remembered in what a haughtier guise
      He had flung an alms to leprosie,
When he caged his young life up in gilded mail
And set forth in search of the Holy Grail.
The heart within him was ashes and dust;
He parted in twain his single crust,
He broke the ice on the streamlet's brink,
And gave the leper to eat and drink;
'T was a mouldy crust of coarse brown bread,
      'T was water out of a wooden bowl,—
Yet with fine wheaten bread was the leper fed,
      And 't was red wine he drank with his thirsty soul.

VII

As Sir Launfal mused with a downcast face,
A light shone round about the place;
The leper no longer crouched at his side,

But stood before him glorified,
Shining and tall and fair and straight
As the pillar that stood by the Beautiful Gate,—
Himself the Gate whereby men can
Enter the temple of God in Man.

VIII

His words were shed softer than leaves from the pine,
And they fell on Sir Launfal as snows on the brine,
Which mingle their softness and quiet in one
With the shaggy unrest they float down upon;
And the voice that was calmer than silence said,
"Lo, it is I, be not afraid!
In many climes, without avail,
Thou hast spent thy life for the Holy Grail;
Behold, it is here,—this cup which thou
Didst fill at the streamlet for me but now;
This crust is my body broken for thee,
This water His blood that died on the tree;
The Holy Supper is kept, indeed,
In whatso we share with another's need,—
Not that which we give, but what we share,—
For the gift without the giver is bare;
Who bestows himself with his alms feeds three,—
Himself, his hungering neighbor, and me."

IX

Sir Launfal awoke, as from a swound:[17]—
"The Grail in my castle here is found!
Hang my idle armor up on the wall,
Let it be the spider's banquet-hall;
He must be fenced with stronger mail
Who would seek and find the Holy Grail."

X

The castle-gate stands open now,
        And the wanderer is welcome to the hall
As the hangbird is to the elm-tree bough;

---

17. Swoon.

No longer scowl the turrets tall,
The Summer's long siege at last is o'er;
When the first poor outcast went in at the door,
She entered with him in disguise,
And mastered the fortress by surprise;
There is no spot she loves so well on ground,
She lingers and smiles there the whole year round;
The meanest serf on Sir Launfal's land
Has hall and bower at his command;
And there 's no poor man in the North Countree
But is lord of the earldom as much as he.

The Antique Ring

by

NATHANIEL HAWTHORNE

"Yes, indeed; the gem is as bright as a star, and curiously set," said Clara Pemberton, examining an antique ring, which her betrothed lover had just presented to her, with a very pretty speech. "It needs only one thing to make it perfect."

"And what is that?" asked Mr. Edward Caryl, secretly anxious for the credit of his gift. "A modern setting, perhaps?"

"Oh, no! That would destroy the charm at once," replied Clara. "It needs nothing but a story. I long to know how many times it has been the pledge of faith between two lovers, and whether the vows, of which it was the symbol, were always kept or often broken. Not that I should be too scrupulous about facts. If you happen to be unacquainted with its authentic history, so much the better. May it not have sparkled upon a queen's finger? Or who knows, but it is the very ring which Posthumus received from Imogen?[1] In short, you must kindle your imagination at the lustre of this diamond, and make a legend for it."

Now such a task—and doubtless Clara knew it—was the most acceptable that could have been imposed on Edward Caryl. He was one of that multitude of young gentlemen—limbs, or rather twigs, of the law—whose names appear in gilt letters on the front of Tudor's Buildings,[2] and other places in the vicinity of the Court-House, which seem to be the haunt of the gentler, as well as the

---

1. In Shakespeare's *Cymbeline* Imogen, the daughter of Cymbeline, marries Posthumous secretly. When her father learns of the marriage, he banishes Posthumous. Before he leaves, Posthumous is given a ring by Imogen. The ring plays an important part in the rest of the plot.

2. William Tudor (1779–1830) was the founder and first editor of the *North American Review* and an original member of the Anthology Club, a Boston literary society, the reading room of which was the foundation of the Boston Athenaeum, a library, art museum, and laboratory. In 1845 the library was provided with its own building.

severer muses. Edward, in the dearth of clients, was accustomed to employ his much leisure in assisting the growth of American literature; to which good cause he had contributed not a few quires of the finest letter paper, containing some thought, some fancy, some depth of feeling, together with a young writer's abundance of conceits. Sonnets, stanzas of Tennysonian sweetness, tales imbued with German mysticism, versions from Jean Paul,[3] criticisms of the old English poets, and essays smacking of Dialistic[4] philosophy, were among his multifarious productions. The editors of the fashionable periodicals were familiar with his autography, and inscribed his name in those brilliant bead-rolls of ink-stained celebrity, which illustrate the first page of their covers. Nor did fame withhold her laurel. Hillard[5] had included him among the lights of the New-England metropolis, in his Boston Book; Bryant[6] had found room for some of his stanzas, in the Selections from American Poetry; and Mr. Griswold,[7] in his recent assemblage of the sons and daughters of song, had introduced Edward Caryl into the inner court of the temple, among his fourscore choicest bards. There was a prospect, indeed, of his assuming a still higher and more independent position. Interviews had been held with Ticknor,[8] and a correspondence with the Harpers,[9] respecting a proposed volume, chiefly to consist of Mr. Caryl's fugitive pieces in the Magazines, but

---

3. Johann Paul Friedrich Richter (1763–1825), a German Romantic novelist.

4. *The Dial* (published from July 1840 to April 1844) was a primary outlet for the writings of the New England Transcendentalists. It was first edited by Margaret Fuller and then by Ralph Waldo Emerson.

5. George Stillman Hillard (1808–1879) compiled *The Boston Book: Being Specimens of Metropolitan Literature* (1840).

6. American poet William Cullen Bryant (1794–1878) edited *Selections from the American Poets* (1840). (No poet named Edward Caryl appears in this collection.)

7. Rufus Wilmot Griswold (1815–1857) compiled anthologies of *The Poets and Poetry of America* (1842) and *The Female Poets of America* (1849). (No poet named Edward Caryl appeared in the former publication.)

8. William Davis Ticknor (1810–1864) founded a publishing company in 1832. In 1854 it became Ticknor and Fields, publisher of Hawthorne's novels as well as the writings of many of the important New England authors of the nineteenth century.

9. James Harper (1795–1869) and his brother John (1797–1875) in 1817 founded a print shop that, by 1818, had developed into Harper's publishing house. Two other brothers, Joseph Wesley (1801–1870) and Fletcher (1806–1877), subsequently joined the firm. In 1833 the name was changed to Harper and Brothers.

to be accompanied with a poem of some length, never before published. Not improbably, the public may yet be gratifed with this collection.

Meanwhile, we sum up our sketch of Edward Caryl, by pronouncing him, though somewhat of a carpet knight[10] in literature, yet no unfavorable specimen of a generation of rising writers, whose spirit is such that we may reasonably expect creditable attempts from all, and good and beautiful results from some. And, it will be observed, Edward was the very man to write pretty legends, at a lady's instance, for an old-fashioned diamond ring. He took the jewel in his hand, and turned it so as to catch its scintillating radiance, as if hoping, in accordance with Clara's suggestion, to light up his fancy with that star-like gleam.

"Shall it be a ballad?—a tale in verse?" he inquired. "Enchanted rings often glisten in old English poetry, I think something may be done with the subject; but it is fitter for rhyme than prose."

"No, no," said Miss Pemberton.—"We will have no more rhyme than just enough for a posy to the ring. You must tell the legend in simple prose; and when it is finished, I will make a little party to hear it read."

The young gentleman promised obedience; and going to his pillow, with his head full of the familiar spirits that used to be worn in rings, watches, and sword-hilts, he had the good fortune to possess himself of an available idea in a dream. Connecting this with what he himself chanced to know of the ring's real history, his task was done. Clara Pemberton invited a select few of her friends, all holding the stanchest faith in Edward's genius, and therefore the most genial auditors, if not altogether the fairest critics, that a writer could possibly desire. Blessed be woman for her faculty of admiration, and especially for her tendency to admire with her heart, when man, at most, grants merely a cold approval with his mind!

Drawing his chair beneath the blaze of a solar lamp,[11] Edward Caryl untied a roll of glossy paper, and began as follows:

---

10. A knight who has spent his life in ease away from battle.

11. Also called an Argand lamp, an oil lamp with a tubular wick that permits air to reach the center of the flame.

The Legend

After the death-warrant had been read to the Earl of Essex,[12] and on the evening before his appointed execution, the Countess of Shrewsbury paid his lordship a visit, and found him, as it appeared, toying childishly with a ring. The diamond, that enriched it, glittered like a little star, but with a singular tinge of red. The gloomy prison-chamber in the Tower, with its deep and narrow windows piercing the walls of stone, was now all that the earl possessed of worldly prospect; so that there was the less wonder that he should look stedfastly into the gem, and moralize upon earth's deceitful splendor, as men in darkness and ruin seldom fail to do. But the shrewd observations of the countess,—an artful and unprincipled woman,—the pretended friend of Essex, but who had come to glut her revenge for a deed of scorn, which he himself had forgotten;—her keen eye detected a deeper interest attached to this jewel. Even while expressing his gratitude for her remembrance of a ruined favorite, and condemned criminal, the earl's glance reverted to the ring, as if all that remained of time and its affairs were collected within that small golden circlet.

"My dear lord," observed the countess, "there is surely some matter of great moment wherewith this ring is connected, since it so absorbs your mind. A token, it may be, of some fair lady's love,—alas, poor lady, once richest in possessing such a heart! Would you that the jewel be returned to her?"

"The queen! the queen! It was her majesty's own gift," replied the earl, still gazing into the depths of the gem. "She took it from her finger, and told me, with a smile, that it was an heir-loom from her Tudor ancestors, and had once been the property of Merlin, the British wizard, who gave it to the lady of his love. His art had made this diamond the abiding-place of a spirit, which, though of fiendish nature, was bound to work only good, so long as the ring

---

12. Robert Devereux, second Earl of Essex (1567–1601) was a favorite of Queen Elizabeth I, with whom he had a stormy relationship. After a series of falling-outs and reconciliations he tried to arouse popular support for his cause but failed. He was executed in 1601. There is an apocryphal story that Elizabeth gave Essex a ring and promised to pardon any offense if he sent it to her. According to the story, when imprisoned in the Tower Essex entrusted the ring to a page boy to give to one of the queen's ladies friendly to him, but the boy mistakenly gave it to the Countess of Nottingham, the wife of one of Essex's enemies. Of course, she never delivered it. Hawthorne has Edward Caryl change the story so that it is the Countess of Shrewsbury, a woman with a reputation as a slanderer and liar, who betrays Essex.

was an unviolated pledge of love and faith, both with the giver and receiver. But should love prove false, and faith be broken, then the evil spirit would work his own devilish will, until the ring were purified by becoming the medium of some good and holy act, and again the pledge of faithful love. The gem soon lost its virtue; for the wizard was murdered by the very lady to whom he gave it."

"An idle legend!" said the countess.

"It is so," answered Essex, with a melancholy smile. "Yet the queen's favor, of which this ring was the symbol, has proved my ruin. When death is nigh, men converse with dreams and shadows. I have been gazing into the diamond, and fancying—but you will laugh at me,—that I might catch a glimpse of the evil spirit there. Do you observe this red glow—dusky, too, amid all the brightness? It is the token of his presence; and even now, methinks, it grows redder and duskier, like an angry sunset."

Nevertheless, the earl's manner testified how slight was his credence in the enchanted properties of the ring. But there is a kind of playfulness that comes in moments of despair, when the reality of misfortune, if entirely felt, would crush the soul at once. He now, for a brief space, was lost in thought, while the countess contemplated him with malignant satisfaction.

"This ring," he resumed, in another tone, "alone remains, of all that my royal mistress's favor lavished upon her servant. My fortunes once shone as brightly as the gem. And now, such a darkness has fallen around me, methinks it would be no marvel if its gleam,—the sole light of my prison-house, were to be forthwith extinguished; inasmuch as my last earthly hope depends upon it."

"How say you, my lord?" asked the Countess of Shrewsbury. "The stone is bright; but there should be strange magic in it, if it can keep your hopes alive, at this sad hour. Alas! these iron bars and ramparts of the Tower, are unlike to yield to such a spell."

Essex raised his head, involuntarily; for there was something in the countess's tone that disturbed him, although he could not suspect that an enemy had intruded upon the sacred privacy of a prisoner's dungeon, to exult over so dark a ruin of such once brilliant fortunes. He looked her in the face, but saw nothing to awaken his distrust. It would have required a keener eye than even Cecil's[13] to read the secret of a countenance, which had been worn so long in the false light of a court, that it was now little better than

---

13. William Cecil (1520–1598) was an adviser to Queen Elizabeth I.

a masque, telling any story save the true one. The condemned nobleman again bent over the ring, and proceeded:

"It once had power in it—this bright gem—the magic that appertains to the talisman of a great queen's favor. She bade me, if hereafter I should fall into her disgrace—how deep soever, and whatever might be my crime—to convey this jewel to her sight, and it should plead for me. Doubtless, with her piercing judgment, she had even then detected the rashness of my nature, and foreboded some such deed as has now brought destruction upon my head. And knowing, too, her own hereditary rigor, she designed, it may be, that the memory of gentler and kindlier hours should soften her heart in my behalf, when my need should be the greatest. I have doubted—I have distrusted—yet who can tell, even now, what happy influence this ring might have?"

"You have delayed full long to show the ring, and plead her majesty's gracious promise," remarked the countess—"your state being what it is."

"True," replied the earl; "but for my honor's sake, I was loth to entreat the queen's mercy, while I might hope for life, at least, from the justice of the laws. If, on a trial by my peers, I had been acquitted of meditating violence against her sacred life, then would I have fallen at her feet, and presenting the jewel, have prayed no other favor than that my love and zeal should be put to the severest test. But now, it were confessing too much—it were cringing too low—to beg the miserable gift of life, on no other score than the tenderness which her majesty deems me to have forfeited!"

"Yet it is your only hope," said the countess.

"And besides," continued Essex, pursuing his own reflections, "of what avail will be this token of womanly feeling, when, on the other hand are arrayed the all-prevailing motives of state policy, and the artifices and intrigues of courtiers, to consummate my downfall? Will Cecil or Raleigh[14] suffer her heart to act for itself, even if the spirit of her father were not in her? It is in vain to hope it."

But still Essex gazed at the ring with an absorbed attention, that proved how much hope his sanguine temperament had concentrated here, when there was none else for him in the wide world, save what lay in the compass of that hoop of gold. The spark of brightness within the diamond, which gleamed like an intenser

---

14. Sir Walter Raleigh (?1552–1618) was an English explorer and author and a favorite of Elizabeth I.

than earthly fire, was the memorial of his dazzling career. It had not paled with the waning sunshine of his mistress's favor; on the contrary, in spite of its remarkable tinge of dusky red, he fancied that it had never shone so brightly. The glow of festal torches—the blaze of perfumed lamps—the bonfires that had been kindled for him, when he was the darling of the people—the splendor of the royal court, where he had been the peculiar star—all seemed to have collected their moral or material glory into the gem, and to burn with a radiance caught from the future, as well as gathered from the past. That radiance might break forth again. Bursting from the diamond, into which it was now narrowed, it might beam first upon the gloomy walls of the Tower—then wider, wider, wider—till all England, and the seas around her cliffs, should be gladdened with the light. It was such an ecstasy as often ensues after long depression, and has been supposed to precede the circumstances of darkest fate that may befall mortal man. The earl pressed the ring to his heart as if it were indeed a talisman, the habitation of a spirit, as the queen had playfully assured him—but a spirit of happier influences than her legend spake of.

"Oh, could I but make my way to her footstool!" cried he, waving his hand aloft, while he paced the stone pavement of his prison-chamber with an impetuous step.—"I might kneel down, indeed, a ruined man, condemned to the block—but how should I rise again? Once more the favorite of Elizabeth!—England's proudest noble!—with such prospects as ambition never aimed at! Why have I tarried so long in this weary dungeon? The ring has power to set me free! The palace wants me! Ho, jailer, unbar the door!"

But then occurred the recollection of the impossibility of obtaining an interview with his fatally estranged mistress, and testing the influence over her affections, which he still flattered himself with possessing.—Could he step beyond the limits of his prison, the world would be all sunshine; but here was only gloom and death.

"Alas!" said he, slowly and sadly, letting his head fall upon his hands.—"I die for lack of one blessed word."

The Countess of Shrewsbury, herself forgotten amid the earl's gorgeous visions, had watched him with an aspect that could have betrayed nothing to the most suspicious observer; unless that it was too calm for humanity, while witnessing the flutterings, as it were, of a generous heart in the death-agony. She now approached him.

"My good lord," she said, "what mean you to do?"

"Nothing—my deeds are done!" replied he, despondingly.— "Yet, had a fallen favorite any friends, I would entreat one of them to lay this ring at her majesty's feet; albeit with little hope, save that, hereafter, it might remind her that poor Essex, once far too highly favored, was at last too severely dealt with."

"I will be that friend," said the countess. "There is no time to be lost. Trust this precious ring with me. This very night, the queen's eye shall rest upon it; nor shall the efficacy of my poor words be wanting, to strengthen the impression which it will doubtless make."

The earl's first impulse was to hold out the ring. But looking at the countess, as she bent forward to receive it, he fancied that the red glow of the gem tinged all her face, and gave it an ominous expression. Many passages of past times recurred to his memory. A preternatural insight, perchance caught from approaching death, threw its momentary gleam, as from a meteor, all round his position.

"Countess," he said, "I know not wherefore I hesitate, being in a plight so desperate, and having so little choice of friends. But have you looked into your own heart? Can you perform this office with the truth—the earnestness—the zeal, even to tears, and agony of spirit—wherewith the holy gift of human life should be pleaded for? Wo be unto you, should you undertake this task, and deal towards me otherwise than with utmost faith! For your own soul's sake, and as you would have peace at your death-hour, consider well in what spirit you receive this ring!"

The countess did not shrink.

"My lord!—my good lord!" she exclaimed, "wrong not a woman's heart by these suspicions. You might choose another messenger; but who, save a lady of her bed-chamber, can obtain access to the queen at this untimely hour? It is for your life—for your life—else I would not renew my offer."

"Take the ring," said the earl.

"Believe that it shall be in the queen's hands before the lapse of another hour," replied the countess, as she received this sacred trust of life and death.—"To-morrow morning, look for the result of my intercession."

She departed. Again the earl's hopes rose high. Dreams visited his slumber, not of the sable-decked scaffold in the Tower-yard, but of canopies of state, obsequious courtiers, pomp, splendor, the smile of the once more gracious queen, and a light beaming from the magic gem, which illuminated his whole future.

History records, how foully the Countess of Shrewsbury betrayed the trust, which Essex, in his utmost need, confided to her. She kept the ring, and stood in the presence of Elizabeth, that night, without one attempt to soften her stern hereditary temper, in behalf of the former favorite. The next day, the earl's noble head rolled upon the scaffold. On her death-bed, tortured, at last, with a sense of the dreadful guilt which she had taken upon her soul, the wicked countess sent for Elizabeth, revealed the story of the ring, and besought forgiveness for her treachery. But the queen, still obdurate, even while remorse for past obduracy was tugging at her heart-strings, shook the dying woman in her bed, as if struggling with death for the privilege of wreaking her revenge and spite. The spirit of the countess passed away, to undergo the justice, or receive the mercy, of a higher tribunal; and tradition says, that the fatal ring was found upon her breast, where it had imprinted a dark red circle, resembling the effect of the intensest heat. The attendants, who prepared the body for burial, shuddered, whispering one to another, that the ring must have derived its heat from the glow of infernal fire. They left it on her breast, in the coffin, and it went with that guilty woman to the tomb.

Many years afterwards, when the church that contained the monuments of the Shrewsbury family, was desecrated by Cromwell's soldiers, they broke open the ancestral vaults, and stole whatever was valuable from the noble personages who reposed there. Merlin's antique ring passed into the possession of a stout serjeant of the Ironsides,[15] who thus became subject to the influences of the evil spirit that still kept his abode within the gem's enchanted depths. The serjeant was soon slain in battle, thus transmitting the ring, though without any legal form of testatment, to a gay cavalier,[16] who forthwith pawned it, and expended the money in liquor, which speedily brought him to the grave. We next catch the sparkle of the magic diamond at various epochs of the merry reign of Charles the Second.[17] But its sinister fortune still attended it.

---

15. "Ironsides" was a nickname of Oliver Cromwell, the key figure in the British government from the beheading of Charles I in 1649 until the Restoration of Charles II in 1660. The term came to be applied to the soldiers serving under Cromwell.

16. A supporter of Charles I of England in his struggles with Parliament.

17. Charles II (1630–1685), son of Charles I, was restored to the British throne in 1660, after an interregnum that had lasted since 1649, when Charles I was beheaded.

From whatever hand this ring of portent came, and whatever finger it encircled, ever it was the pledge of deceit between man and man, or man and woman, of faithless vows, and unhallowed passion; and whether to lords and ladies, or to village-maids—for sometimes it found its way so low,—still it brought nothing but sorrow and disgrace. No purifying deed was done, to drive the fiend from his bright home in this little star. Again, we hear of it at a later period, when Sir Robert Walpole[18] bestowed the ring, among far richer jewels, on the lady of a British legislator, whose political honor he wished to undermine. Many a dismal and unhappy tale might be wrought out of its other adventures. All this while, its ominous tinge of dusky red had been deepening and darkening, until, if laid upon white paper, it cast the mingled hue of night and blood, strangely illuminated with scintillating light, in a circle round about. But this peculiarity only made it the more valuable.

Alas, the fatal ring! When shall its dark secret be discovered, and the doom of ill, inherited from one possessor to another, be finally revoked?

The legend now crosses the Atlantic, and comes down to our own immediate time. In a certain church of our city, not many evenings ago, there was a contribution for a charitable object. A fervid preacher had poured out his whole soul in a rich and tender discourse, which had at least excited the tears, and perhaps the more effectual sympathy, of a numerous audience. While the choristers sang sweetly, and the organ poured forth its melodious thunder, the deacons passed up and down the aisles, and along the galleries, presenting their mahogany boxes, in which each person deposited whatever sum he deemed it safe to lend to the Lord, in aid of human wretchedness. Charity became audible—chink, chink, chink,—as it fell, drop by drop, into the common receptacle. There was a hum—a stir,—the subdued bustle of people putting their hands into their pockets; while, ever and anon, a vagrant coin fell upon the floor, and rolled away, with long reverberation, into some inscrutable corner.

At length, all having been favored with an opportunity to be generous, the two deacons placed their boxes on the communion-table, and thence, at the conclusion of the services, removed them into the vestry. Here these good old gentlemen sat down together, to reckon the accumulated treasure.

---

18. Prime Minister of England from 1721 to 1742.

"Fie, fie, brother Tilton," said Deacon Trott, peeping into Deacon Tilton's box, "what a heap of copper you have picked up! Really, for an old man, you must have had a heavy job to lug it along. Copper! copper! copper! Do people expect to get admittance into Heaven at the price of a few coppers?"

"Don't wrong them, brother," answered Deacon Tilton, a simple and kindly old man. "Copper may do more for one person, than gold will for another. In the galleries, where I present my box, we must not expect such a harvest as you gather among the gentry in the broad-aisle, and all over the floor of the church. My people are chiefly poor mechanics and laborers, sailors, seamstresses, and servant-maids, with a most uncomfortable intermixture of roguish school-boys."

"Well, well," said Deacon Trott;—"but there is a great deal, brother Tilton, in the method of presenting a contribution-box. It is a knack that comes by nature, or not at all."

They now proceeded to sum up the avails of the evening, beginning with the receipts of Deacon Trott. In good sooth,[19] that worthy personage had reaped an abundant harvest, in which he prided himself no less, apparently, than if every dollar had been contributed from his own individual pocket. Had the good deacon been meditating a jaunt to Texas, the treasures of the mahogany-box might have sent him on his way rejoicing. There were bank-notes, mostly, it is true, of the smallest denominations in the giver's pocket-book, yet making a goodly average upon the whole. The most splendid contribution was a check for a hundred dollars, bearing the name of a distinguished merchant, whose liberality was duly celebrated in the newspapers of the next day. No less than seven half eagles,[20] together with an English sovereign,[21] glittered amidst an indiscriminate heap of silver; the box being polluted with nothing of the copper kind; except a single bright new cent, wherewith a little boy had performed his first charitable act.

"Very well! very well indeed!" said Deacon Trott, self-approvingly. "A handsome evening's work! And now, brother Tilton, let's see whether you can match it."

Here was a sad contrast! They poured forth Deacon Tilton's treasure upon the table, and it really seemed as if the whole copper

---

19. Truth.

20. Five-dollar gold coins.

21. A British gold coin.

coinage of the country, together with an amazing quantity of shopkeepers' tokens, and English and Irish half-pence, mostly of base metal, had been congregated into the box. There was a very substantial pencil-case, and the semblance of a shilling; but the latter proved to be made of tin, and the former of German silver. A gilded brass button was doing duty as a gold coin, and a folded shop-bill had assumed the character of a bank-note. But Deacon Tilton's feelings were much revived, by the aspect of another bank-note, new and crisp, adorned with beautiful engravings, and stamped with the indubitable word, TWENTY, in large black letters. Alas! it was a counterfeit. In short, the poor old Deacon was no less unfortunate than those who trade with fairies, and whose gains are sure to be transformed into dried leaves, pebbles, and other valuables of that kind.

"I believe the Evil One is in the box," said he, with some vexation.

"Well done, Deacon Tilton!" cried his brother Trott, with a hearty laugh.—"You ought to have a statue in copper."

"Never mind, brother," replied the good Deacon, recovering his temper. "I'll bestow ten dollars from my own pocket, and may Heaven's blessing go along with it! But look! what do you call this?"

Under the copper mountain, which it had cost them so much toil to remove, lay an antique ring! It was enriched with a diamond, which, so soon as it caught the light, began to twinkle and glimmer, emitting the whitest and purest lustre that could possibly be conceived. It was as brilliant as if some magician had condensed the brightest star in heaven into a compass fit to be set in a ring, for a lady's delicate finger.

"How is this?" said Deacon Trott, examining it carefully, in the expectation of finding it as worthless as the rest of his colleague's treasure. "Why, upon my word, this seems to be a real diamond, and of the purest water.[22] Whence could it have come?"

"Really, I cannot tell," quoth Deacon Tilton, "for my spectacles were so misty that all faces looked alike. But now I remember, there was a flash of light came from the box, at one moment; but it seemed a dusky red, instead of a pure white, like the sparkle of this gem. Well; the ring will make up for the copper; but I wish the giver had thrown its history into the box along with it."

---

22. "Water" is the degree of transparency and brilliancy of a diamond or other precious stone.

It has been our good luck to recover a portion of that history. After transmitting misfortune from one possessor to another, ever since the days of British Merlin, the identical ring which Queen Elizabeth gave to the Earl of Essex was finally thrown into the contribution-box of a New-England church. The two deacons deposited it in the glass-case of a fashionable jeweller, of whom it was purchased by the humble rehearser of this legend, in the hope that it may be allowed to sparkle on a fair lady's finger. Purified from the foul fiend, so long its inhabitant, by a deed of unostentatious charity, and now made the symbol of faithful and devoted love, the gentle bosom of its new possessor need fear no sorrow from its influence.

"Very pretty!—Beautiful!—How original!—How sweetly written!—What nature!—What imagination!—What power!—What pathos!—What exquisite humor!"—were the exclamations of Edward Caryl's kind and generous auditors, at the conclusion of the legend.

"It is a pretty tale," said Miss Pemberton, who, conscious that her praise was to that of all others as a diamond to a pebble, was therefore the less liberal in awarding it. "It is really a pretty tale, and very proper for any of the Annuals. But, Edward, your moral does not satisfy me. What thought did you embody in the ring?"

"Oh, Clara, this is too bad!" replied Edward, with a half-reproachful smile.—"You know that I can never separate the idea from the symbol in which it manifests itself. However, we may suppose the Gem to be the human heart, and the Evil Spirit to be Falsehood, which, in one guise or another, is the fiend that causes all the sorrow and trouble in the world. I beseech you, to let this suffice."

"It shall," said Clara, kindly. "And believe me, whatever the world may say of the story, I prize it far above the diamond which enkindled your imagination."

Kathanal

by
KATRINA TRASK

The sky was one unbroken pall of gray,
Casting a gloom upon the restless sea,
Dulling her sapphire splendour to a dark
And minor beauty. All the rock-bound shore
Was silent, save a widowed song-bird sang
Far off at intervals a mournful note,
And on the broken crags of dark gray rock
The waves dashed ceaselessly. Sir Kathanal[1]
Stood with uncovered head and folded arms,
His soul as restless as the surging sea
Lashed into passion by the coming storm.
His helmet lay upon the sand; its crest,
A floating plume of deep-hued violet,
Was tossed and torn in fury by the wind
Until it seemed a thing of life. He stood
And watched it, only half aware at first
That it was there, then scarce aware of aught
Besides the plume. As in the room of death
Some iterated sound or motion holds
Attent the stricken mind, benumbed, and keeps
The horror of its grief awhile at bay
As by a spell, so now, though Kathanal
Had sought the sea-shore to be free of men
Because of his sore agony of heart,
And all the passion of his daring soul
Was tossing like the sea in fierce revolt,
His thoughts and gaze were centred on his crest.

---

1. A knight at the court of King Constantine, the king said by Malory to have taken over the rule of England when Arthur died. There is no precedent in earlier literature for Kathanal or for the other characters placed at Constantine's court by Trask.

Before the gray of sea and sky he saw
Naught but the waving, waving of the plume;
Before the vision of his love, Leorre,
Her tender eyes aglow with changeless light,
The golden splendour of her sunny hair,
Her winning smiles of grace and sweetness blent,
There came the waving, waving, of the plume;
Between his sorrow and his weary soul,
Between his trouble and his clear-eyed self,
There came the waving, waving of the plume;
Until he felt, in some half-conscious way,
It was his heart, and he a stranger there
That looked down, from a height, indifferent
Upon it at the mercy of the wind.

Sudden, with that long lingering trace of youth
That gave to him the fascinating charm
Which other men were fain to emulate,
He quickly stooped, and tore it from his helm,
And cast it far out on the tossing sea.
It lighted on the waves a purple bird,
Floating with swan-like grace before the wind.
The action quenched impatience. Kathanal,
Impulsive, passionate and sensitive,
In moods was ever ready with response
To omen and to change of circumstance.
He stood a moment, and then forward sprang
To catch it ere it vanished out of reach.
It was too late—the outward-flowing tide
Bore it from wave to wave beyond his sight.

"Ah, God!" he cried aloud, "what have I done?
It is the omen of a curse to me;
My crest is gone, my knightly symbol lost,
My helm dishonoured through an act of mine."

Then came the memory of early youth,
The recollection of a high resolve
To keep his manhood free from touch of stain,
To be a knight like Galahad, pure and true.
So few short years had passed since that resolve,
And yet he had forgotten loyalty

And truth and honour for the fair Leorre,
The wife of Reginault, his patron knight,—
The brave old man who treated him as son.
Long had he loved her with a knightly love,
And fought for her, and chosen her the queen
Of many a tournament. She still was young,
Fairer than morning in the early spring.
When she had come, a gladsome bride, to grace
The castle of old Reginault, and warm
His grand old spirit into youth again,
Sir Kathanal had bowed before her, saying,
"My gracious lady, take me as your knight";
And she had answered, with her winning smile,
"You are Sir Reginault's, and therefore mine."
Well had he loved her from that very hour,
Giving her honour as his old friend's bride,
Making the castle ring with merriment
To do her service, and fulfil the hest[2]
Of Reginault, who bade him use his grace
To make her life a round of holidays.
But day by day his selfish love had grown
From friendly service to a lover's claim,
Until he had forgotten Reginault
In her fair eyes, and all things else but her,
Who granted him no boon, no smallest act
Of love or tenderness.

                    At last the strife
Between deep yearning for some touch of love,
And brave endeavour for self-mastery,
Had driven him to madness and despair.
To the lone sea he brought his agony
To face it boldly, and his spirit, quick
To wear new moods, caught a despondent gloom
From the dark omen that oppressed his soul.

"Love is divine," he said, "and it is well
To love Leorre, wife though she be, for love
Is free to noble natures; but at last,
When in her shining eyes I see response,

---

2. Command.

Albeit unconscious, to my longing pain,
I cannot rest content with boonless love,
Although divine. I fear me, if I stay
Within the circle of her tempting charm,
I shall, through some wild impulse, wantonly
Fling my unsullied knighthood to the winds,
As now I flung the plume from out my helm."

He went at even-song time to Leorre,
And told her of his struggle by the sea,
Of his determined purpose and resolve.

"Leorre, I love you with a love unsung
By poets, and unknown by other men,
Undreamed by women; I must leave you, dear;
I cannot see you fair for Reginault,
I cannot watch your sweetness not for me.
I will go far upon some distant quest
Until this frenzy ceases, and the quest
Shall be for you, my love, for you alone.

"Dear, sunny head that lights my darkened way
With its bright, golden glory, let me seek
A crown that well befits it for my quest.
Fair waist that curves beneath the heart I love,
I shall engirdle you with priceless gems
Won by my prowess for your perfect grace.
O wondrous neck! great lustrous, flawless pearls,
That shall be royal in their worth, to match
The white enchantment of your beauty fair,
Shall be my quest for you.

                          "I will not come
Back to the court of Constantine, Leorre,
Until I bring that which shall honour you,
And winning which, I shall have cooled my pain."

She came and knelt beside him, took his hand,
Looked deep into his ardent eyes,—her own
Like stars that shone into his inmost soul.

"Will you, indeed, go forth," she answered low,
"Across the world upon a quest for me?

And will you falter not, nor swerve, nor fail,
Nor turn aside from seeking, night nor day,
Until you conquer with your prowess rare
The prize for me? And may I choose the quest
I most desire?"

          "Ah! surely, what you will,"
Said Kathanal, as echo to his eyes,
Which answered ere the words could form themselves.

She waited, silently; the room was still;
Sir Kathanal was faint from drinking deep,
With thirsty eyes, the beauty of her face.

At last she spoke, almost inaudibly,
But evermore the thought of her low speech
Made melody within his memory.

"Go forth, my knight of love, o'er land and sea,
And purify your spirit and your life,
And seek until you find the Holy Grail,
Keeping the vision ever in your thought,
The inspiration ever in your soul.
Let Tristram yield his loyalty and honour
For fair Isoud, and die inglorious,—
Let Launcelot in Guenever's embrace
Forget the consecrated vows he swore,
And bring dark desolation on the land,—
My knight must grow the greater through his love,
The better for my favour, the more pure!
More than all gifts, or wealth of royal dower,
I want, I crave, I claim this boon of thee."

Between the bronze-brown of his eyes and her,
There sudden came a faint and misty veil;
Through the wide-open window a sun's beam
Flashed on it, making o'er her bowèd head
A halo from his own unfallen tears.
He rose and lifted her, loosed her sweet hands,
And fell upon his knees low at her feet.

"Leorre, my love, my queen, my woman-saint,
I am not worthy, but I take your quest;

I will not falter and I will not swerve
Until I see the Grail, or pass to where
I see the glory it but symbols here,
In Paradise. Beloved, all the world
Is better for your living, all the air
Is sweeter for your breathing, and all love
Is holier, purer, that you may be loved."

"Rise, Kathanal, stand still and let me gaze
Upon you with that purpose in your face!
So brave, so resolute! I love you, Kathanal!
Nay! do not touch me, listen to my words!
Surely it cannot be a sin to speak,
Perchance it is a debt I owe my knight
For his life's consecration, once to say
To him, as I have said to my own heart,
Just how I love him.

                    "I would follow you
Across the world, if it might be, a slave,
To serve you at your bidding night and day;
Or I would rouse me to my highest pride
That I might be your queen, and lead you on
To glory. I am strong to do and bear
The uttermost my mind can think, for you,
To cheer you, help you, strengthen you; and yet—
I am a woman, and my senses thrill
If you but touch the border of my robe,
And if you take my hand, before the court,
And raise it to your lips, I faint, I die,
With the vast tide of my unconquered love."

"Great Christ! how can I hear you and depart?
I did not know you loved me. O my sweet,
Here by your side I stay; my quest shall be
The love-light dawning in your shining eyes."

"Is this your answer, Kathanal," she sighed,
"To the unveiling of my heart of hearts?
No! now, if ever, you will surely go
On the sole quest that makes that action right."

"Leorre, come once to me!" he said with arms
Outstretched to her. Quickly she backward drew
With one swift whispered "Kathanal!"

                                        "Leorre,
You cannot love and be so calm and still;
My soul would sacrifice both earth and heaven
For one full, rapturous kiss from those sweet lips
That lure me on to madness by their spell."

"It is my love that keeps me calm," she said;
"Love makes us strong for what is bitterest;
Were we faint-hearted through imperfect love
We could not part; but loving perfectly
We are full strong for that, and all things else.

"Farewell, my Kathanal, take as you go
This spotless scarf, the girdle from my robe,
And put it where the purple plume has been,
And wear it as my favour in your helm.
If that lost plume was darksome omen ill,
Let this defy it with an omen fair,
A prophecy to spur you on your quest.
My heart says it is better as it is;
I joy me that you flung into the sea
That purple plume my loving, longing gaze
Has often followed in the tournament.
Remember, purple doth betoken pain,
And white betokens conquest, purity;
Look, Kathanal, beloved, in my eyes!
I know that you will find the Holy Grail."

She stood immaculate, and from those eyes
That oft had kindled passionate desire
He drew an inspiration high and pure,
A prescient sense of victory and peace;
And falling on his knees once more, he bowed,
Kissed her white robe, and left her standing there.

Then followed days of struggle and dark gloom.
Far from the court he found a lonely cell,
Where morn and night he prayed, and, praying, wrought

A score of earnest, unrecorded deeds
To purify and cleanse himself from sin.

Oft the old passion would arise and sweep
His spirit bare of every conquest. Once
The longing and the yearning were so great,
So strong beyond all thought of holiness,
He sprang up from his bed at dead of night
And stopped not, night nor day, until he reached
His old home by the sea, and saw Leorre.
Her hair had its untarnished golden glow,
Her beauty was unchanged, but her sweet mouth
Had caught a touch of pathos in its smile;
She wore a purple robe, and stood in state
Beside Sir Reginault,—who greeted him
With tender, grave, and kind solicitude,—
And lifted eyes that smote upon his heart
With a long gaze of passionate appeal
That held a pain at bay deep in their depths.

"So weak," he whispered to his heart, "for self,
I will be strong for her; she needs my strength."

Again he hurried from her sight, half glad
For the remembered pain within her eyes;
Ashamed of his own soul that it was glad.

For years he struggled, prayed, and fought his fight;
And sometimes when his soul was desolate
And he was weary from his eager quest,
When such a sense of deep humility
Would fall upon his praying, watching heart
That he would fain[3] forego all in despair,
A marvellous ray of light, mysterious,
Would slant athwart the darkness of his cell,
Then he would rouse him to his quest once more
And say, "Perchance the Holy Grail is near!"

One night at midnight came the ray again,
And with it came a strange expectancy

---

3. Gladly.

Of spirit as the light waxed radiant.
The cell was filled with spicy odours sweet,
And on the midnight stillness song was borne
As sweet as heaven's harmony—the words,—
The same Sir Launcelot had heard of old,—
"Honour and joy be to the Father of Heaven."
With wide eyes searching his lone cell for cause
He waited: as the ray became more clear
And more effulgent than the mid-day sun,
He trembled with that chill of mortal flesh
Beholding spiritual things. At last—
Now vaguely as though veiled by light, and then
With shining clearness, perfectly—he saw
The sight unspeakable, transcending words.

Forth from his barren cell came Kathanal,
Strong and inspired, born anew for deeds.
Straightway he grew to be the bravest knight
Under King Constantine, since Sir Sanpeur;[4]
The boldest in the battles for the right;
The kindest in his judgment of the wrong.
His eyes that held the vision of the Grail
Were ever clear to see and know the truth;
His lips that had been touched by holy chrism[5]
Were strong to utter holy living words;
He sang of life in life, and life in death,
And taught the lesson that his heart had learned—
All love should be a glory, not a doom;
Love for love's sake, albeit bliss-denied.

To his old home beside the sapphire sea
Floated his songs and his far-reaching fame;
For in the land no name was loved so well
As Kathanal the peerless Minstrel Knight.

Lone in her chamber sat Leorre, and heard
The songs of Kathanal by courtiers sung—

---

4. Sanpeur, the hero of the first and longest of the three narrative poems in Trask's volume, is the greatest of the knights of Constantine's court.

5. A mixture of oil and balsam consecrated by a bishop and used for anointing in various church sacraments.

Arousing words, like a clear clarion call
To truth and virtue, purity and faith.
She clasped her hands and bent her head, and wept
In silent passion pent-up tears, for joy;
For now she knew—far off, beyond her sight—
Her love had seen the sacred Holy Grail.
And as she listened, inspiration came,
Irradiating all her spirit, lifting it
Beyond her sorrow and her daily want
Of Kathanal. Soft through her soul there crept
The echo of a benedicite,[6]
Enwrapping her in calm, triumphant peace.

Then she arose, put on her whitest robe,
And went out radiant, strong, and full of joy.

---

6. Invocation of a blessing.

From:
The Story of King Arthur and His Knights

by

HOWARD PYLE

How King Arthur Became Lost in the Forest, and How He Fell Into a Very Singular Adventure in a Castle Unto Which He Came.

Now, it befell upon a time some while after this, that King Arthur was at Tintagalon[1] upon certain affairs of state. And Queen Guinevere and her Court and the King's Court made progression from Camelot unto Carleon,[2] and there they abided until the King should be through his business at Tintagalon and should join them at Carleon.

Now that time was the spring of the year, and all things were very jolly and gay, wherefore King Arthur became possessed with a great desire for adventure. So he called unto him a certain favorite esquire, hight Boisenard,[3] and he said to him, "Boisenard, this day is so pleasant that I hardly know how I may contain myself because of the joy I take in it, for it seems to be that my heart is nigh ready to burst with a great pleasure of desiring. So I am of a mind to go a-gadding[4] with only thee for companion."

To this Boisenard said, "Lord, I know of nothing that would give to me a greater pleasure than that."

So King Arthur said, "Very well, let us then go away from this place in such a manner that no one will be aware of our departure. And so we will go to Carleon and surprise the Queen by coming unexpectedly to that place."

---

1. Tintagel, a castle on the coast of Cornwall and the legendary site of Arthur's conception and birth.

2. A town on the River Usk and one of the traditional places where Arthur held court.

3. Named Boisenard. There is no precedent for this name for Arthur's squire.

4. Wandering.

So Boisenard brought armor, without device,[5] and he clad the King in that armor; and then they two rode forth together, and no one wist[6] that they had left the castle.

And when they came forth into the fields, King Arthur whistled and sang and jested and laughed and made himself merry; for he was as a war-horse turned forth upon the grass that taketh glory in the sunshine and the warm air and becometh like unto a colt again.

So by and by they came into the forest and rode that way with great content of spirit; and they took this path and they took that path for no reason but because the day was so gay and jolly. So, by and by, they lost their way in the mazes of the woodland and knew not where they were.

Now when they found themselves to be lost in that wise they journeyed with more circumspection, going first by this way and then by that, but in no manner could they find their way out from their entanglement. And so fell night-time and they knew not where they were; but all became very dark and obscure, with the woodland full of strange and unusual sounds around about them.

Then King Arthur said, "Boisenard, this is a very perplexing pass and I do not know how we shall find lodging for this night."

To this Boisenard said, "Lord, if I have thy permission to do so, I will climb one of these trees and see if I can discover any sign of habitation in this wilderness." And King Arthur said, "Do so, I pray thee."

So Boisenard climbed a very tall tree and from the top of the tree he beheld a light a great distance away, and he said, "Lord, I see a light in that direction." And therewith he came down from the tree again.

So King Arthur and Boisenard went in the direction that Boisenard had beheld the light, and by and by they came out of the forest and into an open place where they beheld a very great castle with several tall towers, very grim and forbidding of appearance. And it was from this castle that the light had appeared that Boisenard had seen. So they two rode up to the castle and Boisenard called aloud and smote upon the gate of the castle. Then immediately there came a porter and demanded of them what they would have. Unto him Boisenard said, "Sirrah, we would come in to

---

5. Heraldic emblem, by which a knight could be identified.

6. Knew.

lodge for to-night, for we are a-weary." So the porter said, "Who are you?"—speaking very roughly and rudely to them, for he could not see of what condition they were because of the darkness. Then Boisenard said, "This is a knight of very good quality and I am his esquire, and we have lost our way in the forest and now we come hither seeking shelter."

"Sir," said the porter, "if ye know what is good for you, ye will sleep in the forest rather than come into this place, for this is no very good retreat for errant knights to shelter themselves."

Upon this King Arthur bespake the porter, for that which the porter said aroused great curiosity within him. So he said, "Nay, we will not go away from here and we demand to lodge here for this night."

Then the porter said, "Very well; ye may come in." And thereupon he opened the gate and they rode into the court-yard of that castle.

Now at the noise of their coming, there appeared a great many lights within the castle, and there came running forth divers attendants. Some of these aided King Arthur and Boisenard to dismount, and others took the horses, and others again brought basins of water for them to wash withal. And after they had washed their faces and hands, other attendants brought them into the castle.

Now as they came into the castle, they were aware of a great noise of very many people talking and laughing together, with the sound of singing and of harping. And so they came into the hall of the castle and beheld that it was lighted with a great number of candles and tapers and torches. Here they found a multitude of people gathered at a table spread for a feast, and at the head of the table there sat a knight, well advanced in years and with hair and beard white as milk. Yet he was exceedingly strong and sturdy of frame, having shoulders of wonderful broadness and a great girth of chest. This knight was of a very stern and forbidding appearance, and was clad altogether in black, and he wore around his neck a chain of gold, with a locket of gold hanging pendant[7] from it.

Now when this knight beheld King Arthur and Boisenard come into the hall, he called aloud to them in a very great voice bidding them to come and sit with him at the head of the table; and

---

7. Suspended.

they did so, and those at the head of the table made place for them, and thus they sat there beside the knight.

Now King Arthur and Boisenard were exceedingly hungry, wherefore they ate with great appetite and made joy of the entertainment which they received, and meantime the knight held them in very pleasant discourse, talking to them of such things as would give them the most entertainment. So after a while the feast was ended and they ceased from eating.

Then, of a sudden, the knight said to King Arthur, "Messire,[8] thou art young and lusty of spirit and I doubt not but thou hath a great heart within thee. What say you now to a little sport betwixt us two?" Upon this King Arthur regarded that knight very steadily and he believed that his face was not so old as it looked; for his eyes were exceedingly bright and shone like sparks of light; wherefore he was a-doubt and he said, "Sir, what sport would you have?" Upon this the knight fell a-laughing in great measure and he said, "This is a very strange sport that I have in mind, for it is this: That thou and I shall prove the one unto the other what courage each of us may have." And King Arthur said, "How shall we prove that?" Whereunto the knight made reply, "This is what we shall do: Thou and I shall stand forth in the middle of this hall, and thou shalt have leave to try to strike off my head; and if I can receive that blow without dying therefrom, then I shall have leave to strike thy head off in a like manner."

Upon this speech King Arthur was greatly a-dread and he said, "That is very strange sport for two men to engage upon."

Now when King Arthur said this, all those who were in the hall burst out laughing beyond all measure and as though they would never stint[9] from their mirth. Then, when they had become in a measure quiet again, the knight of that castle said, "Sir, art thou afraid of that sport?" Upon which King Arthur fell very angry and he said, "Nay, I am not afeared, for no man hath ever yet had reason to say that I showed myself afeared of anyone." "Very well," said the knight of the castle; "then let us try that sport of which I spake." And King Arthur said, "I am willing."

Then Boisenard came to King Arthur where he was, and he said, "Lord, do not thou enter into this thing, but rather let me undertake this venture in thy stead, for I am assured that some great

---

8. Sir.

9. Cease.

treachery is meditated against thee." But King Arthur said, "Nay; no man shall take my danger upon himself, but I will assume mine own danger without calling upon any man to take it." So he said to the knight of the castle, "Sir, I am ready for that sport of which thou didst speak, but who is to strike that first blow and how shall we draw lots therefor?" "Messire," said the knight of the castle, "there shall be no lots drawn. For, as thou art the guest of this place, so shall thou have first assay at that sport."

Therewith that knight arose and laid aside his black robe, and he was clad beneath in a shirt of fine linen very cunningly worked. And he wore hosen of crimson. Then he opened that linen undergarment at the throat and he turned down the collar thereof so as to lay his neck bare to the blow. Thereupon he said, "Now, Sir Knight, thou shalt have to strike well if thou wouldst win at this sport."

But King Arthur showed no dread of that undertaking, for he arose and drew Excalibur so that the blade of the sword flashed with exceeding brightness. Then he measured his distance, and lifted the sword, and he smote the knight of the castle with all his might upon the neck. And, lo! the blade cut through the neck of the knight of the castle with wonderful ease, so that the head flew from the body to a great distance away.

But the trunk of the body of that knight did not fall, but instead of that it stood, and it walked to where the head lay, and the hands of the trunk picked up the head and they set the head back upon the body, and, lo! that knight was as sound and whole as ever he had been in all his life.

Upon this all those of the castle shouted and made great mirth, and they called upon King Arthur that it was now his turn to try that sport. So the King prepared himself, laying aside his surcoat and opening his undergarment at the throat, as the knight of the castle had done. And at that Boisenard made great lamentation. Then the knight of the castle said, "Sir, art thou afeared?" And King Arthur said, "No, I am not afeared, for every man must come to his death some time, and it appears that my time hath now come, and that I am to lay down my life in this foolish fashion for no fault of mine own."

Then the knight of the castle said, "Well, stand thou away a little distance so that I may not strike thee too close, and so lose the virtue of my blow."

So King Arthur stood forth in the midst of the hall, and the knight of the castle swung his sword several times, but did not strike.

Likewise, he several times laid the blade of the sword upon King Arthur's neck, and it was very cold. Then King Arthur cried out in great passion, "Sir, it is thy right to strike, but I beseech thee not to torment me in this manner." "Nay," said the knight of the castle, "it is my right to strike when it pleases me, and I will not strike any before that time. For if it please me I will torment thee for a great while ere I slay thee." So he laid his sword several times more upon King Arthur's neck, and King Arthur said no more, but bore that torment with a very steadfast spirit.

Then the knight of the castle said, "Thou appearest to be a very courageous and honorable knight, and I have a mind to make a covenant with thee." And King Arthur said, "What is that covenant?" "It is this," said the knight of the castle, "I will spare thee thy life for a year and a day if thou wilt pledge me thy knightly word to return hither at the end of that time."

Then King Arthur said, "Very well; it shall be so." And therewith he pledged his knightly word to return at the end of that time, swearing to that pledge upon the cross of the hilt of Excalibur.

Then the knight of the castle said, "I will make another covenant with thee." "What is it?" said King Arthur. "My second covenant is this," quoth the knight of the castle, "I will give to thee a riddle, and if thou wilt answer that riddle when thou returnest hither, and if thou makest no mistake in that answer, then will I spare thy life and set thee free." And King Arthur said, "What is that riddle?" To which the knight made reply, "The riddle is this: What is it that a woman desires most of all in the world?"

"Sir," said King Arthur, "I will seek to find the answer to that riddle, and I give thee gramercy for sparing my life for so long a time as thou hast done, and for giving me the chance to escape my death." Upon this the knight of the castle smiled very sourly, and he said, "I do not offer this to thee because of mercy to thee, but because I find pleasure in tormenting thee. For what delight canst thou have in living thy life when thou knowest that thou must, for a surety, die at the end of one short year? And what pleasure canst thou have in living even that year when thou shalt be tormented with anxiety to discover the answer to my riddle?"

Then King Arthur said, "I think thou art very cruel." And the knight said, "I am not denying that."

So that night King Arthur and Boisenard lay at the castle, and the next day they took their way thence. And King Arthur was very heavy and troubled in spirit; ne'theless he charged Boisenard that he should say nothing concerning that which had befallen, but that he should keep it in secret. And Boisenard did as the King commanded, and said nothing concerning that adventure.

Now in that year which followed, King Arthur settled his affairs. Also he sought everywhere to find the answer to that riddle. Many there were who gave him answers in plenty, for one said that a woman most desired wealth, and another said she most desired beauty, and one said she desired power to please, and another said that she most desired fine raiment; and one said this, and another said that; but no answer appeared to King Arthur to be good and fitting for his purpose.

So the year passed by, until only a fortnight remained; and then King Arthur could not abide to stay where he was any longer, for it seemed to him his time was very near at hand, and he was filled with a very bitter anxiety of soul, wherefore he was very restless to be away.

So he called Boisenard to him, and he said, "Boisenard, help me to arm, for I am going away."

Then Boisenard fell a-weeping in very great measure, and he said, "Lord, do not go."

At this King Arthur looked very sternly at his esquire, and said, "Boisenard, how is this? Wouldst thou tempt me to violate mine honor? It is not very hard to die, but it would be very bitter to live my life in dishonor; wherefore tempt me no more, but do my bidding and hold thy peace. And if I do not return in a month from this time, then mayst thou tell all that hath befallen. And thou mayst tell Sir Constantine of Cornwall that he is to search the papers in my cabinet, and that there he will find all that is to be done should death overtake me."

So Boisenard put a plain suit of armor upon King Arthur, though he could hardly see what he was about for the tears that flowed down out of his eyes in great abundance. And he laced upon the armor of the King a surcoat without device, and he gave the King a shield without device. Thereupon King Arthur rode away without considering whither his way took him. And of everyone whom he met he inquired what that thing was that a woman most desired, and no one could give him an answer that appeared to him to be what it should be, wherefore he was in great doubt and torment of spirit.

Now the day before King Arthur was to keep his covenant at that castle, he was wandering through the adjacent forest in great travail of soul, for he wist[10] not what he should do to save his life. As he wandered so, he came of a sudden upon a small hut built up under an overhanging oak-tree so that it was very hard to tell where the oak-tree ended and the hut began. And there were a great many large rocks all about covered with moss, so that the King might very easily have passed by the hut only that he beheld a smoke to arise therefrom as from a fire that burned within. So he went to the hut and opened the door and entered. At first he thought there was no one there, but when he looked again he beheld an old woman sitting bent over a small fire that burned upon the hearth. And King Arthur had never beheld such an ugly beldame[11] as that one who sat there bending over that fire, for her ears were very huge and flapped, and her hair hung down over her head like to snakes, and her face was covered all over with wrinkles so that there were not any places at all where there was not a wrinkle; and her eyes were bleared and covered over with a film, and the eyelids were red as with the continual weeping of her eyes, and she had but one tooth in her mouth, and her hands, which she spread out to the fire, were like claws of bone.

Then King Arthur gave her greeting and she gave the King greeting, and she said to him, "My lord King, whence come ye? and why do ye come to this place?"

Then King Arthur was greatly astonished that that old woman should know him, who he was, and he said, "Who are you that appeareth to know me?" "No matter," said she, "I am one who meaneth you well; so tell me what is the trouble that brings you here at this time." So the King confessed all his trouble to that old woman, and he asked her if she knew the answer to that riddle, "What is it that a woman most desires?" "Yea," said the old woman, "I know the answer to that riddle very well, but I will not tell it to thee unless thou wilt promise me something in return."

At this King Arthur was filled with very great joy that the old woman should know the answer to that riddle, and he was filled with doubt of what she would demand of him, wherefore he said, "What is it thou must have in return for that answer?"

Then the old woman said, "If I aid thee to guess thy riddle aright, thou must promise that I shall become wife unto one of the

---

10. Knew.
11. Lady.

knights of thy Court, whom I may choose when thou returnest homeward again."

"Ha!" said King Arthur, "how may I promise that upon the behalf of anyone?" Upon this the old woman said, "Are not the knights of thy Court of such nobility that they will do that to save thee from death?" "I believe they are," said King Arthur. And with that he meditated a long while, saying unto himself, "What will my kingdom do if I die at this time? I have no right to die." So he said to the old woman, "Very well, I will make that promise."

Then she said unto the King, "This is the answer to that riddle: That which a woman most desires is to have her will." And the answer seemed to King Arthur to be altogether right. Then the old woman said, "My lord King, thou hast been played upon by that knight who hath led thee into this trouble, for he is a great conjurer and a magician of a very evil sort. He carrieth his life not within his body, but in a crystal globe which he weareth in a locket hanging about his neck; wherefore it was that when thou didst cut the head from off his body, his life remained in that locket and he did not die. But if thou hadst destroyed that locket, then he would immediately have died."

"I will mind me of that," said King Arthur.

So King Arthur abided with that old woman for that night, and she refreshed him with meat and drink and served him very well. And the next morning he set forth unto that castle where he had made his covenant, and his heart was more cheerful than it had been for a whole year.

How King Arthur Overcame the Knight-Enchanter, and How Sir Gawaine Manifested the High Nobility of His Knighthood.

Now, when King Arthur came to the castle, the gateway thereof was immediately opened to him and he entered. And when he had entered, sundry attendants came and conducted him into the hall where he had aforetime been. There he beheld the knight of that castle and a great many people who had come to witness the conclusion of the adventure. And when the knight beheld King Arthur he said to him, "Sir, hast thou come to redeem thy pledge?" "Yea," said King Arthur, "for so I made my vow to thee." Then the knight of the castle said, "Sir, hast thou guessed that riddle?" And King Arthur said, "I believe that I have." The knight of the castle said, "Then let me hear thy answer thereto. But if thou makest any mistake, or if thou dost not guess aright, then is thy life forfeit."

"Very well," said King Arthur, "let it be that way. Now this is the answer to thy riddle: That which a woman most desires is to have her will."

Now when the lord of the castle heard King Arthur guess aright he wist not what to say or where to look, and those who were there also perceived that the King had guessed aright.

Then King Arthur came very close to that knight with great sternness of demeanor, and he said, "Now, thou traitor knight! thou didst ask me to enter into thy sport with thee a year ago, so at these present it is my turn to ask thee to have sport with me. And this is the sport I will have, that thou shalt give me that chain and locket that hang about thy neck, and that I shall give thee the collar which hangeth about my neck."

At this, the face of that knight fell all pale, like to ashes, and he emitted a sound similar to the sound made by a hare when the hound lays hold upon it. Then King Arthur catched him very violently by the arm, and he catched the locket and brake it away from about the knight's neck, and upon that the knight shrieked very loud, and fell down upon his knees and besought mercy of the King, and there was great uproar in that place. Then King Arthur opened the locket and lo! there was a ball as of crystal, very clear and shining. And King Arthur said, "I will have no mercy," and therewith he flung the ball violently down upon the stone of the pavement so that it brake with a loud noise. Then, upon that instant, the knight-conjurer gave a piercing bitter cry and fell down upon the ground; and when they ran to raise him up, behold! he was entirely dead.

Now when the people of that castle beheld their knight thus suddenly dead, and when they beheld King Arthur how he stood in the fury of his kingly majesty, they were greatly afeared so that they shrunk away from the King where he stood. Then the King turned and went out from that castle and no one stayed him, and he mounted his horse and rode away, and no one gave him let or hindrance in his going.

Now when the King had left the castle in that wise, he went straight to the hut where was the old beldame and he said to her, "Thou hast holpen[12] me a very great deal in mine hour of need, so now will I fulfil that pledge which I made unto thee, for I will take thee unto my Court and thou shalt choose one of my knights for thy

---

12. Helped.

husband. For I think there is not one knight in all my Court but would be very glad to do anything that lieth in his power to reward one who hath saved me as thou hast done this day."

Therewith he took that old woman and he lifted her up upon the crupper[13] of his horse; then he himself mounted upon his horse, and so they rode away from that place. And the King comported himself to that aged beldame in all ways with the utmost consideration as though she had been a beautiful dame of the highest degree in the land. Likewise he showed her such respect that had she been a lady of royal blood, he could not have shown greater respect to her.

So in due time they reached the Court, which was then at Carleon. And they came there nigh about mid-day.

Now about that time it chanced that the Queen and a number of the lords of the Court, and a number of the ladies of the Court, were out in the fields enjoying the pleasantness of the Maytime; for no one in all the world, excepting the esquire, Boisenard, knew anything of the danger that beset King Arthur; hence all were very glad of the pleasantness of the season. Now as King Arthur drew nigh to that place, these lifted up their eyes and beheld him come, and they were astonished beyond all measure to see King Arthur come to them across that field with that old beldame behind him upon the saddle, wherefore they stood still to wait until King Arthur reached them.

But when King Arthur had come to them, he did not dismount from his horse, but sat thereon and regarded them all very steadfastly; and Queen Guinevere said, "Sir, what is this? Hast thou a mind to play some merry jest this day that thou hast brought hither that old woman?"

"Lady," said King Arthur, "excepting for this old woman it were like to have been a very sorry jest for thee and for me; for had she not aided me I would now have been a dead man and in a few days you would doubtless all have been in great passion of sorrow."

Then all they who were there marvelled very greatly at the King's words. And the Queen said, "Sir, what is it that hath befallen thee?"

Thereupon King Arthur told them all that had happened to him from the very beginning when he and Boisenard had left the

---

13. Rump.

castle of Tintagalon. And when he had ended his story, they were greatly amazed.

Now there were seventeen lords of the Court there present. So when King Arthur had ended his story, he said unto these, "Messires, I have given my pledge unto this aged woman that any one of you whom she may choose, shall take her unto him as his wife, and shall treat her with all the regard that it is possible for him to do; for this was the condition that she laid upon me. Now tell me, did I do right in making unto her my pledge that I would fulfil that which she desired?" And all of those who were present said, "Yea, lord, thou didst right, for we would do all in the world for to save thee from such peril as that from which thou hast escaped."

Then King Arthur said to that old woman, "Lady, is there any of these knights here whom you would choose for to be your husband?" Upon this, the old woman pointed with her very long, bony finger unto Sir Gawaine, saying, "Yea, I would marry that lord, for I see by the chain that is around his neck and by the golden circlet upon his hair and by the haughty nobility of his aspect, that he must be the son of a king."

Then King Arthur said unto Sir Gawaine, "Sir, art thou willing to fulfil my pledge unto this old woman?" And Sir Gawaine said, "Yea, lord, whatsoever thou requirest of me, that will I do." So Sir Gawaine came to the old woman and took her hand into his and set it to his lips; and not one of all those present so much as smiled. Then they all turned their faces and returned unto the King's castle; and they were very silent and downcast, for this was sore trouble that had come upon that Court.

Now after they had returned unto the Court, they assigned certain apartments therein to that old woman, and they clad her in rich raiment such as a queen might wear, and they assigned unto her a Court such as was fit for a queen; and it seemed to all the Court that, in the rich robes which she wore, she was ten times more ugly than she was before. So when eleven days had passed, Sir Gawaine was wedded to that old woman in the chapel of the King's Court with great ceremony and pomp of circumstance, and all of those who were there were as sad and as sorrowful as though Sir Gawaine had been called upon to suffer his death.

Afterward that they were married, Sir Gawaine and the old woman went to Sir Gawaine's house and there Sir Gawaine shut himself off from all the world and suffered no one to come nigh him; for he was proud beyond all measure, and in this great humiliation he suffered in such a wise that words cannot tell how great was that humiliation. Wherefore he shut himself away from the world that no one might behold his grief and his shame.

And all the rest of that day he walked continually up and down his chamber, for he was altogether in such despair that it came unto his mind that it would be well if he took his own life; for it seemed to him impossible for to suffer such shame as that which had come upon him. So after a while it fell the dark of the early night and therewith a certain strength came to Sir Gawaine and he said, "This is a shame for me for to behave in this way; for since I have married that lady she is my true wedded wife and I do not treat her with that regard unto which she hath the right." So he went out of that place and sought the apartment of that old woman who was his wife, and by that time it was altogether dark. But when Sir Gawaine had come into that place where she was, that old woman upbraided him, crying out upon him, "So, Sir! You have treated me but ill upon this our wedding-day, for you have stayed all the afternoon away from me and now only come to me when it is dark night." And Sir Gawaine said, "Lady, I could not help it, for I was very sore oppressed with many cares. But if I have disregarded thee this day, I do beseech thy forgiveness therefore, and I will hold myself willing to do all that is in my power to recompense thee for any neglect that I have placed upon thee." Then the lady said, "Sir, it is very dark in this place; let us then have a light." "It shall be as thou dost desire," said Sir Gawaine, "and I, myself, will go and fetch a light for thee."

So Sir Gawaine went forth from that place and he brought two waxen tapers, one in either hand, and he bore them in candlesticks of gold; for he was minded to show all respect unto that old woman. And when he came into the room he perceived that she was at the farther end of the apartment and he went toward her, and she arose and stood before him as he approached.

But when the circle of light fell upon that old woman, and when Sir Gawaine beheld her who stood before him, he cried out aloud in a very great voice because of the great marvel and wonder of that which he saw. For, instead of that old woman whom he had left, he beheld a lady of extraordinary beauty and in the very flower of her youth. And he beheld that her hair was long and glossy and very black, and that her eyes were likewise black like to black jewels, and that her lips were like coral, and her teeth were like pearls. So, for a while, Sir Gawaine could not speak, and then he cried out, "Lady! lady! who art thou?"

Then that lady smiled upon Sir Gawaine with such loving-kindness that he wist not what to think, other than that this was an angel who had descended to that place out of paradise. Wherefore he stood before her for a long time and could find no more words to say, and she continued to smile upon him very kindly in that wise. Then by and by Sir Gawaine said to her, "Lady, where is that dame who is my wife?" And the lady said, "Sir Gawaine, I am she." "It is not possible," cried out Sir Gawaine, "for she was old and extraordinarily ugly, but I believe that thou art beautiful beyond any lady whom I have beheld." And the lady said, "Nevertheless, I am she and because thou hast taken me for thy wife with thine own free will and with great courtesy, so is a part of that enchantment that lay upon me removed from me. For I will now be able to appear before thee in mine own true shape. For whiles I was a little while ago so ugly and foul as thou didst behold me to be, now am I to be as thou seest me, for one-half the day—and the other half thereof I must be ugly as I was before."

Then Sir Gawaine was filled beyond all words with great joy. And with that joy there came an extreme passion of loving regard for that lady. So he cried out aloud several times, "This is surely the most wonderful thing that ever befell any man in all the world." Therewith he fell down upon his knees and took that lady's hands into his own hands, and kissed her hands with great fervor, and all the while she smiled upon him as she had done at first.

Then again the lady said, "Come, sit thee down beside me and let us consider what part of the day I shall be in the one guise, and what part of the day I shall be in the other guise; for all day I may have the one appearance, and all night I may have the other appearance."

Then Sir Gawaine said, "I would have thee in this guise during the night time, for then we are together at our own inn; and since thou art of this sort that I now see thee, I do not at all reckon how the world may regard thee."

Upon this the lady spake with great animation, saying, "No, sir, I would not have it in that wise, for every woman loveth the regard of the world, and I would fain enjoy such beauty as is mine before the world, and not endure the scorn and contempt of men and women."

To this Sir Gawaine said, "Lady, I would have it the other way."

And she said, "Nay, I would have it my way."

Then Sir Gawaine said, "So be it. For since I have taken thee for my wife, so must I show thee respect in all matters; wherefore thou shalt have thy will in this and in all other things."

Then that lady fell a-laughing beyond all measure and she said, "Sir, I did but put this as a last trial upon thee, for as I am now, so shall I always be."

Upon this Sir Gawaine was so filled with joy that he knew not how to contain himself.

So they sat together for a long time, hand in hand. Then after a while Sir Gawaine said, "Lady, who art thou?" Unto which she made reply, "I am one of the Ladies of the Lake; but for thy sake I have become mortal like to other women and have quit that very beautiful home where I one time dwelt. I have kept thee in my heart for a considerable while, for I was not very far distant at that time when thou didst bid adieu to Sir Pellias beside the lake. There I beheld how thou didst weep and bewail thyself when Sir Pellias left thee,[14] wherefore my heart went out to thee with great pity. So, after a while, I quitted that lake and became mortal for thy sake. Now, when I found the trouble into which King Arthur had fallen I took that occasion to have him fetch me unto thee so that I might test the entire nobility of thy knighthood; and, lo! I have found it all that I deemed it possible to be. For though I appeared to thee so aged, so ugly, and so foul, yet hast thou treated me with such kind regard that I do not believe that thou couldst have behaved with more courtesy to me had I been the daughter of a king. Wherefore it doth now afford me such pleasure for to possess thee for my knight and my true lord, that I cannot very well tell thee how great is my joy therein."

Then Sir Gawaine said, "Lady, I do not think it can be so great as my joy in possessing thee." And thereupon he came to her and laid his hand upon her shoulder and kissed her upon the lips.

Then, after that, he went forth and called with a great voice all through that house, and the people of the house came running from everywhere. And he commanded that the people should bring lights and refreshments, and they brought the lights, and when they had brought them and beheld that beautiful lady instead of the

---

14. Earlier in Pyle's story, after Gawaine (because of enchantment and not because he is dishonorable) has betrayed Sir Pellias, he finds him on the shore of a lake. Pellias has become "not all human, but part fay" and is about to depart for the realm of the Lady of the Lake. Sir Gawaine weeps "with great passion" because of Pellias' departure.

aged dame, they were filled with great wonder and joy; wherefore they cried out aloud and clapped their hands together and made much sound of rejoicing. And they set a great feast for Sir Gawaine and his lady, and in place of the sorrow and darkness that had been, there was joy and light, and music and singing; wherefore those of the King's Court, beholding this from a distance, said, "It is very strange that Sir Gawaine should have taken so much joy of having wedded that old beldame."

But when the next morning had come, that lady clad herself in raiment of yellow silk, and she hung about her many strands of precious stones of several colors, and she set a golden crown upon her head. And Sir Gawaine let call his horse, and he let call a snow-white palfrey[15] for the lady, and thereupon they rode out from that place and entered the Court of the King. But when the King and the Queen and their several Courts beheld that lady, they were filled with such great astonishment that they wist not what to say for pure wonder. And when they heard all that had happened, they gave great joy and loud acclaim so that all their mourning was changed into rejoicing. And, indeed, there was not one knight there of all that Court who would not have given half his life to have been so fortunate in that matter as was Sir Gawaine, the son of King Lot of Orkney.

Such is the story of Sir Gawaine, and from it I draw this significance: as that poor ugly beldame appeared unto the eyes of Sir Gawaine, so doth a man's duty sometimes appear to him to be ugly and exceedingly ill-favored unto his desires. But when he shall have wedded himself unto that duty so that he hath made it one with him as a bridegroom maketh himself one with his bride, then doth that duty become of a sudden very beautiful unto him and unto others.

So may it be with ye that you shall take duty unto yourselves no matter how much it may mislike ye to do so. For indeed a man shall hardly have any real pleasure in his life unless his inclination becometh wedded unto his duty and cleaveth[16] unto it as a husband cleaveth unto his wife. For when inclination is thus wedded unto duty, then doth the soul take great joy unto itself as though a

---

15. A riding horse.
16. Is faithful.

wedding had taken place betwixt a bridegroom and a bride within its tabernacle.

Likewise, when you shall have become entirely wedded unto your duty, then shall you become equally worthy with that good knight and gentleman Sir Gawaine; for it needs not that a man shall wear armor for to be a true knight, but only that he shall do his best endeavor with all patience and humility as it hath been ordained for him to do. Wherefore, when your time cometh unto you to display your knightness by assuming your duty, I do pray that you also may approve yourself as worthy as Sir Gawaine approved himself in this story which I have told you of as above written.

Guenevere

by

SARA TEASDALE

I was a queen, and I have lost my crown;
A wife, and I have broken all my vows;
A lover, and I ruined him I loved:—
There is no other havoc left to do.
A little month ago I was a queen,
And mothers held their babies up to see
When I came riding out of Camelot.
The women smiled, and all the world smiled too.
And now, what woman's eyes would smile on me?
I am still beautiful, and yet what child
Would think of me as some high, heaven-sent thing,
An angel, clad in gold and miniver?[1]
The world would run from me, and yet I am
No different from the queen they used to love.
If water, flowing silver over stones,
Is forded, and beneath the horses' feet
Grows turbid suddenly, it clears again,
And men will drink it with no thought of harm.
Yet I am branded for a single fault.

I was the flower amid a toiling world,
Where people smiled to see one happy thing,
And they were proud and glad to raise me high;
They only asked that I should be right fair,
A little kind, and gownèd wondrously,
And surely it were little praise to me
If I had pleased them well throughout my life.

I was a queen, the daughter of a king.
The crown was never heavy on my head,

---

1. A white or light-gray fur used as a rich trim on medieval robes.

It was my right, and was a part of me.
The women thought me proud, the men were kind,
And bowed down gallantly to kiss my hand,
And watched me as I passed them calmly by,
Along the halls I shall not tread again.
What if, to-night, I should revisit them?
The warders at the gates, the kitchen-maids,
The very beggars would stand off from me,
And I, their queen, would climb the stairs alone,
Pass through the banquet-hall, a hated thing,
And seek my chambers for a hiding-place,
And I should find them but a sepulchre,
The very rushes rotted on the floors,
The fire in ashes on the freezing hearth.

I was a queen, and he who loved me best
Made me a woman for a night and day,
And now I go unqueened forevermore.

A queen should never dream on summer nights,
When hovering spells are heavy in the dusk:—
I think no night was ever quite so still,
So smoothly lit with red along the west,
So deeply hushed with quiet through and through.
And strangely clear, and sharply dyed with light,
The trees stood straight against a paling sky,
With Venus burning lamp-like in the west.
I walked alone among a thousand flowers,
That drooped their heads and drowsed beneath the dew,
And all my thoughts were quieted to sleep.
Behind me, on the walk, I heard a step—
I did not know my heart could tell his tread,
I did not know I loved him till that hour.
The garden reeled a little, I was weak,
And in my breast I felt a wild, sick pain.
Quickly he came behind me, caught my arms,
That ached beneath his touch; and then I swayed,
My head fell backward and I saw his face.

All this grows bitter that was once so sweet,
And many mouths must drain the dregs of it,
But none will pity me, nor pity him
Whom Love so lashed, and with such cruel thongs.

Merlin

by

EDWIN ARLINGTON ROBINSON

I

"Gawaine, Gawaine, what look ye for to see,
So far beyond the faint edge of the world?
D'ye look to see the lady Vivian,
Pursued by divers ominous vile demons
That have another king more fierce than ours?
Or think ye that if ye look far enough
And hard enough into the feathery west
Ye'll have a glimmer of the Grail itself?
And if ye look for neither Grail nor lady,
What look ye for to see, Gawaine, Gawaine?"

So Dagonet, whom Arthur made a knight
Because he loved him as he laughed at him,
Intoned his idle presence on a day
To Gawaine, who had thought himself alone,
Had there been in him thought of anything
Save what was murmured now in Camelot
Of Merlin's hushed and all but unconfirmed
Appearance out of Brittany. It was heard
At first there was a ghost in Arthur's palace,
But soon among the scullions[1] and anon
Among the knights a firmer credit held
All tongues from uttering what all glances told—
Though not for long. Gawaine, this afternoon,
Fearing he might say more to Lancelot
Of Merlin's rumor-laden resurrection
Than Lancelot would have an ear to cherish,

---

1. Servants who perform menial tasks in the kitchen.

Had sauntered off with his imagination
To Merlin's Rock, where now there was no Merlin
To meditate upon a whispering town
Below him in the silence.—Once he said
To Gawaine: "You are young; and that being so,
Behold the shining city of our dreams
And of our King."—"Long live the King," said Gawaine.—
"Long live the King," said Merlin after him;
"Better for me that I shall not be King;
Wherefore I say again, Long live the King,
And add, God save him, also, and all kings—
All kings and queens. I speak in general.
Kings have I known that were but weary men
With no stout appetite for more than peace
That was not made for them."—"Nor were they made
For kings," Gawaine said, laughing.—"You are young,
Gawaine, and you may one day hold the world
Between your fingers, knowing not what it is
That you are holding. Better for you and me,
I think, that we shall not be kings."

                                    Gawaine,
Remembering Merlin's words of long ago,
Frowned as he thought, and having frowned again,
He smiled and threw an acorn at a lizard:
"There's more afoot and in the air to-day
Than what is good for Camelot. Merlin
May or may not know all, but he said well
To say to me that he would not be King.
Nor more would I be King." Far down he gazed
On Camelot, until he made of it
A phantom town of many stillnesses,
Not reared for men to dwell in, or for kings
To reign in, without omens and obscure
Familiars to bring terror to their days;
For though a knight, and one as hard at arms
As any, save the fate-begotten few
That all acknowledged or in envy loathed,
He felt a foreign sort of creeping up
And down him, as of moist things in the dark,—
When Dagonet, coming on him unawares,
Presuming on his title of Sir Fool,

Addressed him and crooned on till he was done:
"What look ye for to see, Gawaine, Gawaine?"

"Sir Dagonet, you best and wariest
Of all dishonest men, I look through Time,
For sight of what it is that is to be.
I look to see it, though I see it not.
I see a town down there that holds a king,
And over it I see a few small clouds—
Like feathers in the west, as you observe;
And I shall see no more this afternoon,
Than what there is around us every day,
Unless you have a skill that I have not
To ferret the invisible for rats."

"If you see what's around us every day,
You need no other showing to go mad.
Remember that and take it home with you;
And say tonight, 'I had it of a fool—
With no immediate obliquity[2]
For this one or for that one, or for me.'"
Gawaine, having risen, eyed the fool curiously:
"I'll not forget I had it of a knight,
Whose only folly is to fool himself;
And as for making other men to laugh,
And so forget their sins and selves a little,
There's no great folly there. So keep it up,
As long as you've a legend or a song,
And have whatever sport of us you like
Till havoc is the word and we fall howling.
For I've a guess there may not be so loud
A sound of laughing here in Camelot
When Merlin goes again to his gay grave
In Brittany. To mention lesser terrors,
Men say his beard is gone."

                              "Do men say that?"
A twitch of an impatient weariness
Played for a moment over the lean face
Of Dagonet, who reasoned inwardly:

---

2. Indirect reference.

"The friendly zeal of this inquiring knight
Will overtake his tact and leave it squealing,
One of these days."—Gawaine looked hard at him:
"If I be too familiar with a fool,
I'm on the way to be another fool,"
He mused, and owned a rueful qualm within him:
"Yes, Dagonet," he ventured, with a laugh,
"Men tell me that his beard has vanished wholly,
And that he shines now as the Lord's anointed,
And wears the valiance of an ageless youth
Crowned with a glory of eternal peace."

Dagonet, smiling strangely, shook his head:
"I grant your valiance of a kind of youth
To Merlin, but your crown of peace I question;
For, though I know no more than any churl
Who pinches any chambermaid soever
In the King's palace, I look not to Merlin
For peace, when out of his peculiar tomb
He comes again to Camelot. Time swings
A mighty scythe, and some day all your peace
Goes down before its edge like so much clover.
No, it is not for peace that Merlin comes,
Without a trumpet—and without a beard,
If what you say men say of him be true—
Nor yet for sudden war."

                              Gawaine, for a moment,
Met then the ambiguous gaze of Dagonet,
And, making nothing of it, looked abroad
As if at something cheerful on all sides,
And back again to the fool's unasking eyes:
"Well, Dagonet, if Merlin would have peace,
Let Merlin stay away from Brittany,"
Said he, with admiration for the man
Whom Folly called a fool: "And we have known him;
We knew him once when he knew everything."

"He knew as much as God would let him know
Until he met the lady Vivian.
I tell you that, for the world knows all that;
Also it knows he told the King one day

That he was to be buried, and alive,
In Brittany; and that the King should see
The face of him no more. Then Merlin sailed
Away to Vivian in Broceliande,
Where now she crowns him and herself with flowers
And feeds him fruits and wines and many foods
Of many savors, and sweet ortolans.[3]
Wise books of every lore of every land
Are there to fill his days, if he require them,
And there are players of all instruments—
Flutes, hautboys,[4] drums, and viols; and she sings
To Merlin, till he trembles in her arms
And there forgets that any town alive
Had ever such a name as Camelot.
So Vivian holds him with her love, they say,
And he, who has no age, has not grown old.
I swear to nothing, but that's what they say.
That's being buried in Broceliande
For too much wisdom and clairvoyancy.
But you and all who live, Gawaine, have heard
This tale, or many like it, more than once;
And you must know that Love, when Love invites
Philosophy to play, plays high and wins,
Or low and loses. And you say to me,
'If Merlin would have peace, let Merlin stay
Away from Brittany.' Gawaine, you are young,
And Merlin's in his grave."

        "Merlin said once
That I was young, and it's a joy for me
That I am here to listen while you say it.
Young or not young, if that be burial,
May I be buried long before I die.
I might be worse than young; I might be old."—
Dagonet answered, and without a smile:
"Somehow I fancy Merlin saying that;
A fancy—a mere fancy." Then he smiled:
"And such a doom as his may be for you,

---

3. Small brownish birds of the Old World, eaten as a delicacy.
4. Oboes.

Gawaine, should your untiring divination
Delve in the veiled eternal mysteries
Too far to be a pleasure for the Lord.
And when you stake your wisdom for a woman,
Compute the woman to be worth a grave,
As Merlin did, and say no more about it.
But Vivian, she played high. Oh, very high!
Flutes, hautboys, drums, and viols,—and her love.
Gawaine, farewell."

                    "Farewell, Sir Dagonet,
And may the devil take you presently."
He followed with a vexed and envious eye,
And with an arid laugh, Sir Dagonet's
Departure, till his gaunt obscurity
Was cloaked and lost amid the glimmering trees.
"Poor fool!" he murmured. "Or am I the fool?
With all my fast ascendency in arms,
That ominous clown is nearer to the King
Than I am—yet; and God knows what he knows,
And what his wits infer from what he sees
And feels and hears. I wonder what he knows
Of Lancelot, or what I might know now,
Could I have sunk myself to sound a fool
To springe[5] a friend. . . . No, I like not this day.
There's a cloud coming over Camelot
Larger than any that is in the sky,—
Or Merlin would be still in Brittany,
With Vivian and the viols. It's all too strange."

And later, when descending to the city,
Through unavailing casements he could hear
The roaring of a mighty voice within,
Confirming fervidly his own conviction:
"It's all too strange, and half the world's half crazy!"—
He scowled: "Well, I agree with Lamorak."
He frowned, and passed: "And I like not this day."

---

5. Ensnare.

II

Sir Lamorak, the man of oak and iron,
Had with him now, as a care-laden guest,
Sir Bedivere, a man whom Arthur loved
As he had loved no man save Lancelot.
Like one whose late-flown shaft of argument
Had glanced and fallen afield innocuously,
He turned upon his host a sudden eye
That met from Lamorak's an even shaft
Of native and unused authority;
And each man held the other till at length
Each turned away, shutting his heavy jaws
Again together, prisoning thus two tongues
That might forget and might not be forgiven.
Then Bedivere, to find a plain way out,
Said, "Lamorak, let us drink to some one here,
And end this dryness. Who shall it be—the King,
The Queen, or Lancelot?"—"Merlin," Lamorak growled;
And then there were more wrinkles round his eyes
Than Bedivere had said were possible.
"There's no refusal in me now for that,"
The guest replied; "so, 'Merlin' let it be.
We've not yet seen him, but if he be here,
And even if he should not be here, say 'Merlin.'"
They drank to the unseen from two new tankards,
And fell straightway to sighing for the past,
And what was yet before them. Silence laid
A cogent finger on the lips of each
Impatient veteran, whose hard hands lay clenched
And restless on his midriff, until words
Were stronger than strong Lamorak:

                                        "Bedivere,"
Began the solid host, "you may as well
Say now as at another time hereafter
That all your certainties have bruises on 'em,
And all your pestilent asseverations
Will never make a man a salamander—
Who's born, as we are told, so fire won't bite him,—

Or a slippery queen a nun who counts[6] and burns
Herself to nothing with her beads and candles.
There's nature, and what's in us, to be sifted
Before we know ourselves, or any man
Or woman that God suffers to be born.
That's how I speak; and while you strain your mazard,[7]
Like Father Jove, big with a new Minerva,[8]
We'll say, to pass the time, that I speak well.
God's fish![9] The King had eyes; and Lancelot
Won't ride home to his mother, for she's dead.
The story is that Merlin warned the King
Of what's come now to pass; and I believe it
And Arthur, he being Arthur and a king,
Has made a more pernicious mess than one,
We're told, for being so great and amorous:
It's that unwholesome and inclement cub
Young Modred I'd see first in hell before
I'd hang too high the Queen or Lancelot;
The King, if one may say it, set the pace,
And we've two strapping bastards here to prove it.
Young Borre,[10] he's well enough; but as for Modred,
I squirm as often as I look at him.
And there again did Merlin warn the King,
The story goes abroad; and I believe it."

Sir Bedivere, as one who caught no more
Than what he would of Lamorak's outpouring,
Inclined his grizzled head and closed his eyes
Before he sighed and rubbed his beard and spoke:
"For all I know to make it otherwise,
The Queen may be a nun some day or other;
I'd pray to God for such a thing to be,
If prayer for that were not a mockery.

---

6. A reference to counting the beads on a rosary.

7. Head.

8. Minerva was the Roman goddess of wisdom, the arts, and martial prowess. She is said to have sprung full-grown and in armor from the head of Jove (or Jupiter).

9. Oaths commonly referred to God's body, blood, etc. From this practice there arose jocular oaths, such as "God's hat" or "God's fish."

10. Illegitimate son of Arthur and Lyonors, daughter of Earl Sanam.

We're late now for much praying, Lamorak,
When you and I can feel upon our faces
A wind that has been blowing over ruins
That we had said were castles and high towers—
Till Merlin, or the spirit of him, came
As the dead come in dreams. I saw the King
This morning, and I saw his face. Therefore,
I tell you, if a state shall have a king,
The king must have the state, and be the state;
Or then shall we have neither king nor state,
But bones and ashes, and high towers all fallen:
And we shall have, where late there was a kingdom,
A dusty wreck of what was once a glory—
A wilderness whereon to crouch and mourn
And moralize, or else to build once more
For something better or for something worse.
Therefore again, I say that Lancelot
Has wrought a potent wrong upon the King,
And all who serve and recognize the King,
And all who follow him and all who love him.
Whatever the stormy faults he may have had,
To look on him today is to forget them;
And if it be too late for sorrow now
To save him—for it was a broken man
I saw this morning, and a broken king—
The God who sets a day for desolation
Will not forsake him in Avilion,[11]
Or whatsoever shadowy land there be
Where peace awaits him on its healing shores."

Sir Lamorak, shifting in his oaken chair,
Growled like a dog and shook himself like one:
"For the stone-chested, helmet-cracking knight
That you are known to be from Lyonnesse
To northward, Bedivere, you fol-de-rol
When days are rancid, and you fiddle-faddle
More like a woman than a man with hands
Fit for the smiting of a crazy giant
With armor an inch thick, as we all know

---

11. Avalon.

You are, when you're not sermonizing at us.
As for the King, I say the King, no doubt,
Is angry, sorry, and all sorts of things,
For Lancelot, and for his easy Queen,
Whom he took knowing she'd thrown sparks already
On that same piece of tinder, Lancelot,
Who fetched her with him from Leodogran
Because the King—God save poor human reason!—
Would prove to Merlin, who knew everything
Worth knowing in those days, that he was wrong.
I'll drink now and be quiet,—but, by God,
I'll have to tell you, Brother Bedivere,
Once more, to make you listen properly,
That crowns and orders, and high palaces,
And all the manifold ingredients
Of this good solid kingdom, where we sit
And spit now at each other with our eyes,
Will not go rolling down to hell just yet
Because a pretty woman is a fool.
And here's Kay coming with his fiddle face
As long now as two fiddles. Sit ye down,
Sir Man, and tell us everything you know
Of Merlin—or his ghost without a beard.
What mostly is it?"

           Sir Kay, the seneschal,
Sat wearily while he gazed upon the two:
"To you it mostly is, if I err not,
That what you hear of Merlin's coming back
Is nothing more or less than heavy truth.
But ask me nothing of the Queen, I say,
For I know nothing. All I know of her
Is what her eyes have told the silences
That now attend her; and that her estate
Is one for less complacent execration
Than quips and innuendoes of the city
Would augur for her sin—if there be sin—
Or for her name—if now she have a name.
And where, I say, is this to lead the King,
And after him, the kingdom and ourselves?
Here be we, three men of a certain strength
And some confessed intelligence, who know

That Merlin has come out of Brittany—
Out of his grave, as he would say it for us—
Because the King has now a desperation
More strong upon him than a woman's net
Was over Merlin—for now Merlin's here,
And two of us who knew him know how well
His wisdom, if he have it any longer,
Will by this hour have sounded and appraised
The grief and wrath and anguish of the King,
Requiring mercy and inspiring fear
Lest he forego the vigil now most urgent,
And leave unwatched a cranny where some worm
Or serpent may come in to speculate."

"I know your worm, and his worm's name is Modred—
Albeit[12] the streets are not yet saying so,"
Said Lamorak, as he lowered his wrath and laughed
A sort of poisonous apology
To Kay: "And in the meantime, I'll be gyved![13]
Here's Bedivere a-wailing for the King,
And you, Kay, with a moist eye for the Queen.
I think I'll blow a horn for Lancelot;
For by my soul a man's in sorry case
When Guineveres are out with eyes to scorch him:
I'm not so ancient or so frozen certain
That I'd ride horses down to skeletons
If she were after me. Has Merlin seen him—
This Lancelot, this Queen-fed friend of ours?"

Kay answered sighing, with a lonely scowl:
"The picture that I conjure leaves him out;
The King and Merlin are this hour together,
And I can say no more; for I know nothing.
But how the King persuaded or beguiled
The stricken wizard from across the water
Outriddles my poor wits. It's all too strange."

"It's all too strange, and half the world's half crazy!"
Roared Lamorak, forgetting once again

---

12. Although.
13. Fettered or shackled.

The devastating carriage of his voice.
"Is the King sick?" he said, more quietly;
"Is he to let one damned scratch be enough
To paralyze the force that heretofore
Would operate a way through hell and iron,
And iron already slimy with his blood?
Is the King blind—with Modred watching him?
Does he forget the crown for Lancelot?
Does he forget that every woman mewing
Shall some day be a handful of small ashes?"

"You speak as one for whom the god of Love
Has yet a mighty trap in preparation.
We know you, Lamorak," said Bedivere:
"We know you for a short man, Lamorak,—
In deeds, if not in inches or in words;
But there are fens and heights and distances
That your capricious ranging has not yet
Essayed in this weird region of man's love.
Forgive me, Lamorak, but your words are words.
Your deeds are what they are; and ages hence
Will men remember your illustriousness,
If there be gratitude in history.
For me, I see the shadow of the end,
Wherein to serve King Arthur to the end,
And, if God have it so, to see the Grail
Before I die."

                But Lamorak shook his head:
"See what you will, or what you may. For me,
I see no other than a stinking mess—
With Modred stirring it, and Agravaine
Spattering Camelot with as much of it
As he can throw. The Devil got somehow
Into God's workshop once upon a time,
And out of the red clay that he found there
He made a shape like Modred, and another
As like as eyes are to this Agravaine.
'I never made 'em,' said the good Lord God,
'But let 'em go, and see what comes of 'em.'
And that's what we're to do. As for the Grail,

I've never worried it, and so the Grail
Has never worried me."

             Kay sighed. "I see
With Bedivere the coming of the end,"
He murmured; "for the King I saw today
Was not, nor shall he ever be again,
The King we knew. I say the King is dead;
The man is living, but the King is dead.
The wheel is broken."

             "Faugh!" said Lamorak;
"There are no dead kings yet in Camelot;
But there is Modred who is hatching ruin,—
And when it hatches I may not be here.
There's Gawaine too, and he does not forget
My father, who killed his. King Arthur's house
Has more divisions in it than I like
In houses; and if Modred's aim be good
For backs like mine, I'm not long for the scene."

III

King Arthur, as he paced a lonely floor
That rolled a muffled echo, as he fancied,
All through the palace and out through the world,
Might now have wondered hard, could he have heard
Sir Lamorak's apathetic disregard
Of what Fate's knocking made so manifest
And ominous to others near the King—
If any, indeed, were near him at this hour
Save Merlin, once the wisest of all men,
And weary Dagonet, whom he had made
A knight for love of him and his abused
Integrity. He might have wondered hard
And wondered much; and after wondering,
He might have summoned, with as little heart
As he had now for crowns, the fond, lost Merlin,

Whose Nemesis[14] had made of him a slave,
A man of dalliance, and a sybarite.[15]

"Men change in Brittany, Merlin," said the King;
And even his grief had strife to freeze again
A dreary smile for the transmuted seer
Now robed in heavy wealth of purple silk,
With frogs and foreign tassels. On his face,
Too smooth now for a wizard or a sage,
Lay written, for the King's remembering eyes,
A pathos of a lost authority
Long faded, and unconscionably gone;
And on the King's heart lay a sudden cold:
"I might as well have left him in his grave,
As he would say it, saying what was true,—
As death is true. This Merlin is not mine,
But Vivian's. My crown is less than hers,
And I am less than woman to this man."

Then Merlin, as one reading Arthur's words
On viewless tablets in the air before him:
"Now, Arthur, since you are a child of mine—
A foster-child, and that's a kind of child—
Be not from hearsay or despair too eager
To dash your meat with bitter seasoning,
So none that are more famished than yourself
Shall have what you refuse. For you are King,
And if you starve yourself, you starve the state;
And then by sundry looks and silences
Of those you loved, and by the lax regard
Of those you knew for fawning enemies,
You may learn soon that you are King no more,
But a slack, blasted, and sad-fronted man,
Made sadder with a crown. No other friend
Than I could say this to you, and say more;
And if you bid me say no more, so be it."

---

14. The goddess of retributive justice or vengeance; thus one who inflicts retribution or vengeance.

15. A person devoted to pleasure and luxury.

The King, who sat with folded arms, now bowed
His head and felt, unfought and all aflame
Like immanent hell-fire, the wretchedness
That only those who are to lead may feel—
And only they when they are maimed and worn
Too sore to covet without shuddering
The fixed impending eminence where death
Itself were victory, could they but lead
Unbitten by the serpents they had fed.
Turning, he spoke: "Merlin, you say the truth:
There is no man who could say more to me
Today, or say so much to me, and live.
But you are Merlin still, or part of him;
I did you wrong when I thought otherwise,
And I am sorry now. Say what you will.
We are alone, and I shall be alone
As long as Time shall hide a reason here
For me to stay in this infested world
Where I have sinned and erred and heeded not
Your counsel; and where you yourself—God save us!—
Have gone down smiling to the smaller life
That you and your incongruous laughter called
Your living grave. God save us all, Merlin,
When you, the seer, the founder, and the prophet,
May throw the gold of your immortal treasure
Back to the God that gave it, and then laugh
Because a woman has you in her arms . . .
Why do you sting me now with a small hive
Of words that are all poison? I do not ask
Much honey; but why poison me for nothing,
And with a venom that I know already
As I know crowns and wars? Why tell a king—
A poor, foiled, flouted, miserable king—
That if he lets rats eat his fingers off
He'll have no fingers to fight battles with?
I know as much as that, for I am still
A king—who thought himself a little less
Than God; a king who built him palaces
On sand and mud, and hears them crumbling now,
And sees them tottering, as he knew they must.
You are the man who made me to be King—
Therefore, say anything."

                    Merlin, stricken deep
With pity that was old, being born of old
Foreshadowings, made answer to the King:
"This coil of Lancelot and Guinevere
Is not for any mortal to undo,
Or to deny, or to make otherwise;
But your most violent years are on their way
To days, and to a sounding of loud hours
That are to strike for war. Let not the time
Between this hour and then be lost in fears,
Or told in obscurations and vain faith
In what has been your long security;
For should your force be slower then than hate,
And your regret be sharper than your sight,
And your remorse fall heavier than your sword,—
Then say farewell to Camelot, and the crown.
But say not you have lost, or failed in aught
Your golden horoscope of imperfection
Has held in starry words that I have read.
I see no farther now than I saw then,
For no man shall be given of everything
Together in one life; yet I may say
The time is imminent when he shall come
For whom I founded the Siege Perilous;
And he shall be too much a living part
Of what he brings, and what he burns away in,
To be for long a vexed inhabitant
Of this mad realm of stains and lower trials.
And here the ways of God again are mixed:
For this new knight who is to find the Grail
For you, and for the least who pray for you
In such lost coombs[16] and hollows of the world
As you have never entered, is to be
The son of him you trusted—Lancelot,
Of all who ever jeopardized a throne
Sure the most evil-fated, saving one,
Your son, begotten, though you knew not then
Your leman[17] was your sister, of Morgause;

---

16. Deep hollows or valleys.

17. Lover.

For it is Modred now, not Lancelot,
Whose native hate plans your annihilation—
Though he may smile till he be sick, and swear
Allegiance to an unforgiven father
Until at last he shake an empty tongue
Talked out with too much lying—though his lies
Will have a truth to steer them. Trust him not,
For unto you the father, he the son
Is like enough to be the last of terrors—
If in a field of time that looms to you
Far larger than it is you fail to plant
And harvest the old seeds of what I say,
And so be nourished and adept again
For what may come to be. But Lancelot
Will have you first; and you need starve no more
For the Queen's love, the love that never was.
Your Queen is now your Kingdom, and hereafter
Let no man take it from you, or you die.
Let no man take it from you for a day;
For days are long when we are far from what
We love, and mischief's other name is distance.
Let that be all, for I can say no more;
Not even to Blaise the Hermit,[18] were he living,
Could I say more than I have given you now
To hear; and he alone was my confessor."

The King arose and paced the floor again.
"I get gray comfort of dark words," he said;
"But tell me not that you can say no more:
You can, for I can hear you saying it.
Yet I'll not ask for more. I have enough—
Until my new knight comes to prove and find
The promise and the glory of the Grail,
Though I shall see no Grail. For I have built
On sand and mud, and I shall see no Grail."—

"Nor I," said Merlin. "Once I dreamed of it,
But I was buried. I shall see no Grail,
Nor would I have it otherwise. I saw

18. Merlin's master, to whom, according to some sources, Merlin dictated the
story of Joseph of Arimathea and the story of the quest for the Holy Grail.

Too much, and that was never good for man.
The man who goes alone too far goes mad—
In one way or another. God knew best,
And he knows what is coming yet for me.
I do not ask. Like you, I have enough."

That night King Arthur's apprehension found
In Merlin an obscure and restive guest,
Whose only thought was on the hour of dawn,
When he should see the last of Camelot
And ride again for Brittany; and what words
Were said before the King was left alone
Were only darker for reiteration.
They parted, all provision made secure
For Merlin's early convoy to the coast,
And Arthur tramped the past. The loneliness
Of kings, around him like the unseen dead,
Lay everywhere; and he was loath to move,
As if in fear to meet with his cold hand
The touch of something colder. Then a whim,
Begotten of intolerable doubt,
Seized him and stung him until he was asking
If any longer lived among his knights
A man to trust as once he trusted all,
And Lancelot more than all. "And it is he
Who is to have me first," so Merlin says,—
"As if he had me not in hell already.
Lancelot! Lancelot!" He cursed the tears
That cooled his misery, and then he asked
Himself again if he had one to trust
Among his knights, till even Bedivere,
Tor,[19] Bors,[20] and Percival, rough Lamorak,
Griflet,[21] and Gareth, and gay Gawaine, all
Were dubious knaves,—or they were like to be,
For cause to make them so; and he had made

---

19. The son of King Pellinore. He is killed by Lancelot's followers in the rescue of Guinevere from the stake.

20. Cousin of Lancelot and one of the three knights who is successful in the quest for the Holy Grail (the other two being Galahad and Percival).

21. A knight of the Round Table who is later slain by Lancelot in his rescue of Guinevere from the stake.

Himself to be the cause. "God set me right,
Before this folly carry me on farther,"
He murmured; and he smiled unhappily,
Though fondly, as he thought: "Yes, there is one
Whom I may trust with even my soul's last shred;
And Dagonet will sing for me tonight
An old song, not too merry or too sad."

When Dagonet, having entered, stood before
The King as one affrighted, the King smiled:
"You think because I call for you so late
That I am angry, Dagonet? Why so?
Have you been saying what I say to you,
And telling men that you brought Merlin here?
No? So I fancied; and if you report
No syllable of anything I speak,
You will have no regrets, and I no anger.
What word of Merlin was abroad today?"

"Today have I heard no man save Gawaine,
And to him I said only what all men
Are saying to their neighbors. They believe
That you have Merlin here, and that his coming
Denotes no good. Gawaine was curious,
But ever mindful of your majesty.
He pressed me not, and we made light of it."

"Gawaine, I fear, makes light of everything,"
The King said, looking down. "Sometimes I wish
I had a full Round Table of Gawaines.
But that's a freak[22] of midnight,—never mind it.
Sing me a song—one of those endless things
That Merlin liked of old, when men were younger
And there were more stars twinkling in the sky.
I see no stars that are alive tonight,
And I am not the king of sleep. So then,
Sing me an old song."

                    Dagonet's quick eye
Caught sorrow in the King's; and he knew more,

---

22. A capricious thought or a whim.

In a fool's way, than even the King himself
Of what was hovering over Camelot.
"O King," he said, "I cannot sing tonight.
If you command me I shall try to sing,
But I shall fail; for there are no songs now
In my old throat, or even in these poor strings
That I can hardly follow with my fingers.
Forgive me—kill me—but I cannot sing."
Dagonet fell down then on both his knees
And shook there while he clutched the King's cold hand
And wept for what he knew.

                    "There, Dagonet;
I shall not kill my knight, or make him sing.
No more; get up, and get you off to bed.
There'll be another time for you to sing,
So get you to your covers and sleep well."
Alone again, the King said, bitterly:
"Yes, I have one friend left, and they who know
As much of him as of themselves believe
That he's a fool. Poor Dagonet's a fool.
And if he be a fool, what else am I
Than one fool more to make the world complete?
'The love that never was!' . . . Fool, fool, fool, fool!"

The King was long awake. No covenant
With peace was his tonight; and he knew sleep
As he knew the cold eyes of Guinevere
That yesterday had stabbed him, having first
On Lancelot's name struck fire, and left him then
As now they left him—with a wounded heart,
A wounded pride, and a sickening pang worse yet
Of lost possession. He thought wearily
Of watchers by the dead, late wayfarers,
Rough-handed mariners on ships at sea,
Lone-yawning sentries, wastrels, and all others
Who might be saying somewhere to themselves,
"The King is now asleep in Camelot;
God save the King."—"God save the King, indeed,
If there be now a king to save," he said.
Then he saw giants rising in the dark,
Born horribly of memories and new fears

That in the gray-lit irony of dawn
Were partly to fade out and be forgotten;
And then there might be sleep, and for a time
There might again be peace. His head was hot
And throbbing; but the rest of him was cold,
As he lay staring hard where nothing stood,
And hearing what was not, even while he saw
And heard, like dust and thunder far away,
The coming confirmation of the words
Of him who saw so much and feared so little
Of all that was to be. No spoken doom
That ever chilled the last night of a felon
Prepared a dragging anguish more profound
And absolute than Arthur, in these hours,
Made out of darkness and of Merlin's words;
No tide that ever crashed on Lyonnesse
Drove echoes inland that were lonelier
For widowed ears among the fisher-folk,
Than for the King were memories tonight
Of old illusions that were dead for ever.

IV

The tortured King—seeing Merlin wholly meshed
In his defection, even to indifference,
And all the while attended and exalted
By some unfathomable obscurity
Of divination, where the Grail, unseen,
Broke yet the darkness where a king saw nothing—
Feared now the lady Vivian more than Fate;
For now he knew that Modred, Lancelot,
The Queen, the King, the Kingdom, and the World,
Were less to Merlin, who had made him King,
Than one small woman in Broceliande.
Whereas the lady Vivian, seeing Merlin
Acclaimed and tempted and allured again
To service in his old magnificence,
Feared now King Arthur more than storms and robbers;
For Merlin, though he knew himself immune
To no least whispered little wish of hers
That might afflict his ear with ecstasy,
Had yet sufficient of his old command

Of all around him to invest an eye
With quiet lightning, and a spoken word
With easy thunder, so accomplishing
A profit and a pastime for himself—
And for the lady Vivian, when her guile
Outlived at intervals her graciousness;
And this equipment of uncertainty,
Which now had gone away with him to Britain
With Dagonet, so plagued her memory
That soon a phantom brood of goblin doubts
Inhabited his absence, which had else
Been empty waiting and a few brave fears,
And a few more, she knew, that were not brave,
Or long to be disowned, or manageable.
She thought of him as he had looked at her
When first he had acquainted her alarm
At sight of the King's letter with its import;
And she remembered now his very words:
"The King believes today as in his boyhood
That I am Fate," he said; and when they parted
She had not even asked him not to go;
She might as well, she thought, have bid the wind
Throw no more clouds across a lonely sky
Between her and the moon,—so great he seemed
In his oppressed solemnity, and she,
In her excess of wrong imagining,
So trivial in an hour, and, after all
A creature of a smaller consequence
Than kings to Merlin, who made kings and kingdoms
And had them as a father; and so she feared
King Arthur more than robbers while she waited
For Merlin's promise to fulfil itself,
And for the rest that was to follow after:
"He said he would come back, and so he will.
He will because he must, and he is Merlin,
The master of the world—or so he was;
And he is coming back again to me
Because he must and I am Vivian.
It's all as easy as two added numbers:
Some day I'll hear him ringing at the gate,
As he rang on that morning in the spring,
Ten years ago; and I shall have him then

For ever. He shall never go away
Though kings come walking on their hands and knees
To take him on their backs." When Merlin came,
She told him that, and laughed; and he said strangely:
"Be glad or sorry, but no kings are coming.
Not Arthur, surely; for now Arthur knows
That I am less than Fate."

                                    Ten years ago
The King had heard, with unbelieving ears
At first, what Merlin said would be the last
Reiteration of his going down
To find a living grave in Brittany:
"Buried alive I told you I should be,
By love made little and by woman shorn,
Like Samson,[23] of my glory; and the time
Is now at hand. I follow in the morning
Where I am led. I see behind me now
The last of crossways, and I see before me
A straight and final highway to the end
Of all my divination. You are King,
And in your kingdom I am what I was.
Wherever I have warned you, see as far
As I have seen; for I have shown the worst
There is to see. Require no more of me,
For I can be no more than what I was."
So, on the morrow, the King said farewell;
And he was never more to Merlin's eye
The King than at that hour; for Merlin knew
How much was going out of Arthur's life
With him, as he went southward to the sea.

Over the waves and into Brittany
Went Merlin, to Broceliande. Gay birds
Were singing high to greet him all along
A broad and sanded woodland avenue
That led him on forever, so he thought,
Until at last there was an end of it;

---

23. In Judges 13-16 Samson is described as a hero whose great strength is
dependent upon the fact that his hair had never been cut. When Delilah learns his
secret and has his hair cut off, Samson loses his strength.

And at the end there was a gate of iron,
Wrought heavily and invidiously barred.
He pulled a cord that rang somewhere a bell
Of many echoes, and sat down to rest,
Outside the keeper's house, upon a bench
Of carven stone that might for centuries
Have waited there in silence to receive him.
The birds were singing still; leaves flashed and swung
Before him in the sunlight; a soft breeze
Made intermittent whisperings around him
Of love and fate and danger, and faint waves
Of many sweetly-stinging fragile odors
Broke lightly as they touched him; cherry-boughs
Above him snowed white petals down upon him,
And under their slow falling Merlin smiled
Contentedly, as one who contemplates
No longer fear, confusion, or regret,
May smile at ruin or at revelation.

A stately fellow with a forest air
Now hailed him from within, with searching words
And curious looks, till Merlin's glowing eye
Transfixed him and he flinched: "My compliments
And homage to the lady Vivian.
Say Merlin from King Arthur's Court is here,
A pilgrim and a stranger in appearance,
Though in effect her friend and humble servant.
Convey to her my speech as I have said it,
Without abbreviation or delay,
And so deserve my gratitude forever."
"But Merlin?" the man stammered; "Merlin? Merlin?"—
"One Merlin is enough. I know no other.
Now go you to the lady Vivian
And bring to me her word, for I am weary."
Still smiling at the cherry-blossoms falling
Down on him and around him in the sunlight,
He waited, never moving, never glancing
This way or that, until his messenger
Came jingling into vision, weighed with keys,
And inly shaken with much wondering
At this great wizard's coming unannounced
And unattended. When the way was open

The stately messenger, now bowing low
In reverence and awe, bade Merlin enter;
And Merlin, having entered, heard the gate
Clang back behind him; and he swore no gate
Like that had ever clanged in Camelot,
Or any other place if not in hell.
"I may be dead; and this good fellow here,
With all his keys," he thought, "may be the Devil,—
Though I were loath to say so, for the keys
Would make him rather more akin to Peter;
And that's fair reasoning for this fair weather."

"The lady Vivian says you are most welcome,"
Said now the stately-favored servitor,
"And are to follow me. She said, 'Say Merlin—
A pilgrim and a stranger in appearance,
Though in effect my friend and humble servant—
Is welcome for himself, and for the sound
Of his great name that echoes everywhere.'"—
"I like you and I like your memory,"
Said Merlin, curiously, "but not your gate.
Why forge for this elysian wilderness
A thing so vicious with unholy noise?"—
"There's a way out of every wilderness
For those who dare or care enough to find it,"
The guide said: and they moved along together,
Down shaded ways, through open ways with hedgerows,
And into shade again more deep than ever,
But edged anon with rays of broken sunshine
In which a fountain, raining crystal music,
Made faery magic of it through green leafage,
Till Merlin's eyes were dim with preparation
For sight now of the lady Vivian.
He saw at first a bit of living green
That might have been a part of all the green
Around the tinkling fountain where she gazed
Upon the circling pool as if her thoughts
Were not so much on Merlin—whose advance
Betrayed through his enormity of hair
The cheeks and eyes of youth—as on the fishes.
But soon she turned and found him, now alone,
And held him while her beauty and her grace

Made passing trash of empires, and his eyes
Told hers of what a splendid emptiness
Her tedious world had been without him in it
Whose love and service were to be her school,
Her triumph, and her history: "This is Merlin,"
She thought; "and I shall dream of him no more.
And he has come, he thinks, to frighten me
With beards and robes and his immortal fame;
Or is it I who think so? I know not.
I'm frightened, sure enough, but if I show it,
I'll be no more the Vivian for whose love
He tossed away his glory, or the Vivian
Who saw no man alive to make her love him
Till she saw Merlin once in Camelot,
And seeing him, saw no other. In an age
That has no plan for me that I can read
Without him, shall he tell me what I am,
And why I am, I wonder?" While she thought,
And feared the man whom her perverse negation
Must overcome somehow to soothe her fancy,
She smiled and welcomed him; and so they stood,
Each finding in the other's eyes a gleam
Of what eternity had hidden there.

"Are you always all in green, as you are now?"
Said Merlin, more employed with her complexion,
Where blood and olive made wild harmony
With eyes and wayward hair that were too dark
For peace if they were not subordinated;
"If so you are, then so you make yourself
A danger in a world of many dangers.
If I were young, God knows if I were safe
Concerning you in green, like a slim cedar,
As you are now, to say my life was mine:
Were you to say to me that I should end it,
Longevity for me were jeopardized.
Have you your green on always and all over?"

"Come here, and I will tell you about that,"
Said Vivian, leading Merlin with a laugh
To an arbored seat where they made opposites:
"If you are Merlin—and I know you are,

For I remember you in Camelot,—
You know that I am Vivian, as I am;
And if I go in green, why, let me go so,
And say at once why you have come to me
Cloaked over like a monk, and with a beard
As long as Jeremiah's.[24] I don't like it.
I'll never like a man with hair like that
While I can feed a carp with little frogs.
I'm rather sure to hate you if you keep it,
And when I hate a man I poison him."

"You've never fed a carp with little frogs,"
Said Merlin; "I can see it in your eyes."—
"I might then, if I haven't," said the lady;
"For I'm a savage, and I love no man
As I have seen him yet. I'm here alone,
With some three hundred others, all of whom
Are ready, I dare say, to die for me;
I'm cruel and I'm cold, and I like snakes;
And some have said my mother was a fairy,
Though I believe it not."

                        "Why not believe it?"
Said Merlin; "I believe it. I believe
Also that you divine, as I had wished,
In my surviving ornament of office
A needless imposition on your wits,
If not yet on the scope of your regard.
Even so, you cannot say how old I am,
Or yet how young. I'm willing cheerfully
To fight, left-handed, Hell's three headed hound[25]
If you but whistle him up from where he lives;
I'm cheerful and I'm fierce, and I've made kings;
And some have said my father was the Devil,
Though I believe it not. Whatever I am,
I have not lived in Time until to-day."

---

24. Jeremiah is an Old Testament prophet, whose prophecies are found in the biblical books of Jeremiah and Lamentations.

25. In classical mythology the entrance to the infernal regions is guarded by Cerberus, a three-headed dog.

A moment's worth of wisdom there escaped him,
But Vivian seized it, and it was not lost.

Embroidering doom with many levities,
Till now the fountain's crystal silver, fading,
Became a splash and a mere chilliness,
They mocked their fate with easy pleasantries
That were too false and small to be forgotten,
And with ingenious insincerities
That had no repetition or revival.
At last the lady Vivian arose,
And with a crying of how late it was
Took Merlin's hand and led him like a child
Along a dusky way between tall cones
Of tight green cedars: "Am I like one of these?
You said I was, though I deny it wholly."—
"Very," said Merlin, to his bearded lips
Uplifting her small fingers.—"O, that hair?"
She moaned, as if in sorrow: "Must it be?
Must every prophet and important wizard
Be clouded so that nothing but his nose
And eyes, and intimations of his ears,
Are there to make us know him when we see him?
Praise heaven I'm not a prophet! Are you glad?"—

He did not say that he was glad or sorry;
For suddenly came flashing into vision
A thing that was a manor and a castle,
With walls and roofs that had a flaming sky
Behind them, like a sky that he remembered,
And one that had from his rock-sheltered haunt
Above the roofs of his forsaken city
Made flame as if all Camelot were on fire.
The glow brought with it a brief memory
Of Arthur as he left him, and the pain
That fought in Arthur's eyes for losing him,
And must have overflowed when he had vanished.
But now the eyes that looked hard into his
Were Vivian's, not the King's; and he could see,
Or so he thought, a shade of sorrow in them.
She took his two hands: "You are sad," she said.—
He smiled: "Your western lights bring memories

Of Camelot. We all have memories—
Prophets, and women who are like slim cedars;
But you are wrong to say that I am sad."—
"Would you go back to Camelot?" she asked,
Her fingers tightening. Merlin shook his head.
"Then listen while I tell you that I'm glad,"
She purred, as if assured that he would listen:
"At your first warning, much too long ago,
Of this quaint pilgrimage of yours to see
'The fairest and most orgulous[26] of ladies'—
No language for a prophet, I am sure—
Said I, 'When this great Merlin comes to me,
My task and avocation for some time
Will be to make him willing, if I can,
To teach and feed me with an ounce of wisdom.'
For I have eaten to an empty shell,
After a weary feast of observation
Among the glories of a tinsel world
That had for me no glory till you came,
A life that is no life. Would you go back
To Camelot?"—Merlin shook his head again,
And the two smiled together in the sunset.

They moved along in silence to the door,
Where Merlin said: "Of your three hundred here
There is but one I know, and him I favor;
I mean the stately one who shakes the keys
Of that most evil sounding gate of yours,
Which has a clang as if it shut forever."—
"If there be need, I'll shut the gate myself,"
She said. "And you like Blaise? Then you shall have him.
He was not born to serve, but serve he must,
It seems, and be enamoured of my shadow.
He cherishes the taint of some high folly
That haunts him with a name he cannot know,
And I could fear his wits are paying for it.
Forgive his tongue, and humor it a little."—
"I knew another one whose name was Blaise,"
He said; and she said lightly, "Well, what of it?"—

---

26. Proud.

"And he was nigh the learnedest of hermits;
His home was far away from everywhere,
And he was all alone there when he died."—
"Now be a pleasant Merlin," Vivian said,
Patting his arm, "and have no more of that;
For I'll not hear of dead men far away,
Or dead men anywhere this afternoon.
There'll be a trifle in the way of supper
This evening, but the dead shall not have any.
Blaise and this man will tell you all there is
For you to know. Then you'll know everything."
She laughed, and vanished like a humming-bird.

V

The sun went down, and the dark after it
Starred Merlin's new abode with many a sconced
And many a moving candle, in whose light
The prisoned wizard, mirrored in amazement,
Saw fronting him a stranger, falcon-eyed,
Firm-featured, of a negligible age,
And fair enough to look upon, he fancied,
Though not a warrior born, nor more a courtier.
A native humor resting in his long
And solemn jaws now stirred, and Merlin smiled
To see himself in purple, touched with gold,
And fledged with snowy lace.—The careful Blaise,
Having drawn some time before from Merlin's wallet
The sable raiment of a royal scholar,
Had eyed it with a long mistrust and said:
"The lady Vivian would be vexed, I fear,
To meet you vested in these learned weeds
Of gravity and death; for she abhors
Mortality in all its hues and emblems—
Black wear, long argument, and all the cold
And solemn things that appertain to graves."—
And Merlin, listening, to himself had said,
"This fellow has a freedom, yet I like him;"
And then aloud: "I trust you. Deck me out,
However, with a temperate regard
For what your candid eye may find in me
Of inward coloring. Let them reap my beard,

Moreover, with a sort of reverence,
For I shall never look on it again.
And though your lady frown her face away
To think of me in black, for God's indulgence,
Array me not in scarlet or in yellow."—
And so it came to pass that Merlin sat
At ease in purple, even though his chin
Reproached him as he pinched it, and seemed yet
A little fearful of its nakedness.
He might have sat and scanned himself for ever
Had not the careful Blaise, regarding him,
Remarked again that in his proper judgment,
And on the valid word of his attendants,
No more was to be done. "Then do no more,"
Said Merlin, with a last look at his chin;
"Never do more when there's no more to do,
And you may shun thereby the bitter taste
Of many disillusions and regrets.
God's pity on us that our words have wings
And leave our deeds to crawl so far below them;
For we have all two heights, we men who dream,
Whether we lead or follow, rule or serve."—
"God's pity on us anyhow," Blaise answered,
"Or most of us. Meanwhile, I have to say,
As long as you are here, and I'm alive,
Your summons will assure the loyalty
Of all my diligence and expedition.
The gong that you hear singing in the distance
Was rung for your attention and your presence."—
"I wonder at this fellow, yet I like him,"
Said Merlin; and he rose to follow him.

The lady Vivian in a fragile sheath
Of crimson, dimmed and veiled ineffably
By the flame-shaken gloom wherein she sat,
And twinkled if she moved, heard Merlin coming,
And smiled as if to make herself believe
Her joy was all a triumph; yet her blood
Confessed a tingling of more wonderment
Than all her five and twenty worldly years
Of waiting for this triumph could remember;
And when she knew and felt the slower tread

Of his unseen advance among the shadows
To the small haven of uncertain light
That held her in it as a torch-lit shoal
Might hold a smooth red fish, her listening skin
Responded with a creeping underneath it,
And a crinkling that was incident alike
To darkness, love, and mice. When he was there,
She looked up at him in a whirl of mirth
And wonder, as in childhood she had gazed
Wide-eyed on royal mountebanks who made
So brief a shift of the impossible
That kings and queens would laugh and shake themselves;
Then rising slowly on her little feet,
Like a slim creature lifted, she thrust out
Her two small hands as if to push him back—
Whereon he seized them. "Go away," she said;
"I never saw you in my life before."—
"You say the truth," he answered; "when I met
Myself an hour ago, my words were yours.
God made the man you see for you to like,
If possible. If otherwise, turn down
These two prodigious and remorseless thumbs
And leave your lions to annihilate him."—

"I have no other lion than yourself,"
She said; "and since you cannot eat yourself,
Pray do a lonely woman, who is, you say,
More like a tree than any other thing
In your discrimination, the large honor
Of sharing with her a small kind of supper."—
"Yes, you are like a tree,—or like a flower;
More like a flower to-night." He bowed his head
And kissed the ten small fingers he was holding,
As calmly as if each had been a son;
Although his heart was leaping and his eyes
Had sight for nothing save a swimming crimson
Between two glimmering arms. "More like a flower
To-night," he said, as now he scanned again
The immemorial meaning of her face
And drew it nearer to his eyes. It seemed
A flower of wonder with a crimson stem
Came leaning slowly and regretfully

To meet his will—a flower of change and peril
That had a clinging blossom of warm olive
Half stifled with a tyranny of black,
And held the wayward fragrance of a rose
Made woman by delirious alchemy.
She raised her face and yoked his willing neck
With half her weight; and with hot lips that left
The world with only one philosophy
For Merlin or for Anaxagoras,[27]
Called his to meet them and in one long hush
Of capture to surrender and make hers
The last of anything that might remain
Of what was now their beardless wizardry.
Then slowly she began to push herself
Away, and slowly Merlin let her go
As far from him as his outreaching hands
Could hold her fingers while his eyes had all
The beauty of the woodland and the world
Before him in the firelight, like a nymph
Of cities, or a queen a little weary
Of inland stillness and immortal trees.
"Are you to let me go again sometime,"
She said,—"before I starve to death, I wonder?
If not, I'll have to bite the lion's paws,
And make him roar. He cannot shake his mane,
For now the lion has no mane to shake;
The lion hardly knows himself without it,
And thinks he has no face, but there's a lady
Who says he had no face until he lost it.
So there we are. And there's a flute somewhere,
Playing a strange old tune. You know the words:
'The Lion and the Lady are both hungry.'"

Fatigue and hunger—tempered leisurely
With food that some devout magician's oven
Might after many failures have delivered,
And wine that had for decades in the dark

27. Anaxagoras (?500-428 B.C.) was a Greek philosopher who taught that a controlling mind (*Nous*) gave order to the world by combining the unlimited number of material elements that made up the universe into actual objects.

Of Merlin's grave been slowly quickening,
And with half-heard, dream-weaving interludes
Of distant flutes and viols, made more distant
By far, nostalgic hautboys blown from nowhere,—
Were tempered not so leisurely, may be,
With Vivian's inextinguishable eyes
Between two shining silver candlesticks
That lifted each a trembling flame to make
The rest of her a dusky loveliness
Against a bank of shadow. Merlin made,
As well as he was able while he ate,
A fair division of the fealty due
To food and beauty, albeit more times than one
Was he at odds with his urbanity
In honoring too long the grosser viand.
"The best invention in Broceliande
Has not been over-taxed in vain, I see,"
She told him, with her chin propped on her fingers
And her eyes flashing blindness into his:
"I put myself out cruelly to please you,
And you, for that, forget almost at once
The name and image of me altogether.
You needn't, for when all is analyzed,
It's only a bird-pie that you are eating."

"I know not what you call it," Merlin said;
"Nor more do I forget your name and image,
Though I do eat; and if I did not eat,
Your sending out of ships and caravans
To get whatever 'tis that's in this thing
Would be a sorrow for you all your days;
And my great love, which you have seen by now,
Might look to you a lie; and like as not
You'd actuate some sinewed mercenary
To carry me away to God knows where
And seal me in a fearsome hole to starve,
Because I made of this insidious picking
An idle circumstance. My dear fair lady—
And there is not another under heaven
So fair as you are as I see you now—
I cannot look at you too much and eat;
And I must eat, or be untimely ashes,

Whereon the light of your celestial gaze
Would fall, I fear me, for no longer time
Than on the solemn dust of Jeremiah—
Whose beard you likened once, in heathen jest,
To mine that now is no man's."

                              "Are you sorry?"
Said Vivian, filling Merlin's empty goblet;
"If you are sorry for the loss of it,
Drink more of this and you may tell me lies
Enough to make me sure that you are glad;
But if your love is what you say it is,
Be never sorry that my love took off
That horrid hair to make your face at last
A human fact. Since I have had your name
To dream of and say over to myself,
The visitations of that awful beard
Have been a terror for my nights and days—
For twenty years. I've seen it like an ocean,
Blown seven ways at once and wrecking ships,
With men and women screaming for their lives;
I've seen it woven into shining ladders
That ran up out of sight and so to heaven,
All covered with white ghosts with hanging robes
Like folded wings,—and there were millions of them,
Climbing, climbing, climbing, all the time;
And all the time that I was watching them
I thought how far above me Merlin was,
And wondered always what his face was like.
But even then, as a child, I knew the day
Would come some time when I should see his face
And hear his voice, and have him in my house
Till he should care no more to stay in it,
And go away to found another kingdom."—
"Not that," he said; and, sighing, drank more wine;
"One kingdom for one Merlin is enough."—
"One Merlin for one Vivian is enough,"
She said. "If you care much, remember that;
But the Lord knows how many Vivians
One Merlin's entertaining eye might favor,
Indifferently well and all at once,
If they were all at hand. Praise heaven they're not."

"If they were in the world—praise heaven they're not—
And if one Merlin's entertaining eye
Saw two of them, there might be left him then
The sight of no eye to see anything—
Not even the Vivian who is everything,
She being Beauty, Beauty being She,
She being Vivian, and so on for ever."—
"I'm glad you don't see two of me," she said;
"For there's a whole world yet for you to eat
And drink and say to me before I know
The sort of creature that you see in me.
I'm withering for a little more attention,
But, being woman, I can wait. These cups
That you see coming are for the last there is
Of what my father gave to kings alone,
And far from always. You are more than kings
To me; therefore I give it all to you,
Imploring you to spare no more of it
Than a small cockle-shell would hold for me
To pledge your love and mine in. Take the rest,
That I may see tonight the end of it.
I'll have no living remnant of the dead
Annoying me until it fades and sours
Of too long cherishing; for Time enjoys
The look that's on our faces when we scowl
On unexpected ruins, and thrift itself
May be a sort of slow unwholesome fire
That eats away to dust the life that feeds it.
You smile, I see, but I said what I said.
One hardly has to live a thousand years
To contemplate a lost economy;
So let us drink it while it's yet alive
And you and I are not untimely ashes.
My last words are your own, and I don't like 'em."—
A sudden laughter scattered from her eyes
A threatening wisdom. He smiled and let her laugh,
Then looked into the dark where there was nothing:
"There's more in this than I have seen," he thought,
"Though I shall see it."—"Drink," she said again;
"There's only this much in the world of it,
And I am near to giving all to you
Because you are so great and I so little."

With a long-kindling gaze that caught from hers
A laughing flame, and with a hand that shook
Like Arthur's kingdom, Merlin slowly raised
A golden cup that for a golden moment
Was twinned in air with hers; and Vivian,
Who smiled at him across their gleaming rims,
From eyes that made a fuel of the night
Surrounding her, shot glory over gold
At Merlin, while their cups touched and his trembled.
He drank, not knowing what, nor caring much
For kings who might have cared less for themselves,
He thought, had all the darkness and wild light
That fell together to make Vivian
Been there before them then to flower anew
Through sheathing crimson into candle-light
With each new leer of their loose, liquorish eyes.
Again he drank, and he cursed every king
Who might have touched her even in her cradle;
For what were kings to such as he, who made them
And saw them totter—for the world to see,
And heed, if the world would? He drank again,
And yet again—to make himself assured
No manner of king should have the last of it—
The cup that Vivian filled unfailingly
Until she poured for nothing. "At the end
Of this incomparable flowing gold,"
She prattled on to Merlin, who observed
Her solemnly, "I fear there may be specks."—
He sighed aloud, whereat she laughed at him
And pushed the golden cup a little nearer.
He scanned it with a sad anxiety,
And then her face likewise, and shook his head
As if at her concern for such a matter:
"Specks? What are specks? Are you afraid of them?"
He murmured slowly, with a drowsy tongue;
"There are specks everywhere. I fear them not.
If I were king in Camelot, I might
Fear more than specks. But now I fear them not.
You are too strange a lady to fear specks."

He stared a long time at the cup of gold
Before him but he drank no more. There came

Between him and the world a crumbling sky
Of black and crimson, with a crimson cloud
That held a far off town of many towers,
All swayed and shaken, till at last they fell,
And there was nothing but a crimson cloud
That crumbled into nothing, like the sky
That vanished with it, carrying away
The world, the woman, and all memory of them,
Until a slow light of another sky
Made gray an open casement, showing him
Faint shapes of an exotic furniture
That glimmered with a dim magnificence,
And letting in the sound of many birds
That were, as he lay there remembering,
The only occupation of his ears
Until it seemed they shared a fainter sound,
As if a sleeping child with a black head
Beside him drew the breath of innocence.

One shining afternoon around the fountain,
As on the shining day of his arrival,
The sunlight was alive with flying silver
That had for Merlin a more dazzling flash
Than jewels rained in dreams, and a richer sound
Than harps, and all the morning stars together,—
When jewels and harps and stars and everything
That flashed and sang and was not Vivian,
Seemed less than echoes of her least of words—
For she was coming. Suddenly, somewhere
Behind him, she was coming; that was all
He knew until she came and took his hand
And held it while she talked about the fishes.
When she looked up he thought a softer light
Was in her eyes than once he had found there;
And had there been left yet for dusky women
A beauty that was heretofore not hers,
He told himself he must have seen it then
Before him in the face at which he smiled
And trembled. "Many men have called me wise,"
He said, "but you are wiser than all wisdom
If you know what you are."—"I don't," she said;
"I know that you and I are here together;

I know that I have known for twenty years
That life would be almost a constant yawning
Until you came; and now that you are here,
I know that you are not to go away
Until you tell me that I'm hideous;
I know that I like fishes, ferns, and snakes,—
Maybe because I liked them when the world
Was young and you and I were salamanders;
I know, too, a cool place not far from here,
Where there are ferns that are like marching men
Who never march away. Come now and see them,
And do as they do—never march away.
When they are gone, some others, crisp and green,
Will have their place, but never march away."—
He smoothed her silky fingers, one by one:
"Some other Merlin, also, do you think,
Will have his place—and never march away?"—
Then Vivian laid a finger on his lips
And shook her head at him before she laughed:
"There is no other Merlin than yourself,
And you are never going to be old."

Oblivious of a world that made of him
A jest, a legend, and a long regret,
And with a more commanding wizardry
Than his to rule a kingdom where the king
Was Love and the queen Vivian, Merlin found
His queen without the blemish of a word
That was more rough than honey from her lips,
Or the first adumbration of a frown
To cloud the night-wild fire that in her eyes
Had yet a smoky friendliness of home,
And a foreknowing care for mighty trifles.
"There are miles and miles for you to wander in,"
She told him once: "Your prison yard is large,
And I would rather take my two ears off
And feed them to the fishes in the fountain
Than buzz like an incorrigible bee
For always around yours, and have you hate
The sound of me; for some day then, for certain,
Your philosophic rage would see in me
A bee in earnest, and your hand would smite

My life away. And what would you do then?
I know: for years and years you'd sit alone
Upon my grave, and be the grieving image
Of lean remorse, and suffer miserably;
And often, all day long, you'd only shake
Your celebrated head and all it holds,
Or beat it with your fist the while you groaned
Aloud and went on saying to yourself:
'Never should I have killed her, or believed
She was a bee that buzzed herself to death,
First having made me crazy, had there been
Judicious distance and wise absences
To keep the two of us inquisitive.'"—
"I fear you bow your unoffending head
Before a load that should be mine," said he;
"If so, you led me on by listening.
You should have shrieked and jumped, and then fled yelling;
That's the best way when a man talks too long.
God's pity on me if I love your feet
More now than I could ever love the face
Of any one of all those Vivians
You summoned out of nothing on the night
When I saw towers. I'll wander and amend."—
At that she flung the noose of her soft arms
Around his neck and kissed him instantly:
"You are the wisest man that ever was,
And I've a prayer to make: May all you say
To Vivian be a part of what you knew
Before the curse of her unquiet head
Was on your shoulder, as you have it now,
To punish you for knowing beyond knowledge.
You are the only one who sees enough
To make me see how far away I am
From all that I have seen and have not been;
You are the only thing there is alive
Between me as I am and as I was
When Merlin was a dream. You are to listen
When I say now to you that I'm alone.
Like you, I saw too much; and unlike you
I made no kingdom out of what I saw—
Or none save this one here that you must rule,
Believing you are ruled. I see too far

To rule myself. Time's way with you and me
Is our way, in that we are out of Time
And out of tune with Time. We have this place,
And you must hold us in it or we die.
Look at me now and say if what I say
Be folly or not; for my unquiet head
Is no conceit of mine. I had it first
When I was born; and I shall have it with me
Till my unquiet soul is on its way
To be, I hope, where souls are quieter.
So let the first and last activity
Of what you say so often is your love
Be always to remember that our lyres
Are not strung for Today. On you it falls
To keep them in accord here with each other,
For you have wisdom, I have only sight
For distant things—and you. And you are Merlin.
Poor wizard! Vivian is your punishment
For making kings of men who are not kings;
And you are mine, by the same reasoning,
For living out of Time and out of tune
With anything but you. No other man
Could make me say so much of what I know
As I say now to you. And you are Merlin!"

She looked up at him till his way was lost
Again in the familiar wilderness
Of night that love made for him in her eyes,
And there he wandered as he said he would;
He wandered also in his prison-yard,
And, when he found her coming after him,
Beguiled her with her own admonishing
And frowned upon her with a fierce reproof
That many a time in the old world outside
Had set the mark of silence on strong men—
Whereat she laughed, not always wholly sure,
Nor always wholly glad, that he who played
So lightly was the wizard of her dreams:
"No matter—if only Merlin keep the world
Away," she thought. "Our lyres have many strings,
But he must know them all, for he is Merlin."

And so for years, till ten of them were gone,—
Ten years, ten seasons, or ten flying ages—
Fate made Broceliande a paradise,
By none invaded, until Dagonet,
Like a discordant, awkward bird of doom,
Flew in with Arthur's message. For the King,
In sorrow cleaving to simplicity,
And having in his love a quick remembrance
Of Merlin's old affection for the fellow,
Had for this vain, reluctant enterprise
Appointed him—the knight who made men laugh,
And was a fool because he played the fool.

"The King believes today, as in his boyhood,
That I am Fate; and I can do no more
Than show again what in his heart he knows,"
Said Merlin to himself and Vivian:
"This time I go because I made him King,
Thereby to be a mirror for the world;
This time I go, but never after this,
For I can be no more than what I was,
And I can do no more than I have done."
He took her slowly in his arms and felt
Her body throbbing like a bird against him:
"This time I go; I go because I must."

And in the morning, when he rode away
With Dagonet and Blaise through the same gate
That once had clanged as if to shut for ever,
She had not even asked him not to go;
For it was then that in his lonely gaze
Of helpless love and sad authority
She found the gleam of his imprisoned power
That Fate withheld; and, pitying herself,
She pitied the fond Merlin she had changed,
And saw the Merlin who had changed the world.

VI

"No kings are coming on their hands and knees,
Nor yet on horses or in chariots,
To carry me away from you again,"

Said Merlin, winding around Vivian's ear
A shred of her black hair. "King Arthur knows
That I have done with kings, and that I speak
No more their crafty language. Once I knew it,
But now the only language I have left
Is one that I must never let you hear
Too long, or know too well. When towering deeds
Once done shall only out of dust and words
Be done again, the doer may then be wary
Lest in the complement of his new fabric
There be more words than dust."

                              "Why tell me so?"
Said Vivian; and a singular thin laugh
Came after her thin question. "Do you think
That I'm so far away from history
That I require, even of the wisest man
Who ever said the wrong thing to a woman,
So large a light on what I know already—
When all I seek is here before me now
In your new eyes that you have brought for me
From Camelot? The eyes you took away
Were sad and old; and I could see in them
A Merlin who remembered all the kings
He ever saw, and wished himself, almost,
Away from Vivian, to make other kings,
And shake the world again in the old manner.
I saw myself no bigger than a beetle
For several days, and wondered if your love
Were large enough to make me any larger
When you came back. Am I a beetle still?"
She stood up on her toes and held her cheek
For some time against his, and let him go.

"I fear the time has come for me to wander
A little in my prison-yard," he said.—
"No, tell me everything that you have seen
And heard and done, and seen done, and heard done,
Since you deserted me. And tell me first
What the King thinks of me."—"The King believes
That you are almost what you are," he told her:
"The beauty of all ages that are vanished,

Reborn to be the wonder of one woman."—
"I knew he hated me. What else of him?"—
"And all that I have seen and heard and done,
Which is not much, would make a weary telling;
And all your part of it would be to sleep,
And dream that Merlin had his beard again."—
"Then tell me more about your good fool knight,
Sir Dagonet. If Blaise were not half-mad
Already with his pondering on the name
And shield of his unshielding nameless father,
I'd make a fool of him. I'd call him Ajax;
I'd have him shake his fist at thunder-storms,
And dance a jig as long as there was lightning,
And so till I forgot myself entirely.
Not even your love may do so much as that."—
"Thunder and lightning are no friends of mine,"
Said Merlin slowly, "more than they are yours;
They bring me nearer to the elements
From which I came than I care now to be."—
"You owe a service to those elements;
For by their service you outwitted age
And made the world a kingdom of your will."—
He touched her hand, smiling: "Whatever service
Of mine awaits them will not be forgotten,"
He said; and the smile faded on his face.—
"Now of all graceless and ungrateful wizards—"
But there she ceased, for she found in his eyes
The first of a new fear. "The wrong word rules
Today," she said; "and we'll have no more journeys."

Although he wandered rather more than ever
Since he had come again to Brittany
From Camelot, Merlin found eternally
Before him a new loneliness that made
Of garden, park, and woodland, all alike,
A desolation and a changelessness
Defying reason, without Vivian
Beside him, like a child with a black head,
Or moving on before him, or somewhere
So near him that, although he saw it not
With eyes, he felt the picture of her beauty
And shivered at the nearness of her being.

Without her now there was no past or future,
And a vague, soul-consuming premonition
He found the only tenant of the present;
He wondered, when she was away from him,
If his avenging injured intellect
Might shine with Arthur's kingdom a twin mirror,
Fate's plaything, for new ages without eyes
To see therein themselves and their declension.
Love made his hours a martyrdom without her;
The world was like an empty house without her,
Where Merlin was a prisoner of love
Confined within himself by too much freedom,
Repeating an unending exploration
Of many solitary silent rooms,
And only in a way remembering now
That once their very solitude and silence
Had by the magic of expectancy
Made sure what now he doubted—though his doubts,
Day after day, were founded on a shadow.

For now to Merlin, in his paradise,
Had come an unseen angel with a sword
Unseen, the touch of which was a long fear
For longer sorrow that had never come,
Yet might if he compelled it. He discovered,
One golden day in autumn as he wandered,
That he had made the radiance of two years
A misty twilight when he might as well
Have had no mist between him and the sun,
The sun being Vivian. On his coming then
To find her all in green against a wall
Of green and yellow leaves, and crumbling bread
For birds around the fountain while she sang
And the birds ate the bread, he told himself
That everything today was as it was
At first, and for a minute he believed it.
"I'd have you always all in green out here,"
He said, "if I had much to say about it."—
She clapped her crumbs away and laughed at him:
"I've covered up my bones with every color
That I can carry on them without screaming,
And you have liked them all—or made me think so."—

"I must have liked them if you thought I did,"
He answered, sighing; "but the sight of you
Today as on the day I saw you first,
All green, all wonderful" . . . He tore a leaf
To pieces with a melancholy care
That made her smile.—"Why pause at 'wonderful'?
You've hardly been yourself since you came back
From Camelot, where that unpleasant King
Said things that you have never said to me."—
He looked upon her with a worn reproach:
"The King said nothing that I keep from you."—
"What is it then?" she asked, imploringly;
"You man of moods and miracles, what is it?"—
He shook his head and tore another leaf:
"There is no need of asking what it is;
Whatever you or I may choose to name it,
The name of it is Fate, who played with me
And gave me eyes to read of the unwritten
More lines than I have read. I see no more
Today than yesterday, but I remember.
My ways are not the ways of other men;
My memories go forward. It was you
Who said that we were not in tune with Time;
It was not I who said it."—"But you knew it;
What matter then who said it?"—"It was you
Who said that Merlin was your punishment
For being in tune with him and not with Time—
With Time or with the world; and it was you
Who said you were alone, even here with Merlin;
It was not I who said it. It is I
Who tell you now my inmost thoughts." He laughed
As if at hidden pain around his heart,
But there was not much laughing in his eyes.
They walked, and for a season they were silent:
"I shall know what you mean by that," she said,
"When you have told me. Here's an oak you like,
And here's a place that fits me wondrous well
To sit in. You sit there. I've seen you there
Before; and I have spoiled your noble thoughts
By walking all my fingers up and down
Your countenance, as if they were the feet
Of a small animal with no great claws.

Tell me a story now about the world,
And the men in it, what they do in it,
And why it is they do it all so badly."—
"I've told you every story that I know,
Almost," he said.—"O, don't begin like that."—
"Well, once upon a time there was a King."—
"That has a more commendable address;
Go on, and tell me all about the King;
I'll bet the King had warts or carbuncles,
Or something wrong in his divine insides,
To make him wish that Adam had died young."

Merlin observed her slowly with a frown
Of saddened wonder. She laughed rather lightly,
And at his heart he felt again the sword
Whose touch was a long fear for longer sorrow.
"Well, once upon a time there was a king,"
He said again, but now in a dry voice
That wavered and betrayed a venturing.
He paused, and would have hesitated longer,
But something in him that was not himself
Compelled an utterance that his tongue obeyed,
As an unwilling child obeys a father
Who might be richer for obedience
If he obeyed the child: "There was a king
Who would have made his reign a monument
For kings and peoples of the waiting ages
To reverence and remember, and to this end
He coveted and won, with no ado
To make a story of, a neighbor queen
Who limed[28] him with her smile and had of him,
In token of their sin, what he found soon
To be a sort of mongrel son and nephew—
And a most precious reptile in addition—
To ornament his court and carry arms,
And latterly to be the darker half
Of ruin. Also the king, who made of love
More than he made of life and death together,
Forgot the world and his example in it

---

28. Snared.

For yet another woman—one of many—
And this one he made Queen, albeit he knew
That her unsworn allegiance to the knight
That he had loved the best of all his order
Must one day bring along the coming end
Of love and honor and of everything;
And with a kingdom builded on two pits
Of living sin,—so founded by the will
Of one wise counsellor who loved the king,
And loved the world and therefore made him king
To be a mirror for it,—the king reigned well
For certain years, awaiting a sure doom;
For certain years he waved across the world
A royal banner with a Dragon on it;
And men of every land fell worshipping
The Dragon as it were the living God,
And not the living sin."

                  She rose at that,
And after a calm yawn, she looked at Merlin:
"Why all this new insistence upon sin?"
She said; "I wonder if I understand
This king of yours, with all his pits and dragons;
I know I do not like him." A thinner light
Was in her eyes than he had found in them
Since he became the willing prisoner
That she had made of him; and on her mouth
Lay now a colder line of irony
Than all his fears or nightmares could have drawn
Before today: "What reason do you know
For me to listen to this king of yours?
What reading has a man of woman's days,
Even though the man be Merlin and a prophet?"

"I know no call for you to love the king,"
Said Merlin, driven ruinously along
By the vindictive urging of his fate;
"I know no call for you to love the king,
Although you serve him, knowing not yet the king
You serve. There is no man, or any woman,
For whom the story of the living king
Is not the story of the living sin.

I thought my story was the common one,
For common recognition and regard."

"Then let us have no more of it," she said;
"For we are not so common, I believe,
That we need kings and pits and flags and dragons
To make us know that we have let the world
Go by us. Have you missed the world so much
That you must have it in with all its clots
And wounds and bristles on to make us happy—
Like Blaise, with shouts and horns and seven men
Triumphant with a most unlovely boar?
Is there no other story in the world
Than this one of a man that you made king
To be a moral for the speckled ages?
You said once long ago, if you remember,
'You are too strange a lady to fear specks';
And it was you, you said, who feared them not.
Why do you look at me as at a snake
All coiled to spring at you and strike you dead?
I am not going to spring at you, or bite you;
I'm going home. And you, if you are kind,
Will have no fear to wander for an hour.
I'm sure the time has come for you to wander;
And there may come a time for you to say
What most you think it is that we need here
To make of this Broceliande a refuge
Where two disheartened sinners may forget
A world that has today no place for them."

A melancholy wave of revelation
Broke over Merlin like a rising sea,
Long viewed unwillingly and long denied.
He saw what he had seen, but would not feel,
Till now the bitterness of what he felt
Was in his throat, and all the coldness of it
Was on him and around him like a flood
Of lonelier memories than he had said
Were memories, although he knew them now
For what they were—for what his eyes had seen,
For what his ears had heard and what his heart
Had felt, with him not knowing what it felt.

But now he knew that his cold angel's name
Was Change, and that a mightier will than his
Or Vivian's had ordained that he be there.
To Vivian he could not say anything
But words that had no more of hope in them
Than anguish had of peace: "I meant the world . . .
I meant the world," he groaned; "not you—not me."

Again the frozen line of irony
Was on her mouth. He looked up once at it.
And then away—too fearful of her eyes
To see what he could hear now in her laugh
That melted slowly into what she said,
Like snow in icy water: "This world of yours
Will surely be the end of us. And why not?
I'm overmuch afraid we're part of it,—
Or why do we build walls up all around us,
With gates of iron that make us think the day
Of judgment's coming when they clang behind us?
And yet you tell me that you fear no specks!
With you I never cared for them enough
To think of them. I was too strange a lady.
And your return is now a speckled king
And something that you call a living sin—
That's like an uninvited poor relation
Who comes without a welcome, rather late,
And on a foundered[29] horse."

                              "Specks? What are specks?"
He gazed at her in a forlorn wonderment
That made her say: "You said, 'I fear them not.'
'If I were king in Camelot,' you said,
'I might fear more than specks.' Have you forgotten?
Don't tell me, Merlin, you are growing old.
Why don't you make somehow a queen of me,
And give me half the world? I'd wager thrushes
That I should reign, with you to turn the wheel,
As well as any king that ever was.
The curse on me is that I cannot serve
A ruler who forgets that he is king."

-----

29. Lame.

In his bewildered misery Merlin then
Stared hard at Vivian's face, more like a slave
Who sought for common mercy than like Merlin:
"You speak a language that was never mine,
Or I have lost my wits. Why do you seize
The flimsiest of opportunities
To make of what I said another thing
Than love or reason could have let me say,
Or let me fancy? Why do you keep the truth
So far away from me, when all your gates
Will open at your word and let me go
To some place where no fear or weariness
Of yours need ever dwell? Why does a woman,
Made otherwise a miracle of love
And loveliness, and of immortal beauty,
Tear one word by the roots out of a thousand,
And worry it, and torture it, and shake it,
Like a small dog that has a rag to play with?
What coil of an ingenious destiny
Is this that makes of what I never meant
A meaning as remote as hell from heaven?"

"I don't know," Vivian said reluctantly,
And half as if in pain; "I'm going home.
I'm going home and leave you here to wander,
Pray take your kings and sins away somewhere
And bury them, and bury the Queen in also.
I know this king; he lives in Camelot,
And I shall never like him. There are specks
Almost all over him. Long live the king,
But not the king who lives in Camelot,
With Modred, Lancelot, and Guinevere—
And all four speckled like a merry nest
Of addled eggs together. You made him King
Because you loved the world and saw in him
From infancy a mirror for the millions.
The world will see itself in him, and then
The world will say its prayers and wash its face,
And build for some new king a new foundation.
Long live the King! . . . But now I apprehend
A time for me to shudder and grow old
And garrulous—and so become a fright

For Blaise to take out walking in warm weather—
Should I give way to long considering
Of worlds you may have lost while prisoned here
With me and my light mind. I contemplate
Another name for this forbidden place,
And one more fitting. Tell me, if you find it,
Some fitter name than Eden. We have had
A man and woman in it for some time,
And now, it seems, we have a Tree of Knowledge."
She looked up at the branches overhead
And shrugged her shoulders. Then she went away;
And what was left of Merlin's happiness,
Like a disloyal phantom, followed her.

He felt the sword of his cold angel thrust
And twisted in his heart, as if the end
Were coming next, but the cold angel passed
Invisibly and left him desolate,
With misty brow and eyes. "The man who sees
May see too far, and he may see too late
The path he takes unseen," he told himself
When he found thought again. "The man who sees
May go on seeing till the immortal flame
That lights and lures him folds him in its heart,
And leaves of what there was of him to die
An item of inhospitable dust
That love and hate alike must hide away;
Or there may still be charted for his feet
A dimmer faring, where the touch of time
Were like the passing of a twilight moth
From flower to flower into oblivion,
If there were not somewhere a barren end
Of moths and flowers, and glimmering far away
Beyond a desert where the flowerless days
Are told in slow defeats and agonies,
The guiding of a nameless light that once
Had made him see too much—and has by now
Revealed in death, to the undying child
Of Lancelot, the Grail. For this pure light
Has many rays to throw, for many men
To follow; and the wise are not all pure,
Nor are the pure all wise who follow it.

There are more rays than men. But let the man
Who saw too much, and was to drive himself
From paradise, play too lightly or too long
Among the moths and flowers, he finds at last
There is a dim way out; and he shall grope
Where pleasant shadows lead him to the plain
That has no shadow save his own behind him.
And there, with no complaint, nor much regret,
Shall he plod on, with death between him now
And the far light that guides him, till he falls
And has an empty thought of empty rest;
Then Fate will put a mattock[30] in his hands
And lash him while he digs himself the grave
That is to be the pallet and the shroud
Of his poor blundering bones. The man who saw
Too much must have an eye to see at last
Where Fate has marked the clay; and he shall delve,
Although his hand may slacken, and his knees
May rock without a method as he toils;
For there's a delving that is to be done—
If not for God, for man. I see the light,
But I shall fall before I come to it;
For I am old. I was young yesterday.
Time's hand that I have held away so long
Grips hard now on my shoulder. Time has won.
Tomorrow I shall say to Vivian
That I am old and gaunt and garrulous,
And tell her one more story: I am old."

There were long hours for Merlin after that,
And much long wandering in his prison-yard,
Where now the progress of each heavy step
Confirmed a stillness of impending change
And imminent farewell. To Vivian's ear
There came for many days no other story
Than Merlin's iteration of his love
And his departure from Broceliande,
Where Merlin still remained. In Vivian's eye,
There was a quiet kindness, and at times

---

30. A digging tool used for loosening hard ground, grubbing up trees, etc.

A smoky flash of incredulity
That faded into pain. Was this the Merlin—
This incarnation of idolatry
And all but supplicating deference—
This bowed and reverential contradiction
Of all her dreams and her realities—
Was this the Merlin who for years and years
Before she found him had so made her love him
That kings and princes, thrones and diadems,
And honorable men who drowned themselves
For love, were less to her than melon-shells?
Was this the Merlin whom her fate had sent
One spring day to come ringing at her gate,
Bewildering her love with happy terror
That later was to be all happiness?
Was this the Merlin who had made the world
Half over, and then left it with a laugh
To be the youngest, oldest, weirdest, gayest,
And wisest, and sometimes the foolishest
Of all the men of her consideration?
Was this the man who had made other men
As ordinary as arithmetic?
Was this man Merlin who came now so slowly
Towards the fountain where she stood again
In shimmering green? Trembling, he took her hands
And pressed them fondly, one upon the other,
Between his:

            "I was wrong that other day,
For I have one more story. I am old."
He waited like one hungry for the word
Not said; and she found in his eyes a light
As patient as a candle in a window
That looks upon the sea and is a mark
For ships that have gone down. "Tomorrow," he said;
"Tomorrow I shall go away again
To Camelot; and I shall see the King
Once more; and I may come to you again
Once more; and I shall go away again
For ever. There is now no more than that
For me to do; and I shall do no more.
I saw too much when I saw Camelot;

And I saw farther backward into Time,
And forward, than a man may see and live,
When I made Arthur king. I saw too far,
But not so far as this. Fate played with me
As I have played with Time; and Time, like me,
Being less than Fate, will have on me his vengeance.
On Fate there is no vengeance, even for God."
He drew her slowly into his embrace
And held her there, but when he kissed her lips
They were as cold as leaves and had no answer;
For Time had given him then, to prove his words,
A frozen moment of a woman's life.

When Merlin the next morning came again
In the same pilgrim robe that he had worn
While he sat waiting where the cherry-blossoms
Outside the gate fell on him and around him
Grief came to Vivian at the sight of him;
And like a flash of a swift ugly knife,
A blinding fear came with it. "Are you going?"
She said, more with her lips than with her voice;
And he said, "I am going. Blaise and I
Are going down together to the shore,
And Blaise is coming back. For this one day
Be good enough to spare him, for I like him.
I tell you now, as once I told the King,
That I can be no more than what I was,
And I can say no more than I have said.
Sometimes you told me that I spoke too long
And sent me off to wander. That was good.
I go now for another wandering,
And I pray God that all be well with you."

For long there was a whining in her ears
Of distant wheels departing. When it ceased,
She closed the gate again so quietly
That Merlin could have heard no sound of it.

VII

By Merlin's Rock, where Dagonet the fool
Was given through many a dying afternoon

To sit and meditate on human ways
And ways divine, Gawaine and Bedivere
Stood silent, gazing down on Camelot.
The two had risen and were going home:
"It hits me sore, Gawaine," said Bedivere,
"To think on all the tumult and affliction
Down there, and all the noise and preparation
That hums of coming death, and, if my fears
Be born of reason, of what's more than death.
Wherefore, I say to you again, Gawaine,—
To you—that this late hour is not too late
For you to change yourself and change the King:
For though the King may love me with a love
More tried, and older, and more sure, may be,
Than for another, for such a time as this
The friend who turns him to the world again
Shall have a tongue more gracious and an eye
More shrewd than mine. For such a time as this
The King must have a glamour[31] to persuade him."

"The King shall have a glamour, and anon,"
Gawaine said, and he shot death from his eyes;
"If you were King, as Arthur is—or was—
And Lancelot had carried off your Queen,
And killed a score or so of your best knights—
Not mentioning my two brothers, whom he slew
Unarmored and unarmed—God save your wits!
Two stewards with skewers could have done as much,
And you and I might now be rotting for it."

"But Lancelot's men were crowded,—they were crushed;
And there was nothing for them but to strike
Or die, not seeing where they struck. Think you
They would have slain Gareth and Gaheris,
And Tor, and all those other friends of theirs?
God's mercy for the world he made, I say,
And for the blood that writes the story of it.
Gareth and Gaheris, Tor and Lamorak,—
All dead, with all the others that are dead!

---

31. Magic spell.

These years have made me turn to Lamorak
For counsel—and now Lamorak is dead."

"Why do you fling those two names in my face?
'Twas Modred made an end of Lamorak,
Not I; and Lancelot now has done for Tor.
I'll urge no king on after Lancelot
For such a two as Tor and Lamorak:
Their father killed my father, and their friend
was Lancelot, not I. I'll own my fault—
I'm living; and while I've a tongue can talk,
I'll say this to the King: 'Burn Lancelot
By inches till he give you back the Queen;
Then hang him—drown him—or do anything
To rid the world of him.' He killed my brothers,
And he was once my friend. Now damn the soul
Of him who killed my brothers! There you have me."

"You are a strong man, Gawaine, and your strength
Goes ill where foes are. You may cleave their limbs
And heads off, but you cannot damn their souls;
What you may do now is to save their souls,
And bodies too, and like enough your own.
Remember that King Arthur is a king,
And where there is a king there is a kingdom.
Is not the kingdom any more to you
Than one brief enemy? Would you see it fall
And the King with it, for one mortal hate
That burns out reason? Gawaine, you are king
Today. Another day may see no king
But Havoc, if you have no other word
For Arthur now than hate for Lancelot.
Is not the world as large as Lancelot?
Is Lancelot, because one woman's eyes
Are brighter when they look on him, to sluice
The world with angry blood? Poor flesh! Poor flesh!
And you, Gawaine,—are you so gaffed[32] with hate
You cannot leave it and so plunge away
To stiller places and there see, for once,
What hangs on this pernicious expedition

---

32. Hooked.

The King in his insane forgetfulness
Would undertake—with you to drum him on?
Are you as mad as he and Lancelot
Made ravening into one man twice as mad
As either? Is the kingdom of the world,
Now rocking, to go down in sound and blood
And ashes and sick ruin, and for the sake
Of three men and a woman? If it be so,
God's mercy for the world he made, I say,—
And say again to Dagonet. Sir Fool,
Your throne is empty, and you may as well
Sit on it and be ruler of the world
From now till supper-time."

                        Sir Dagonet,
Appearing, made reply to Bedivere's
Dry welcome with a famished look of pain,
On which he built a smile: "If I were King,
You, Bedivere, should be my counsellor;
And we should have no more wars over women.
I'll sit me down and meditate on that."
Gawaine, for all his anger, laughed a little,
And clapped the fool's lean shoulder; for he loved him
And was with Arthur when he made him knight.
Then Dagonet said on to Bedivere,
As if his tongue would make a jest of sorrow:
"Sometime I'll tell you what I might have done
Had I been Lancelot and you King Arthur—
Each having in himself the vicious essence
That now lives in the other and makes war.
When all men are like you and me, my lord,
When all are rational or rickety,
There may be no more war. But what's here now?
Lancelot loves the Queen, and he makes war
Of love; the King, being bitten to the soul
By love and hate that work in him together,
Makes war of madness; Gawaine hates Lancelot,
And he, to be in tune, makes war of hate;
Modred hates everything, yet he can see
With one damned illegitimate small eye
His father's crown, and with another like it
He sees the beauty of the Queen herself;

He needs the two for his ambitious pleasure,
And therefore he makes war of his ambition;
And somewhere in the middle of all this
There's a squeezed world that elbows for attention.
Poor Merlin, buried in Broceliande!
He must have had an academic eye
For woman when he founded Arthur's kingdom,
And in Broceliande he may be sorry.
Flutes, hautboys, drums, and viols. God be with him!
I'm glad they tell me there's another world,
For this one's a disease without a doctor."

"No, not so bad as that," said Bedivere;
The doctor, like ourselves, may now be learning;
And Merlin may have gauged his enterprise
Whatever the cost he may have paid for knowing.
We pass, but many are to follow us,
And what they build may stay; though I believe
Another age will have another Merlin,
Another Camelot, and another King.
Sir Dagonet, farewell."

                    "Farewell, Sir Knight,
And you, Sir Knight: Gawaine, you have the world
Now in your fingers—an uncommon toy,
Albeit a small persuasion in the balance
With one man's hate. I'm glad you're not a fool,
For then you might be rickety, as I am,
And rational as Bedivere. Farewell.
I'll sit here and be king. God save the King!"

But Gawaine scowled and frowned and answered nothing
As he went slowly down with Bedivere
To Camelot, where Arthur's army waited
The King's word for the melancholy march
To Joyous Gard, where Lancelot hid the Queen
And armed his host, and there was now no joy,
As there was now no joy for Dagonet
While he sat brooding, with his wan cheek-bones
Hooked with his bony fingers: "Go, Gawaine,"
He mumbled: "Go your way, and drag the world
Along down with you. What's a world or so

To you if you can hide an ell[33] of iron
Somewhere in Lancelot, and hear him wheeze
And sputter once or twice before he goes
Wherever the Queen sends him? There's a man
Who should have been a king, and would have been,
Had he been born so. So should I have been
A king, had I been born so, fool or no:
King Dagonet, or Dagonet the King;
King-Fool, Fool-King; 'twere not impossible.
I'll meditate on that and pray for Arthur,
Who made me all I am, except a fool.
Now he goes mad for love, as I might go
Had I been born a king and not a fool.
Today I think I'd rather be a fool;
Today the world is less than one scared woman—
Wherefore a field of waving men may soon
Be shorn by Time's indifferent scythe, because
The King is mad. The seeds of history
Are small, but given a few gouts[34] of warm blood
For quickening, they sprout out wondrously
And have a leaping growth whereof no man
May shun such harvesting of change or death,
Or life, as may fall on him to be borne.
When I am still alive and rickety,
And Bedivere's alive and rational—
If he come out of this, and there's a doubt,—
The King, Gawaine, Modred, and Lancelot
May all be lying underneath a weight
Of bloody sheaves too heavy for their shoulders
All spent, and all dishonored, and all dead;
And if it come to be that this be so,
And it be true that Merlin saw the truth,
Such harvest were the best. Your fool sees not
So far as Merlin sees: yet if he saw
The truth—why then, such harvest were the best.
I'll pray for Arthur; I can do no more."

---

33. An English measure equal to 45 inches.
34. Drops.

"Why not for Merlin? Or do you count him,
In this extreme, so foreign to salvation
That prayer would be a stranger to his name?"

Poor Dagonet, with terror shaking him,
Stood up and saw before him an old face
Made older with an inch of silver beard,
And faded eyes more eloquent of pain
And ruin than all the faded eyes of age
Till now had ever been, although in them
There was a mystic and intrinsic peace
Of one who sees where men of nearer sight
See nothing. On their way to Camelot,
Gawaine and Bedivere had passed him by,
With lax attention for the pilgrim cloak
They passed, and what it hid: yet Merlin saw
Their faces, and he saw the tale was true
That he had lately drawn from solemn strangers.

"Well, Dagonet, and by your leave," he said,
"I'll rest my lonely relics for a while
On this rock that was mine and now is yours.
I favor the succession; for you know
Far more than many doctors, though your doubt
Is your peculiar poison. I foresaw
Long since, and I have latterly[35] been told
What moves in this commotion down below
To show men what it means. It means the end—
If men whose tongues had less to say to me
Than had their shoulders are adept enough
To know; and you may pray for me or not,
Sir Friend, Sir Dagonet."

                          "Sir fool, you mean,"
Dagonet said, and gazed on Merlin sadly:
"I'll never pray again for anything,
And last of all for this that you behold—
The smouldering faggot of unlovely bones
That God has given to me to call Myself.

---

35. Subsequently.

When Merlin comes to Dagonet for prayer,
It is indeed the end."

                    "And in the end
Are more beginnings, Dagonet, than men
Shall name or know today. It was the end
Of Arthur's insubstantial majesty
When to him and his knights the Grail foreshowed
The quest of life that was to be the death
Of many, and the slow discouraging
Of many more. Or do I err in this?"

"No," Dagonet replied; "there was a Light;
And Galahad, in the Siege Perilous,
Alone of all on whom it fell, was calm;
There was a Light wherein men saw themselves
In one another as they might become—
Or so they dreamed. There was a long to-do,
And Gawaine, of all forlorn ineligibles,
Rose up the first, and cried more lustily
Than any after him that he should find
The Grail, or die for it,—though he did neither;
For he came back as living and as fit
For new and old iniquity as ever.
Then Lancelot came back, and Bors came back,—
Like men who had seen more than men should see,
And still come back. They told of Percival
Who saw too much to make of this worn life
A long necessity, and of Galahad,
Who died and is alive. They all saw Something.
God knows the meaning or the end of it,
But they saw Something. And if I've an eye,
Small joy has the Queen been to Lancelot
Since he came back from seeing what he saw;
For though his passion hold him like hot claws,
He's neither in the world nor out of it.
Gawaine is king, though Arthur wears the crown;
And Gawaine's hate for Lancelot is the sword
That hangs by one of Merlin's fragile hairs
Above the world. Were you to see the King,
The frenzy that has overthrown his wisdom,

Instead of him and his upheaving empire,
Might have an end."

                     "I came to see the King,"
Said Merlin, like a man who labors hard
And long with an importunate confession.
"No, Dagonet, you cannot tell me why,
Although your tongue is eager with wild hope
To tell me more than I may tell myself
About myself. All this that was to be
Might show to man how vain it were to wreck
The world for self if it were all in vain.
When I began with Arthur I could see
In each bewildered man who dots the earth
A moment with his days a groping thought
Of an eternal will, strangely endowed
With merciful illusions whereby self
Becomes the will itself and each man swells
In fond accordance with his agency.
Now Arthur, Modred, Lancelot, and Gawaine
Are swollen thoughts of this eternal will
Which have no other way to find the way
That leads them on to their inheritance
Than by the time-infuriating flame
Of a wrecked empire, lighted by the torch
Of woman, who, together with the light
That Galahad found, is yet to light the world."

A wan smile crept across the weary face
Of Dagonet the fool: "If you knew that
Before your burial in Broceliande,
No wonder your eternal will accords
With all your dreams of what the world requires.
My master, I may say this unto you
Because I am a fool, and fear no man;
My fear is that I've been a groping thought
That never swelled enough. You say the torch
Of woman and the light that Galahad found
Are some day to illuminate the world?
I'll meditate on that. The world is done
For me; and I have been, to make men laugh,
A lean thing of no shape and many capers.

I made them laugh, and I could laugh anon
Myself to see them killing one another
Because a woman with corn-colored hair
Has pranked a man with horns.[36] 'Twas but a flash
Of chance, and Lancelot, the other day
That saved this pleasing sinner from the fire
That she may spread for thousands. Were she now
The cinder the King willed, or were you now
To see the King, the fire might yet go out;
But the eternal will says otherwise.
So be it; I'll assemble certain gold
That I may say is mine and get myself
Away from this accurst unhappy court,
And in some quiet place where shepherd clowns
And cowherds may have more respondent ears
Than kings and kingdom-builders, I shall troll
Old men to easy graves and be a child
Again among the children of the earth.
I'll have no more kings, even though I loved
King Arthur, who is mad, as I could love
No other man save Merlin, who is dead."

"Not wholly dead, but old. Merlin is old."
The wizard shivered as he spoke, and stared
Away into the sunset where he saw
Once more, as through a cracked and cloudy glass,
A crumbling sky that held a crimson cloud
Wherein there was a town of many towers
All swayed and shaken, in a woman's hand
This time, till out of it there spilled and flashed
And tumbled, like loose jewels, town, towers, and walls,
And there was nothing but a crumbling sky
That made anon of black and red and ruin
A wild and final rain on Camelot.
He bowed, and pressed his eyes: "Now by my soul,
I have seen this before—all black and red—
Like that—like that—like Vivian—black and red;
Like Vivian, when her eyes looked into mine

---

36. I.e., cuckolded (or been unfaithful) to her husband.

Across the cups of gold. A flute was playing—
Then all was black and red."

                          Another smile
Crept over the wan face of Dagonet,
Who shivered in his turn. "The torch of woman,"
He muttered, "and the light that Galahad found,
Will some day save us all, as they saved Merlin.
Forgive my shivering wits, but I am cold,
And it will soon be dark. Will you go down
With me to see the King, or will you not?
If not, I go tomorrow to the shepherds.
The world is mad, and I'm a groping thought
Of your eternal will; the world and I
Are strangers, and I'll have no more of it—
Except you go with me to see the King."

"No, Dagonet, you cannot leave me now,"
Said Merlin, sadly. "You and I are old;
And, as you say, we fear no man. God knows
I would not have the love that once you had
For me be fear of me, for I am past
All fearing now. But Fate may send a fly
Sometimes, and he may sting us to the grave,
So driven to test our faith in what we see.
Are you, now I am coming to an end,
As Arthur's days are coming to an end,
To sting me like a fly? I do not ask
Of you to say that you see what I see,
Where you see nothing; nor do I require
Of any man more vision than is his;
Yet I could wish for you a larger part
For your last entrance here than this you play
Tonight of a sad insect stinging Merlin.
The more you sting, the more he pities you;
And you were never overfond of pity.
Had you been so, I doubt if Arthur's love,
Or Gawaine's, would have made of you a knight.
No, Dagonet, you cannot leave me now,
Nor would you if you could. You call yourself
A fool, because the world and you are strangers.
You are a proud man, Dagonet; you have suffered

What I alone have seen. You are no fool;
And surely you are not a fly to sting
My love to last regret. Believe or not
What I have seen, or what I say to you,
But say no more to me that I am dead
Because the King is mad, and you are old,
And I am older. In Broceliande
Time overtook me as I knew he must;
And I, with a fond overplus of words,
Had warned the lady Vivian already,
Before these wrinkles and this hesitancy
Inhibiting my joints oppressed her sight
With age and dissolution. She said once
That she was cold and cruel; but she meant
That she was warm and kind, and over-wise
For woman in a world where men see not
Beyond themselves. She saw beyond them all,
As I did; and she waited, as I did,
The coming of a day when cherry-blossoms
Were to fall down all over me like snow
In springtime. I was far from Camelot
That afternoon; and I am farther now
From her. I see no more for me to do
Than to leave her and Arthur and the world
Behind me, and to pray that all be well
With Vivian, whose unquiet heart is hungry
For what is not, and what shall never be
Without her, in a world that men are making,
Knowing not how, nor caring yet to know
How slowly and how grievously they do it,—
Though Vivian, in her golden shell of exile,
Knows now and cares, not knowing that she cares,
Nor caring that she knows. In time to be,
The like of her shall have another name
Than Vivian, and her laugh shall be a fire,
Not shining only to consume itself
With what it burns. She knows not yet the name
Of what she is, for now there is no name;
Some day there shall be. Time has many names,
Unwritten yet, for what we say is old
Because we are so young that it seems old.
And this is all a part of what I saw

Before you saw King Arthur. When we parted,
I told her I should see the King again,
And, having seen him, might go back again
To see her face once more. But I shall see
No more the lady Vivian. Let her love
What man she may, no other love than mine
Shall be an index of her memories.
I fear no man who may come after me,
And I see none. I see her, still in green,
Beside the fountain. I shall not go back.
We pay for going back; and all we get
Is one more needless ounce of weary wisdom
To bring away with us. If I come not,
The lady Vivian will remember me,
And say: 'I knew him when his heart was young,
Though I have lost him now. Time called him home,
And that was as it was; for much is lost
Between Broceliande and Camelot.'"

He stared away into the west again,
Where now no crimson cloud or phantom town
Deceived his eyes. Above a living town
There were gray clouds and ultimate suspense,
And a cold wind was coming. Dagonet,
Now crouched at Merlin's feet in his dejection,
Saw multiplying lights far down below,
Where lay the fevered streets. At length he felt
On his lean shoulder Merlin's tragic hand
And trembled, knowing that a few more days
Would see the last of Arthur and the first
Of Modred, whose dark patience had attained
To one precarious half of what he sought:
"And even the Queen herself may fall to him,"
Dagonet murmured.—"The Queen fall to Modred?
Is that your only fear tonight?" said Merlin;
"She may, but not for long."—"No, not my fear;
For I fear nothing. But I wish no fate
Like that for any woman the King loves,
Although she be the scourge and the end of him
That you saw coming, as I see it now."
Dagonet shook, but he would have no tears,
He swore, for any king, queen, knave, or wizard—

Albeit he was a stranger among those
Who laughed at him because he was a fool.
"You said the truth, I cannot leave you now,"
He stammered, and was angry for the tears
That mocked his will and choked him.

                              Merlin smiled,
Faintly, and for the moment: "Dagonet,
I need your word as one of Arthur's knights
That you will go on with me to the end
Of my short way, and say unto no man
Or woman that you found or saw me here.
No good would follow, for a doubt would live
Unstifled of my loyalty to him
Whose deeds are wrought for those who are to come;
And many who see not what I have seen,
Or what you see tonight, would prattle on
For ever, and their children after them,
Of what might once have been had I gone down
With you to Camelot to see the King.
I came to see the King,—but why see kings?
All this that was to be is what I saw
Before there was an Arthur to be king,
And so to be a mirror wherein men
May see themselves, and pause. If they see not,
Or if they do see and they ponder not,—
I saw; but I was neither Fate nor God.
I saw too much; and this would be the end,
Were there to be an end. I saw myself—
A sight no other man has ever seen;
And through the dark that lay beyond myself
I saw two fires that are to light the world."

On Dagonet the silent hand of Merlin
Weighed now as living iron that held him down
With a primeval power. Doubt, wonderment,
Impatience, and a self-accusing sorrow
Born of an ancient love, possessed and held him
Until his love was more than he could name,
And he was Merlin's fool, not Arthur's now:
"Say what you will, I say that I'm the fool
Of Merlin, King of Nowhere; which is Here.

With you for king and me for court, what else
Have we to sigh for but a place to sleep?
I know a tavern that will take us in;
And on the morrow I shall follow you
Until I die for you. And when I die . . ."—
"Well, Dagonet, the King is listening."—
And Dagonet answered, hearing in the words
Of Merlin a grave humor and a sound
Of graver pity, "I shall die a fool."
He heard what might have been a father's laugh,
Faintly behind him; and the living weight
Of Merlin's hand was lifted. They arose,
And, saying nothing, found a groping way
Down through the gloom together. Fiercer now,
The wind was like a flying animal
That beat the two of them incessantly
With icy wings, and bit them as they went.
The rock above them was an empty place
Where neither seer nor fool should view again
The stricken city. Colder blew the wind
Across the world, and on it heavier lay
The shadow and the burden of the night;
And there was darkness over Camelot.

IV.
The Modern Period

Introduction

In the twentieth century there has been and continues to be a rich variety of Arthurian literature. In the early part of the century, partly because of the influence of Carr's *King Arthur*, more plays based on the Arthurian legend were written than at any other time. Writers like Laurence Binyon, Ernest Rhys, Gordon Bottomley, John Masefield, Thomas Hardy, and many others looked to the legends for their subject matter. One of the most popular themes was the love of Tristan and Isolt. Seventeen plays on this subject were written in England and America in the first half of the century, including some of the most interesting Arthurian plays, works like *Tristram & Isoult* by Martha Kinross, *Out of the Sea* by American author Don Marquis, *Tristram & Isoult: A Dramatic Poem* by An Pilibin (pseudonym of John Hackett Pollock), and *Tristan and Isolt* by John Masefield.

Masefield's version, *Tristan and Isolt: A Play in Verse* (1927), attempts to give new life to the legend by combining elements from various sources. As he does in his collection of Arthurian poetry, *Midsummer Night and Other Tales in Verse* (1928), Masefield tries to get close to the historical origins of his subject at the same time that he acknowledges the medieval literary tradition. He devotes a major portion of his play to reenacting an event described in the Welsh *Triads*, which tells of "Three Powerful Swineherds of the Island of Britain," one of whom was "Drystan son of Tallwch," who kept watch over the swine of "March" (the Mark of later legend) while the swineherd delivered a message from him to "Essyllt."

The play is exceptional because it presents Isolt as a tragic figure. By omitting Isolt of Brittany from his story, Masefield removes any possibility of jealousy or other base motive for Isolt's actions. Tristan is unswervingly devoted to her, and only her recognition of Marc's nobility and of her obligation to him makes her reject Tristan and order the punishment that ultimately causes his death. (Masefield's Marc is a good man who dies fighting the heathen at the Battle of Mount Badon.) Thus the play is really the tragedy of Isolt, who is caught between her love and her sense of duty. Through this conflict Masefield's reason for introducing the preromantic material from the *Triads* becomes apparent. It is precisely the blend of the Celtic material with the later romantic elements that creates the tragic dilemma for Isolt. The sense of duty she feels and the harsh justice she administers, both consistent with the heroic world of early Celtic literature, are in conflict in her character and in the action of the play with her romantic love for Tristan.

History, legend, and romance do not blend quite as smoothly in *Midsummer Night and Other Tales in Verse* (1928). The volume as a whole never achieves the unity that Masefield's *Tristan and Isolt* does. Nevertheless, it is an important collection because of its attempt to bring together three different approaches. As one of the first modern authors to incorporate historical material into his verse and as author of an Arthurian historical novel himself, *Badon Parchments* (1947), Masefield foreshadows the great interest in the historical novel in the latter part of the twentieth century.

Yet Masefield's historical verse, such as "The Fight at Camlan," though important, is not his best poetry or even his best narrative in *Midsummer Night*. As a story "The Sailing of Hell Race," based on Celtic myth, is better. And as poetry pieces like "Gwenivere Tells" and "The Death of Lancelot" are better. These poems, which attempt to give Gwenivere her own voice, describe the persistence of her love and provide a perspective that seems truer than her typical rejection of Lancelot, though not as morally correct. In the former Gwenivere tells of her love, symbolized by a rose, which contrasts with the withered, gray olive spray that Lancelot sends her after his pilgrimage to the Holy Land.

The sense of a love that outlasts tragedy and repentance also appears in "The Death of Lancelot," in which Gwenivere leaves the convent when she hears that Lancelot is dying. In this reversal of the typical pattern it is she who arrives too late to see him before his death. The sorrow of the situation is conveyed nicely in the image of the dead Lancelot's not being able to hold the crucifix placed in his sword-hand as he is fitted out for burial. But an equally powerful image is that of Gwenivere, having left the convent to see him, gathering flowers, a visual reiteration of her statement that "April will out," that is, that love will endure because it is a natural force stronger than even the "nun's and marriage-vows" that she has broken because of it.

A decade after Masefield's book of Arthurian verse was first published, there appeared *Taliessin Through Logres* (1938) by Charles Williams. This book and its companion volume, *The Region of the Summer Stars* (1944), formed a cycle of poems telling the story of Logres, Arthurian Britain, and its inhabitants. In these two collections Williams employs a complex of symbols centering on the Grail. The focal characters in the cycle are Taliessin and Galahad. Their roles, and some idea of the ways in which Williams uses symbolism, can be seen in the poems "Mount Badon" and "The Coming of Galahad."

"Mount Badon" is unlike Masefield's *Badon Parchments* or his poem "Badon Hill" from *Midsummer Night*, where the intent is to present a narrative of a battle that seems to be going against the British forces until Arthur leads the charge. In Williams's poem Taliessin is both "king's poet" and "captain of horse in the wars." The dual roles merge because the warrior is engaged in a battle to bring order to Logres just as the poet is always engaged in an attempt to bring the order of the Logos (for Williams, both the written word and Christ) to Arthur's realm. This coalescence is emphasized in "Mount Badon" by Taliessin's vision of Vergil seeking both "the word" and "the invention of the City," that is, the order of civilization that poetry represents. The vision comes to Taliessin as he is seeking a weakness in the enemy's defenses. Poetry and battle, pen and sword, become mixed in the poem's imagery because at this moment they are one, both means of imposing order. Williams writes that Taliessin saw "the hexameter spring and the King's sword swing," thus equating the verse of Vergil with the sword wielded by Arthur. And when Taliessin "fetched the pen of his spear from its bearer," his functions as poet and military leader blend.

Taliessin also plays a role in "The Coming of Galahad," a poem that reflects Williams's concern with uniting the spiritual and the natural. The occasion of the poem is the arrival of Galahad, the chosen knight who is able to sit in the Siege Perilous and thus complete the circle of knights at the Round Table. But most of the poem is devoted to a conversation Taliessin has with Gareth and a slave girl. When Gareth asks who it is who has been allowed to sit in the forbidden seat, Taliessin speaks of the "the double dance of a stone and a shell," a notion that Williams took from Wordsworth. In *The Prelude* Wordsworth speaks of a dream of an Arab, a "semi-Quixote," who shows him a stone that represents "geometric truth" and a shell that represents "poetry." These images suggest the typical romantic opposition between reason and imagination, science and poetry. Williams extends the meaning of these symbols to the natural and the supernatural. Galahad, as Grail knight, unites the two. His sitting in the "perilous sell" is like the fitting of the stone to the shell.

This union is an important concept in "The Coming of Galahad" and indeed in Williams's poetry in general. The strange site of the conversation, "among the jakes and latrines," is explained by this notion. As much a part of the natural world as the porphyry stair in the palace, the baser elements are necessary to the achieving of the Grail, as Taliessin's words imply: "without this alley-way how can man prefer? / and without preference can the Grail's grace be stored?"

The union of the natural and the spiritual in Galahad is alluded to again in the image of his hands: "when he washed his hands, the water became phosphorescent." The "sanctity" implied here is absent from Guinevere, whose hand "lying on her heart" is quite the opposite. Her fingers are like claws, and represent "the stone / fitting itself to its echo" and not to the shell.

Williams's symbolism can be difficult and cryptic at times, but his poems in *Taliessin Through Logres* and *The Region of the Summer Stars* are a significant contribution to Arthurian poetry. They present a very different picture of the Grail than that in the other major modern poetic treatment of the subject, T. S. Eliot's *Waste Land*. Whereas Eliot uses the myth to emphasize the sterility of modern society, Williams uses it to suggest the possibility of integrating the natural and supernatural world and thus finding the grace of the Grail.

In the second half of the twentieth century Arthurian drama became less common, partly because it was replaced by spectacular movies such as *Knights of the Round Table* (1953) and *The Black Knight* (1954). This is a trend that continues in such productions as John Boorman's *Excalibur* (1981). And even the function of parody, earlier served by plays like Fielding's *Tom Thumb* and Fawcett's *The New King Arthur*, is fulfilled by a movie like *Monty Python and the Holy Grail* (1975). Arthurian poetry, however, has remained popular throughout the century; and as drama wanes as a form for treating Arthurian material, the novel is more frequently employed, due largely to the influence of T. H. White's *The Once and Future King*, one of the most widely read Arthurian works of all time. Other novelists considered among the best of literary artists have written about the legends, like John Steinbeck in his incomplete *The Acts of*

King Arthur and His Noble Knights (1976) and Walker Percy in
Lancelot (1978). Other popular novels, like Mary Stewart's Merlin
trilogy (*The Crystal Cave, The Hollow Hills,* and *The Last Enchantment*
[1970, 1973, and 1979]), and Marion Zimmer Bradley's *The Mists of
Avalon* (1982), have inspired the writing of a large number of
historical and feminist Arthurian novels, respectively. White's book
is, of course, a fantasy, a genre that inspired one of the finest of the
modern retellings of the legends, Thomas Berger's *Arthur Rex: A
Legendary Novel* (1978).[1]

Berger's treatment of the great Middle English poem *Sir
Gawain and the Green Knight* exemplifies his approach to the
legendary material. He turns the Gothic castle of the medieval
poem into Liberty Castle, a place where "the freedom of [the] guest
is absolute." In keeping with this directive the castle is full of
luxuries and pleasures: scantily clad women or young men, for those
so inclined, and exotic foods, including "lark's eyes in jelly,"
"coddled serpent-eggs," and "pickled testicles of tiger." Gawaine
tries nobly to resist the temptations by rejecting sexual pleasures
and preferring, in good British fashion, "cold mutton and small
beer" to the unusual delicacies.

At last, however, he does succumb to the advances of the
woman he believes to be his host's wife. Since the terms of his
bargain with his host require the exchange of whatever each has
won during the day, Gawaine lies. He chooses to say he gained
nothing rather than to return to a man the pleasure he won from a
woman. For Berger the issue is not saving one's life by keeping a
green girdle presumed to have magical powers but rather
preserving one kind of virtue by yielding another. The dilemma

---

1. Since a collection like this volume would, in any study of the
development of the Arthurian legends after the Middle Ages, most likely be
supplemented by the reading of one or more complete novels and since I have tried
to include as few abridged works as possible, I have chosen not to select passages
from key novels like *A Connecticut Yankee in King Arthur's Court, The Once and Future
King, The Crystal Cave,* or *The Mists of Avalon.* I have, however, included a retelling of
Sir Gawain and the Green Knight from Thomas Berger's *Arthur Rex* as an example of
the treatment of Arthurian themes by modern novelists. This seemed a likely
selection since it appeared in a slightly different form as a story in *Playboy* before its
inclusion in the published novel. The minor changes in the present selection (based
on the novel and not on the *Playboy* story, in which editorial changes were made
without the author's approval) are by Mr. Berger himself, who kindly agreed to edit
the chapter so that it would read as a self-contained unit.

faced by Gawaine points up the moral complexity of Berger's tale of the Green Knight (and indeed of *Arthur Rex* as a whole).

The Green Knight, who turns out to be the Lady of the Lake, recognizes that Gawaine's failing was small and so gives him, as in the medieval poem, a small nick on the neck instead of beheading him. She explains that "a knight does better to break his word than, keeping it, to behave unnaturally. And a liar, sir, is preferable to a monster." She also sanctions Gawaine's conclusion that "sometimes justice is better served by a lie than by the absolute and literal truth."

The events of this tale fit into a larger pattern in the book. It is a theme, perhaps *the* theme, of *Arthur Rex* that extreme adherence to moral rules can be more damaging than lapses in morality. This is not to say that the desire to be and to make things better is wrong. Berger seems to have a great admiration for the legend of Arthur, even as he modernizes, at times parodies, and radically revises it. But in Berger's novel the desire to make things perfect without admitting human failings causes more trouble than outright imperfection does. As the Lady of the Lake says in an earlier chapter, "To have a purpose is good, but to be so intent upon it as to see only its end is folly." And later in the book, after the tragic downfall of Arthur's kingdom, Guinevere says that it occurred "because of men and their laws and their principles." Even Morgan la Fey decides in the end to join the Little Sisters of Poverty and Pain because "after a long career in the service of evil she had come to believe that corruption were sooner brought amongst humankind by the forces of virtue, and from this moment on she was notable for her piety."

The continuing relevance of the Arthurian legends is evident not only in a book like *Arthur Rex* but also in the fine poems that are still written on the Matter of Britain. "Launcelot in Hell" by John Ciardi, for example, is a modern treatment of the love between Launcelot and Guinevere and of the final days of Camelot. Ciardi deromanticizes the events. His Launcelot has killed Arthur in the final battle and then thrown the King's sword into a swamp where "No fairy arm reached out of the muck to catch it." Worst of all, from the romantic perspective, is Launcelot's attitude towards the Queen. He refers to her as a "mare" that he mounted and is disgusted by her turning to religion. This harshly realistic view of the bitter end of the Arthurian realm seems to justify Launcelot's statement that "there is no moral"; and yet the title provides an ironic comment on his statement that shows that Ciardi's Launcelot does not fully comprehend, or at least does not fully explain, the events even in their demystified form.

Richard Wilbur's account of Merlin's entrapment, on the other hand, symbolizes a necessary end. In a poem that exemplifies Wilbur's brilliant use of language and imagery, he shows that, though "Fate would be fated" and "Dreams desire to sleep," the "forsaken will not understand" their loss. So the king and the knights go in quest of Merlin. They go out "aimlessly riding," but not with the Providence-directed aimlessness of the traditional quest. And they leave "their drained cups on the table round," a wonderful phrase that suggests on the one hand a striking contrast to the ever-full cup of the Grail and on the other the lack of order that negates the wholeness and purpose of the Round Table. The body of the poem develops a pattern of water imagery that culminates when Niniane receives Merlin "as the sea receives a stream." The flow of the water is perfectly appropriate to the flow of events that results in the passing of the glory of Camelot. The poem ends in an image that sums up and concretizes the passing: the mail of the questing knights "grew quainter as they clopped along. / The sky became a still and woven blue." The word "clopped" turns the war-horses of the knights into tired nags; and as the sky becomes a "still and woven blue," the heroes become figures in a tapestry.

Just as many modern novelists revitalize the legends by focusing on the female characters or telling the tales from their perspectives, so too do a number of poets. A treatment of the Merlin and Nimue story even more recent than Wilbur's transports the legendary figures to modern America and shifts the focus and the voice from Merlin to Nimue. Valerie Nieman Colander's "The Naming of the Lost," a gem of modern Arthurian literature, infuses a West Virginia countryside with myth. A simple oak chair with a broken rung becomes a Siege Visionary in which a lost and nameless wanderer discovers her identity as Nimue and is reconciled with Merlin. Their reconciliation is presented in beautiful imagery and a blank verse that flows as smoothly as the river and "water-flow" with which Nimue is associated. She tells Merlin:

But I remain
the water-flow, and you the lasting stone.

> Can you embrace and not be worn away?
> Can I be held and not break free to foam,
> or chafe myself, confined, to stagnancy?

Merlin's reply is that their incompatibility was in the former time, the age of Camelot, but that "there are times between the stars / when all the elements are joined." Merlin, with a touch, lifts Nimue from the chair and says, "We'll sing together a song, and arches raise / of a new Camelot which shall not fall." In a deft contrast of images, "The chair crumbles, falls fine to ash and sifts / upon the flowered lawn," just as the two mythic figures raise through their reunion the new Camelot of personal union and happiness.

Another poem that gives a voice to a female character from the legends is Wendy Mnookin's "Guenever Speaks" (which becomes two poems in her cycle *Guenever Speaks,* published in 1991). The poem masterfully maintains Guenever's royal dignity at the same time that it presents her as a real person, a woman who works and feels, desires and regrets like all women and all people. This sense is achieved through the imagery that shows Guenever's physical condition deteriorating because of the emotional stress she feels. As she reads a holy book, she has Lancelot's letter to her in its pages; and the words "tilt on the page." Her inner conflict prevents her from eating and sleeping, so she swoons at vespers and then in the garden as she watches the carefree Caroline skipping ahead of her on the path. As she faints, the red leaves of the trees turn to blackness.

The poem ends with a wonderfully human touch. Guenever resolves, as in Malory, never to leave Almesbury, but for Mnookin it is not because she has found religion and not only because she is too remorseful to allow herself to live out her life with Lancelot. Rather it is because "I cannot lose him / again." Overwhelmed by her first loss, she will not let herself be placed in a position where she will be separated from him again. Of course, this resolution adds poignance to the closing quotation from Malory, which speaks of Guenever's death. If she never lost him again, she also never saw him. The fact that she had to pray constantly not to see him shows that her inner struggle did not end because of the separation. And therein lies the tragedy of Mnookin's Guenever.

That the poems of Colander and Mnookin look to Malory, the former for an epigraph and the latter for its framing quotations, emphasizes that even the newest and most innovative works of

Arthurian literature are part of a vital tradition. For a true understanding of the literary, historical, moral, and social significance of the Arthurian legends it is necessary both to look to the past, to the historical origins of the legends and the medieval sources, and also to appreciate the wide range of Arthurian literature written after the Middle Ages.

Gwenivere Tells

by

JOHN MASEFIELD

So Arthur passed, but country-folk believe
He will return, to triumph and achieve;
Men watch for him on each Midsummer Eve.

They watch in vain, for ere that night was sped,
That ship reached Avalon with Arthur dead;
I, Gwenivere, helped cere[1] him, within lead.

I, Gwenivere, helped bury him in crypt,
Under cold flagstones that the ringbolts shipped;
The hangings waved, the yellow candles dripped.

Anon I made profession, and took vows
As nun encloistered: I became Christ's spouse,
At Amesbury, as Abbess to the house.

I changed my ermines for a goat-hair stole,
I broke my beauty there, with dule and dole,[2]
But love remained a flame within my soul.

What though I watched and fasted and did good
Like any saint among my sisterhood,
God could not be deceived, God understood

How night and day my love was as a cry
Calling my lover out of earth and sky
The while I shut the bars against reply.

---

1. To wrap in a cere-cloth, a cloth coated with wax, formerly used for
wrapping the dead.

2. Grief and sorrow.

Years thence a message came: I stood to deal
The lepers' portions through the bars of steel;
A pilgrim thrust me something shut with seal.

I could not know him in his hoodings hid;
Besides, he fled: his package I undid;
Lancelot's leopard-crest was on the lid.

Within, on scarlet ivory, there lay
A withered branchlet, having leaves of gray.
A writing said: "This is an olive spray

Picked for your blessing from a deathless tree
That shades the garden of Gethsemane;
May it give peace, as it has given me."

Did it give peace? Alas, a woman knows
The rind without may deaden under blows;
But who has peace when all within's a rose?

The Death of Lancelot
As Told by Gwenivere

by

JOHN MASEFIELD

Then, after many years, a rider came,
An old lame man upon a horse as lame,
Hailing me "Queen" and calling me by name.

I knew him; he was Bors of Gannis,[1] he.
He said that in his chapel by the sea
My lover on his death-bed longed for me.

No vows could check me at that dying cry,
I cast my abbess-ship and nunhood by . . .
I prayed, "God, let me see him ere he die."

We passt the walls of Camelot: we passt
Sand-raddled Severn[2] shadowing many a mast,
And bright Caerleon[3] where I saw him last.

Westward we went, till, in an evening, lo,
A bay of bareness with the tide at flow,
And one green headland in the sunset's glow.

There was the chapel, at a brooklet's side.
I galloped downhill to it with my guide.
I was too late, for Lancelot had died.

---

1. Cousin of Sir Lancelot.

2. A river running through parts of Wales and western England.

3. A town on the River Usk and one of the traditional sites where Arthur
held court.

I had last seen him as a flag in air,
A battle banner bidding men out-dare.
Now he lay dead; old, old, with silver hair.

I had not ever thought of him as old . . .
This hurt me most: his sword-hand could not hold
Even the cross upon the sacking-fold.[4]

They had a garden-close[5] outside the church
With Hector's[6] grave, where robins came to perch.
When I could see again, I went to search

For flowers for him dead, my king of men.
I wandered up the brooklet, up the glen:
A robin watched me and a water-hen.

There I picked honeysuckles, many a bine[7]
Of golden trumpets budding red as wine,
With dark green leaves, each with a yellow spine.

We buried him by Hector, covered close
With these, and elder-flower, and wild rose.
His friends are gone thence now: no other goes.

He once so ringing glad among the spears,
Lies where the rabbit browses with droppt ears
And shy-foot stags come when the moon appears.

Myself shall follow, when it be God's will;
But whatso'er my death be, good or ill,
Surely my love will burn within me still.

Death cannot make so great a fire drowse;
What though I broke both nun's and marriage-vows,
April will out, however hard the boughs:

---

4. Burial cloth.

5. Enclosed garden.

6. Malory's Ector de Marys, half-brother of Lancelot.

7. The flexible stem of any of various climbing and twining plants.

And though my spirit be a lost thing blown,
It, in its waste, and, in the grave, my bone,
Will glimmer still from Love, that will atone.

Mount Badon

by

CHARLES WILLIAMS

The king's poet was his captain of horse in the wars.
He rode over the ridge; his force
sat hidden behind, as the king's mind had bidden.
The plain below held the Dragon in the centre,
Lancelot on the left, on the right Gawaine,
Bors in the rear commanding the small reserve:
the sea's indiscriminate host roared at the City's wall.
As with his household few Taliessin[1] rode over the ridge,
the trumpets blew, the lines engaged.

Staring, motionless, he sat;
who of the pirates saw? none stopped;
they cropped and lopped Logres; they struck deep,
and their luck held; only support lacked:
neither for charge nor for ruse could the allied crews
abide the civilized single command;
each captain led his own band and each captain unbacked;
but numbers crashed; Taliessin saw Gawaine
fail, recover, and fail again;
he saw the Dragon sway; far away
the household of Lancelot was wholly lost in the fray;
he saw Bors fling
company after company to the aid of the king,
till the last waited the word alone.

Staring, motionless, he sat.
Dimly behind him he heard how his staff stirred.
One said: "He dreams or makes verse"; one: "Fool,

---

1. A sixth-century Celtic bard who has been presented as Arthur's court poet
in a number of modern works.

all lies in a passion of patience—my lord's rule."
In a passion of patience he waited the expected second.
Suddenly the noise abated, the fight vanished, the last
few belated shouts died in a new quiet.
In the silence of a distance, clear to the king's poet's sight,
Virgil[2] was standing on a trellised path by the sea.
Taliessin saw him negligently leaning; he felt
the deep breath dragging the depth of all dimension,
as the Roman sought for the word, sought for his thought,
sought for the invention of the City by the phrase.
He saw Virgil's unseeing eyes; his own,
in that passion of all activity but one suspended,
leaned on those screened ports of blind courage.
Barbaric centuries away, the ghostly battle contended.

Civilized centuries away, the Roman moved.
Taliessin saw the flash of his style
dash at the wax; he saw the hexameter[3] spring
and the king's sword swing; he saw, in the long field,
the point where the pirate chaos might suddenly yield,
the place for the law of grace to strike.
He stood in his stirrups; he stretched his hand;
he fetched the pen of his spear[4] from its bearer;
his staff behind signed to their men.

The Aeneid's beaked lines swooped on Actium;[5]
the stooped horse charged; backward blown,
the flame of song streaked the spread spears
and the strung faces of words on a strong tongue.
The household of Taliessin swung on the battle;
hierarchs of freedom, golden candles of the solstice
that flared round the golden-girdled Logos,[6] snowy-haired,
brazen-footed, starry-handed, the thigh banded with the Name.

---

2. Virgil (or Vergil; 70–19 B.C.) was the Roman poet who wrote the *Aeneid*.

3. Dactylic hexameter is the meter in which the *Aeneid* is written.

4. Taliessin's fighting the forces of chaos is like his creation of poetry, an assertion of order over chaos. Thus pen and spear merge in this image.

5. The lines of the poem (the *Aeneid*), compared to the beaked (prowed) ships by which the Romans defeated Antony and Cleopatra at Actium, become the weapon or the force by which the City (a symbol of order) overcomes chaos.

6. The Word (both poetry and Christ).

The trumpets of the City blared through the feet of brass;
the candles flared among the pirates; their mass broke;
Bors flung his company forward; the horse and the reserve
caught the sea's host in a double curve;
the paps of the day were golden-girdled;[7]
hair, bleached white by the mere stress of the glory,
drew the battle through the air up threads of light.
The tor[8] of Badon heard the analytical word;
the grand art mastered the thudding hammer of Thor,[9]
and the heart of our lord Taliessin determined the war.

The lord Taliessin kneeled to the king;
the candles of new Camelot shone through the fought field.

---

7. This image, like several of those preceding and following it, comes from the Apocalypse (cf. Revelations 1:10–20).

8. Hill.

9. Germanic god of thunder.

The Coming of Galahad

by

CHARLES WILLIAMS

In the hall all had what food they chose;
they rose then, the king, Lancelot, the queen;
they led the young man Galahad to Arthur's bed.
The bishops and peers, going with the royalties, made
ceremony; they created a Rite. When he was laid,
and the order done, the lords went to their rooms.
The queen all night lay thinking of Lancelot's son.

At their rising the king's poet alone had gone
another way; he took the canals of the palace,
the lower corridors, between maids and squires,
past the offices and fires of the king's kitchens,
till he came by a door cleft in a smooth wall
into the outer yards, the skied hall of the guards,
grooms, and scullions.[1] He looked above; he saw
through the unshuttered openings of stairs and rooms
the red flares of processional torches and candles
winding to the king's bed; where instead
of Arthur Galahad that night should lie,
Helayne's[2] son instead of the king's, Lancelot's
instead of Guinevere's, all taken at their word,
their professions, their oaths; the third heaven[3] heard
their declarations of love, and measured them the medium of
      exchange.

---

1. Servants who perform menial tasks in the kitchen.

2. Helayne or Elayne is the daughter of King Pelles and the mother of
Galahad by Lancelot.

3. The third heaven is the sphere of Venus.

He stood looking up among the jakes[4] and latrines;
he touched his harp, low-chanting a nursery rhyme:
"Down the porphyry stair the queen's child ran;
there he played with his father's crown . . ."
A youth came up in the dark, the king's scavenger,
large-boned, fresh-coloured, flame-haired,
Gareth, a prince and a menial,[5] the son of Morgause,
sent from Orkney and the skull-stone in the sea,
to be for cause of obedience set to the worst work.
None at Caerleon knew him but his brother Gawaine
and the king's poet who saw the profile of his mother,
in a grace of fate and a face too soon to be dead.
Hearing him now, Taliessin half-turned his head,
saying: "Sir?" Gareth said, looking at the light:
"Lord, tell me of the new knight."

Taliessin answered, sounding the strings still:
"Is it not known he is strange, being nurtured till,
men say, but yesterday, among the White Nuns,
by the sister of Percivale, the"—his harp sang—"princess
          Blanchefleur?"

Gareth said: "Lord, bless me with more.
Among the slaves I saw from the hall's door
over a meal a mystery sitting in the air—
a cup with a covered fitting under a saffron veil,
as of the Grail itself: what man
is this for whom the Emperor lifts the Great Ban?"[6]

Taliessin stayed the music; he said:
"My lords and fathers the Druids between the hazels
touched poems in chords; they made tell
of everywhere a double dance of a stone and a shell,
and the glittering sterile smile of the sea that pursues."

Gareth answered: "I heard it read from a book

---

4. Privies or outhouses.

5. Gareth served for a year as a scullion in Arthur's kitchen, a condition of his being allowed to go to Camelot imposed on him by his mother, who wished to keep her son from the dangers of knighthood.

6. The "Great Ban" is the injunction against sitting in the Siege Perilous.

by a Northern poet, and once I seemed to look
on Logres[7] pouring like ocean after a girl
who ran in the van, and her hands before her stretched
shone—bright shell, transparent stone,
and the sea touched her, and suddenly by a wind was blown
back, and she mounted a wind and rode away,
and measurement went with her and all sound,
and I found myself weeping there like a fool."

                                        "To-day
the stone was fitted to the shell," the king's poet said;
"when my lord Sir Lancelot's son sat in the perilous sell,[8]
if he be Sir Lancelot's; in Logres the thing is done,
the thing I saw wherever I have gone—
in five houses, and each house double: the boughs
of the Druid oak,[9] the cover of gay strokes in the play
of Caucasia, the parchments of Gaul, the altar-stone
in Lateran or Canterbury, the tall Byzantine hall—
O the double newels[10] at the ground of the porphyry stair!
O there the double categories of shell and stone,
and the Acts of Identity uttered out of the Throne."

"And I among dung and urine—am I one
with shell or stone," Gareth asked, "in the jakes?"
But Taliessin: "And what makes the City? to-morrow
you shall be a prince of Orkney again; to-night
abandon the degrees of Gawaine your brother; consent
to be nothing but the shape in the gate of excrement,
while Galahad in peace and the king's protection sleeps:
question and digestion, rejection and election,
winged shapes of the Grail's officers, double
grand equality of the State, common of all lives,

---

7. The realm of Arthur.

8. Seat.

9. C. S. Lewis comments on these lines: "As Williams says in one of his notes 'The shell must be fitted to the stone to breed there and burst from it; this is the finding of Identity; without it we remain pseudo-romantics.' Taliessin claims to have seen this 'fitting' achieved in five different Houses; in the House of Poetry (the Druid Oak), in the life of the flesh (Caucasia), in the intellect (Gaul), in the Church (Lateran or Canterbury) and even in the vision itself (Byzantium)" (in *Arthurian Torso* [London: Oxford University Press, 1948], p. 168).

10. Posts.

common of all experience, sense and more;
adore and repent, reject and elect. Sir,
without this alley-way how can man prefer?
and without preference can the Grail's grace be stored?"

A girl said suddenly beside them: "Lord,
tell me the food you preferred—"; and he: "More
choice is within the working than goes before.
The good that was there—and did I well then? yes?"
She said: "Yes; yet has all food one taste?
felicity does not alter?" He answered in haste:
"Felicity alters from its centre; but I—free
to taste each alteration, and that within reach
then and there; why change till the range twirls?" The girl's
eyes turned to the black palace and back.
She said: "This morning when the Saracen prince[11] was christened
dimly the lord Percivale's pentagram glistened
in the rain-dark stones of his eyes: what food there?"

Taliessin answered: "Five cells the world
gave me, five shells of multiple sound;
but when I searched for the paths that joined the signs,
lines of the pentagram's frame, the houses fled
instead to undimensioned points; their content slid
through the gate of the winged prince of the jakes; pale
they fluttered in an empty fate; the Child lay dead
in his own gate of growth—and what then,
lady, for you or me or the Saracen,
when the cut hazel has nothing to measure?" "I have known,"
she said, with the scintillation of a grave smile,
"the hazel's stripes on my shoulders; the blessed luck
of Logres has a sharp style, since I was caught free
from the pirate chaos savaging land and sea;
is the shell thus also hidden in the stone?"
"Also thus," he said, "if the heart fare
on what lies ever now on the board, stored
meats of love, laughter, intelligence, and prayer.
Is it thus?" and she: "Who knows?—and who does not care?—
yet my heart's cheer may hope, if Messias[12] please.

---

11. Palomides.
12. Messiah.

Is this the colour of my lord Galahad's eyes?"

He said: "The eyes of my lord are the measure of intensity
and his arms of action; the hazel, Blanchefleur, he.
The clerks of the Emperor's house study the redaction
of categories into identity: so we.
Give me your hand." Lightly she obeyed, and he
as lightly kissed: "O office of all lights
from the king's scavenger to the king's substitute, mean
of the merciful Child, common of all rites,
winged wonder of shell and stone, here
a shoot of your own third heaven takes root in Logres."

Gareth said: "Lord, before the meal,
when he washed his hands, the water became phosphorescent;
did you not see?" and he: "Sanctity
common and crescent! I have seen it flushed anew
in each motion and mode of the princess Blanchefleur;
who walked dropping light, as all our beloved do.
It is the shell of adoration and the grand art.
But I looked rather to-night at the queen's hand
lying on her heart, and the way her eyes scanned
the unknown lord who sat in the perilous sell.
The bone of the fingers showed through the flesh; they were claws
wherewith the queen's grace gripped: this was the stone
fitting itself to its echo."
                              He turned to the gate
into the outer air; she let cry:
"Lord, make us die as you would have us die."

But he: "Proofs were; roofs were: I
what more? creeds were; songs were. Four
zones divide the empire from the Throne's firmament,
slanted to each cleft in each wall, with planets planted:
Mercury, thinning and thickening, thirsting to theft;
Venus preference—though of the greatest, preference;
O Earth between, O seen and strewn by the four!
Jupiter with a moon of irony and of defeated irony,
and Saturn circled, girdled by turned space.
The moon of irony shone on Lancelot at Carbonek,[13]

---

13. The Grail chapel where Lancelot was denied the vision of the Holy Grail.

the moon of defeated irony on Blanchefleur at Almesbury;[14]
her hands and head were the shell bursting from the stone
after it has bred in the stone; she was bright with the moon's light
when truth sped from the taunt; well she nurtured Galahad.
Logres is come into Jupiter; all the zones
circle Saturn, spinning against the glory,
all the Throne's points, themes of the Empire."

Emeralds of fire, blank to both, his eyes
were points of the Throne's foot that sank through Logres.

---

14. The convent to which Guinevere retreats and becomes a nun.

Merlin Enthralled

by

RICHARD WILBUR

In a while they rose and went out aimlessly riding,
Leaving their drained cups on the table round.
Merlin, Merlin, their hearts cried, where are you hiding?
In all the world was no unnatural sound.

Mystery watched them riding glade by glade;
They saw it darkle[1] from under leafy brows;
But leaves were all its voice, and squirrels made
An alien fracas in the ancient boughs.

Once by a lake-edge something made them stop.
Yet what they found was the thumping of a frog,
Bugs skating on the shut water-top,
Some hairlike algae bleaching on a log.

Gawen thought for a moment that he heard
A whitethorn breathe *Niniane*.[2] That Siren's daughter
Rose in a fort of dreams and spoke the word
Sleep, her voice like dark diving water;

And Merlin slept, who had imagined her
Of water-sounds and the deep unsoundable swell
A creature to bewitch a sorcerer,
And lay there now within her towering spell.

Slowly the shapes of searching men and horses
Escaped him as he dreamt on that high bed:
History died; he gathered in its forces;
The mists of time condensed in the still head

---

1. Show itself indistinctly.
2. The woman (in other versions Vivien or Nimue) who entraps Merlin.

Until his mind, as clear as mountain water,
Went raveling toward the deep transparent dream
Who bade him sleep. And then the Siren's daughter
Received him as the sea receives a stream.

Fate would be fated; dreams desire to sleep.
This the forsaken will not understand.
Arthur upon the road began to weep
And said to Gawen *Remember when this hand*

Once haled[3] *a sword from stone; now no less strong*
It cannot dream of such a thing to do.
Their mail grew quainter as they clopped along.
The sky became a still and wove.. blue.

---

3. Drew.

Launcelot in Hell

by

JOHN CIARDI

That noon we banged like tubs in a blast from Hell's mouth.
Axes donged on casques, and the dead steamed through their
    armor,
their wounds frying. Horses screamed like cats, and men
ran through their own dust like darks howling. My country
went up in flames to the last rick and roof, and the smoke
was my own breath in me scorching the world bare.

We fought. May the clerk eat his own hand in fire forever
who wrote I would not face Arthur. Iron sparks iron.
We fought as we had been made, iron to iron. Who takes
a field from me tastes his own blood on it.
Three times I knocked him from the saddle. What's a king?—
he'd had the best mare ever danced on turf

and couldn't sit *that* saddle. Well, I rode her:
king's mount from bell to cockcrow while bed, castle and country
shook under us, and he snored holiness to a sleeping sword
from the fairies. Excalibur's ex-horseman. Yes, I fought him:
I took my damnation as it came and would have hacked
a thousand Arthurs small to mount her again.

He did better by a warhorse. That saddle, at least, he knew
how to climb into. Iron to iron he charged, and could have knocked
a castle over. But still a fool, too pure for a feint
or sidestep. Three times I dumped him with his ribs stove
and could have finished him backhand, but reined and waited
with my own head split and a puddle of blood in my pants.

The fourth, he hove[1] dead already into the saddle and came on.
But even a king won't work with no blood in him:
his point dropped till it grounded, and poled him
over his horse's rump. And I did not rein but took him
clean in air, though I broke my arm to do it. And there he lay:
my two horns on his head, my third through his back.

What can a clerk know of the day of dead kings and dead countries?
I blew and no one answered. The men were dead
and scarcely boys enough left to carry a king's bones
to the smoke of the burned chapel. What other burial
was done that day was done by crows and gypsies. And in my heart:
where would I find another worth damnation?

I never turned back and I never looked back. My country
burned behind me and a king lay skewered on a charred altar,
his sword in blood at my feet. I took it up and flung it
into a swamp. He had bled into it: why hold back his sword?
No fairy arm reached out of the muck to catch it. That
was another life and spent, and what was there left to save?

Except the mare! Even bled down to dust and my bones shivered,
my veins pumped at the thought of her. Why else
had I cracked king, castle, and my own head? I rode,
and mended as I rode—mended enough—enough to be still alive—
or half alive—when I found her. And when I had waited
a cool two hours at her door, what came to meet me?

A nun! Eight thousand men dead and the best iron in England
black in the burned stones of a burned shire, and my own bones
stitched in by nothing but scars, and there she stood,
black as the day we had made of the world, and gave me
—a litany of tears! A whore of heaven wailing
from a black cassock as if she stood naked in a hollow tree!

With her eyes turned in unseeing: as if to Heaven:
as if there were no world and we had not dared it
beyond damnation! That was the death of all:
she dared not even look at what we were! And for *this*

---

1. Rose, i.e., mounted.

I had fed the best meat in England to carrion crows
and left a crown in mud for a gypsy's picking.

I did not turn back and I did not look back.
I had left a king and country dead without turning.
Should I turn now for a mare? Let Heaven ride her spavined:[2]
I had the heat of her once, and I'd sooner
have turned Saracen and ripped the crosses from Europe
than deny my blood spilled into his in the field that made us.

Once of a world she danced like flame, and the man who would not
die to be scorched there was dead already. Dead as the clerk
who rhymed us to a moral. There is no moral. I was. He was. She
          was.
Blood is a war. I broke my bones on his, iron to iron.
And would again. Without her. Stroke for stroke. For his own sake.
Because no other iron dared me whole.

---

2. Decrepit or broken-down (from "spavin," a disease of the hock joint of
horses in which enlargement occurs due to collection of fluids).

From: Book IX of *Arthur Rex*

by

THOMAS BERGER

Now a twelvemonth[1] having passed, it was time for Sir Gawaine to go and keep his fell appointment with the Green Knight. Therefore he bade good-by to his brothers, his friend Launcelot, and Arthur his king and uncle. And to all he said, "God alone knows when we shall meet again, whether on earth or in Heaven."

For he believed it likely that in return for beheading the Green Knight he would lose his own head, and his own could not be returned to his neck.

Now, as in all true quests, though he had no precise sense of where the Green Knight could be sought, he knew he would find him eventually by allowing his horse its head, and when at dawn he reached a castle, before which his steed stopped and pawed the ground and neighed, he applied for entrance to it.

But when the drawbridge was lowered and the portcullis raised, and he rode within, he was greeted not by the Green Knight but rather by a fine tall lord who welcomed him graciously and invited him to spend the night.

"I thank you, most noble sir," said Gawaine, "but I can not linger here. For I must needs meet an obligation within the next four days, and I do not know how much farther I must travel." And, because this handsome lord looked an honest man, he told him of his appointment with his verdant adversary.

"Sir knight," said the lord, "I tell you that I know this green man, whose Green Chapel is just near by, and it is there that you will find him, four days hence and in good time! Meanwhile you must accept my hospitality." And he led Sir Gawaine within the castle, which was the most sumptuously furnished place that Gawaine had ever seen, and the chamber where he was led was

---

1. Year.

hung with silks and carpeted in fur soft as foam, and nightingales sang in golden cages, and hanging lamps burned Arabic oils with a delicious fragrance and in their glow, on a couch of wine-purple velvet, lay an exquisite woman whose robes were of pale-violet gauze and transparent, so that her voluptuous body was revealed in every particular.

Now Sir Gawaine was taken aback, for he believed that he had been conducted into a bordel and that this seemingly fine lord was rather a loathsome pander. But before he could draw his sword and smite him with the flat of it for this insult to a knight of the Round Table, the lord said, "Most noble Sir Gawaine, may I present my wife."

And therefore Gawaine was constrained by the laws of courtesy to greet this lady as he would any other, and he endeavored to ignore the indecency of her costume as she smiled at him and welcomed him to the castle, for her ivory body, scarcely screened, was far more beautiful than any he had ever seen in many years of intimate congress with maids.

"Now, Sir Gawaine," said the lord, "whilst you are under my roof, all that I possess is yours, and the only offense that you can commit against me is to refrain from using that which you desire. For this is Liberty Castle, and the freedom of my guest is absolute."

"My lord," said he, "do I understand that you are so addicted to the giving of freedom that you would impose it upon him who doth not seek it?"

"Ah," said the lord, "there is no such mortal upon the earth, for all are born free and become captives through denial."

Now Gawaine believed this an impious theory, but having a generous heart, he determined to ponder on it further. Therefore he now said only, "My sole desire currently is but for a basin of water and a towel, for my journey hath been dusty and I would wash."

"Then come with me, my dear sir," said the lord, and he conducted Gawaine to another chamber, which was even more sumptuously appointed than the one in which his wife lolled, and it gave onto a walled garden in which every sort of flower did bloom under a warm sun (though elsewhere the day had been damp and dreary), and in this garden was a pool in the center of which was the alabaster statue of a nude woman, and from each of her paps flowed a fountain of silvery water. And lovely soft music was heard there, though no musicians could be seen.

And saying, "Here you may bathe," the lord did clap his hands and a peacock spread its resplendent fan and strutted to him, carrying in its beak a little silver bell, the which he took, and he rang it, and three naked small boys, all with golden hair and very white skin, came to Sir Gawaine, bearing towels as fluffy as clouds.

"Now," said the lord, "these tiny retainers will dry you, and kiss you as well, and when you have taken your pleasure with them, please ring the bell."

But Sir Gawaine did start back in dismay. "My lord," said he, "kindly remove these juvenile persons."

"Very well," said the lord, smiling. "I shall summon my wife to wash you."

"Nay, my lord, with all respect," said Sir Gawaine. But before he could say he would wash alone, the lord rang the bell again and a robust young man appeared, unclad except for an iron helmet and brass greaves,[2] and carrying a bundle of birches, he smote his other hand with them whilst smirking in genial cruelty.

"This fellow," said the lord, "is late masseur to the court of Rome, and can soon obliterate the loins' memory of an arduous day in the saddle."

"Sir," said Gawaine, "I would wash me alone, and in a simple tin basin filled with cold water."

"I can deny you nothing," said the lord, and he summoned these things, and they were brought by a withered hag, and Sir Gawaine dismissed her and was left by himself.

Now when he had finished his bathe, he realized he had nought to wear but his smallclothes[3] and steel armor, and therefore he reluctantly rang for his host, for to request the loan of a house coat. But in answer to his summons came instead a lovely young maid, her flaxen hair flowing over her white shoulders to part at her high round breasts so that the orchidaceous tips were revealed, for she was naked, and Sir Gawaine, who was an authority on such matters, judged she was in years sixteen, and in former times she would have been to him as a goblet of cool water to a parched throat, but now he hastily concealed his secrets with the coarse homespun cloth brought him by the hag to dry himself on, and he commanded her to fetch her master to him.

And when, as required by the laws of Liberty Castle, she complied instantly with his wishes, Sir Gawaine knew the first faint

---

2. Leg armor worn below the knees.

3. Underwear.

pangs of regret, for though he was no longer the unrestrained lecher of old, neither had he become as enervate as an eunuch.

Now the lord brought him a robe of fine silken stuff and trimmed with soft fur, and then he led him to a magnificent dining hall, where the table was laden with delicacies from all over the earth and the dishes were of pure gold, while the goblets were each cut from a solid diamond, and when they sat down they were served by a corps of unfledged maidens, delicate as primroses and with smooth bodies clad only in sheer lawn.[4]

And hearing some slight stirring near his knees beneath the table, Sir Gawaine lifted the cloth and saw a beautiful child with a face of old ivory and dark eyes shaped like almonds.

"At the very edge of the world," said the lord his host, "on the brink of nothingness, live in great luxury a golden-skinned people called the Chinee. Now it is their practice to use infantile entertainers beneath the table top at banquets, to stir one appetite by provoking another. This can be especially amusing as prelude to an Oriental dish we shall presently be offered: live monkey. I shall strike off its crown, and we shall eat his smoking brains." And here the lord brandished a little silver ax. "I promise you that nothing is more aphrodisiac, and that soon you will be delirious with lust."

But Sir Gawaine declined to partake of the pleasure beneath the cloth, and he begged to have the dish withheld, but though he believed this lord monstrously unnatural he would not denounce him under his own roof, for after all no vileness had yet been imposed upon him, but rather merely offered.

And Gawaine also spurned the lark's eyes in jelly, the coddled serpent-eggs, the pickled testicles of tiger, the lot, and he asked instead for cold mutton and small beer, which he instantly was brought.

Now after this feast the lord led Sir Gawaine to a chamber where a lovely maid, dressed in many veils, played sweetly upon a flute while dancing gracefully, and one by one she dropped her veils until with the last one she was revealed to be a willowy young man, and when the dance was done, he bowed to the floor before Sir Gawaine but facing away.

But Gawaine said to his host, "My lord, I am no bugger."[5]

---

4. "Lawn" is a sheer linen or cotton fabric.

5. Sodomite.

Therefore the lord dismissed the young man, and then he said to Sir Gawaine, "Well, I would know what I might do for you."

And Gawaine said, "Nothing, my lord."

"So be it," said the lord. "And now I must leave you, for to go hunting, and I shall be away until nightfall. Pray remember that even in my absence you can be denied nothing at Liberty Castle." And he gave Gawaine the silver bell that had been fetched by the peacock. "Ring this for whatever you desire. But now I propose to you a bargain: that when I return we each exchange with the other that which we have got during the course of the day when we were apart."

Now Sir Gawaine could see no reason to do this, but he was aware by now that the ways of this castle were strange, so strange indeed as to suggest magic, but whether white or black he could not yet say: for though the beastly amusements offered him were evil, they may well have been temptations in the service of a higher good. And surely courtesy required that he respond amiably to this lord, until such time as he could determine his purpose.

Therefore he agreed to this bargain, for anyway he had no intention to do ought all day but prepare himself spiritually for the ordeal to come, when he must face the Green Knight.

"Good," said the lord. "Perhaps I shall bring you a brace of partridges."

"And if I have nothing to return?" asked Sir Gawaine.

"Then nothing shall be my reward," said the lord in a merry voice. "But do not forget that our agreement is to be considered literally, and that to conceal *anything* you have received would be to violate your pledge."

"My lord," said Gawaine reproachfully, "I am a knight of the Round Table."

"Indeed," the lord said, "and I should strike a bargain with no other!"

Then he left to go a-hunting, and scarcely was he gone when Sir Gawaine regretted not having asked where the chapel was situated within the castle, for he wished to pray there. But remembering the little silver bell, he rang it, and in answer to his summons the lord's wife appeared and she was no more abundantly dressed than she had been when he had seen her first.

"Lady," said he, "please direct me to your chapel, for I would fain pray."

But the lady came to press against him, and she put her arms about his neck, and she said, "Sweet Sir Gawaine, be kind to me, I beg of you."

And though Gawaine was far from being immune to the sensations caused by the pressure of her luxuriant body (and graciousness would not allow him to thrust her away), he had the strength of soul to remain modest, and he said, "Lady, this is not proper."

"I speak of kindness and not propriety," cried the lady, and she held him tightly and her warm breath was against the hollow of his neck.

"Lady," said Gawaine, "methinks I now understand the test to which I am being put at Liberty Castle, where all temptations of the flesh have been offered me, but in fact not even when I was a notable lecher did I frequent children, persons of mine own gender, nor other men's wives."

Now this beautiful lady did fall against him weeping. "You are the defender of women," said she, "and I am in distress."

"Then let me get mine armor and weapons," said Sir Gawaine, "and tell me who would abuse you."

"'Tis no person," said the lady. "I am rather tormented by a sense that my kisses are obnoxious, for my lord hath avoided me lately." And she lifted her mouth to him, the which was moist and red.

"Your breath, lady," said Gawaine, "is fragrant as the zephyrs of spring. I cannot believe that your kisses are repulsive."

"Well," said the lady, "then there must be something offensive in the touch of my lips." And she pursed these for his inspection.

"Nay," said Sir Gawaine. "They are flawless as the rose."

"Yet," said she, "you can not be certain unless you press them to your own."

"Perhaps that is true," said Sir Gawaine. "But should I be the one to make this test?"

"But who other?" asked the lady. "I can not subject my husband to it, for it is precisely he who I fear finds me obnoxious. And any man who is not a knight of the Round Table could never be trusted."

"Trusted, lady?" asked Gawaine, endeavoring to loosen her clasp, which had now been lowered to his waist, to the end that their bellies were joined.

"A knight of lesser virtue, enflamed by my kiss, alone with me, my lord being in the remote forest, I attired lightly as I am, he in a

robe of fine thin stuff that betrays the least stirring of his loins—"
And so said the lady, and she heaved with the horror of it.

And Sir Gawaine said hastily, "Certes,[6] I am trustworthy in this
regard. Now, lady, your argument hath moved me. I shall accept
one kiss from you, for the purpose of examining it."

And the lady forthwith crushed her hot mouth against his lips
and had he not clenched his jaws and so erected a barrier of teeth,
she would have thrust her tongue into his throat so far as it would
go, for it battered against his gums with great force.

And when he at last broke free, he said, "Your kiss is sweet, I
assure you. But perhaps it is given too strenuously." (And truly, his
lips were full sore.) And then he said, "As guest in Liberty Castle I
have this wish, which must be honored, and it is that this test be
taken as concluded." Therefore, as she was constrained to do by the
laws of the place, the lady went away.

Now when the lord returned from his hunt he came to Sir
Gawaine, saying, "Well, here you are, sir knight, a brace of fine fat
partridges, the which are my gain, and all of it, from a day in the
forest. Now, what have you got here that, according to our
agreement, you shall give to me?"

"As I predicted," said Sir Gawaine, "I have nothing to give
you, having received nothing."

"I beg you to re-examine your memory," said the lord. "Surely
you received something during my absence that you had not
previously possessed?"

And Sir Gawaine was ashamed, first for his failure of recall,
and then for what he must needs confess.

"I received a kiss, my lord," said he, coloring. But then he
realized that he was not obliged to say who had kissed him (and the
situation at Liberty Castle was such that there were many possible
candidates).

"Very well, then," said the lord smiling. "Pray give it me."

Now Gawaine's shame was increased, for he understood that
the terms of the agreement were absolute, but manfully he did
purse his lips and press them to the cheek of the lord.

"Now," said the lord, "is this precisely how you received this
kiss, and did the giver thereof make a similar grimace?"

Sir Gawaine hung his head and said, "Nay, my lord." And
then gathering his strength he lifted his mouth to the lord's and,

---

6. Surely.

doing his best to simulate the tender expression of the lady, he kissed him full upon the lips.

"Splendid!" said the lord. "You are a truthful knight of much worship."

Now the following day the lord came to Sir Gawaine once again, and he announced to him that he would make the same exchange with him as he had done the day before. But Gawaine did protest against this.

"Sir," said the lord, "I took you for a courteous knight. Are Arthur's men given to such rudeness?"

"With all respect, my lord," said Gawaine, "I am fasting for my appointment with the Green Knight, and therefore I can not eat game."

"Then I shall bring to you some other goods of the forest," said the lord, and then he looked narrowly at Sir Gawaine. "Sir," said he, "methinks you worry that you will have to give me another kiss."

Now though this was quite true, Sir Gawaine could hardly confess to it without being discourteous in the extreme, and therefore he bowed and said, "My lord, I make this pact with you once again."

But so soon as the lord left the castle this time, Gawaine, eschewing the use of the silver bell and hoping thereby to elude the lady, went alone in search of the chapel, but though he looked everywhere he could not find it. Therefore he returned to the chamber where he had spent the night and he knelt by his bed clasping his hands in the attitude of prayer, but before he could begin his orisons the lady appeared from nowhere and embraced him.

Then he rose with difficulty and freeing himself gently from her, he said, "Lady, it would be indecent for me to talk with you at this time. Pray let us wait until your husband returns from the hunt."

But the lady said, "Sir, remember your sworn duty to all women! Once again I require your aid, and the vows you have taken will never allow you to deny me." And she drew aside the transparent stuff that swathed her bosom, and she bared her breasts absolutely.

"Ah," she cried, "you start back, just as does my husband when I undress before him! Then it is as I fear: my bosom is hideous."

"No, that is not true, lady," said Sir Gawaine. "Between waist and shoulders you are very beautiful."

"Do you say my mammets are round?" asked the lady.

"Very round," said sir Gawaine.

"And full?"

"Very full."

"Yet high."

"Oh, indeed high," said Sir Gawaine as he walked backwards, for she continued to approach him.

"But think you that the paps are discolored?" And now she held herself in two hands, so that the pink nipples did peek through the white fingers.

"Never discolored," said Gawaine, who was now against the arras[7] and could retreat no farther.

"Not brown then?"

"Certes," said Sir Gawaine, "they are rather of the hue of the Afric orchid."

"Oh," said the lady, taking her hands away, "but they are cold! Methinks breasts should be warm, or if not, then warmed." And before Sir Gawaine knew what he did, she had taken his fingers and put them onto her bosoms. "Now tell me if they are cold."

"Lady," said Gawaine, "they are quite near burning." And for a dreadful moment he could not control his fingers, and finally it was she who drew back, saying haughtily, "Sir, I did not seek kneading. I wished only to know my temperature."

And Sir Gawaine was chagrined. "Forgive me, lady." He sighed with great feeling. "Now, by my privilege as guest, I wish to be alone." Therefore she vanished, and he fell to praying ardently.

Now when the lord returned from the forests he presented to Sir Gawaine the flayed hide of a bear, and he said, "There you have my day's spoil, and all of it. What shall you give me in return?"

And this time Sir Gawaine was ready for him, and he was relieved that it was not so distasteful a thing as a kiss. "I have for you a touch of the chest," said he. "Therefore if you will remove your hauberk[8] and breastplate and raise your doublet,[9] I shall give it you."

Now the lord did these things, and Sir Gawaine groped at his chest, which was covered with a thick mat of hair very like that of the bearskin.

---

7. Tapestry.

8. A tunic of chain mail.

9. A man's close-fitting jacket.

Then the lord began to laugh, for he was ticklish, and when Sir Gawaine was done the lord said, "And is that all? Did I not know you as a truthful knight, I should wonder at this. Nor is it evident as to whose chest was so tickled in the original episode: your own, or that of another?"

"Mine obligation, methinks," said Sir Gawaine, "is but to give you what I had got, and so have I done. I am not required to explain it."

"Aha," said the lord, "methinks not even a sodomite doth toy with a hairy chest, and certes you are anyway not a sod. May I then assume it was rather a woman's full bosom which you fondled?"

"My lord," said Gawaine, "our agreement is to be kept to the letter, no more and no less."

And the lord did laugh merrily, saying, "Well put, my dear sir."

"And now," said Sir Gawaine, "may I ask you to show me to the chapel, for 'tis there I intend to stay at prayers until my appointment with the Green Knight, which is now but two mornings away."

But the lord said, "I'm afraid there is no chapel at Liberty Castle, good Sir Gawaine. We are pagans here, and furthermore we make no apology for so being."

Sir Gawaine crossed himself. "I should have understood that," said he. "Absolute liberty is the freedom to be depraved."

"But only if you choose to make it so," said the lord. "One can also see it as the only situation in which principles may be put to the proof. No strength of character is needed to stay virtuous under restraint."

"But only God, sir, hath perfect strength," said Gawaine. And he was now vexed, and he said, "And how dare you, as a paynim,[10] to test the virtue of a Christian?"

"Because I have no shame!" merrily replied the lord. "Which is a Christian invention."

Now Sir Gawaine began to suspect that this lord was the Devil, for never had he heard so much wickedness from any man. "Methinks," said he, "that you would weaken me for my encounter with the Green Knight."

"Well," said the lord, "if you are honest you will admit that it is a ridiculous thing. A charlatan dyes his skin and hair and dressed in

---

10. Pagan.

green clothes bursts into Arthur's court to make a preposterous challenge. Would that be taken seriously anywhere but at Camelot? Now you are likely to die of this buffoonery, and *cui bono*?"[11]

"For the Green Knight I care not a bean," said Sir Gawaine. "But to keep my oath I should go to Hell. And methinks I have done so in coming here."

But the lord did make much mirth. "It is so only if you choose to make it such, I say again," said he, "the which can be said of any other place on earth but especially of your Britain. But enough of this colloquy! And pray never believe that I do not admire you withal."

"Despite such flattery," said Sir Gawaine, "I shall leave you now."

"Ah," the lord said, "you well may leave me, but the one freedom not available at Liberty Castle is to leave it before the proper time hath come."

And Gawaine found that what he had said was true, for when he sought to go out of the gate he was arrested by a strange unseen force and could move only in the direction of the castle behind him. Therefore willy-nilly he stayed the final night, and the next morning the lord came to him again with the familiar proposal.

"Do I have a choice?" asked Gawaine.

And the lord answered, "Well, it is the last time." And promising to exchange with his guest what they each had come into possession of during the day, he went a-hunting in the forest.

Now Gawaine determined no longer to wait passively for the lady to seek him out, for he knew that she would do so, according to the pattern of the previous days: and all things in Heaven and on earth come in threes, and only the tripod is ever stable even though its legs be of unequal lengths. Therefore taking the virile initiative he did go in search of her, and you may be sure he was not long in finding her, for her sole purpose was to try his virtue (to which end all women, even the chaste, are dedicated) and thus all corridors at Liberty Castle soon led to the most private of her chambers, the walls of which were lined with quilted velvet of pink, the which color deepened and darkened as he penetrated the room, and the couch on which she lay was of magenta. But her body for once was fully covered, in a robe of the richest dark red and of many folds and trimmed with the sleek fur of the otter.

---

11. For what good [purpose]?

"Good day to you, sir knight," said she. "And for what have you come to me?"

"To offer my services," said Sir Gawaine, "the which you have previously required each day at just this time."

"Of that I have no memory," said the lady sternly. "And can your purpose be decent, so to seek me out when mine husband is away?" And crying, "Villainy!" she did clap her hands, and soon a brace of huge knights, armed cap-à-pie, burst into the chamber through a secret door and made at Sir Gawaine.

Now Gawaine understood that he had been tricked and mostly by himself, for he had come here voluntarily and unarmored and unweaponed. But being the truest of knights, what he feared was not the death that he might well be dealt here (for he expected to be killed on the morrow by the Green Knight, and we each of us owe God but one life), but rather that if he were not alive to meet his appointment with the verdant giant he would cause great shame to be brought upon the Round Table, for death were never a good excuse for breaking a pledge.

Therefore he seized a tall candlestick of heavy bronze, and he swung its weighted base with such force that the flange not only split the helm of the first knight to reach him, but also cracked his skull to the very brainpan, and his wits spewed out through his ears. Now taking the halberd[12] that this man dropped, Sir Gawaine brought it up from the floor just as the other knight came at him, and he cut him from the crotch to the wishbone, and his guts hung out like ropes.

"Well," said the lady when this short fight was done, "do not suppose you have me at your mercy." And she found a dagger within her clothes and leaping at Sir Gawaine she sought to do him grievous injury.

But though he was the protector of women Gawaine saw no obligation to suffer being assailed by a female to whom he had offered no harm. Therefore he seized the dagger from her, and then, because she next tried to claw him with the sharp nails of her fingers, he restrained her hands behind her waist.

But hooking her toe behind his ankle the lady tripped him up, so that he fell onto the couch, and she was underneath him.

"Lady," he said, "I would not hurt you for all the world."

---

12. A weapon with an axelike blade and a steel spike mounted on the end of a long shaft.

"Then release mine hands so that I might feel whether I have broken anything," said she. And he did so, but when her fingers were free she used them rather to bare her thighs, the which she then spread on either side of him. And whilst he was stunned with amazement at her strange behavior, she lifted his own robe to the waist, saying, "I fear I may have smote your belly with my knee, and I would soothe your bruises." And then she went to that part and farther with her white fingers.

"Lady," said Gawaine, "I assure you that I am not sore."

"Yet you have a swelling," said she, and she did forthwith apply a poultice to him.

And to his horror Sir Gawaine discovered that his strength of will was as nothing in this circumstance, and therefore he must needs submit to this lady altogether. But this was a defeat which it was the more easy to accept with every passing instant, and before many had gone by he had quite forgot why he had resisted so long, in the service of a mere idea, for such is the eloquence with which the flesh first speaketh to him who ceases to withstand temptation, God save him.

But when the lady was done with him, and they lay resting, he knew great shame, and this grew even worse when he remembered he had agreed to exchange the spoils of the day with the lord of the castle.

Therefore when the lord returned from his hunting and presented to Sir Gawaine a splendid rack of antlers from a stag, and asked in exchange whatever Gawaine had got, his guest did prevaricate and say he had spent all day in prayer and therefore could give the lord only the peace he had thereby obtained.

"I am prevented by the laws of hospitality," said his host, "from impugning the veracity of a knight to whom I am giving shelter. Yet it seems remarkable to me that you have got no more tangible rewards during a day at Liberty Castle."

"Well," said Gawaine, "I cannot call it a reward when I am attacked by two of your armed men. Should you like me to assail you with a halberd and a mace?"

"Hardly," said the lord, but he smiled. "Yet you appear whole, whereas I passed their bodies being hauled away in a cart."

"My lord," said Sir Gawaine, "on the morrow I meet the Green Knight, and though I thank you for your hospitality, I shall be relieved to have it come to an end, for between us there is no common language."

And so he retired for the night. But while he slept he had bad dreams.

Therefore when Sir Gawaine awoke, he went to find the lord for to tell him everything that had happened on the previous day. But nowhere could he find him throughout the castle, nor indeed did he see the lady or anyone else, nor the scented pleasure-chambers. In fact, the entire castle was but a ruin and covered in years of moss and vines, and it was apparent that no one had inhabited it since the days of the giants who lived in Britain before the first men came there after the fall of Troy.[13]

Thus it was in sadness that Sir Gawaine rode to seek the Green Knight, for he realized that the last three days of his life had been spent in some magical test at which he had proved himself untrustworthy, mendacious, and adulterous.

Now he was not long in reaching a valley where a green chapel stood, and before it was tethered a green-colored stallion. And when he dismounted and went within he saw the same huge green knight who had come to Camelot one year before.

"Sir Gawaine," said the Green Knight, brandishing his great green battle-ax, "are you prepared to keep our bargain?"

"I have come here only for that reason," said Gawaine, removing his helm and baring his neck. "And I would fain have you get it over with quickly."

"Why for?" cried the green man. "Who rushes to his death?"

"Our bargain, sir," said Gawaine, "will be completed when you strike off my head. There is no provision in it for argument."

"I am no quotidian[14] headsman," said the Green Knight, "and I do not crop necks for profit nor pleasure. Tell me why you are in haste to lose your self, the which is truly the only thing a man possesseth, if but temporarily."

"I am not pleased with mine," said Gawaine. "I have not done well. I have lately broken a vow and lied."

"Which is no more than to say, you have been a man," said the Green Knight and in a jovial voice. "And with only these failings, are better than most."

"And worse," said Gawaine, "I have adulterated with the wife of mine host." And with a groan he threw himself into the stones of

---

13. According to medieval legend Britain was founded by and named for Brutus, great-grandson of Aeneas, who together with others of the Trojan race founded Troynovant (New Troy), later named London.

14. Commonplace.

the floor of the chapel so that the Green Knight could chop off his head.

"Sir Gawaine," said the Green Knight, raising his ax high over his head, "you are the most humane of all the company of the Round Table, and therefore, unlike the others, you are never immodest. To be greater than you is to be tragic; to be less, farcical."

And with a great rush of air he brought the ax down onto Gawaine's bare neck and the blade struck the stones with a great clangor, and red sparks sputtered in the air.

But Gawaine was still sensible, and he flexed his shoulders and stretched his neck, and then he felt with his hands that his head was yet in place.

Therefore he sprang to his feet and drew his sword. "Well, sir," he said, "you have had your one blow. I am not to be held at fault if you missed me! Then have at you!"

But the Green Knight threw down his ax and laughed most merrily. "Feel your neck," said he, "and you will find that you have been wounded slightly."

And Gawaine did as directed, and there was a slight cut in the skin, the which bled onto his fingers.

"That is your punishment," said the Green Knight. "You are no adulterer, dear sir, for that was no one's wife but rather the Lady of the Lake. You did however break your pledge to the lord of Liberty Castle, and you did prevaricate. But had you told the full and literal truth and fulfilled to the letter the terms of your agreement, you would have been obliged to use the lord as you did the lady."

"Yes," said Sir Gawaine, and having escaped the death for which he had been prepared, he felt an unique joy though his demeanor remained sober. "But I had done better to explain that at the time."

"Indeed," said the Green Knight. "And therefore, your slight wound. But in the large you performed well: a knight does better to break his word than, keeping it, to behave unnaturally. And a liar, sir, is preferable to a monster."

"Then can it be said, think you," asked Sir Gawaine, "that sometimes justice is better served by a lie than by the absolute and literal truth?"

"That may indeed be so," said the Green Knight, "when trafficking with humanity, but I should not think that God could be ever deluded."

Then Sir Gawaine knelt to pray, and when he rose he saw that the Green Knight had lost his greenness and had dwindled in size, and in fact was no longer a man, but a woman, and she was the Lady of the Lake.

"My dear Gawaine," said she, "do not hide thy face. Thou hast done nothing for which to be ashamed."

"Lady," said Sir Gawaine, "'tis not all of it shame. I confess that I am vexed that once again you have chosen to gull me. Remember that on the first occasion I did seemingly kill a woman and now I apparently made love to another. Yet each of them was you, and both events were delusions."

"And from neither have you come away without some reward," said the Lady of the Lake, who in her true appearance was even more beautiful than in any of her guises. "And would you rather that each time the woman had been real?"

"No, my lady!" cried Gawaine. "But I might ask why my natural addiction to women must invariably be the cause of my difficulties. Methinks I was happier as the lecher of old. I have since been only miserable. And for that matter, what service did I render to Elaine of Astolat, whom I did love without carnality? Better I had made to her lewd advances, the rejection of which would not have altered her fate, but would have freed me!"

"Why," asked the Lady of the Lake, "didst thou assume thine overtures would have been rejected? Gawaine, thou wert never commanded to be a prude."

And so having made her favorite knight the more puzzled, the Lady of the Lake did void that place in the form of a golden gossamer,[15] the which floated from the door of the chapel and rose high into the soft air without.

---

15. A fine film of cobwebs often seen floating in the air.

The Naming of the Lost

by

VALERIE NIEMAN COLANDER

". . . so by her subtle working she made Merlin to go under that
stone to let her wit of the marvels there. . . . And so she departed
and left Merlin."

—Le Morte D'Arthur

I call myself the lost one. I walk the rails
below the mountain, above the water's curve,
companioned only by my steady breath.
I, I—there is no soul behind that word,
a cry against a time which even my flesh
and hidden bones cannot recall to me.
My face is the one which I saw reflected,
without a name. And it may be this day
that I will walk myself down, or tomorrow.

The rails are rusted, brown as the hillside,
but the sun strikes an echo from the steel,
keen of ten thousand steps of stretched metal,
twisting upon its spikes. My ear against
the rail, I hear distance, distance, distance.

This dress, lilac flowers now stained by sweat,
I took from a woman's line of drying clothes.
I took it the way I'll take a name. Perhaps
the place I walk to, Catawba,[1] that will be
my name. On the beating under-skin of my wrist
I taste the day. I am river water
which flows swift deep and green, carrying more
than itself, secrets, not knowing more

---

1. A small community on the Monongahela River north of Fairmont, West
Virginia.

than tangled currents and the rub of the banks.
I feel pregnant, as if a river's child
were growing hidden by this borrowed skirt,
but I remember no lust, and no man's arms.

In the heat of the late of summer, cool on my back
a shadow's thrown. An edge of an echo, steps.
"Is someone there?" I call. The shade moves on,
slowly passing like the shadow of a cloud
that is not there. The sky is hot, hazy.
I look back, to find no one behind. Again,
without a reason, I had thought that one
for whom I seem to wait was following me.
But there's no one, not least myself, who has
the name by which to spin me clear around,
to make my feet daintily dance, my hands
weave gold from the summer-straw air. My path
follows along the steps that I have found.

The land broadens, mountains rise on the smell
of sassafras, of tree bark spice, green juice
sweet in the stems of rock maples and beech.
I feel the sandstone ribs of the country like
the bones of a lover. I, the nameless one,
will love only one sure as rock in himself,
his name pressed in every cell. When he
dies, his bones will cry his name in the wind
that lifts the tipping wings of the red-tailed hawk.

Upon my left there widens a bay of land,
a green lawn down from the tracks to the river bank,
and sunk to its rungs in the meadow soil, a chair,
alone, with neither house nor barn nearby.
The chair looks out across the flowing stream.
I go down, stepping from cinders to grass and mounds
of starry flowers foaming here, and here.

A kitchen chair, and turned from oak—one rung
is broken where a farmer's foot would rest.
Seven rods support the rounded back, the gray
wood carved to show an open pair of hands.
I rest my hands upon the back and watch

the river flowing north, nestling against
the near bank, gnawing it from beneath. One day
it will devour the meadow, this chair, and all.

I lift my feet from broken shoes and stand,
the grass blades bend, soft edges unblooded
against my ankles. The heat goes from my skin.
Ahead, Catawba lies, and they say there
that white and glistening salt is hilled beside
the tracks, burning under the sun, waiting
for rain to run it into sterile earth.
A long walk, yet, and so I sit and rest,
my shoulder-blades within the back's embrace.

In the river's deepest bend, I see bottom,
and broken hulls of sunken barges finned
with heavy carp upon the bows. Silt stirs.
Quickened with the raw Appalachian earth
which ran down red in spring rain, three dragons rise,
their wings unfurling, up from the barges' depth.
The dragons rest suspended in the stream,
great fish with golden scales. Watching, I scarcely
hear the tread of feet on the railroad ties.

"Good day."
                    I turn. An old man stands where I
had left the tracks; he holds one hand above
his eyes, blocking the river's reflected light.
"Who are you?" I call. He cocks his head.
"A farmer here. My name is Merle." He waits
for mine. I fold my hands on emptiness.

He takes long strides in high, brown boots, pushing
aside the grass and starlike flowers, the steps
of a younger man. White hair hangs collar-long
on his blue-sky shirt of faded plaid, and white
his beard as well, but streaks with black. "My chair,"
he says, a resonant voice. "D'ye like it, girl?"

What can I say but that I do? He kneels
beside me. "And what d'ye see from sitting there?"
I motion, nothing, and the old man steadies

himself with a hand on the seat and gazes out
across the water. My lips, my throat grow cold,
as after chewing mint. "I see dragons,
their scales like light, all golden in the stream."
"A good eye, girl—your name?"
                              "The lost one," I say.

"I've found a name in every place I've been,
where the pale moon has faded flowers, where
the sun is old and copper-dark. And now
I walk to Catawba landing, and that, perhaps,
will be my name, or hold a name for me."

And though his years lie worn and plain on him
he rises smoothly, and kneels before my feet.
He clasps my hand in his. "Welcome," he says,
"my Nimue,[2] after a long and barren time."
I try to rise, but feel my shoulders held
firmly within the chair. "I say again,
welcome. A new Siege Perilous,[3] I made
this to wait until you'd stray across the world."

I struggle, cry, "I wish to leave!" Then feel
myself untutored, rude. "You left before,"
he says, "and then I could not follow you.
But came the time appointed for the spell
to end—a water spell which found an end
as water must. And since, I ever watched
your path. For you, like all who spurn their hearts,
have lost yourself."
                     "And where have you followed?"
"I have been many places behind you. Steps,
and half-heard sounds, and shadows that soon passed."

I find some corner of myself within
that name, Nimue, Nimue, a place dusty
and cool with shadows lying thick at noon.

---

2. The enchantress who seals Merlin in a cave or a tree (Tennyson's Vivien).

3. The seat (from the French *siège*) at the Round Table at which no one but
the Grail Knight can sit without suffering great harm.

It may be I recall a long night's dream,
or a name I once had taken, or refused.

The weight of his hands on mine is warm as summer
in my lap, his dark eyes deep as August shade.
"Remember, then"—a distant image flares
of a slow stream, green banks, and two riders,
their horses gray. "Oh!"
                           "Remember, then."

The riders halt beside a waiting cave,
ragged darkness guarded by an unshaped stone.
The woman slips to the dark man's arms, and she
is robed in green. Her hair, all free, is gold.
The woman waits; the man goes forward. Dark
around him closes as she sings of sleep
flowing north, weaves a spell of stream and brook.
The stone rolls closed to seal away the cave.
She smiles, a secret warm beneath her ribs
as a child not born. I push the memory
away—a vision, no more. "It is not I,
this water-singer, green-eyed maker of spells."
His hands are firm. "Nimue," he says,
"it was a far time away."
                           "I won't believe."

But light ebbs from white, to gold, to red,
and merciful tears arise from a hollow place,
and I can cry for days from dawn to dusk
and each relinquished past, long slipped away.

"You knew me as Merlin, then, and you were mine,
as Arthur was who passed to Avalon,
noble still. But you were dangerous,
a lake reflecting fair, bright skies while all
below is rocks and shards. And so I fell,
knowing that time must wear away that taint
before our stricken lives could be renewed."
His fingers touch my cheek and gather there
the tears. "River-child, my Nimue, look."

A teardrop rests, silver, in the palm of his hand:
he breathes upon it, speaks familiar slow
commanding words. And where the tear had been,
a green pearl-gem appears, faintly glowing
with evening light. "Take it, an orient
layered of long forgetting." He lets go
my hands. "Is it some spell to bind me, now,
within a flowered meadow? Do you give
me sleep as I awake to myself?"
                                        "Would I,
who have so long followed all your paths?"

I take the tear-jewel in my lips, perfect
roundness. Layer by layer it dissolves,
the sharp of anguish, bitter salt of remorse,
at center, sweet. And memory speaks as reeds
at water's edge and water tumbling down
to green and silent pools. I see, I see
the ageless through the old, Merlin, ancient
Myrddin who wears no more a farmer's face.

I learn again the names of things, the words
to free the winter's ice-bound streams, and warm
them clear, and freshening. My beating flesh
recalls a thousand thousand paths I walked
alone, and each a long night's longest dream.

"Ah, Nimue, this time we'll thread the nighting
stars upon our chains. This time we shall
become the rulers of all powers, of earth
and air, and fire, water, since we at last
have come to rule ourselves."
                                        "But I remain
the water-flow, and you the lasting stone.
Can you embrace, and not be worn away?
Can I be held and not break free to foam,
or chafe myself, confined, to stagnancy?"

"In time that was, my river-child, in time
when Camelot burned, new-pulled from imagining's
flame. But there are times between the stars
when all the elements are joined." A light

wind comes between us, lifts his hair, and falls,
is gone. "Yet if a teacher may regain
an erring student," I ask, "can a lover forgive
such a betrayal?"
                    "Have you not lost yourself
and found yourself again?" He lifts me from
the charmed chair by his hand's warm touch on mine.
"We'll sing together a song, and arches raise
of a new Camelot which shall not fall."

The chair crumbles, falls fine to ash and sifts
upon the flowered lawn. A new wind bears
the ash across the slow, north-flowing stream.
Three dragons wing from their water-nest to fly
in patterns tangled as ancient auguries.
The stars come out like salt, strewn, and fill
the night from north to south. I match my heart
to his, his breath to mine.
                    Soft-bladed grass
closes above the place our feet had been.

Guenever Speaks

by

WENDY M. MNOOKIN

I
Guenever Learns of Arthur's Death

And when Queen Guenever understood
King Arthur was slain,
she stole away to Almesbury
and ware white clothes and black.

Great penance she took,
as ever did sinful lady in this land.
She lived in fasting, prayers, and alms-deeds.
Never creature could make her merry.

All manner of people marvelled
how virtuously she was changed.

—Thomas Malory, *Le Morte d'Arthur*

II
Guenever Retreats to Almesbury

The sisters say walk, walk
in the garden, so I do. I work
in the garden, raking fingers
through thick blankets of thyme,
pinching off tops of basil. Smell
makes me dizzy. I hold my head.
Fingers smell rich.

       spice fingers
       unsullied with food

saved for dipping in
cinnamon
                    sweet basil

                              honey

not me
I save the smell of you
on fingers

I thin the sage and tie up mint.

          fresh rushes
          on floors at festivals
          roses
                    lilies

                              mint
          soft crush

                              turns brittle

                              filthy

The sisters say read, why
don't you read?
          I have your letter
in the pages of my book.

          Guenever,
          in you I have my earthly joy,
          Leave Almesbury now
          and be with me.

Words tilt on the page.
I turn my head to follow them
scramble up
                    down.
I snap the book shut to keep the words
still.

          do not write
          no use
          in sending letters
          I will not read them

          I cannot read your letters

The sisters say rest,
get some sleep. I lie awake
and wait for Matins.[1]

> awake I do not see
> Gaheris Gareth
> unarmed
>   slain
> by you in my rescue

The nuns return from morning prayers
to sleep. Three hours
until Prime.[2] Three hours
to lie awake.

> entombed
> a stone house built around her:
> Crazy Anne: killed her husband

> eyes closed
> I see you
> fighting Arthur lying dead

Air cuts my eyes
like broken glass.

I will not close my eyes.

The sisters say eat, you must eat
to stay well. I move the food around
and smile.

>   Yesterday I swooned at Vespers.[3]
> I must eat some bread. A little bread
> so I won't swoon. So I can stay awake.

> lying in bed
> hip bones push
> against skin

---

1. The canonical hour at which morning prayers are said.
2. The second of the canonical hours.
3. The canonical hour at which evening prayers are said.

it is my time
I bleed

(I see their bodies

        bones   blood)

III
Guenever Speaks

Sister Margaret and I
walk with Caroline
back from the garden.

We walk in silence,
though now I speak.
There is little need
for talk,
and the sisters observe
silence.

Caroline skips ahead.
Her hair floats
up and down
        until she's lost

in leaves
as she rounds
a tree
    my eyes strain
to find her
I see the bough
that closed
around her
      leaves
orange gold

but Caroline is gone

leaves
where hair should be
I see red

       black

Margaret eases me
down
I breathe
in gasps
      a voice
from far away
a voice
I do not recognize
           my voice
speaks
of things I have not said before

Margaret listens.
It grows late, and cold,
and still she listens.

My voice comes back
from far away.
My breath comes easy.

Then I say—
just under the quiet—
I will stay at Almesbury

till I die.
I cannot look
at Lancelot's face

again.
I cannot lose him
again.

IV
The Sisters Tell Lancelot of Guenever's Last Words

"Hither he cometh as fast as he may.
Wherefore I beseech Almighty God:
may I never have the power
to see Lancelot
with my worldly eyen."

And thus was ever her prayer
these two days,
till she was dead.

         —Thomas Malory, *Le Morte d'Arthur*

Bibliography

Works Cited in the Introductions
Further Readings on Postmedieval Arthurian Literature

Abbott, Charles D. *Howard Pyle: A Chronicle.* New York: Harper, 1925.

Agosta, Lucien L. *Howard Pyle.* Boston: Twayne, 1987.

Alaya, Flavia M. "Tennyson's 'The Lady of Shalott': The Triumph of Art." *Victorian Poetry,* 8 (1970), 273–89.

Altieri, Joanne. "Baroque Hieroglyphics: Dryden's *King Arthur.*" *Philological Quarterly,* 61.4 (Fall 1982), 431–451.

Armistead, J. M. "Dryden's *King Arthur* and the Literary Tradition: A Way of Seeing." *Studies in Philology,* 85.1 (Winter 1988), 53–72.

Balch, Dennis R. "Guenevere's Fidelity to Arthur in 'The Defence of Guenevere' and 'King Arthur's Tomb.'" *Victorian Poetry,* 13.3–4 (Fall–Winter 1975), 61–70.

Berkove, Lawrence I. "The Reality of the Dream: Structural and Thematic Unity in *A Connecticut Yankee.*" *Mark Twain Journal,* 22.1 (Spring 1984), 8–14.

Boardman, Phillip C. "Arthur Redivivus: A Reader's Guide to Recent Arthurian Fiction." *Halcyon* 2 (1980), 41–56.

Brinkley, Roberta Florence. *Arthurian Legend in the Seventeenth Century.* 1932; rpt. New York: Octagon Books, 1970.

Buckley, Jerome Hamilton. *Tennyson: The Growth of a Poet.* Cambridge: Harvard University Press, 1960.

Bugge, John. "Arthurian Myth Devalued in Walker Percy's *Lancelot.*" In *The Arthurian Tradition: Essays in Convergence.* Ed. Mary Flowers Braswell and John Bugge. Tuscaloosa: University of Alabama Press, 1988.

——. "Merlin and the Movies in Walker Percy's *Lancelot.*" *Studies in Medievalism,* 2.4 (Fall 1983), 39–55.

Carley, James P. "'Heaven's Colour, the Blue': Morris's Guenevere and the Choosing Cloths Reread." *The Journal of the William Morris Society*, 9.1 (Autumn 1990), 20–22.

———. "Polydore Vergil and John Leland on King Arthur: The Battle of the Books." *Interpretations*, 15.2 (Spring 1984), 86–100.

Carter, Everett. "The Meaning of *A Connecticut Yankee*." *American Literature*, 50.3 (November 1978), 418–40.

Cavaliero, Glen. *Charles Williams: Poet of Theology*. Grand Rapids, Michigan: Eerdmans, 1983.

Cochran, Rebecca. "Edwin Arlington Robinson's Arthurian Poems: Studies in Medievalisms." *Arthurian Interpretations*, 3.1 (Fall 1988), 49–60.

———. "Swinburne's Concept of the Hero in *The Tale of Balen*." *Arthurian Interpretations*, 1.1 (Fall 1986), 47–53.

Collins, William J. "Hank Morgan in the Garden of Forking Paths: *A Connecticut Yankee in King Arthur's Court* as Alternative History." *Modern Fiction Studies*, 32.1 (Spring 1986), 109–14.

Crane, John K. *T. H. White*. New York: Twayne, 1974.

Davis, Bertram H. *Thomas Percy: A Scholar-Cleric in the Age of Johnson*. Philadelphia: University of Pennsylvania Press, 1989.

Dilworth, Thomas. "Arthur's Wake: The Shape of Meaning in David Jones's *The Sleeping Lord*." *The Anglo-Welsh Review*, 76 (1984), 59–71.

Eggers, J. Philip. *King Arthur's Laureate: A Study of Tennyson's Idylls of the King*. New York: New York University Press, 1971.

The Figure of Merlin in the Nineteenth and Twentieth Centuries. Ed. Jeanie Watson and Maureen Fries. Lewiston: Mellen, 1989.

Fisher, Benjamin Franklin, IV. "King Arthur Plays from the 1890s." *Victorian Poetry*, 28.3–4 (Autumn–Winter 1990), 153–76.

Franchere, Hoyt C. *Edwin Arlington Robinson*. New York: Twayne, 1968.

Fries, Maureen. "What Tennyson Really Did to Malory's Women." *Quondam et Futurus: A Journal of Arthurian Interpretations*, 1.1 (Spring 1991), 44–55.

Gallix, François. "T. H. White et le legende du roi Arthur: De la fantaisie animale au moralisme politique." *Études Anglaises*, 34.2 (April–June 1981), 192–203.

Gamerschlag, Kurt. "Arthur Coming Alive Again: 18th-Century Medievalism and the Beginnings of a Modern Myth." In *The Vitality of the Arthurian Legend: A Symposium.* Ed. Mette Pors. Odense: Odense University Press, 1988. Pp. 91–103.

Gardiner, Jane. "'A More Splendid Necromancy': Mark Twain's *Connecticut Yankee* and the Electrical Revolution." *Studies in the Novel,* 19.4 (Winter 1987), 448–58.

Göller, Karl Heinz. "From Logres to Carbonek: The Arthuriad of Charles Williams." *Arthurian Literature,* 1 (1981), 121–73.

Goodman, Jennifer. "The Last of Avalon: Henry Irving's *King Arthur* of 1895." *Harvard Library Bulletin,* 32.3 (Summer 1984), 239–55.

Hadfield, Alice Mary. *Charles Williams: An Exploration of His Life and Work.* New York: Oxford University Press, 1983.

Hansen, Chadwick. "The Once and Future Boss: Mark Twain's Yankee." *Nineteenth-Century Fiction,* 28.1 (June 1973), 62–73.

Hardy, John Edward. *The Fiction of Walker Percy.* Urbana: University of Illinois Press, 1987.

Hodges, Laura F. "Steinbeck's Dream Sequence in *The Acts of King Arthur and His Noble Knights.*" *Arthurian Interpretations,* 4.2 (Spring 1990), 35–49.

Hough, Graham. *A Preface to the Faerie Queene.* New York: Norton, 1963.

Jankofsky, Klaus P. "'America' in Parke Godwin's Arthurian Novels." *Arthurian Interpretations,* 4.2 (Spring 1990), 65–80.

———. "Sir Gawaine at Liberty Castle: Thomas Berger's Comic Didacticism in *Arthur Rex: A Legendary Novel.*" In *Theorie und Praxis im Erzählen des 19. und 20. Jahrhunderts: Studien zur englischen und amerikanischen Literatur zu Ehren von Willi Erzgräber.* Ed. Winfried Herget, Klaus Peter Jochum, and Ingeborg Weber. Tübingen: Gunger Narr, 1986.

Kendall, J. L. "The Unity of Arnold's *Tristram and Iseult.*" *Victorian Poetry,* 1 (1963), 140–45.

Kenney, Alice P. "Yankees in Camelot: The Democratization of Chivalry in James Russell Lowell, Mark Twain, and Edwin Arlington Robinson." *Studies in Medievalism,* 1.2 (Spring 1982), 73–78.

King Arthur Through the Ages. 2 vols. Ed. Valerie M. Lagorio and Mildred Leake Day. New York: Garland, 1990.

Knight, Stephen. *Arthurian Literature and Society*. New York: St. Martin's, 1983.

Kordecki, Lesley C. "Twain's Critique of Malory's Romance: *Forma tractandi* and *A Connecticut Yankee*." *Nineteenth-Century Literature*, 41.3 (December 1986), 329–48.

Lacy, Norris J., and Geoffrey Ashe. *The Arthurian Handbook*. New York: Garland, 1988.

Leavy, Barbara Fass. "Iseult of Brittany: A New Interpretation of Matthew Arnold's *Tristram and Iseult*." *Victorian Poetry*, 18 (1980), 1–22.

Lupack, Alan. "The Americanization of Merlin." *Avalon to Camelot*, 2.4 (1987), 13–16.

———. "Arthurian Poetry and the Modern World." *Avalon to Camelot*, 2.3 (1987), 27–29.

———. "Beyond the Model: Howard Pyle's Arthurian Books." *Arthurian Yearbook*, 1 (1991), 215–34.

———. "Merlin in America." *Arthurian Interpretations*, 1.1 (Fall 1986), 64–74.

———. "Modern Arthurian Novelists on the Arthurian Legend." *Studies in Medievalism*, 2.4 (Fall 1983), 79–88.

Macdonald, Allan Houston. *Richard Hovey: Man & Craftsman*. Durham, North Carolina: Duke University Press, 1957.

Maynadier, Howard. *The Arthur of the English Poets*. 1907; rpt. New York: Haskell House, 1966.

Merriman, James Douglas. *The Flower of Kings: A Study of the Arthurian Legend in England Between 1485 and 1835*. Lawrence: University Press of Kansas, 1973.

———. "The Last Days of the Eighteenth-Century Epic: Bulwer-Lytton's Arthuriad." *Studies in Medievalism*, 2.4 (Fall 1983), 15–37.

Millican, Charles Bowie. *Spenser and the Table Round: A Study in the Contemporaneous Background for Spenser's Use of the Arthurian Legend*. Cambridge: Harvard University Press, 1932.

Moorman, Charles. *Arthurian Triptych: Mythic Materials in Charles Williams, C. S. Lewis, and T. S. Eliot*. Berkeley: University of California Press, 1960.

Nastali, Daniel P. "The Decline of the British Enchanter: Merlin in Eighteenth-Century Popular Culture." *Avalon to Camelot*, 2.4 (1987), 35–37.

The New Arthurian Encyclopedia. Ed. Norris J. Lacy et al. New York: Garland, 1991.

Oliver, Nancy S. "New Manifest Destiny in *A Connecticut Yankee in King Arthur's Court.*" *Mark Twain Journal*, 21.4 (Fall 1983), 28–32.

Owens, Louis. "Camelot East of Eden: John Steinbeck's *Tortilla Flat.*" *Arizona Quarterly*, 38.3 (Autumn 1982), 203–16.

The Passing of Arthur: New Essays in Arthurian Tradition. Ed. Christopher Baswell and William Sharpe. New York: Garland Publishing, 1988.

Peacock, John. "Jonson and Jones Collaborate on *Prince Henry's Barriers.*" *Word & Image*, 3.2 (April–June 1987), 172–94.

Perrine, Laurence. "The Sources of Robinson's *Merlin.*" *American Literature*, 44 (1972–73), 313–21.

Pitz, Henry C. *Howard Pyle: Writer, Illustrator, Founder of the Brandywine School.* New York: Potter, 1975.

Pressman, Richard S. "A Connecticut Yankee in Merlin's Cave: The Role of Contradiction in Mark Twain's Novel." *American Literary Realism*, 16.1 (Spring 1983), 58–72.

Probert, K. G. "Nick Carraway and the Romance of Art." *English Studies in Canada*, 10.2 (June 1984), 188–208.

Rosenberg, John D. "Tennyson and the Passing of Arthur." In *The Passing of Arthur: New Essays in Arthurian Tradition.* Ed. Christopher Baswell and William Sharpe. New York: Garland, 1988. Pp. 221–34.

Sibley, Agnes. *Charles Williams.* Boston: Twayne, 1982.

Smith, Henry Nash. *Mark Twain's Fable of Progress: Political and Economic Ideas in "A Connecticut Yankee."* New Brunswick, New Jersey: Rutgers University Press, 1964.

Spivack, Charlotte. *Merlin's Daughters: Contemporary Women Writers of Fantasy.* Westport, Connecticut: Greenwood, 1987.

Staines, David. "Swinburne's Arthurian World: Swinburne's Arthurian Poetry and Its Medieval Sources." *Studia Neophilologica*, 50 (1978), 53–70.

———. *Tennyson's Camelot: The Idylls of the King and Its Medieval Sources.* Waterloo, Ontario: Wilfrid Laurier University Press, 1982.

Starr, Nathan Comfort. "Edwin Arlington Robinson's Arthurian Heroines: Vivian, Guinevere and the Two Isolts." *Philological Quarterly*, 56 (1977), 231–49.

———. *King Arthur Today: The Arthurian Legend in English and American Literature, 1901–1953*. Gainesville: University of Florida Press, 1954.

Taylor, Beverly, and Elisabeth Brewer. *The Return of King Arthur: British and American Literature Since 1900* [for *1800*]. Cambridge: Brewer, 1983.

Thompson, Raymond H. "Humor and Irony in Modern Arthurian Fantasy: Thomas Berger's *Arthur Rex*." *Kansas Quarterly*, 16.3 (Summer 1984), 45–49.

———. *The Return from Avalon: A Study of the Arthurian Legend in Modern Fiction*. Westport, Connecticut: Greenwood, 1985.

Williams, Charles, and C. S. Lewis. *Arthurian Torso: Containing the Posthumous Fragment of the Figure of Arthur by Charles Williams and a Commentary on the Arthurian Poems of Charles Williams by C. S. Lewis*. London: Oxford University Press, 1952.

Williams, Mary C. "Lessons from Ladies in Steinbeck's 'Gawain, Ewain, and Marhalt.'" *Avalon to Camelot* (1984), 40–41.

Winters, Yvor. *Edwin Arlington Robinson*. Norfolk, Connecticut: New Directions, 1946.